GO WOKE, GO BROKE

GO WOKE, GO BROKE

THE INSIDE STORY of the RADICALIZATION OF CORPORATE AMERICA

Charles Gasparino

CENTER STREET
NEW YORK NASHVILLE

Center Street
Hachette Book Group
1290 Avenue of the Americas, New York, NY 10104
centerstreet.com
@CenterStreet/@CenterStreetBooks

First Edition: August 2024

Center Street is a division of Hachette Book Group, Inc. The Center Street name and logo are registered trademarks of Hachette Book Group, Inc.
The publisher is not responsible for websites (or their content) that are not owned by the publisher.

Print book interior design by Sheryl Kober

Library of Congress Cataloging-in-Publication Data
Names: Gasparino, Charles, author.
Title: Go woke, go broke: the inside story of the radicalization of corporate America / Charles Gasparino.
Description: First edition. | New York: Center Street, 2024. | Includes bibliographical references and index.
Identifiers: LCCN 2024002714 | ISBN 9781546007418 (hardcover) | ISBN 9781546007432 (ebook)
Subjects: LCSH: Social responsibility of business—United States | Industries—Social aspects—United States. | Business and politics—United States.
Classification: LCC HD60.5.U5 G377 2024 | DDC 306.30973—dc23/eng/20240226
LC record available at https://lccn.loc.gov/2024002714

ISBNs: 978-1-5460-0741-8 (hardcover), 978-1-5460-0743-2 (ebook)

Printed in Canada

LSC-MRQ

Printing 1, 2024

To Gin: Thanks for the push

Contents

Introduction *1*

CHAPTER ONE: The Great Goldman Chick-fil-A Debate 7
CHAPTER TWO: The Wokening of Corporate America 23
CHAPTER THREE: DEI or DIE? 47
CHAPTER FOUR: The Summer of Love 73
CHAPTER FIVE: Woke and Broke 113
CHAPTER SIX: The Fight Begins 127
CHAPTER SEVEN: "Who the Fuck Are These People?!?!" 137
CHAPTER EIGHT: The Boys from Brazil (and Belgium) 163
CHAPTER NINE: This Bud Is Not for You 181
CHAPTER TEN: The Not So Wonderful World of Woke Disney . 191
CHAPTER ELEVEN: The Biggest Woke Target in the World 223
CHAPTER TWELVE: Woke Is Finally Broken 239

Notes *263*
Index *293*

Introduction

Go woke, and you just might go broke.

This is my first book after a ten-year hiatus. Before that, I'd written five, including two national bestsellers. Book writing is grueling work because it's more than writing. It's the art of reporting something fairly and accurately. It's about checking facts and sources. It's about giving people a chance to respond to criticism.

Then it's about rewriting multiple times.

You don't do this simply for the money; you do this because in your heart you really want to tell a story about something important. You believe your end product will spark a debate and enact change.

That's why I wrote this book: Something does need to change in the ethos of corporate America for the good of the economy and the country's well-being. The noxious ideology of progressive politics in the boardroom—aka corporate wokeness—needs to die a thousand deaths. And you do that only by exposing its ugly truth.

You also don't do that overnight. The left-wing indoctrination and the acquiescence of our CEO class and the companies they run didn't occur overnight; it started small and grew incrementally until it became the monster that it is today. It's entrenched in the fabric of just about every public company, and it's at least as dangerous as the left-wing bias in the media or the progressive takeover of the university.

Yes, you slay the beast by exposing it—truthfully and journalistically, which is what I tried to do with *Go Woke, Go Broke*: a full journalistic account of how corporate America became something close to a foot soldier in the progressive movement.

In this book, I have attempted to provide a sweeping account of this madness: from its humble beginnings with CEOs taking mild political stands to their full-on embrace of far-left causes like BLM to where we are today, a nation finally coming to grips with the destructive capacity of corporate wokeism amid a backlash from the American public.

A sprawling account of corporate leftism, though, wasn't the original idea. It began with Jonathan Bronitsky having seen my reporting on Fox and my columns in the *New York Post* on the demise of Silicon Valley Bank. He suggested a book that focused on the once high-flying, tech-savvy lender to the rich and the aspiring wealthy in our ever-expanding land of all things internet-related, where management seemed to luxuriate in progressive causes as a side hustle.

It was an interesting story because, for a while, going woke didn't seem to matter. SVB was printing money until one day it wasn't. Someone seemed to have forgotten some of the basics of risk management, and in a few days, the place was toes up.

Conventional wisdom was that SVB blew up because managers couldn't read a balance sheet and extended too many risky loans to start-up tech firms that in 2022 and early 2023 were facing their first cash crunch in years. Jonathan saw, as did I, that what plagued SVB was bigger and scarier—it was a commentary on how corporate America had succumbed to left-wing agitprop.

While the bank was engaging in risky behavior, top executives were touting stuff you might hear come out of the mouth of AOC or Bernie Sanders. Endless Diversity Equity and Inclusion, devotion to the gospel of Environmental Social Governance investing. Its regulator, the San Francisco Fed, was cheering on the radically leftist Black Lives Matter movement.

Corporate wokeness was as much a part of its DNA as was making loans.

Great story until we realized that SVB was bad but small-fry compared to the monstrosity of corporate wokeness in the American economic ecosystem, the proverbial tip of the iceberg. Soon news of SVB was eclipsed by stories about Budweiser turning to a transwoman influencer in its marketing of the nation's then-top-selling beer, Bud Light. Bud's parent company was so obsessed with DEI metrics that someone in middle management thought it would be a great idea to appeal to biological men dressed as women to expand the beer's customer base.

Yikes! Then came news out of Disney—another American cultural icon, no less—that it was using shareholder money to thwart a Florida law that prevented something seemingly innocuous: the teaching of sex ed to children, a parental prerogative if ever there was one.

One of the nation's largest companies, which appeals in its programming and theme park experience to children, wanted to overturn the will of the people in Florida to make sure kids knew about gender reassignment therapy and intercourse between various sexes. I was pretty shocked, but I shouldn't have been, because for years Disney has been sexualizing content in its movies and animated programming aimed at children.

So why should the lefty Disney suits just stop there?

As I kept digging, the examples of boardroom politics veering into culturally progressive territory kept piling up: Companies turning to purveyors of the noxious critical race theory during HR sessions, branding many of their employees as racist oppressors. Corporate donations to radical leftist groups like Black Lives Matter surged, depriving other real charities of money because the left's version of social justice had become a boardroom priority.

So did the endless celebrations of gender and gender fluidity. To celebrate Gay Pride Month, the big retailer Target displayed so-called tuck-friendly bathing suits for men transitioning to women near rainbow-colored onesies for toddlers—all to be seen by parents shopping for inexpensive goods and clothing with their children.

De-facto and probably illegal hiring quotas imposed at most major companies were increasingly common after the tragic death of George Floyd. The death of the ex-con while resisting arrest in Minneapolis was used by the radical left, BLM, Antifa, et cetera, as proof of our country's systemic racism for their warped political purposes—with a huge assist from corporate America.

No less a figure than Jamie Dimon, the top banker in the country and CEO of JP Morgan, took a knee during the summer of 2020 in apparent solidarity.

Big money managers like BlackRock, a company I've covered for years because it holds more assets than any other financial firm in the world, used to be in the business of helping people save for retirement. Now it was in the business of imposing strict mandates the left believes will save the environment, so-called Environmental Social Governance's investing metrics.

ESG was a huge moneymaker for BlackRock, but it was also costly for the American consumer. ESG edicts force energy companies to invest in "sustainable" and inefficient sources of energy like windmills and solar. They were imposed on oil companies at a time when oil prices shot up after the Russian invasion of Ukraine, further squeezing supply and spurring massive inflation.

Wall Street was essentially getting rich off of ESG investing (such funds charge higher fees) while average Americans were being taxed at the gas pump to finance their wealth.

Then came the backlash because the American people aren't the woke monolith corporate America either assumed or sought to create. Some courageous business types like Ed Rensi, the retired CEO of McDonald's USA, and Bernie Marcus, the founder of Home Depot, took up the fight against corporate wokeness, as did the American people, as this book demonstrates.

The results should be a wake-up call to the woke American CEO class. Bud Light is no longer the nation's No. 1 selling beer; Target still faces boycotts; Disney is looking to take politics out of its programming and corporate imperatives (it was forced to list its history of wokeness as a risk factor for shareholders). BlackRock is closing down ESG funds. Dimon's flacks, nearly four years later, swear their boss took a knee merely to fit into a photo with other JPM execs. Liberal Wall Street types are refusing to endow their alma maters because of left-wing and antisemitic bias at these elite schools, which has led to protests in favor of the brutal Hamas massacre on October 7, 2023.

Go Woke, Go Broke, I hope, provides a compelling account of how progressive ideology infected an important cultural institution—corporate America: something that was supposed to be focused on selling products and employing the masses, not marketing a left-wing vision for America.

I also hope it's a teachable moment for the executive class. As you will discover, the American public is mad as hell and doesn't like being proselytized to wokeness while downing a cold one or sitting through a cartoon with their kids.

I couldn't have written this book without the support of friends and family. My wife, Virginia Juliano, is at the top of the list for convincing me I had at least one more in me; she truly has been my secret weapon throughout my career. My agent, Jonathan Bronitsky, my editor, Alex Pappas, with his team at Hachette, and the people at Fox Business and the *New York Post* all provided tremendous support, as did Eleanor Terrett, my producer at Fox Business, who assisted throughout the process of writing, editing, and fact-checking.

CHAPTER ONE

The Great Goldman Chick-fil-A Debate

It was around 2019 or so, during the last year of the highly volatile Trump presidency, that a strange and telling debate broke out inside the hallowed halls of Goldman Sachs, the big and until recently prestigious investment bank. No, not one about the crazy orange-haired dude in the White House, or Donald Trump's often globalist-defying economic policies, his trade war with Communist China (a huge Goldman client, mind you). Not even the propriety of "tax cuts for the rich," as progressives love to ding the Trump tax plan that provided years of strong economic and, finally, wage growth for average Americans.

This debate involved something more absurd, even surreal, but obviously existentially important to a handful of young Goldman associates discussing dinner plans as they prepared for another marathon evening of deal processing: whether it would be bigoted to chow down on those delicious (but too greasy for my taste buds) chicken sandwiches from the local Chick-fil-A restaurant.

Yes, you read that right, racism and Chick-fil-A.

Again, I'm not a fan of these fried chicken sandwiches. Still, I never thought eating one would cause the type of mental anguish and psychological heartburn that transpired in a conference room at Goldman's Manhattan global headquarters. Or the management response that followed.

The great Goldman Chick-fil-A debate began with a tip to my then Fox Business colleague Lydia Moynihan, though the term "debate" gives this anti-intellectual woke food fight too much heft. I grew up in an era where debates among young financial professionals centered on meaty subjects: the efficacy of tax cuts in spurring economic growth; the future of interest rates and the chances of a recession; what presidential candidate is best suited to face the challenges of a dangerously chaotic world; how we should combat terrorism at home and abroad. Or on a slow day, why do the Mets suck so much?

But what captured the imagination of some of Goldman's best and brightest that night was whether eating a Chick-fil-A sandwich would signal a significant step in America's racial de-evolution, sending the nation back to the dark times of the antebellum South.

A little background on why Chick-fil-A became such a hot-button issue for these gentle, woke souls at Goldman, who, in case you don't know it, are also the firm's and corporate America's future leaders.

Decades ago, someone named S. Truett Cathy started Chick-fil-A. He was a World War II vet who created what would become a billion-dollar franchise business nearly from scratch. He was also a southern white man. Back in the day, that didn't matter, because he had a vision, successfully executed, creating thousands upon thousands of jobs both inner-city and rural, and tax revenues from his significant wealth.

As pillars of the American establishment went "woke"—the sometimes overused term that so perfectly describes the progressive groupthink that seeks to remake the country and its culture into a left-wing hellhole—being southern, white, and conservative makes you a triple threat to mankind. Even at a business dinner.

Based on my research, Truett devised his signature chicken sandwich in a small grillroom outside Atlanta, and he confined his beliefs largely to preachy little sayings on his company's website that signaled his Baptist beliefs. The most offensive thing I found about him was a statement extolling the company's "purpose" is "to glorify God by being a faithful steward of all that is entrusted to us."

You get the picture on old Truett. Under his leadership, Chick-fil-A donated to conservative causes and plenty of other charities as well. "The Cathy family is one of the most generous out there," is how one philanthropic fundraiser described the clan. Occasionally, he was known to make statements in support of traditional marriage, and that's about it. Truett & co. wanted his employees to take off on Sunday so they could go to church or do whatever (Chick-fil-As still close on the Christian holy day). By all accounts, he was a live-and-let-live type of southern religious dude.

As wokeness spread from the febrile backwaters of university safe spaces to cliques of young bankers and the C-suites of corporate America, achievements like these are being erased. S. Truett Cathy is considered the embodiment of evil. His whiteness and conservative religious beliefs are a scarlet letter. Being white, male, and a conservative Christian in academic culture, then popular culture, and now the culture of corporate America is to be on the wrong side of history. In recent years, the Cathys faced immense media coverage on how they were allegedly using their wealth for sinister means; the vaulted Rainbow was being vandalized because a couple of dudes from Georgia who made chicken sandwiches think marriage should be between a man and a woman.

Truett died a billionaire in 2014 at the age of ninety-three and left the company to his son Dan Cathy, also an evangelical Christian. Again, if you know anything about Baptists in the South, you also know they're not that keen on same-sex marriage. Don't get them started on the propriety of gender-affirming operations (sex changes) for children, both key elements of the new enlightenment known as wokeism.

That's why all hell broke out inside a conference room at Goldman Sachs when someone suggested that Chick-fil-A was needed to power through another deal night. As it was relayed to us, the enthusiastic suggestion sounded like a good idea until someone brought up Cathy's alleged anti-gay beliefs. So did another and another, we discovered in our reporting. A voice of semi-reason reminded the group that Cathy might be a bad dude, a bigot no less, but there was no blanket ban at Chick-fil-A on same-sex marriage. Chick-fil-A, he said, might just pass the woke litmus test. That just riled up the anti-Chick-fil-A contingent even more, according to our reporting.

A couple of things stand out in addition to the idiocy of this debate. First, you would think, being young financiers, that the Goldman crew would know Chick-fil-A is a franchise business with three thousand locations across the country. The Cathy clan doesn't own the restaurants; they're owned and operated by entrepreneurs from all walks of life. The man or woman or trans person who owns the Manhattan franchise they might be ordering from could be an Asian or Hispanic immigrant, or some dude from Ghana, not a real or imagined southern redneck.

They should also know that Chick-fil-A has also gone a bit woke lately. It never barred its employees from same-sex marriage; now it no longer donates to organizations that are deemed, in the lexicon of the woke, "LGBTQ+ unfriendly." The company has transitioned from culturally conservative to something that might soon be embracing pronouns and has begun condemning systemic racism in America.

It couldn't be determined if any of these high-minded souls kept arguing and did without dinner that night, or if they decided to split the baby and order something more culturally progressive like Chinese food. Either way, sources at the bank said the debate was intense enough that it made its way to Goldman management, themselves an increasingly woke bunch.

Fearing a dreaded call by Goldman's hyper-woke human resources department—which had long embraced everything from mandatory diversity sessions to pronoun guides describing the ever-changing woke gender classifications—management checked in with HR to get a ruling on where eating Chick-fil-A passed the proverbial woke smell test.

It did.

Whew.

When we asked Goldman for comment on this matter, a company flack said she couldn't rule out the Chick-fil-A brouhaha but found no "evidence" it occurred. Someone at Goldman later asked why I thought this story was worth reporting.

Good question. My answer: Read *Go Woke, Go Broke.* You will understand the horrific corrosive effect corporate wokeness is having on American business and our culture. It manifests not just in the weird mindset of a few Millennials and Gen-Zers debating the racism of eating a chicken sandwich. It can be found throughout Goldman management and elsewhere in corporate boardrooms and in the workplace, where racialized indoctrination sessions masquerading as diversity training have become the norm. So have hiring quotas, progressive causes embraced in corporate advertisements, and gender fluidity in children's programming.

Corporate wokeness is about every major publicly traded company these days adhering to the left-wing dictates of ESG (environmental, social, and governance) investment techniques, along with its kissing cousin, DEI, or diversity, equity, and inclusion, among the most heinously anti-American management philosophies ever developed.

It's the nation's biggest companies joining the likes of Alexandria Ocasio-Cortez, also known as AOC, Bernie Sanders, the hyperactive woke far-left congresswoman Rashida Tlaib, BLM, and assorted members of the progressive movement to change America, and not for the better.

As columnist and author Gerard Baker so frighteningly and poetically described this mass hysteria, it's "business leaders using their companies...as vehicles for cultural and social change."

It's both infuriating and sad how we got here, because corporate America once stood for something better—America's industrial, technological, intellectual, and financial might. Politics had no place in a system that encouraged innovation and drive and was focused on making money no matter who you were. CEOs once fixated on delivering returns for shareholders; they now see themselves as global citizens working for "stakeholders." They're not just businessmen but political leaders charged with carrying out progressivism even though no one elected them to advance the cause.

The damage wokeness has done is everywhere but let us focus on Goldman Sachs for a moment. The firm was once an exemplar for much of what worked in the American economy. Its top executives served in the military, got rich through years of hard work, and then often served at the pinnacle of government. Yes, serious people ran Goldman, and that was one of the reasons it became one of the most efficient and effective investment banks in the nation's history. Goldman was about as close to a pure meritocracy as exists in the corporate world. It did not just recruit from the Ivy League, though there are plenty of Harvard graduates who have filtered through the bank. It looked for hungry, smart people willing to work long hours to contribute to the firm.

Its top partners—Gus Levy, John Whitehead, Jon Corzine, Hank Paulson, Gary Cohn, Lloyd Blankfein, and Robert Rubin—conferred with presidents and prime ministers. After his career at Goldman, Cohn added significant sanity and stability to the sometimes chaotic Trump White House as head of the former president's National Economic Council. Blankfein and Cohn saved the company from annihilation during the 2008 financial crisis. Rubin and Paulson also became top government officials, Treasury secretaries during Democrat and Republican administrations. Corzine was the governor and US senator from New Jersey after his Goldman years.

It's fair to say that the culture of hard work, merit, and achievement is why Goldman has been one of the most impactful banks—and companies—in American history. Its traders sniffed out the early stages of the 2008 Wall Street collapse, saving the firm by working day and night crunching numbers. They adroitly traded through mini crashes over the past three decades.

Bankers like Paulson—who didn't drink and rarely slept—would dial up clients across the globe at all hours of the day and night when chasing a deal. Corzine served in the Marines; Whitehead stormed the beaches of Normandy. They advised iconic American companies during the tech revolution, underwriting public offerings for Microsoft, Google, Apple, and Amazon. Partners became wealthy men; some left to start hedge funds, others private equity firms.

Yes, Goldman was quite a place; it was a culture of hard work, and striving for excellence is no doubt the reason why Goldman is what it is.

Or maybe what it was.

I say this because a good case can be made that Goldman's glory days are slipping away. Sure, it remains profitable and a top dealmaker, but management turmoil is a constant and its place among the elite shaky. Its embrace of so-called corporate wokeism, a term popularized by author, entrepreneur, and recently presidential candidate Vivek Ramaswamy, is partially, if not largely, to blame, my reporting shows.

Today, a veteran investment banker named David Solomon runs Goldman. He has a side hustle as a high-end DJ under the name DJ D-Sol. He was dubbed "one woke dude" by *Vanity Fair* writer William Cohan when he took the CEO job in 2018 because he cares about woke stuff like the environment, diversity in management, and so on. He wanted Goldman to be more humane.

At first, he wore the moniker proudly. These days, having spent several years navigating the increasing wokeness of corporate America, and the even woker young bankers that now populate Goldman, I'm not too sure.

Solomon faces crises both existential and internal. The existential crisis is simply that Goldman—despite its white-shoe investment bank and high-powered trading operations—might now be too small to compete with mega-banks like JP Morgan.

That's easier to fix through a merger even if it means giving up control to another suitor in order to survive. More difficult is the bank's internal crisis of confidence. The Goldman culture is under siege from the pernicious disease of corporate wokeism even worse than that Chick-fil-A garbage.

Solomon is dealing with societal changes that the firm's legendary leaders would never contemplate, and, yes, some of his own making, since it was his idea to embrace wokeness in the first place. All those leaders I mentioned toiled through the associate Goldman boot camp, working on deals around the clock was mandatory. Critics have likened it to a sweatshop, but there wasn't much time or tolerance for Chick-fil-A debates. Solomon upon taking over tried to make nice with a new breed of Goldman employee. He vowed to make certain that associates weren't put through the infamous Goldman deal grinder. He wanted a kinder, gentler Goldman, and one that's more woke.

He supported other cultural changes at the firm. DEI—one of the pillars of corporate wokeness—is big inside the Goldman human resources department, sources there say. Like most things woke, DEI in the corporate setting started with good intentions. Civil rights laws in the 1960s outlawed race- and gender-based discrimination. HR departments began pushing management to embrace something known as affirmative action—the recruitment of employees from underrepresented communities. Sometime in the 2000s, DEI began to take off when the notion of diversity took an even more dramatic and totalitarian interpretation. The journalist Bari Weiss has studied DEI, and she describes it as a management theory that doles out benefits based on "extraordinarily crude racial categories." People are not judged based on "the merits or demerits of your deeds but...on [the] identity of the person carrying them out," which places white men at the bottom of the pecking order for all kinds of benefits, including employment and advancement.

Some of DEI sounds noble—seeking out diverse workers, suppliers from underserved communities—until you see how it is practiced in the real world. DEI officers can be found at most major corporations, and they are dogmatic in their approach. The result is not just hiring quotas; until recently, there's been a near ban on hiring and promoting white men at many large corporations, according to interviews and news reports. Corporate DEI mandates have filtered into our culture so much that they've infected the image making of Madison Avenue. Major advertising companies, according to my sources, must vet every single ad through the DEI department to determine if it meets a woke diversity litmus test. That's why a straight white dude in a TV ad these days is about as rare as Halley's Comet, and even more rarely do you see an all-white traditional family. Most recently, the trans community has been included as a victimized group that gets special treatment in the DEI framework, which accounts for the obsession with everything trans at companies like the big retailer, Target and AB InBev, the holding company for Anheuser-Bush and its beer Budweiser, as we will discuss shortly.

At Goldman, for instance, DEI places significant emphasis on race, but also on types of gender preferences. "I was basically asked if I was bisexual," one woman applicant told me. She didn't get the job despite a stellar résumé at big banks in marketing financial products, because she said she was insulted by the question and wouldn't answer it.

Truth be told, I was skeptical of her account until I discovered that Goldman's HR department has published a guide on gender pronouns, presumably so that cis-male bankers don't offend the gender-fluid fat cats when they're on deadline processing deals.

A snippet of the Goldman pronoun guide per the *New York Post* describes how to properly address a colleague in the new world of woke capitalism: "Ze went to the store. I spoke with zir/zem. The apple was zirs/zes," it instructs.

I'd love to be a fly on the wall during deal night at Goldman!

In all seriousness, DEI (and corporate wokeness in general) is both cultist and quite scary. If you oppose these bizarre mandates, you're branded a racist, sexist, or anti-trans, and out of a job, so most people just go along. It's also counterproductive. Goldman—once a legendary eat-what-you-kill firm—is supposed to be in the business of making money for itself and its shareholders. Now it won't underwrite initial public offerings for companies it deems not diverse. (Except of course for Chinese companies, which are exempt from much of this nonsense. More on that to come.) In the past, the legendary General Electric CEO Jack Welch and other corporate titans came to the firm to dispense their wisdom. Today, Goldman's woke-inspired speaker list, it has been reported, includes leading figures in something called the critical race theory (CRT) movement. No one complained, except under his or her breath.

CRT, another key tenet of corporate wokeness, is an odd thing to find in the workplace, because it stresses the opposite of team building, the necessary ingredient for any company to survive and thrive. Companies are like armies; people need to work together to achieve a common goal. CRT, frankly, teaches people to hate each other.

On one level CRT is a difficult concept to grasp because there is no concrete or fixed definition. There is plenty of scholarship on the subject, but it's highly subjective and the standards would fail the scientific smell test. It can be whatever the CRT scholar says it is.

That said, there are some defining characteristics; like pornography, you know it when you see or hear it. Its devotees agree on several broad sets of principles, starting with the contention that the white American majority is inherently racist and in need of reform through any means necessary, including brainwashing children in grade school, young adults in college, and adults while at work.

It also offers an odious brand of historical reinterpretation of America's founding principles and evolution by ignoring the great strides in race relations that have occurred over the years. It demands immediate atonement for past sins. And of course, there must be reparations based on race and, increasingly, gender. CRT in one form or another is infused in the corporate diversity, equity, inclusion framework.

Yet CRT is both one of the most counterproductive aspects of corporate life these days and a mainstay at places like American Express, Bank of America, and most of the nation's and even the world's big companies.

When you talk to people at Goldman and even Solomon himself (as I have) about what's happening culturally at the firm, and throughout corporate America, they concede it's a bizarre spectacle. They also concede they're powerless to turn back the clock on wokeness. The schools from which they recruit inculcate students in every left-wing fad imaginable (hence the Chick-fil-A debate). Fighting wokeness can be expensive. The plaintiff bar has targeted every Wall Street firm and every company for various forms of discrimination, both real and imagined.

I say "imagined" because proof of racism or gender bias is often statistical, and simplistically so—such as the preponderance of straight white males in management jobs, not necessarily actual instances of discrimination. Companies would rather just settle these lawsuits than go through what could be a costly and embarrassing defense to explain that just because white dudes are in charge doesn't mean the place is run like the KKK.

People at Goldman and elsewhere in moments of candor will also explain their impotence to thwart the power of the almighty corporate HR departments. Boards of directors have seen to it that HR has been equipped with stroke, even overriding the CEO when it comes to matters of wokeness, like DEI. That's one reason why nearly every public company in America mandates what's euphemistically known as "diversity training." Under the guise of teaching people how to respect one another, diversity training infused with the DEI/CRT groupthink devolves into something more perverse. Moderators demand that employees explore their inner racist self and read up on it from the alleged scholars in CRT.

I asked a top executive at American Express why CRT zealots were lecturing employees about the evils of capitalism at a credit card company named "American," no less. He blamed it on a "runaway HR department, obsessed with DEI."

DEI's counterpart is something known as ESG, or environmental, social, and governance—a key metric assigned by asset managers to Goldman and every major public company in the United States. In fact, DEI would be largely defanged if ESG didn't exist, according to my reporting.

Like DEI, ESG is another key element in the foundation of corporate wokeism. Also like DEI, its stated purpose is something noble: using the power of investable assets to force companies to do good while they make money for shareholders. CEOs must take concrete steps to save the environment, hire more historically discriminated races, and give back to local communities instead of focusing only on the bottom line.

In practice, ESG warps the investment process and rational corporate decision making to achieve a political result most Americans would abhor and any sentient shareholder should despise. Asset management firms direct their investment dollars to companies only if they meet certain woke metrics. The companies' ability to grow and create shareholder value becomes a secondary or even tertiary investment concern. Management's desire to grow their business and hire the best people takes a backseat to the demands of ESG money managers that companies focus their efforts on increasingly inefficient ways of cleaning up the environment (such as using windmills to generate electricity) and barely legal methods of creating statistical diversity in their workforce (aka quotas).

It also reeks of elitism: That a bunch of number-crunching Wall Street geeks can gin up an investing formula to save the planet from environmental Armageddon and make the races live in harmony is patently absurd. To achieve this utopian fantasy, working-class people must suffer from higher energy costs because ESG demands less oil exploration; the white working class must be disadvantaged when competing for jobs with the offspring of wealthy South American dictators.

Under ESG, the American public must accept hardship to achieve this greater good, and unqualified people must be placed in some of the nation's most important jobs for no other reason than that they meet ESG's racial litmus test. No better proof of ESG's diversity pitfalls is the sad story of now former Harvard president Claudine Gay; yes, colleges adopt ESG measures to their own detriment, as we will discuss in later chapters.

On top of it all, it's a shitty investment strategy. ESG-tailored funds are wickedly expensive, charging much higher fees than any actively managed investment fund. No fund manager can outsmart the collective wisdom of the markets; price discovery is reached by millions of actors exercising free will every minute of every day (it's why most active managers can't beat simple indexes unless they cheat with insider trading). If Wall Street money managers were so smart, they wouldn't have crunched all those numbers and taken all that risk with weird investments that caused the 2008 financial crisis, and lots of bad stuff before that.

So how did we get to an investment world so utterly obsessed with something that, frankly, sucks? The historical context of corporate wokeness, and its ESG and DEI spawn, began with changes in boardroom ethos in the late 1980s and the 1990s when corporate CEOs began running companies along the lines of so-called corporate social responsibility, using shareholder money to donate to various charities, or end world hunger. Then came the rise of stakeholder capitalism; the central mission of the CEO went from managing their business to bringing about positive (often woke) social change.

By the mid-2000s, CEOs began to feel the heat from the left, politically connected activist groups, and far-left politicians, including the community organizer turned president Barack Obama, to go even further. The 2008 banking crisis and the bailouts that followed made Wall Street—the biggest recipient of the government handouts—vulnerable to big government and ripe for such woke intervention.

Yes, corporate wokeism began with a heavy dose of Wall Street CEO guilt. In the lead-up to the 2008 crash, the big banks were creating dubious financial products predicated on the notion that everyone should own a home and the riskiest loans could be made risk-free by packing them together through a process known as securitization. It was a very big, lucrative, and, some critics would contend, borderline illegal business. Mortgage bonds and other variations of securitized debt were sold as riskless investments. Big banks held this debt for its high interest income, unaware the bonds were about to implode in value. Soon the irrational exuberance gave way to reality: Those allegedly riskless investments crashed because owning a home requires a down payment and a job by the borrower. No amount of securitization could stop people from defaulting on loans they couldn't afford. The bonds defaulted in gargantuan numbers, and a full-on financial panic was in motion when the banks fell into insolvency.

The government stepped in and bailed out the big banks—the biggest government intervention in US history. The country paid the price, with taxpayer money bailing out some of the biggest businesses in the world. The Great Recession followed, an economic collapse not seen since the Great Depression.

Main Street was hurting. Wall Street not so much, as it turned out. The bailouts were both fast and efficient, so much so that by early 2009, banks and all of Wall Street were making money and were preparing to hand out bonuses again.

It laid the groundwork for the next stage in corporate America's embrace of all things woke.

The banks needed cover for their greed and possible illegality during the run-up to the big collapse while they faced populist pressure from the right (the burgeoning Tea Party movement), but mostly from the left. Occupy Wall Street began large-scale protests in major cities, including the epicenter of market capitalism in New York. It's no accident that Occupy's squalid headquarters was Zuccotti Park, a few blocks from the New York Stock Exchange and the HQ of major brokerages. It gave the protestors the opportunity to harass and harangue bankers and even working-class back-office staffers, and they did. Other forms of corporate harassment came from progressive pols like Massachusetts senator Elizabeth Warren, who appeared to want all CEOs in jail for allegedly decimating the working class. Left-wing activist investors began buying shares of major companies, demanding they conform to progressive edicts. Big and powerful pension funds in liberal blue states manage trillions of dollars of money and they too joined in on the action, pressuring their portfolio companies to do the same. With its influenced neutered, big companies went all in on woke politics. Corporate wokeism was the ultimate Faustian bargain, my reporting shows.

Yet corporate wokeness is now failing, as I will show in *Go Woke, Go Broke.* Some of its demise is attributable to cultural reasons. People hate it and won't buy products from companies that immerse themselves in the cultural rot I describe in the coming chapters.

It's also dying because corporate America is still a bottom-line-driven entity. CEOs and investors are paid on performance, which is why, as you will discover, even ESG's biggest practitioners are running for cover these days.

If companies like Goldman won't underwrite the stocks of those it deems non-ESG-compliant, or if the firm doesn't attract good people because management is too obsessed with gender pronouns, its bottom line will eventually suffer. If Goldman's deal associates are wasting too much time debating Chick-fil-A, that same cultural rot will destroy what it took David Solomon's predecessors a century and a half to build.

Solomon will also be toast as CEO.

That's exactly what is happening. Shares of Goldman have risen modestly over the past three years, while markets have soared. Its stock market value is the smallest of the big money-center financial institutions. Solomon is often despised among his young troops as an out-of-touch Boomer. Millennials and a younger generation of bankers scoff at his attempts to get them back into the office well after Covid has passed, my reporting shows. When they're not arguing about Chick-fil-A, they leak stories to embarrass him, like the time he removed a concession stand that provided free coffee, a move that was framed as a ruthless cost-cutting gesture.

A trivial lawsuit by a former female employee found its way into the media because of a nugget that Solomon allegedly bragged about receiving oral sex in a private meeting she wasn't even at (he denies this). It was an example of toxic masculinity run amok at the increasingly woke firm. He is bashed nearly daily for his now infamous side hustle as a DJ at swanky Hamptons parties, while the hoi polloi toil away on deals.

Wall Street's woke CEO has been derided as dictatorial and resistant to change. A foray into consumer banking was a bust, and Goldman's uneven profitability is said to be the fault of his allegedly brutal management approach and lack of team building. As I write this, a nasty civil war still simmers between Goldman's traders and bankers (Solomon is a banker), further exposing the fault lines of his fractured management ranks.

"I like David," is how one Wall Street CEO described the situation Solomon faces. "But I'd be surprised he makes it another year. He's the worst of both worlds; he wants to be woke, but the young people who work for him think he's not woke enough. With so much dissension in the ranks, he gets blamed for everything and his enemies pile on."

Solomon isn't incompetent. He's a smart banker and, one-on-one, as genial and decent a man as I have personally witnessed. I'm going to offer an alternative explanation for his agonistes: embracing and then giving in to the woke mob that increasingly occupies space inside Goldman. When you're stretched thin mandating pronouns and diversity training, and bypassing deals of companies that aren't diverse, it's hard to execute on consumer banking or much else. Sadly, Goldman's move toward wokeism isn't a one-off in the phenomenon—or hysteria—sweeping corporate America.

I've been a business and financial reporter for decades. Corporate America once shied away from political issues because it could be bad for the bottom line. One person's cause is another's pet peeve. It didn't make business sense to preach politics because you're always pissing off someone. Those days are clearly over. Corporate America went woke; this book will describe both how we got here, and why some are going broke because Americans chose to fight back.

It won't be easy to end the war against wokeism, because the opposition is not just entrenched but well financed. Wokeism's foot soldiers control academia, popular culture, and the media. Activist groups have become quasi-institutional investors buying shares of companies they want to target for "social justice" and invading the so-called proxy process to enforce progressive change in corporate governance through annual shareholder votes.

There was once a time when CEOs were known as "masters of the universe" because they commanded power inside the boardroom and in policymaking for the country. They still do, to some extent, yet they continue to cave to the progressive mob outside their offices. Examples are endless, as you will discover, but several stand out. Former Disney CEO Bob Chapek, a Republican from Middle America, born and raised in Indiana, allowed Disney and its programming to continue to veer into left-wing propaganda, ceding to pressure from the Hollywood elite, advocacy groups, and his own vocally progressive employees.

Brendan Whitworth, another Republican, a former Marine and friend of Donald Trump Jr., no less, extolled the virtues of serving beer to the company's "partners" in the LGBTQ+ community while his company hired a transgender woman social activist to advertise Bud Light on social media.

Following the great Goldman sandwich debate, the allegedly homophobic, racist Dan Cathy held a company seminar to address racial justice at a church in Atlanta, the home city of Chick-fil-A Inc.

It was just after George Floyd's death in May 2020. The death of the ex-con, an African American who was resisting arrest by a white police officer in Minneapolis, triggered some of the most violent riots this country has seen since the 1960s. Chick-fil-A franchises were targeted and ransacked because of the Cathy family's anti-woke rep.

Instead of calling for a greater police presence to protect his stores and his workers, Dan Cathy summoned his inner woke demons. He was onstage with a guest, a Christian African American rapper named Lecrae Moore, and said the following:

"As Caucasians, until we're willing to pick up the baton and fight for our black African American brothers and sisters—which they are as one human race. We are shameful. We are just adding to it. Our silence is so huge this time. We cannot be silent. Someone has to fight."

Maybe Cathy heard about the Goldman Chick-fil-A brawl. Maybe he was tired of the continued media attacks about his conservative views, or the online trolling that he and his dad were racists. Maybe he was suffering from the corporate version of Stockholm syndrome, or he was brainwashed along with his employees in a corporate diversity session.

Alternatively, maybe he was just "virtue signaling"—a term you will see a lot in these pages as it so accurately expresses the spurious public sermonizing about progressive causes, not just in the popular culture or media, but from the C-suite as well.

Either way, after he uttered those banalities, Cathy picked up a shoeshine brush, walked over to Moore, and began shining his shoes.

Not kidding.

CHAPTER TWO

The Wokening of Corporate America

The term "woke," as far as I can tell, is a relatively new addition to the national conversation. It was added to the dictionary around 2017 after radicals used it during the race riots in Ferguson, Missouri, jargonized from the term "stay awake."

"Stay awake" was meant to alert people of color to allegedly widespread police brutality following the killing of a Black man, Michael Brown, in 2014, who, as the story goes, was shot while surrendering to the police with his hands up. Like the word itself, the circumstances of Brown's death have been bastardized.

Brown was hardly a saint; a troubled teen from a poor St. Louis edge city, he had just robbed a convenience store. When the police were called to the scene, the six-foot-four Brown attacked a white cop and tried to grab his service pistol. Brown was shot during the struggle.

The facts didn't prevent days and days of rioting and looting in Ferguson; several progressive political movements emerged from the tragedies. One ultimately involved Colin Kaepernick, a washed-up football player who began taking a knee during the national anthem. Soon it became a big thing; players emulated his one-knee during games, upsetting fans and leading to a boycott of games. Yet Kaepernick, with no future in football, began appearing in Nike ads.

Another movement that blossomed after Ferguson is known as Black Lives Matter. The organization has a national chapter, a "nonprofit" that accepts contributions and has made its leadership incredibly rich in recent years. It also has affiliate organizations, about forty of them around the country, that are basically in the business of protesting, and more recently exploiting, white-CEO guilt, which means beginning in 2020 and particularly in the aftermath of George Floyd, they had a field day in terms of organized outrage, and then corporate fundraising.

Then VP candidate Kamala Harris, looking to tap into the aura of BLM for votes during the 2020 election, praised its "brilliance." Harris called the group's tactics, which included violent protests that year, as "necessary" to help the country repent from its past racist sins. Businesses burned to the ground in minority neighborhoods is a strange way to repent. Someone of Harris's stature praising BLM's tactics only added to the group's allure and gave cover for major corporations like Amazon, DoorDash, and Microsoft to finance the organization or its affiliated nonprofits and its tactics. All very strange. Throwing money at social unrest gives you more of it. Stranger still when you investigate what BLM and its founding members, Patrisse Cullors and Alicia Garza, are all about.

In one interview, Cullors described herself and Garza as "trained Marxists."

"We are super-versed on, sort of, ideological theories," she said. Sounds like the type of radical that would loot and pillage the offices of each of its corporate sponsors and distribute the riches to its members—and to themselves.

BLM, you see, doesn't exactly practice what it preaches. Sure, its leaders peddle a weird form of anti-Americanism and anti-capitalism; they worship the scholars of critical race theory, echo their sentiments that racists built this country and capitalism financed the racist government that continues to this day. They also live lifestyles of the rich and famous; BLM's leadership take in millions of dollars in corporate contributions, pay themselves huge salaries, and own expensive homes.

Even worse, they've been crowding out real charities as wokeism has infused corporate decision making.

"Are you fucking kidding me?" a volunteer fundraiser snapped after hearing from an executive at a major company that he didn't have enough money to give to one of the worthiest causes there is: the Navy SEAL Foundation.

The Navy SEALs, of course, need no introduction; suffice it to say they are the nation's ultimate warriors, risking life and limb for freedom and democracy. The foundation is a real charity that helps Navy SEALs injured in battle cope with life changes like living without limbs and battle fatigue.

Many Wall Street executives, including my source, raise money for the foundation by selling seats to a gala that occurs once a year around March. For years, big companies would take out tables for the event. After 2020, less so. There was just so much money to go around when in boardrooms across corporate America the directive was to make "charities" like BLM and other social justice organizations a priority.

That's not all. My fundraising source did a little digging. He says he discovered that the charitable donations were also supporting causes like the radical defund the police movement and various forms of reparations for allegedly oppressed communities of color. These groups advocated for quotas and strictly mandated DEI.

Yet another way to improve their DEI scores and ESG rankings—even if they had to make the Navy SEALs an afterthought in the process.

"It was the most frustrating thing I've ever experienced," the executive, who asked not to be named, told me. "Depriving real heroes charity so these political idiots can get rich makes me sick."

Who wouldn't be?

What escaped the C-suite woke impulse to support BLM was the truly noxious underpinnings of the movement. Despite its catchy name (who doesn't think Black lives matter?), much of BLM's core mission is decidedly un-American: BLM supports slavery reparations. In its warped world view, working-class people of most races need to be taxed more to pay for reparations to Black people over slavery. The logic of how the offspring of post–Civil War immigrants, most of whom came to the United States well after 1900, much less 1865, should pay even rich Black people for the sins of slavery is twisted. Of the eight athletes who are bona fide billionaires, five are African American: LeBron James, Magic Johnson, Tiger Woods, Michael Jordan, and Floyd Mayweather Jr. Using BLM's reasoning, the West Virginia coal miner needs to pitch in to cut them a check.

How absurd, and who made BLM a suitable arbiter of racial justice in the first place?

Besides being anti-American, the organization is known for being staunchly anti-Israel. Its leaders see the Jewish state as a colonialist oppressor of dark-skinned Arab terrorists on its borders, and a weapon in America's quest for world domination of people of color. The group openly supports the Palestinian cause to the extreme, even if that means at times supporting the murder of Jews in Israel. Some members of the BLM movement believe Israel needs to be abolished, as if Jews never survived the Holocaust, never lived in the Holy Land, and never agreed to two-state solutions that the Palestinians have rejected for decades.

BLM's ideology has spread to major American campuses, as witnessed by the violent protests by students in favor of the gruesome October 7, 2023, Hamas attack in Israel. In the lowest point in the group's history, BLM's Chicago chapter celebrated those Hamas terrorists who beheaded Jewish babies, raped and tortured women, and killed more than a thousand people near Gaza. The chapter issued a social media post of a paraglider with the Palestinian flag as a backdrop. The words "I stand with Palestine" appeared underneath the disturbing image that literally celebrated the monsters who descended on the kibbutzim and committed wanton mass slaughter.

Support for BLM is best described as an updated version of "radical chic," the term invented by the great novelist Tom Wolfe to explain elite fascination with and support of belligerently leftist causes. In 2020, as crime in New York City reached astounding new heights, Mayor Bill de Blasio painted a BLM mural on Fifth Avenue, in front of Trump Tower, no less. Beginning in 2020, it was fashionable for corporations to have BLM-affiliated speakers at conferences and lecture their executives on how to understand concepts like "social justice," radical interpretations of American history, and that capitalism is inherently racist and in desperate need of change.

The 2020 death of George Floyd is a key marker in the evolution of corporate wokeism—and it went far beyond corporate support for groups like BLM. By now, cultural elites had firmly decided that Floyd's death was a testament to endemic systemic racism in this country, in the media, and at the workplace. Companies took the lead in rooting this evil out of American culture through training sessions that included lectures on "microaggressions," or "unconscious bias," because white people, particularly white men, are so racist that they don't even know when they are racist.

Then came the CRT—and lots of it—to root out those demons, aka "white privilege." It is one thing to be radicalized on social media. That's a passive endeavor. According to people I interviewed, companies literally began compelling their employees to go to CRT lectures that forced them to accept the notion that American culture needs to be radically changed; the white majority needs to be reeducated on race.

They also needed to accept as gospel the crazy theory known as "intersectionality," a belief system promoted by the far-left civil rights attorney Kimberlé Crenshaw that individuals don't really exist. People are merely the sum of their oppressed parts, so government can properly dole out reparations proportionate to past discrimination. A lesbian Black woman, for example, should benefit more from the welfare state or in a corporate setting in terms of salary and promotion than, say, a gay white male, because he only checks one oppressed box and she checks three.

How do you build corporate teamwork when your company hands out benefits and assignments based on people's differences? You don't, of course. Still HR departments obsess over this shit, and they have been pushing its limits in hiring and promotion at big public companies for years now, my reporting shows.

The result has been chaos and rank discrimination of the illegal kind. Intersectionality is why the Veterans Administration, the taxpayer-funded government agency created by Congress to support veterans of *all races*, recommended in 2020 that minorities be given preference for receiving Covid vaccines, "considering the disproportionate impact of COVID-19 on racial and ethnicity minority groups." Last I checked, Covid doesn't discriminate based on race. At the workplace, it meant white males need not apply for jobs no matter how qualified, a clear violation of just about every civil rights law ever enacted, but because of corporate wokeism, management often doesn't think about challenging it.

It also meant the people at a company called NextEra had to sit through racialized Town Halls instead of engaging in teamwork-building discussions or hearing about their company's earnings.

I'm withholding the names of employees who provided the following account so they can keep their jobs. "This place takes being woke to another level," is how one NextEra employee described how corporate wokeness is practiced at what is essentially a utility.

NextEra Energy is the holding company for Florida Power & Light. That means its main goal is supposed to be keeping the lights on and the air conditioners working for millions of people in the state. Employees I spoke to say wokeness is also part of the company's mission statement.

Florida, of course, is the state run by a man named Ron DeSantis. The second-term governor and former GOP presidential candidate loves to say, "Florida is where woke goes to die," and he has certainly tried to slay the beast.

In the battle against wokeism, DeSantis has probably done more than anyone to draw attention to its abuses, whether via the passing of laws that prevent the teaching of transgenderism to children or his epic battles with the uber-woke leadership at one of the state's largest employers, the once iconic Walt Disney Company.

In the summer and fall of 2020, NextEra clearly didn't get the DeSantis memo. Around this time, it began to divest its holdings of an oil pipeline to meet ESG standards. It employed an entire department, "The Engagement, Diversity & Inclusion Team," that included among its duties holding a yearly "summit" that employees are "encouraged" to participate in via Zoom or in person to discuss the company's version of race relations, including how America hasn't moved that far beyond Jim Crow.

The summit, I am told by people at the company, isn't mandatory, though you get points with management for attending. Other DEI sessions are *definitely* mandatory. They often appear in the form of so-called Town Halls, a type of corporate gathering popular today where employees hear directly from management about the business and major boardroom initiatives.

One of the biggest initiatives at NextEra turns out to be corporate wokeness.

"I remember one Town Hall in 2020," said another employee, also speaking on the condition of anonymity out of fear of reprisal. "It was just after George Floyd, but we were supposed to hear about quarterly earnings from the CEO, so the entire company was on the call. Instead, the meeting opened up with a Black woman at the company explaining the hardships her dad, a bus driver, had to overcome to raise a family as a Black man in America. How much she overcame as a black woman in a racist country. She was not older than me, so it's safe to say she grew up in the 1980s—not exactly Jim Crow Mississippi. I remember thinking to myself, 'At least you had a father, and why are these people subjecting me to this?'"

Good question.

Here you might ask: What's the harm having people of color or different genders celebrating their stories at work? Well, work is supposed to be a place free of celebrating differences, where people work for a common goal. Moreover, these aren't mere celebrations of identity. As anyone who has sat through one of these sessions will tell you, they are infused with agitprop, administered by lefty HR departments preoccupied with progressive groupthink and looking to sway people to accept a set of political beliefs.

HR departments were once the place that helped guide women through mommy leave, or made layoffs more palatable as they explained severance. Following #MeToo they became more activist, and for good reason. You don't want your CEO wasting time chasing the secretary around her desk.

That's the good news. The bad news is that increasingly over the past two decades, my reporting shows, HR departments have been growing politically woke. Overt celebrations of sexuality and race in the workplace have been the norm for years. So have hiring preferences based on similar stuff. Floyd's death took the radicalization of HR's function to new levels. Justifying the connection between the crimes of the Minneapolis police officers and corporate behavior took a special type of twisted logic, but HR departments are resourceful and have plenty of tools at their disposal. DEI training manuals used in corporate HR settings provide the framework. They commonly teach executives how to "disrupt implicit bias" on the job and guide practitioners in how best to train managers to better understand their inner racist selves, my reporting shows.

If the employees at NextEra objected to being lectured on their white privilege, HR would have them fired. So most people there and elsewhere remain quiet. Not Brian Netzel. He worked for credit card giant American Express from 2018 to around the time that the 2020 cultural revolution reached its peak at the company, he states in a lawsuit against his old firm. I say old firm because he was fired for cause. His crime, according to his lawsuit: speaking up against what he called "race-based indoctrination sessions" that Amex instituted at the time of the Floyd riots, and a policy pushed by CEO Stephen Squeri that mandated that Black employment in each department reflect the percentage of African Americans in the general population.

A senior executive at American Express disputes some of this; there are no racial quotas in hiring, he says. Netzel was fired for what the executive described as noxious social media postings. Okay, but it doesn't take much digging to determine that while Amex doesn't use the words "quotas," it does adhere strictly to DEI. As the company's chief diversity officer explains proudly on the company's website, "At American Express, embracing diversity and standing for equity and inclusion…are at the core of our culture."

Squeri was born and bred in Queens, New York, grew up in the working class, and his work ethic got him to the top of one of the biggest companies. "He never forgot where he came from," is something I heard from a few mutual acquaintances. How you go from striver to woke is something this book explores. One explanation: To move up the management ranks, you need to adopt management's ethos.

A softer type of political progressivism began at Amex under Squeri's boss, the longtime and successful CEO Ken Chenault, I am told. Chenault, one of the nation's few Black CEOs, ran what Netzel said was mostly a meritocracy; hiring and promotion were based on work production and traditional measures of performance. It could be that Squeri, who took over as CEO in 2018, went woke because of white man's guilt. Likelier, he was pressured by his board to cave and meet progressive ESG standards following George Floyd.

Either way, Squeri made wokeness even bigger at Amex than it ever was under Chenault, people there tell me. His HR department brought in purveyors of critical race theory to lecture employees in 2020 around the time of the George Floyd riots, as if dividing people by race and subjecting white employees to charges that they are evil will solve our country's great racial divide.

Again, who is against diversity? Not me and not Netzel; what he spoke out against was what appeared to be racial quotas at a company. He also spoke out about being subjected to lectures that called him a bigot in the name of eliminating inherent racism from the face of the earth.

And all because some cop in Minneapolis killed a Black man after he tried to pass a counterfeit twenty-dollar bill in a convenience store.

Corporate wokeness is infuriating, sometimes exhausting to try to comprehend, but it was also inevitable if you study the zeitgeist of corporate America over the last fifty years. Like all revolutions, the woke one at the workplace started small: woke academics writing papers on the economic benefits; seminars airing those beliefs at places like the World Economic Forum in Davos. Companies increasingly began holding in-house symposiums that discussed soft subjects like "social responsibility," or the need for business to put aside shareholder concerns to address stuff like the environment and to make sure their workforce reflected society. ESG increasingly became ingrained in the corporate balance sheet.

Further propelling corporate wokeism, a new generation of corporate leaders found its way into the executive class. These were men, and a few women, many of whom were schooled at elite colleges that inculcated them with progressivism even as they sought jobs paying tens of millions of dollars a year thanks to the economic boom created by Ronald Reagan.

This new generation began to flex its might at something called Business Roundtable, setting the stage for the great corporate wokening to come. The Roundtable is the nation's biggest lobbying group for corporate America. It's like an exclusive country club, only to gain entry you must be a CEO. Leaders include 181 of the most powerful executives in the world, people like Jamie Dimon, the CEO of mega-bank JP Morgan and part of that newer, more progressive generation.

On August 19, 2019, Dimon, as head of Business Roundtable, did something that just a few years earlier would have seemed improbable, even sacrilegious. He declared that "shareholder capitalism" was dead and cancelled the great economist Milton Friedman, the man who created what history shows to be the most efficient form of corporate governance.

"Since 1978, Business Roundtable has periodically issued Principles of Corporate Governance," the Roundtable advised its members. "Each version of the document issued since 1997 has endorsed principles of shareholder primacy—that corporations exist principally to serve shareholders. With today's announcement, the new Statement supersedes previous statements and outlines a modern standard for corporate responsibility."

Dimon's statement continued, "While each of our individual companies serves its own corporate purpose, we share a fundamental commitment to all of our stakeholders. We commit to...deliver value to all of them, for the future success of our companies, our communities and our country."

In Dimon's telling, shareholder capitalism and Friedman were being replaced by something noble and modern. Also, thoroughly wokeish. If you really want to know why every company today seems like an extension of the Democratic National Committee—committed to far-left green edicts, ESG that destroys oil production and creates inflation, DEI that devolves into quotas—you can trace much of it to stakeholder capitalism as a defining principle of corporate governance. Stakeholder capitalism means that companies don't just make money, they need to take a political stand that is always left of center for reasons that will become apparent. Its embrace of progressivism is all encompassing: hiring, firing, investing, even advertising. In stakeholder capitalism, the corporation doesn't place ads to sell products, it advertises to sell woke politics. That same year Dimon did away with Friedman, and during the height of the #MeToo era (which carried its own bit of hysteria), a razor company named Gillette spent millions of dollars in ads to alert the world that every man alive has the Harvey Weinstein gene of toxic masculinity. Men can do better, the company wanted people to know; its ad buy featured actors portraying various forms of gross and faux male hood, because, they said, "boys will be boys."

Stakeholder capitalism at its finest! Dimon & co. want us to virtue signal while we shave because a male oppressor is born every minute. They wouldn't put it exactly that way, of course. To them stakeholder capitalism is refreshing and righteous. Bold and benevolent. Yet when I ask CEOs or business academics to define it, I get a different answer every time, which is why the woke forces found it so easy to hijack it as a tool of progressive, postmodern corporate groupthink as you will soon find out. Shareholder capitalism, meanwhile, might seem antiquated because its power is in its simplicity—and because it is hard for any activist to fuck with. CEOs had one boss: the shareholder. Do good for the shareholder, put people to work, make money for America, pay your taxes, and the rest will take care of itself. Laws will mandate that everyone gets an equal shot.

It worked for years, until Dimon & Co. began messing with what Uncle Milton created.

A little background on the man who started the shareholder capitalism movement. Milton Friedman specialized in the field of econometrics, or the use of complex mathematical formulas to study inflation, consumption, and how to grow GDP. He was one of the leaders of the Chicago school of economics that rejected the tax-and-spend consensus of Keynesianism and advocated free-market principles like cutting taxes and controlling the money supply to achieve economic goals like full employment.

He also promulgated the theory that CEOs were trained to be good at certain, narrow things, like growing a business, and serving *shareholders*, so they should stick to it. Leave the touchy-feely stuff to the political class. Unlike politicians, CEOs weren't elected to make the world a better place. If they tried, they would fuck it up.

During his many decades in the public eye, Uncle Milton achieved something rare in the field of economics: He was a Renaissance man, a writer, and a public intellectual speaking on cultural issues, advising presidents and prime ministers on public policy. He won the Nobel Prize in Economics in 1976, for his analysis of price stability. He helped give us the economic revival of the Reagan years.

The politicization of the boardroom—grandstanding CEOs taking on political causes that he saw beginning in the 1970s—particularly irked him because Friedman also thought it was morally wrong for CEOs to be taking their eyes off the shareholder ball. In his words, "There is one and only one social responsibility of business—to use its resources and engage in activities designed to increase its profits so long as it stays within the rules of the game, which is to say, engages in open and free competition without deception or fraud."

Friedman, one of history's great economists, died in 2006, but not without leaving his mark—that is, until Business Roundtable came along and tried to make him an economic asterisk. In the 1980s through the 1990s and well into the new millennium, when Friedman's influence reigned supreme, the United States witnessed an economic revival from the malaise of the 1970s. The tech revolutions created wealth like never before. Doing good meant making money, rewarding shareholders for their capital investments, and deploying that capital to expand and hire people, providing them with decent wages and benefits.

What did stakeholder capitalism give us? ESG everywhere. Hiring quotas, uber-powerful DEI advocates inside corporations, and if you haven't already heard, trans influencers in beer advertising, and tuck-friendly bathing suits for men transitioning to be women at the retailer Target. The Goldman Sachs pronoun guide, and Disney CEO Bob Chapek using corporate money to change a Florida law that banned the teaching of sex ed to toddlers.

It always struck me as odd that Dimon, someone I know well and admire, put the stake through the heart of Friedman's shareholder capitalism. The Jamie Dimon I know is a political moderate. He is also a longtime C-suite executive who worked his way from Harvard Business School to assist Sandy Weill, a legendary banking dealmaker, in creating another mega-bank, Citigroup. He is operationally one of the greatest CEOs ever, having steered JP Morgan through the 2008 financial crisis when other big banks needed federal aid, or they would have gone insolvent.

He did this through a lot of creative destruction as opposed to figuring out every conceivable way of maintaining a diverse workforce. He spent his time buying smaller banks and brokerages, scaling them down, and making sure all the parts worked collectively for shareholders. Dimon conducted quite a few mass firings in his time, not very stakeholder friendly.

At least before he went woke, Dimon recognized that businesses that struggle cut costs to survive; they perish when their products are obsolete, and that puts everyone out of work. Henry Ford in the mass production of the car put the buggy whip makers out of work, but those displaced workers got good-paying factory jobs at Ford, and also at GM and Chrysler. The middle and working class got an efficient form of transportation.

Now that Dimon has gone woke, he and the other stakeholder capitalists appear oblivious to the thing that sets us apart from the rest of world—the great and once hypercompetitive US economy. Productivity—the mother's milk of US prosperity—has stalled since 2005. Is it a coincidence that that's about the time corporate America started going woke? What is undeniable is that what Friedman railed against was mild compared to what's going down in woke corporate boardrooms today—propelled at least in part by Jamie Dimon.

And it pains me to say that.

It's no coincidence that with the rise of stakeholder capitalism came the mainstreaming of ESG, for the simple reason that both are built on the same warped set of values: that CEOs aren't in the job to make money, expand their business, and provide a decent return on investment. Their main function is to change America, which needed radical cultural and economic change.

Like the overall march toward corporate wokeism, ESG began slowly and methodically. At the *Wall Street Journal* in the mid-1990s, I covered something known as "socially responsible investing," in which mutual funds picked stocks of companies that provided birth control on demand, supported environmentalism, and advocated that boardrooms become less white and definitely less white male. It was a backwater business, overshadowed by the trillions of investor money flowing into technology funds or internet IPOs.

It was a start, and like all successful political movements, its foot soldiers were dogged and determined. As we will discuss shortly, activist groups like the Center for American Progress and the Human Rights Campaign, known in the boardroom by their acronyms, CAP and HRC, made great strides propelling corporate wokeness in general and ESG in particular by pushing a left-wing agenda through so-called "policy research," and good old-fashioned lobbying.

Increasingly, beginning in the mid- to late 2000s, activists began to target big companies to follow their agenda regarding the environment, diverse boards, and LGBTQ+ rights—key ingredients of the ESG matrix—as separate and distinct from the obvious rights every American worker has under the law.

These groups had money (funded by left-wing billionaire George Soros and other progressive fat cats) and the stroke to influence government officials in the Democratic Party to pressure big business. HRC's president, Kelley Robinson, for instance is tight with Obama and helped run his 2008 campaign. The Obama regulatory regime may have been among the most progressively aggressive until Biden was elected president. Corporate America's way of fighting back against forces like these is to cozy up to them and their proxies with money. It's called buying protection. No wonder HRC's list of donors, or so-called corporate partners, includes Disney, UPS, Pfizer,

Amazon, Google, and JP Morgan, a veritable who's who of corporate America looking to tout wokeness because of the political environment.

Consider the perversity of all of this. The nation's largest bank, JP Morgan, does business in red and blue states alike. Its clients come from all races and represent a spectrum of political beliefs. Many of its top executives vote Republican. It's run by one of history's great bankers, Jamie Dimon. But the bank also proudly supports an organization that brags on its website that it "defeated President Trump" during the 2020 presidential election. HRC is the same group that declared a "state of emergency for LGBTQ+ people" because it says there's been a "spike" in "anti-LGBTQ+ legislative assaults" in various states, which in plain English translates into governors and state legislatures calling it quits on teaching toddlers the finer points of gender fluidity.

All very radical stuff, and it's a testament to the degree that progressivism has infected the boardroom that HRC has a say in corporate governance. But it does. HRC publishes a widely followed list of companies that score highest on its "Corporate Equity Index," a rating system that has become a powerful tool used by the left to enforce its brand politics on corporate America. Big asset managers study HRC's index in measuring the "G," or governance, part of their ESG scoring. Get a low score from HRC and your company is attacked online as being transphobic or racist. ESG scores decline.

Yet ESG gets its imprimatur of respectably not only from the HRCs of the world. ESG gained broader acceptance with the support from globalist and quasi-governmental bodies, like the World Economic Forum in Davos, the yearly gathering of CEOs and one of the incubators of corporate wokeism.

And the United Nations. I found it no surprise that the uber-woke UN, which coddles left-wing dictators but attacks Israel for defending itself from terrorists, is at the forefront of corporate wokeness—and used its own power to influence corporate America to accept the progressive agenda of ESG.

The UN began publishing so-called studies around 2005 on the need for corporate America and multinational companies to embrace a new set of corporate governance standards that don't focus myopically on profits. Yes, the letters ESG came out of the UN. Soon the ideology seeped into every panel discussion at Davos, during public companies' annual meetings, and in CEO discussions. It was off to the races.

That set the stage for ESG being what it is today: a $50 trillion business when you're accounting for all the pigs feeding at the ESG trough. There are the fund managers, the Big Three of ESG: BlackRock, Vanguard, and State Street, which use ESG metrics when investing money for their clients. These companies manage about $22 trillion in combined assets, meaning they hold stocks in every major public company, which also means they can and do control corporate behavior to comply with ESG mandates.

They offer investors ESG funds that charge some of the highest fees in the money management business. That's why ESG has been such a cash cow for so long. They also infuse ESG metrics throughout their investment process even for those portfolios that are not sustainable. The reason? More money. ESG is a key selling point to gain access to lucrative pension money from progressive politicians who oversee retirement funds in places like New York and California.

The so-called outside proxy advisers like Institutional Shareholder Services and Glass, Lewis & Co. have also carved out an interesting and lucrative ESG niche. These companies operate a near duopoly, one of the few remaining in corporate America. They are nominally in the business of advising shareholders on how to vote on matters of corporate governance. They often serve as a "proxy," meaning shareholders just follow their advice on these matters because they don't have the time to sift through every shareholder proposal.

The proxy advisers have been huge proponents of ESG in recent years, and it's easy to see why. They have earned significant sums of money doling out ESG ratings on companies, with a side hustle consulting business that guides companies on how to attain the highest score so they can appeal to ESG-conscious investors.

Conflict of interest? Reps from both firms didn't return requests for comment. Wall Street's top regulator, the Securities and Exchange Commission under GOP chair Jay Clayton, thought so. Clayton sought to rein in this "duopoly," as he referred to them, and passed new disclosure rules of their aforementioned conflicts of interest. They would also have to consent to having their advice regulated like other Wall Street firms, which they did for a time. Clayton's lefty Democrat and ESG-obsessed successor, Gary Gensler, bowed to pressure from progressives and reversed the rule, giving the duopoly a free pass. No wonder ESG has grown into the behemoth it is today.

By 2021, it seemed that nothing could stop the ESG train from rolling. That year, BlackRock, Vanguard, and State Street signed on to something known as the "Net Zero Asset Managers" initiative, a partner of the UN-sponsored "Race to Zero" campaign to make a significant dent in greenhouse gas emissions by 2050.

ESG got further mainstreamed because investors can't help but put some of their money into funds that invest in "sustainable products"—the Wall Street euphemism for corporations that went woke. Investment advisers said ESG was the only way retail investors could get a piece of some of the booming and very ESG-compliant stocks in the tech sector.

Strange, isn't it? You would think that ESG portfolios would focus on the so-called green economy—windmills, solar panels, hydropower, EVs—as well as the stocks of companies dedicated to various social and diversity goals (Ben & Jerry's, to name just one). How is tech part of the green economy? Because the Apple iPhone doesn't emit greenhouse gases, and the Amazon board has a mandate to elect women and minority directors.

You get the picture: Describing exactly what constitutes ESG investing can be like nailing Jell-O to the wall. Sure, there are ESG "screens" offered by outside consultants like those old Good Housekeeping Seals of Approval. The standards are often obtuse and malleable. ESG portfolios also leave out the most sustainable energy source—nuclear power—because the ESG monitors seem to think nuclear energy will lead to the next Hiroshima and all-out nuclear war.

Easier to understand are the manifold downsides of ESG for the average Joe saving for retirement. And how ESG has made Wall Street fat cats much fatter. ESG-styled funds charge fees as much as four times higher than the average actively managed fund. Yet most ESG funds underperform the markets; they're what Gordon Gekko would call a "dog with fleas." Windmills are a horrible investment; they are one of the least efficient ways to produce electrical power, and that's reflected in the stock prices of their manufacturers. Americans love guns, which is why Smith & Wesson remains very profitable despite constant attacks from the left.

Then there's the societal implications. ESG prepares for a future that is probably never coming. Al Gore has been saying the world was about to burn itself out because of greenhouse gas emissions for at least the past two decades, and if he lives long enough maybe the next two as well. The Net

Zero Asset Owner Alliance's ambitious goal of net zero emissions by 2050 is laughably unattainable when you consider that emerging economies—yes, those in China, India, and elsewhere—are burning fossil fuels like crazy. They see it as the fastest way to grow their economies, lifting millions of people out of poverty, no matter how much pollution it creates.

Preserving our country's vast natural beauty, the environment, is a worthy cause, of course. There are laws against dumping waste in rivers, or needlessly polluting the air around us. But ESG takes environmentalism to extreme, nefarious levels. It tries to codify unestablished climate science—mostly the opinions of progressive activists that the world will end in 2050 unless businesses stop doing so much business—into a set of inchoate investment rules. It does so without any acknowledgment of economic dislocations when you curtail oil exploration. It does so without a replacement energy source like nuclear power that could provide a seamless transition to a green economy, because the left sees nuclear as end-of-times stuff.

Average Americans, meanwhile, are left shouldering the cost of this experiment. Even though ESG has no set definition, it does find some degree of common ground. Energy companies get higher grades when they drill less and build green but inefficient energy sources. That has led, as we're all painfully aware, to higher energy prices and runaway inflation. Businesses that decide to cap expansion because they're worried about an expanding corporate footprint get good ESG grades. It doesn't matter that working-class wage rates will suffer.

Most Americans aren't schooled in all the nuances of ESG, but they despise what it's done to the US economy and their paychecks. Notice President Joe Biden's sickeningly low approval ratings. To hear it from Sleepy Joe, the US economy is booming even as his administration thoroughly infuses ESG into the regulation of big business. In his warped worldview, restrictions on energy exploration, forcing companies to adopt ESG business standards, have been great for the average Joe and Jane.

The country isn't buying it—or his poll numbers would be better. The president says he wants rich people to "pay their fair share." But he taxed the working class by accepting the higher inflation that came from government mandating and encouraging various forms of ESG though his war on oil and coal. He did this to make peace with progressives and maintain his shaky governing coalition.

Now the public wants him out.

The idiocy of "E"—cutting back on drilling, for instance, when oil reserves are taxed because of the war in Ukraine—isn't quite rivaled by the farce of "S," but it comes close.

Society matters, right? The social part of ESG is all about "compensating [people] fairly and providing important benefits...supporting them through training and education that help develop new skills for a rapidly changing world," according to Business Roundtable. Sounds like something you might support. But when the automakers decided to embrace the S (even before it was widely known as S), they nearly put themselves out of business offering gold-plated pensions and endless benefits to line workers when they really needed to downsize. It's no wonder that the Big Three automakers have been reduced to shells of their former selves, competing now with Tesla in the electric vehicle business that they see as the future even if most electric cars are too expensive for the vast middle and working class to afford and too cumbersome to power on a daily basis.

That brings us to the "G" in ESG, which leans heavily on the aforementioned DEI practiced in cultlike fashion by HR departments all across corporate America. These screens determine whether companies are committed to diversity in all its forms, whether they are hiring enough women and minorities in the executive ranks or at the board level. Are they supporting the LGBTQ+ community with sufficient zeal? In the world of DEI, the old boys' club still exists, even though anyone who has worked at a major company knows it hasn't for decades.

According to a June 2022 report in *Forbes*, "a whopping 404 of the Fortune 500 companies included the business case for diversity on their corporate website by suggesting that diversity was important because it would contribute to their profits or bottom line in some way." Diversity proponents claim there is a ton of good academic research proving how corporate diversity—in the C-suite or in the boardroom and in the ranks of employees—improves corporate performance, their stock price, more productivity, and so on.

You can also find research on the health benefits of cannibalism. Likewise, most of these academic papers do so without control groups that measure margins of error. Those academics who have applied scientific methodology to diversity and its benefits have found no correlation between having a nonbinary male serving on a corporate board and the company's stock performance.

"Increasing the numbers of traditionally underrepresented people in your workforce does not automatically produce benefits. Taking an 'add diversity and stir' approach, while business continues as usual, will not spur leaps in your firm's effectiveness or financial performance," write Robin Ely and David Thomas of the Harvard Business School. "The research touting the link was conducted by consulting firms and financial institutions and fails to pass muster when subjected to scholarly scrutiny. Meta-analyses of rigorous, peer-reviewed studies found no significant relationships—causal or otherwise—between board gender diversity and firm performance," they write.

If ESG is so bad, what keeps it going? As *Go Woke, Go Broke* will show, power and money. The top ESG asset managers—BlackRock, Vanguard, State Street—are big and powerful. While people at the Big Three of ESG tell me they're just responding to demand for ESG—blue-state pension funds and sovereign wealth funds want ESG portfolios, as do many investors—they also create their own demand, as you will soon discover.

And yet, you could maybe, just maybe, stomach all the phony virtue signaling surrounding ESG from the woke capitalism crowd if they applied it equally to all public companies.

They don't. Not even close.

Take what's happening at the Nasdaq, a big stock exchange that caters to the tech industry. If you're a CEO of a company who wants his stock to trade seamlessly, you apply to "list," or have it traded on a major stock exchange, like the New York Stock Exchange or the Nasdaq Stock Market, the two largest such venues. Meeting Nasdaq's so-called listing standards should be standard stuff like disclosure of profits, losses, and other logical corporate governance metrics to make sure the CEO isn't robbing the place blind.

Not quite. In 2020, Nasdaq's obsession with ESG and wokeness grew to unfathomable levels. The exchange adopted a rule that all but set quotas in the corporate boardroom, forcing all listed companies to disclose boardroom diversity. Critics called it a public shaming exercise; companies are forced to "explain why they do not have at least two diverse directors, including one who self-identifies as female and one who self-identifies as either an underrepresented minority or LGBTQ."

Guess who's exempt from all of this? The Chinese. China's economy is on the verge of rivaling our own in size. Its companies list their shares on all the major exchanges, including the Nasdaq. Chinese companies are also some of the world's biggest polluters; they're controlled by one of the world's most repressive regimes, known as the Chinese Communist Party (CCP). They would fail nearly every ESG metric if they were also held to them, but they're not, by Nasdaq or any other adherent to the dictates of corporate wokeness.

I discovered this devious wrinkle in corporate progressivism a few years ago while covering the IPO of Alibaba, the China-based competitor to our online retailer Amazon. A real entrepreneur, Jack Ma created Alibaba in his Beijing apartment. But even self-made men in China answer to the commie apparatchiks at the CCP. In the IPO docs, there was a not-so-subtle risk factor about the CCP and its tendency to "exercise significant control over China's economic growth…providing preferential treatment to particular industries and companies." Translated into English: If the CCP doesn't like someone at Alibaba, it's off to the gulag, and shareholders might suffer. That's kind of what happened to Ma, who disappeared for months after mildly rebuking the CCP.

Yet Alibaba's ESG score didn't suffer.

Boardroom politics in the woke era is a twisted phenomenon. It allows China Inc. to get rich while it oppresses the LGBTQ community on the mainland and persecutes (some would say commits genocide on) its Uyghur ethnic minority without Nasdaq demanding Uyghur board seats on listed Chinese companies. The reason? It has something to do with money. Nasdaq would lose potentially billions of dollars if these metrics were applied equally. So would Goldman Sachs. David Solomon's Goldman Sachs may channel wokeness at work and love investing according to ESG, but not enough to turn its back on underwriting the stocks of Chinese companies like the Alibaba IPO even if its founder eventually finds himself sitting in a cell.

Disney also preaches some of the most woke politics from its boardroom and C-suites that filter into its programming and theme park experiences. And it also excuses China's human rights abuses as it seeks to expand in the mainland. Ditto for BlackRock, a leader in ESG on its US portfolio companies but that doesn't use ESG screens when buying Chinese stocks. To do so would piss off the Chinese government that approved BlackRock's recent foray into selling its funds to China's massive and growing investor class.

Yes, BlackRock is the first US money manager to offer mutual funds to Chinese investors, and it certainly won't be the last. JP Morgan's CEO, Jamie Dimon, too loves to tout corporate wokeism, even taking what looked like a BLM-inspired knee during the 2020 social unrest. He also loves the Chinese market; JP Morgan is buying stakes in Chinese banks and opening branches. The firm also serves as an underwriter for Alibaba, also ignoring Jack Ma's plight. US tech giant Apple, from woke Silicon Valley, builds its iPhones there; EV sensation Tesla is saving the world, but has plants in China.

Mark Cuban, the billionaire tech entrepreneur and until recently owner of a professional basketball team, attempts to make the case in this book that woke does sell; the younger generation is into social justice and products that reflect progressive politics. He says the NBA is all in on social justice. Its success in attracting a younger fan base that will soon dominate sales is proof no one is going broke on going woke.

Aside from a lack of obvious evidence that woke sells to most Americans, let's explore the hypocrisy of the NBA's progressive virtue signaling. Until recently, Cuban was also the owner of the NBA's Dallas Mavericks. The NBA is the only professional sports league that's in business with the CCP to air games on the mainland. So much money is on the line for pro basketball that the NBA has been known to discipline any executive who speaks up against real oppression in China, the brutal crackdown on pro-Democracy protesters in Hong Kong.

How's that for supporting social justice?

I asked Adena Friedman, the CEO of Nasdaq and the author of those crazy listing rules, how all this makes sense. The morally corrupt CCP—the Chinese Communist Party—runs every Chinese company, even those listed in US exchanges. Will Nasdaq force Chinese companies to institute DEI and meet the same ESG standards she's demanding here in the United States? Her flacks told me progress is achieved incrementally; for now they're willing to accept two female board members on Chinese companies even if they're both hard-core commies.

Okay, but my Wall Street sources say Friedman's new diversity rules aren't purely about achieving some sort of kumbaya moment; she's running cover for some powerful political players in the woke corporate movement. She is close to Gary Gensler, the SEC chair appointed by President Biden, who is leading an effort in Washington to push corporate America to the left, as we discuss in upcoming chapters.

A former official in the Justice Department under George W. Bush, who also serves on corporate boards, tells me that Gensler is behind the Nasdaq effort because these so-called diverse corporate boards channel progressive politics into company policy. And it's working. Roughly since the time the Nasdaq rules took effect, the McKinsey corporate consulting firm says 70 percent of all directors appointed to corporate boards are no longer straight and white and male.

That's one big reason DEI and ESG have become touchstones of corporate behavior: They're being enforced by woker and woker board members. These members owe their jobs to the preservation of the woke circus at some of the nation's largest companies.

Whether it's channeled through ESG or DEI, corporate wokeism is a farce on so many levels that it's hard to keep track. Google is said to be a paragon of ESG compliance (what's the carbon footprint of a search engine?). Yet it's one of the worst enforcers of speech codes among its employees, as the sad situation of James Damore shows. He was a Google engineer until he decided to write a memo assailing the left-wing bias in the Google corporate culture. That's when he was fired. And you wonder why many employees are afraid to speak up when management brings in some CRT scholar to enlighten them on their systemic racism.

Like Google, Apple and Tesla too are the very models that corporate wokeism works; they're companies with soaring valuations and a devotion to doing good (even if they do business with China), particularly when it comes to the environment. iPhones don't pollute, and neither do EVs. Right? Execs at both companies would eagerly agree. Apple, in fact, has signed on to Business Roundtable's stakeholder capitalism pledge to "protect the environment by embracing sustainable practices across our businesses."

Here's the inside scoop on their business models, as explained by none other than Larry Fink, the CEO of BlackRock, the world's largest money management firm.

The popular view, particularly on the right, is that Fink, the most powerful financier on the planet, is also ESG's biggest defender and a progressive zealot. Fink and BlackRock are indeed powerful: $10 trillion in assets under management in 2024 means they own pieces of just about every public company on the planet. That power extends to Fink's political influence; he has major politicians, the president even, on speed dial. He's also been among ESG's most influential advocates.

I've known Fink for years and I can also tell you he's much more of a political moderate than he appears, and his allegiance to ESG has become much more nuanced than his critics contend. He's also among the most astute observers of boardroom behavior alive today.

Fink recently confided to me how ESG is somewhat of an absurdity, though he didn't use those exact words. Instead, he explained how ESG-compliant iPhones and electric car batteries are built. You need to mine minerals like lithium, copper, and even gold. The mining is done in Africa in appalling slave-labor-like conditions. It's also done in a way that produces tremendous greenhouse emissions and pollutes the air and water with chemicals. The biggest companies doing the mining are from China, not exactly our best friends.

And that's Larry Fink.

The repulsive underside to ESG is that while it's making many in corporate America rich, average Americans may be going broke from it. And not just from inflation. Plenty of data shows an interesting correlation between corporate America's embrace of ESG, stakeholder capitalism, and DEI and average Americans suffering from falling wages, analysts say. They referred me to an interesting chart by an outfit called Statista. It tracks the "Aggregated CEO-to-worker compensation ratio for the 350 largest publicly owned companies in the United States from 1965 to 2022."

Indeed, between 2016 and 2022, a time when stakeholder capitalism began and corporate wokeism exploded, the income gap between top earners and the working class exploded as well, expanding a whopping 47 percent. It's the largest spike in income inequality in recent history. You can make a good case that ESG alters corporate incentives enough that productivity declines precipitously under the weight of its various edicts, and the middle and working class suffers as oil companies scale back drilling for oil and car makers are forced to make expensive and inefficient electric vehicles.

Remember: Higher inflation translates into a regressive form of taxation for anyone but the rich, because people with money can speculate in stock investing; the rest of us can't afford to fill up our tanks.

And if ESG and woke capitalism was so good, why are CEOs in corporate America still primarily white and male? And why are so many average dudes collecting unemployment checks because of the fentanyl crisis or racial- and gender-based quotas? Why are Black poverty levels still too high?

Maybe because woke capitalism doesn't work.

CHAPTER THREE

DEI or DIE?

"I'm going to speculate that most executives turn this woke stuff over to some junior person to work on this because they don't want to get their hands dirty," Ed Rensi tells me. "Most CEOs are dealing with a lot of stuff at thirty thousand feet, and they're about as far from the grass roots as you can get."

Rensi, the retired CEO of McDonald's USA, will play a key role in the anti-woke counter-offensive this book will detail. Ed's been around for decades in the fast-food industry. When you eat a Chicken McNugget, remember it was Rensi who created it (with others, he tells me) when he ran the company's US subsidiary in the 1990s. Yes, the guy who formulated little pieces of faux fried chicken is now leading a grassroots effort to combat corporate wokeness. But Rensi is a true believer—not in the health benefits of the McNugget (I know, there aren't any), but in combatting the virus infecting our economy.

I asked him how we got to a place where left-wing causes, demands for reparations, and Greenpeace-like environmental solutions are supported not just by some lefty academics but also by the pillars of capitalism. He believes the real adults in the room—CEOs—don't want to get too involved and they farm out the politics to more progressive types who populate HR and other departments, so they don't have to be bothered.

Based on my reporting there's some truth to what Rensi is saying. CEOs are busy people. They don't have time to do everything, including monitor Chick-fil-A debates and if Pride Month was sufficiently celebrated in and around every cubicle.

That doesn't mean CEOs are unaware of the wokening of their firms and boardrooms, or don't support it. Far from it. In fact, C-suite support is the key reason corporate America has gone so woke. CEOs set the woke agenda at big public companies often because they've convinced themselves of some of the weird benefits of it (more on that to come). Underlings then carry out this agenda through diversity training, hiring quotas, all the stuff that helps the CEO meet various DEI and ESG edicts. It is a wash and repeat loop of sorts, based on the news of the day, whether it's #MeToo, George Floyd, Pride Month, or the endless displays of diversity every time progressive advocates discover a new gender.

Fear drives this vicious cycle as well. Most CEOs these days are cowards. The old-timers, like Jack Welch of GE, Bernie Marcus at Home Depot, John Whitehead at Goldman Sachs, or even the semi-old-timers, like Morgan Stanley's former CEO John Mack, would see fads like DEI or ESG as obstacles to making money and patently un-American. Not these guys. They cower before the progressive left in the activist space and, of course, big government. One reason is that corporate America is highly regulated, increasingly so over the past five decades, thus highly reliant on government for handouts. CEOs I speak to say DEI mandates are enforced in part by the plaintiff bar joining with the Justice Department's Civil Rights Division to bring cases against firms if they can show statistical disparities based on race and sex even without providing actual evidence of discrimination.

All true, though my reporting shows that the new breed of CEO agrees with some of this woke nonsense. It's also just easier to give in to the madness and collect their multi-gazillion-dollar paychecks.

That's why it's no coincidence that the rise of corporate progressivism and its various permutations like DEI reached a fever pitch during the Biden presidency. Joe Biden might just be the most DEI-obsessed president in the nation's history in terms of its enforcing racial and gender diversity mandates in government, and threatening to impose those on the private sector.

"The burden to appoint a white male to a major cabinet post is so high most don't even throw their hat in the ring for consideration," one DC political operative told me. There's an unofficial rule, he said, that for every white cabinet member in the Biden administration, you need to find two or three people of color or someone with gender diversity for other key posts.

The proof? Well, consider the following: Biden's appointee to the Supreme Court was an African American woman, Ketanji Brown Jackson, who once opined in her defense of affirmative action that Black doctors are better at delivering Black babies. Kamala Harris, his deeply unpopular vice president, became Biden's running mate in 2020, and it wasn't because of her immense political talents or likability (she got crushed in the primaries and Biden's wife, Jill, hated her). We may eventually have a President Kamala Harris because, after George Floyd, Biden promised a woman of color as his VP, and she's of Indian and African American descent.

The ultimate diversity hire in the administration is that of a transwoman, Rachel Levine, who until 2011 was Richard Levine, an MD with two children. Levine is a longtime health bureaucrat who somehow was commissioned as a four-star admiral in the US Public Health Service Commissioned Corps, whatever that is. Many firsts appear on Rachel's résumé in terms of her gender, but not a great record of accomplishment as a doctor unless you consider as a "plus" her support of "gender-affirming care" or puberty blockers and mastectomies to gender-dysphoric children.

In a world where DEI rules, Rachel Levine is perfect to serve as assistant secretary of health.

Biden likes to say that because of DEI, his administration reflects the demographics of America. It doesn't, or his cabinet and choices to lead major regulatory agencies would be 75 percent white and many more of them men. He was also once considered a moderate Democrat. Now all he talks about is racial inequality, the green movement, gender-affirming care for kids, and ways to use the federal government to remedy it.

So, what happened? At eighty-one, Biden is old, and at times feeble (the reason he's known as "Sleepy Joe"), but still very ambitious. His trajectory to the left and overt wokeism has everything to do with political expediency—the left these days controls the Democratic Party—and his lust to become president after trying and failing so many times during his long political career.

Corporate wokeism's journey as a dominant boardroom theology, its love affair with DEI, and the progressive movement is more complicated than Sleepy Joe's, but there are similarities. This C-suite political shift began in the 1980s and continued through the 1990s until we had increasingly progressive CEOs sitting in C-suites. For a time, corporate America's luminaries—think Jack Welch, Bernie Marcus, and some of the people who ran Goldman that I mentioned—kept politics away from the boardroom. Merit was the first thing that mattered in hiring and promotion. DEI officers didn't exist, and if they did, they didn't command the attention they do today.

That changed gradually and incrementally over the past thirty-plus years, according to my reporting on boardroom behavior. One important impetus for corporate wokeism: government pressure from the DOJ civil rights department and the threat of costly and embarrassing litigation. Then came progressive activist groups disguised as shareholders descending on boardrooms and demanding various degrees of progressive change through the proxy process and threats of boycotts.

Conservatives have traditionally taken the position that the invisible hand of the free market should dictate how a company behaves. Not the left. And that's why it's better armed for this battle to make business woke, my reporting shows.

Barack Obama's presidency in 2008 also supercharged the progressive movement in America in ways that profoundly influenced the economy and the politics of business. Finally, the far left had one of their own, a community organizer in the mold of Saul Alinsky, in the White House. Business increasingly came under political pressure from the White House because left-wing political activists as opposed to moderate members of the business community filled key regulatory positions.

Joe Biden picked up where Obama left off. Just as Sleepy Joe succumbed to the left-wing pressure in his party to get ahead, corporate America caved and adopted wokeness as a cost of doing business. The pressure on business to conform to left-wing diktat in the form of DEI and ESG was daunting, but it also paid to go woke. Big government and big business have always performed a weird kabuki dance, government beating up rich greedy CEOs, demanding that corporations pay their "fair share" of taxes, and the business community fighting back, explaining how increasing the cost of doing business will slow the economy. The reality is that they find common ground over something called "crony capitalism"—a mutually advantageous relationship where businesses find ways to profit from targeted tax breaks and other incentives handed out by government to engage in certain types of economic activities.

Crony capitalism provides one explanation for Jeff Immelt's conversion from Mitt Romney Republican to proponent of corporate progressivism after replacing Jack Welch as CEO of GE. "Jeff's a Republican, not that he sounds like one these days," one of Immelt's friends and former colleagues once remarked. In 2010, Immelt joined Barack Obama's Council on Jobs and Competitiveness, a group of CEOs that regularly conferred with the president on economic policy. Much of that policy involved enticing big companies to go woke, both environmentally and institutionally. In GE's case, the conglomerate jumped headfirst into the green energy movement, subsidized by the government through various means. It looked like a no-lose proposition, making money from a green new deal with government assistance. It also diverted Immelt and his management team from their day job of growing their traditional business lines of aircraft manufacturing, consumer goods, and so on. About a decade later Immelt (facing criticism from Wall Street and publicly from his old boss, Welch) was out and GE was fighting to stay alive.

Again, as with Goldman, you can't entirely blame wokeness for GE's demise, but, like Goldman, you can see how it played a role. GE feasted off green energy and the subsidies Obama handed out to build highly ineffective solar panels and windmills. Immelt similarly instituted DEI mandates at GE when he should have been laser focused on the company's broken business model and hiring the most talented people regardless of race. Talk to most Americans and they will tell you diversity is a worthy goal; affirmative action should seek out minority candidates, and women should be a corporate priority. It became *the priority*. Around the time of the Obama presidency is when you began to see CEOs and their boards of directors granting vast powers to HR departments to meet hard-and-fast DEI goals, aka quotas.

One corporate lawyer described DEI's stroke in corporate America this way: "There are few if any limiting principles on DEI departments. Many seem to operate outside legal controls because woke boards and CEOs set them up that way."

DEI is so powerful at major companies that Anheuser-Busch's quest for a higher DEI score led to a transwoman pushing its iconic beer brand Budweiser on social media.

Like all things woke, DEI went nuclear after George Floyd. Corporate America's lurch to the left on diversity and wokeness had been happening for years; Floyd's death was a flashpoint in its elevation to new and more dangerous levels. CEOs trotting out Black executives, many of them multimillionaires, to lecture middle-class employees about their terrible lot in life is another level of absurdity. But that was just the beginning; the sinister side of DEI then went into motion. Companies hired consultants to provide "racial equity audits" that graded management on diversity in board membership and the companies' entire workforce.

The CEO of United Airlines in 2021 boasted that his DEI mandates would mean that 50 percent of all new pilots wouldn't be white dudes—they would be chosen based on race and sex. Scary, but not surprising. Boeing stated similarly stringent DEI hiring goals in management and its operations, a corporate priority that takes precedence even above the quality of its aircraft, which increasingly showed signs of disrepair. The carrier was so undeterred in its corporate priorities that not even a door flying off one of its jets in midflight could put a hold on its DEI obsession. DEI became so granular in doling out benefits based on race that it has extended through the corporate supply chain. White-male-owned suppliers to big companies needed to go and be replaced by those deemed oppressed. Boards set supervisory pay to meeting DEI mandates. Translation: You hire, promote, and do business with fewer white people and you get a bonus. Don't hire based on race, and you get a pay cut.

Hooray!

Wokeness and its manifestations like DEI were more Orwellian than anything the great literary thinker wrote. So-called DEI statements became standard, forcing job applicants to describe in writing what they did to make the world more diverse and humane to all races. The reality of these statements was something far worse; they are more like pledges of allegiance to progressivism, a woke litmus test to weed out free-thinking applicants.

Author and policy analyst Andrew Gillen studied the impact of DEI statements at the University of California, Berkeley. "The scale of the resulting purge would make Stalin blush," he writes. "Of 893 nominally qualified candidates, 679 were eliminated solely due to insufficiently woke diversity, equity and inclusion statements. In other words, Berkeley used a political litmus test to eliminate over three-quarters of the applicant pool."

"I can't believe what I had to sign to get considered for a job," said one health care executive after his potential supervisor told him that the DEI statement was as important as his twenty-plus years in the medical field. He needed to provide granular information and proof on how he dedicated his life, his career, but not to saving lives. That was secondary to his work in advancing women and minorities—even better, women who were minorities, because they checked two DEI boxes. In the end, he didn't get the job, after fessing up that he refused to advance people who weren't qualified.

The big consulting firm McKinsey & Company, which advises every major company in the world, is a huge supporter of DEI and the various ways it's enforced. It describes DEI as a way of creating fairness in a corporate environment by adopting "three closely linked values...that are working to be supportive of different groups of individuals including people of different races, ethnicities, religions, abilities, gender and sexual orientations."

In practice, DEI has little to do with fairness and everything to do with a warped definition of "equity," according to my reporting. Scores of midlevel and even upper-level corporate managers tell me DEI enforced by increasingly woke corporate HR departments and their "chief diversity officers" has turned the HR function into a quota machine.

As California debates reparations for slavery, corporate America has already adopted a form of them through the DEI model. Talk to enough lawyers and you might also come away with the notion that DEI is not just silly (is it practical to be doling out jobs solely on the basis of skin color?) but also illegal. The 2023 Supreme Court ruling on affirmative action that stated unequivocally race can't be used in college admissions could mean the end of DEI is just one similar lawsuit away.

"I can't wait to take the DEI case," a veteran corporate lawyer told me after the SCOTUS ruling. Here's his legal reasoning, and it makes sense. The affirmative action ruling's underlying premise was a strict reading of Title VI of the Civil Rights Act, which bars discrimination based on race in "any program or activity receiving federal assistance." That would include public and private universities.

Title VII of the Civil Rights Act specifically involves employment for companies with more than fifteen employees. That's where corporate DEI comes in, he says. And because Title VII is virtually indistinguishable from Title VI, corporate DEI is on dubious legal footing. "It's only a matter of time before DEI goes the same way affirmative action went with this Supreme Court," my legal source says.

His lips to God's ears. In the meantime, DEI has grown to a \$10-billion-a-year business, and despite some recent setbacks, it remains entrenched in the culture of corporate America.

"We were all called to attend a Zoom meeting about a racial incident involving an employee," said one senior manager at a major consulting firm. The manager, whose name I'm withholding, at first thought someone in her department had used a demeaning slur in reference to a Black woman.

When the call began here's what she discovered: The DEI officer said she had asked people at the company to report any "microaggressions" they had experienced on the job. Loosely defined, microaggressions aren't what most people think when they think of racist behavior. They don't involve the use of the N-word or excluding Black people from the company picnic or after-work drinks. They are innocent, even unconscious expressions that someone might on a bad day take offense to. Less loosely defined, a microaggression is a solution in search of a problem that doesn't exist. Either way, rooting them out became an important thing first on college campuses, then more recently at the nation's largest companies in the era of corporate wokeism.

As our manager was about to discover, the all-hands-on-deck discussion was prompted by a report that a white man did something deemed evil when he complimented a Black woman on her new hairstyle one day at work. The woman complained that the compliment was not a compliment but a subtly racist remark, a function of the white male's racist preference for what she said was her new "white-looking" women's hair.

A microaggression.

When people on the call heard all of this, they were shocked, infuriated, and embarrassed to be working at a company that would indulge someone's fantasy about racism. Tolerating hurt feelings at this level, elevating it to a corporate crime, means just about anything anyone says at work or at a work function can lead to dismissal. It's a form of mind control that takes those old college speech codes to a completely new and dangerous level. "It was proof that at the office, you can't say anything," my source told me. "Why would I want to strike up a conversation with a Black employee if I could get fired for something innocent?"

The stupidity of DEI and the entire corporate wokeness hysteria is why it's destined to ultimately fail. How do you innovate products and compete globally when you're spending so much time on microaggressions or are worried about ever more esoteric forms of diversity? For every trans beer drinker you might attract, you're going to lose ten more traditional beer drinkers in Middle America who want to see real women in bikinis sipping cold ones. That's why following Budweiser's infamous Dylan Mulvaney ad, which this book will examine later in greater detail, sales cratered.

Mulvaney is a transwoman activist, very "un-brand" for Bud and its traditional blue-collar customer. Her fame shot to new heights because of one of the weirdest spectacles in recent economic history, when she was hired as a media influencer for Bud Light, through its parent company, AB InBev.

How Mulvaney sitting in a bubble bath and half-naked came to represent a once iconic beer brand is indicative of corporate America's DEI obsession and its pitfalls. Her beer-drinking fame began in April 2023 with a social media ad that made a big splash, and not in a good way for Bud, which is still paying the price as customers, mostly blue-collar, and hardly woke, revolted and boycotted the beer for shoving such politicized nonsense in their collective face. The Budweiser brand that took 150 years to build has been severely tarnished, possibly destroyed, in just a few weeks, because for all the political power behind corporate wokeism, consumers in Middle America, indeed most of America, are starting to rebel against this weird conformity.

Vanitha Swaminathan has spent a lot of time looking into the politicization of brands through DEI, how companies have begun to look at sales and marketing through the lens of what she calls "corporate-social-political action."

Swaminathan, a marketing professor at the University of Pittsburgh, divides what many people call corporate wokeness (not her words) into three phases that began in the 1950s through the 1970s with companies adopting "cause marketing," typically apolitical causes to make the world a better place. Think food drives to war-ravaged countries or calls to donate blood to the Red Cross.

Later, sometime in the 1980s, came companies with brands that identified specifically with a political cause, often of the progressive variety. Think Ben & Jerry's ice cream, a brand devoted to left-wing politics through its stated corporate objectives not just to sell ice cream but to save the earth from (alleged) global warming and promoting social justice through race-based hiring schemes. Or Nike's support of progressive causes that its target demo also supports. The people who run these places don't care if they piss off two-thirds of the country with unrelenting progressivism in ads and marketing—that's the point of the brand that serves a niche audience.

Then, according to Swaminathan, came the third wave sometime in the mid-2000s: "corporate-social-political action." The progressive evolution in corporate groupthink bled into the marketing of products as CEOs and management began to see their role as beyond serving shareholders. They were using their positions to do good, saving the environment, and above all promoting diversity in management and throughout their companies. Product ads and marketing campaigns reflected all of the above. DEI came into vogue.

To understand why Budweiser and then the retailer Target, and many others like Disney, got into such hot water with their traditional customers, you need to understand how corporate-social-political action works, and how Americans are increasingly repulsed by it. It forces companies to view their consumers not as individuals but as part of groups, and subgroups, and even smaller segments of those groups, based on race, sex, and the protean forms of gender that the progressive left is telling Americans redefine inherently real categories like male and female.

Consumers are viewed as members of different tribes where people think alike and display similar buying patterns. At BlackRock, salespeople are given specific instructions on how to peddle various investment products to women, "Latino and Hispanic Investors," "Black Investors," and even "LGBTQ+ Investors," according to internal documents I've obtained.

"Women are an economic powerhouse," BlackRock's manual states. "Yet many feel less confident than men when it comes to financial decision-making and 36% say they feel patronized by advisors. Breaking away from common misperceptions that 'women don't understand finance,'" it instructs, "would benefit both women investors and advisors."

I guess BlackRock sees the need to tell its people that women are good with numbers.

Equally patronizing is the firm's guide to selling to Hispanics. "Hispanic refers to people who originated (or their ancestors originated) from countries where Spanish is the most commonly spoken language...Latino and Latina are the masculine and feminine terms that identify people with a heritage rooted in Latin American countries, irrespective of the language spoken. Given the many Latin American countries where Spanish is the common language, many people are both Hispanic and Latino."

So, knowing that "Latina" refers to a Hispanic woman really might get her to buy one of BlackRock's overpriced and underperforming ESG funds?

The documents alert BlackRock's salesforce that there's something different about Black people, and it goes beyond the color of their skin. "Black Americans may have multiple intersecting identities, such as Black & woman, Black & LGBTQ+, Black & single parent and many others. Each identity can influence an investor's financial beliefs and goals in different ways," it says.

Really? Black LGBTQ+ people really want to grow a retirement account different than white people?

Which brings us to how BlackRock is assisting its salesforce to sell to all variations of the LGBTQ+ rainbow. "The LGBTQ+ community in the U.S. stands at 13 million individuals and represents nearly $7 trillion in wealth," the guide says. LGBTQ+ people face lots of discrimination, so they may not like a slick salesman cold calling them with investment pitches. Here's BlackRock's advice on how to make the sale to the various shades of the rainbow: "Be open and honest. Showing that you are sincere in your desire to understand both the individual and their community sets the stage for a successful client-advisor relationship."

Ummm. Does BlackRock really mean that its salesmen have to be more extra-especially honest with an LGBTQ+ person than a middle-aged white dude?

Okay, when you get through the trite (and clownish) nature of how one of the biggest companies in the world approaches woke DEI-infused marketing, you also might say that some of this sounds legit. Looking to appeal to some differences between people is called target marketing, and businesses have been doing it since the beginning of time. It's also common sense that a lot of this target marketing is tribalized marketing, and absurd. The "Hispanic market" is one of the fastest growing in the country, we are told by marketing experts. Yet what is a Hispanic anyway? Someone from Mexico, Nicaragua, Ecuador, Argentina, or Cuba? We are led to believe that these folks, some of them white, some of them Black, some mixed-race, many of them rich, all of them from different cultures, share the same buying patterns because they're all "Hispanic."

Common sense and real data will tell you that LGBTQ+, Black, Hispanic, and women investors won't buy BlackRock funds no matter how culturally sensitive the sales pitch if those funds suck. Yes, just like some old white guy. Still, there's supposed to be money in this tribalization. Marketing firms that specialize in breaking down consumer behavior along these lines have been making lots of it serving the nation's biggest companies for going on two decades. The theory of this type of market research posits, for example, that white male Baby Boomers (born between 1946 and 1964) won't go for a Pride Month clothing display, so forget about them. They're a dying demographic anyway. Most African Americans, some of this data shows, will accept Pride Month as a cultural norm, despite the deep cultural conservatism found in the Black community. Same with Hispanics, the nation's fastest-growing demo.

Meanwhile, a new generation of white consumers was arriving and ready to consume more than the Boomers and embrace wokeism. This demo is far more open to diversity, particularly gender diversity, than its predecessors. They are the Millennials (born between the early 1980s and mid-1990s), then the Gen-Zers (mid-1990s to 2012).

If you believe any of this, you also believe these groups have "a much greater self-identification with LGBTQ+" than older generations and the white Boomers, explains David Evans, the chief insights officer for Collage Group, a consumer research firm that specializes in cultural marketing for major companies. Evans points out that some smart companies saw this coming. Corporate America began its tentative steps toward marketing in this way sometime around 2016, when Smirnoff Vodka, owned by the Diageo company, ventured significantly into this genre, Evans says.

Who knew there were so many trans people into vodka? Smirnoff did, apparently, when it introduced an ad featuring a Black transwoman. The campaign was heralded as a success in the burgeoning woke marketing business, more proof that cultural-demographic marketing does work if done right, and if existing customers aren't offended.

Of course, trans people make up a tiny demographic, but that's not the point, Evans adds. At bottom, marketing is the business discipline of getting people to buy stuff. This type of marketing posits that younger demos, people in the sweet spot of marketing and advertising, are of the opinion that displays of diversity, equity, and inclusion are necessary for any brand they plan to purchase. Their parents were taught to see America as having a common culture. Now, tribalism has been pounded into the collective consciousness of the younger demos, particularly on the college campus. That's why, if you believe this stuff, non-trans younger people *are demanding* that LGBTQ+ people be seen and heard in product marketing campaigns, Evans says.

The science behind marketing is to attach your product to an emerging demo early on so they keep buying your product in greater numbers as they get older and attain more wealth. Young people are "embracing diversity in ways that are very different than older generations have," Evans said. "They are redefining what it means to have an identity," which in their view is about feeling different from the "the norm," and not being part of a group where everyone looks the same.

They may not be trans, and most aren't, but they want companies to appeal to the trans community. In marketing, it's called the "halo effect," Evans says, an advertising method suggesting that the younger demos have a "desire to connect to people unlike yourself," he adds.

Evans, for his part, concedes that marketing tribalism has its drawbacks; he says he and his team have routinely cautioned clients that this type of stereotyping invites divisiveness that could be bad for the brands. Some listen, some don't. The ones that don't, he says, really think that there is money to be made by cynically appealing to consumers who want to virtue signal as they shop. "We don't agree with that," he tells me. "We advise companies not to get caught up in preaching forms of inclusion, inauthentic representations like thinking all Hispanics think alike."

That said, companies all too often latch on to these broad and woke generalizations. They see the research showing that "there are a lot of young white people, the majority of whom are straight, who want to see a lot of embracing of differences. They want to see brands advertise specifically in this inclusive way," Evans said.

In particular, the marketing approach holds that "we don't see anywhere near the kind of antipathy to LGBTQ+ marketing campaigns within non-white groups as we do with white conservatives." Again, Evans is just laying out the theory of woke marketing, not advocating it, which begs the question: If it works so well, why are people running away from brands like Budweiser and Target (as you will soon discover) that go there? Why are, as you will see in later chapters, so many people not showing up to theaters with their kids for Disney movies strewn with same-sex kissing scenes?

Supporters would say it's mainly that older demo (those damn white Boomers) doing the running. Both companies were also unprepared for the backlash; management's ineptness meant they didn't know how to counter it.

An alternative explanation is that you can't keep looking to appease members of distinct tribes, instead of individuals, and not expect blowback. This type of marketing tribalism, and progressive tribalism in general, has run its course. It can be traced in part to the social and political realignment that took place in 2021 and 2022. Republican Glenn Youngkin, against significant odds, became the governor of Virginia running largely on a plank that would end the gender obsession in Virginia's public elementary and high schools. Ditto for Ron DeSantis's political ascension as he bashed all things woke, including progressive indoctrination of children on sexual matters.

What the people who run these companies chose to ignore is why people shop at Target or drink a Bud. Sorry, it's not for any halo effect; most people drink Bud because they identify with the beer's long-standing brand, which is decidedly male and decidedly straight. Target's core customer shops there not to be hit over the head with gender-fluid clothing, but to be inundated with bargains—decent clothes for women, men, and children at low prices.

In a bit, we will explore how DEI-obsessed marketers at Budweiser read this data and got so woke they're still trying to undo the damage. For now, let's look at Target, and how the big retailer channeled the woke, DEI-focused marketing methodology employed by the geniuses at Budweiser and got the same results when it unveiled its annual Pride Month celebration in June 2023.

I tried to find someone, anyone, who could bring me into a Target meeting where it was agreed that offering products as "diverse" as tuck-friendly bathing suits, along with rainbow-colored onesies for children, was a smart move or why it decided it needed a "Pride Month" clothing and product-line celebration in the first place. Target declined repeated calls for comment on the celebration and the fallout that ensued. The best explanation that I can come up with is something a little more meta, based on interviews with people like Evans, Swaminathan, and executives who know Target's CEO, Brian Cornell (a Target spokesman did review material in this book and made a few marginal suggestions that I included in the text).

Target has been holding Pride Month celebrations—with special-themed clothing displays and other items aimed at the LGBTQ+ community—around June of every year for the past decade. Finding such products is increasingly easy amid corporate America's obsession with meeting DEI mandates. So-called queer fashion, or fashion that is focused on gays, lesbians, trans people, and other genders that blur the distinctions between men and women, is a growing business. If you want mannequins posing with "tuck-friendly" bathing suits (for men who haven't fully transitioned), there is a queer fashion designer ready to create them. A 2021 article on the website *Them* covered the topic and came to this conclusion: "Fashion is getting queerer than ever. And in many ways, all this was inevitable. Millennials and Gen-Z are the queerest generations ever."

The business side of appealing to LGBTQ+ also includes gray areas that many Americans find appalling. You might not know this, but there's a whole genre of LGBTQ+ books aimed at children. *When Aiden Became a Brother* is described as a "sweet groundbreaking picture book, winner of the 2020 Stonewall Book Award, [that] celebrates the changes in a transgender boy's life." There is a line of clothing for children to celebrate gender diversity. Rainbow-colored onesies for infants.

All of the above and more could be found at Target during Pride Month. You might be asking yourself why management didn't weigh if it was going too far in sexualizing the shopping experience for most of its customers, or why someone in power didn't see a potential backlash brewing over gender indoctrination, particularly as it involves children.

The answers: See the top of the management chart, and credit corporate wokeness taken to some of the most absurd levels ever seen.

"The things we've done from a DE and I standpoint, it's adding value, it's helping us drive sales, it's building greater engagement with both our teams and our guests," Brian Cornell, Target's CEO, proudly stated in a podcast hosted by editors of the business publication *Fortune* after the company's 2023 Pride displays. "And those are just the right things for our business today." He added that his "focus on diversity and inclusion and equity has fueled much of our growth over the last nine years."

Interesting comments from a CEO running one of the country's largest retail chains. More interesting, and alarming, because Cornell didn't really comprehend the smoldering customer backlash that would build into such a force that it continues to jeopardize Target's bottom line.

Also interesting because on a personal level Cornell isn't known to be a social justice warrior, according to people I interviewed who know him. Friends of Cornell describe him a fiscal conservative, a moderate on social issues, and a family man. If I asked him to explain intersectionality, or recite gender pronouns, he wouldn't have a clue, they tell me. What he is, they say, is a good executive; he made his managerial chops at several big corporations, including as CEO of the US division of PepsiCo Americas Foods before getting his chance to run a major public company, Target, as its CEO, in 2014.

Not exactly the DNA for steroidal wokeness that Target has become associated with, unless you understand how executives respond to incentives to get ahead, and where they were schooled in the finer points of corporate wokeness. PepsiCo, the soft drink maker and Cornell's prior employer, has been on the cutting edge of wokeness for as long as there has been corporate wokeness. The independent journalist Eric Starkman in his popular blog *Starkman Approved* has done significant reporting on PepsiCo's strict, even maniacal, adherence to DEI in its pursuit of the perfect ESG rating.

"Pepsi is among the most aggressive touting its commitment to ESG metrics...boasting of the great strides it made since launching PepsiCo Positive (pep+), 'a strategic end-to-end business transformation with sustainability and human capital at the center of how the company will create growth and value,'" Starkman writes. "Pepsi's stated accomplishments include 'economically empowering women' with 'gender smart solutions along our agricultural supply chains in Dominican Republic, Ecuador, and Guatemala.'"

From a company that produces the eponymous soft drink that rots out teeth also came something so idiotically woke it's hard to believe. An advertisement in 2017 featured model Kendall Jenner hanging out at what looked like a BLM protest, confronting the enemy—a cop. Do cops drink Pepsi? Probably. Are all cops evil racists? Not even close. The company didn't really care, because that's not the point. Pepsi was looking for some of that halo effect, by stroking the young demo that indulges in social justice, and possibly a boost in its ESG ranking, former employees tell me. A win-win.

Kendall Jenner is famous, but for a narrow set of things; she's of Kardashian reality TV fame. She's an influencer of beauty products, bathing suits, and so on. She is paid up to $300,000 a pop to push merchandise on her social media pages. Here she was in a Pepsi ad attempting to suspend disbelief by hanging at a social justice protest, approaching a menacing-looking riot cop and handing him a can of the shitty soft drink to defuse the situation.

If only someone handed those cops a Pepsi when they were beating the hell out of Rodney King!

Really dopey stuff. A former PepsiCo PR executive told me that after the commercials ran, "angry customers jammed our phone lines for months." But that's where Brian Cornell learned his boardroom wokeness, and by the looks of things, he made sure Target emulated the same garbage practiced at Pepsi as Pride Month approached.

At Target, the buildup to Pride Month takes weeks of intense preparation, people with knowledge of the matter tell me. All two thousand of its stores participate. Hovering above all the plans and preparation should be an inconvenient fact of Target's customer base. The nation's seventh-largest retailer has a demo that is decidedly Middle America. It's people who make $80,000 a year or less, skewing largely to that stay-at-home mom shopping with two kids in a stroller, and not necessarily college educated.

This demo, based on my reporting and plain common sense, isn't really looking to celebrate Pride with the kids. They want to shop at Target to find bargains. They might even be repulsed by the spectacle of seeing rainbow flags replace Old Glory everywhere they look, and Pride-colored onesies for toddlers. They've been saying as much for years now during Target's Pride Month, mostly with social media commentary. The growing consensus, in harsher language than I need to print, was that Target was going beyond just offering LGBTQ+ clothing and branded items. Target was putting its boardroom obsession with gender diversity into people's living rooms.

I'm not saying I agree with these sentiments; I personally have no problem strolling past male mannequins dressed in what's best described as a woman's bathing suit. I'm also not a typical Target customer shopping there with children. The social media commentary from customers appeared most biting when it came to the perception that kids were the focus of Target's displays. Sure, there was plenty of merchandise like home furnishings displaying Pride flags and special gender-neutral clothing for trans people. Nothing wrong with that, per se.

The trouble began, at least according to the customer complaints on social media, when the company's displays seemed to be crossing over to "grooming" or proselytizing of children into the LGBTQ+ lifestyle.

Books for sale included titles like *Bye Bye, Binary*, or *Pride 1 2 3*, and *I'm Not a Girl: A Transgender Story*. All for children as young as two years of age. A T-shirt targeting kids had the words "Girls Gays Theys" displayed on the front. Those aforementioned onesies for infants emblazoned with the Pride colors; those tuck-friendly bathing suits, designed specifically for transwomen who have yet to get reassignment surgery, so they can, ya know, hide their junk. The tuck-friendly bathing suits could always be purchased online or through Target's catalog. Now you could find them not far from where the children's clothing was on display.

WTF?

Target's corporate obsession with gender diversity can be answered in several ways. Cornell reports to a board of directors that demands a woke conformity from the C-suite, and increasingly so in recent years. He might be looking for the "halo effect" demo that Evans mentioned, where younger people demand DEI from the places where they shop.

He and other CEOs also indirectly report to groups like the Human Rights Campaign (HRC), which publishes yearly diversity audits of major companies. The group is backed by billionaire lefties like George Soros. Diversity of this kind is big in the Soros agenda, and journalists who have followed his money trail say he's a stickler for results.

Soros, if you don't know his background, doesn't seem like someone on the cutting edge of wokeness. He is a brilliant student of the markets and one of the best traders in history. He has written books on the subject that are classics about money management. On Wall Street, he might be best known for "shorting," or trading against, the British pound sterling in a move that allegedly "broke" the country's central bank in the early 1990s, forcing it to devalue its currency.

In recent years, Soros's trading prowess has been overshadowed by his left-wing politics. Since semi-retiring from the hedge fund business, he has devoted much of his life to promote progressive causes, including funding groups like HRC and others that have helped elect local prosecutors who want to decriminalize many crimes.

His critics say he has managed to help institutionalize corporate wokeism because he demands results from the people and places he funds. According to independent journalist John Solomon, Soros has spent millions of dollars on campaign contributions and donations to left-wing activist groups and pols. Future contributions are contingent on woke "ROI," or return on equity, Solomon says. If you don't produce woke results, you don't get any more of his money.

In the interest of fairness, I sought out Soros's interpretation of his political activities. Here's the response I received from a spokesman after he reviewed the material about his boss: "The excerpt[s] are a bunch of horse cr...p," he said in an email. "It's just so riddled with errors and ignorant statements there is no point. I'm not going to correct your facts because you are too lazy to do honest research and what you are doing is actually disgusting attempted character assignation." He added that what was provided to him "is vaguely anti-Semitic conspiracy BS," and recommended one of Soros's books to get a better understanding of the man.

I understand that Soros, a Hungarian Jew who survived the Holocaust, is often the target of right-wing paranoia with a dose of antisemitism, which

I won't dignify in these pages. I also am well acquainted with Soros's literary output; I read his book *The Alchemy of Finance: Reading the Mind of the Market* years ago, and I fully appreciate his intellectual gifts and contributions to the understanding of high finance.

That's not what we're talking about here, according to my other sources who track Soros's woke money machinations. They say that activist organizations like the Center for American Progress (CAP) and HRC—both Soros beneficiaries—extend corporate wokeism's reach. Soros helps keep these and other woke activists in business; their lobbying on behalf of progressive boardroom changes in the media and among their contacts in government is an important catalyst for the politicization of corporate behavior.

It is this advocacy that is causing C-suite executives like Cornell to adopt progressive policies like DEI and ESG, with a heavy emphasis on LGBTQ+ issues, my reporting shows. Best that I can tell, that's what Cornell meant when he said corporate wokeism is "good for business."

He also might have meant what's good *for him*. A Target spokesman says that "no part" of Cornell's pay is directly linked to DEI or ESG. Okay, but you can also see how achieving the highest DEI score might also mean more money in Cornell's pocket. His board calculates his "performance driven" yearly bonus that is often paid in stock. For years, stock prices were heavily dependent on ESG scores, because big asset managers demanded adherence to the DEI wokeness metric. Cornell was making lots of money while virtue signaling: $17 million in 2022 as he touted the benefits of DEI, and I have never met a CEO in existence who was looking for a pay cut.

Making a CEO's salary, with its manifold perks and privileges, is great but it also distorts reality. CEOs and their highly paid teams of advisers don't see the real world, the real America, where average folk view the corporate elite as a bunch of left-wing carpetbaggers touting the religion of wokeness to make money and attain a lifestyle separate and unequal from the cultural hellhole they created. Cornell has children who could have been easily shielded from what's happening in his stores, or the endless drag-queen bedtime-stories celebrations and genderless bathrooms in public schools, the teaching of sex acts among children to normalize gender fluidity, because money buys protection, private schools, private shoppers, and more.

Middle America isn't protected—when it shops, when it watches TV, or when it sends its kids to school. It is the guinea pig in this social experiment. Increasingly it's mad as hell and not taking it any longer.

For the record, Target has in news reports denied that it *targeted* its tuck-friendly wear to children, but for many parents it was hard to know for sure, because they said the merchandise seemed to be lumped together. In 2023 a viral social media moment ensued, not that much different from the one involving Dylan Mulvaney at Budweiser. Parents expressed their outrage on Twitter, Instagram, and elsewhere. They called out Target for subjecting children to overt sexuality and grooming.

A full-on boycott of Target began and really hasn't completely ended. Sales sank; Target's stock collapsed. That's what happens when parents liken shopping at Target to a stroll down 42nd Street and Times Square during the heyday of the smut industry. Not a good look. A *New York Post* headline writer captured it best. Target was experiencing "Budweiser 2.0."

Part of me says capitalism is all about choice. If parents hate Target's genuflection to wokeness, shop somewhere else. But there's nowhere to go, so that's why they're choosing to fight and teach all these Harvard MBAs running the nation's biggest companies a lesson, further showing that at the most basic level woke capitalism isn't good for business no matter how much Cornell and other woke CEOs virtue signal for it. In fact, unless you're Ben & Jerry's or Nike it is often bad for business, more and more so lately or the execs at Target and Bud wouldn't be flailing to revive their brands.

The reason wokeness isn't selling more broadly has to do with a different type of shift in consumer behavior, some market executives I spoke to concede. Woke CEOs don't understand it. Market data might not totally capture it, but it is easy to understand if you're following the plight of the working class. Average Americans saw something vile in all those "largely peaceful protests" and Wall Street types applauding BLM during our "Summer of Love" in 2020. A growing number of Americans abhor the racialized image making in television ads of products they consume that is a direct result of strict DEI standards imposed by ad agencies.

Is every family really mixed-race? No, just 10 percent, but you wouldn't know it watching what passes for a depiction of American life as seen through the DEI-focused lens of Madison Avenue. Don't straight white guys drink beer and drive cars? You know the answer. Growing numbers of average folk hate being preached to by elite TV journalists or Hollywood billionaire executives, corporate CEOs, or ad executives that *we must* celebrate our differences as opposed to our national identity. They despise the elites for teaching their kids American history based on the *New York Times*' 1619 Project, the Grey Lady's Pulitzer Prize–winning "reporting" that tried to make the case that America's founding was that of a slave state, that capitalism is inherently racist.

Both are absurd, of course. Slavery was tolerated by our Founders, and yes, that is our country's original sin. It was also fiercely debated because of the founding principles, there was a war to end it, and a civil rights movement put the final nail in its legacy. The southern slave states were hardly a model of free-market capitalism no matter how hard the *New York Times* tries to bastardize the legacy of Adam Smith.

Americans understand American history better than the elites do. They see their way of life coming under assault from the left and they detest how corporate America—the places where they work—joined forces with other progressive movements. They are now rebelling, and for good reason. What is in it for them as the world goes woke? Working-class wages have declined dramatically over the years, yet the richest people on earth tell them they're the spoiled, privileged oppressor.

Plus, Middle America learned a thing or two from the woke social activists. They will use social media to protest. It's now their Arab Spring.

Target discovered that firsthand, as did Budweiser. The anti-woke mass movement has legs for many reasons, but also because while Gen Alpha (born after 2012) might like progressive posturing, Millennials and Gen-Zers are getting older. They're acting more like Boomers in style, and in politics, it seems. They don't want to be indoctrinated into leftism when they see their paychecks eaten away from inflation that was sparked by big government and high taxes that keeps the welfare state in business. Many don't want to be told they're part of an oppressive class of white people when their ancestors came to the United States through Ellis Island, poor and hungry.

The pendulum that brought companies into the "corporate-social-political action" fold is forcing them out of it because the DEI obsession from major corporations has reached a tipping point; the backlash to it is real, as the situation at Target and Budweiser shows.

"This is risky stuff," Swaminathan concedes. "When done right, corporate purpose and brand activism can have win-win outcomes with positive impacts for both brands and the causes that they serve."

The problem is that the impulse, for all the reasons we discuss in this book, is not to do it right and with nuance. The result is often disaster, and as the bank once known as SVB discovered, complete destruction. A good case can be made that the implosion of the San Francisco–based Silicon Valley Bank, or SVB, is one of the more frightening and significant anecdotes for understanding the rot and instability of the financial system that DEI and corporate wokeness has unleashed.

In the words of BlackRock's Larry Fink, SVB was considered a "rock-star bank" just a few short years ago, as it grew astronomically over a short period, and for a time made a ton of money servicing wannabe tech titans. SVB may have been a rock star by some financial metrics, except the most important: risk management. It extended risky loans to start-ups, so-called venture capital, or VC, start-ups, and failed to properly manage its capital—the cushion all banks maintain to weather loan losses.

The bank's balance sheet was a weird conglomeration of undiversified risky products, people who worked there tell me. Such assets perform well when the economy is humming, when credit was cheap as the Fed took interest rates to zero in 2020 and kept them there for most of the next two years. What happens when it's not? Loans like this start to falter, and a contagion that follows—the so-called bank run of depositors yanking their money—often leads to insolvency.

Then came the wokeness: a heavy dose of DEI and corporate virtue signaling at SVB, some former employees say to mollify the guilt of making so much money when the rest of the country was suffering during the pandemic. Once again, it was more than just left-leaning corporate policies that led to this bank's demise in March 2023.

Yet, a good case can be made that the bank spent too much time virtue signaling and not enough time gauging the impact of a likely change in interest rates on its financial stability.

How SVB got through its compliance exams is still something that my Wall Street sources find it hard to explain. On the other hand, the bank's executives and regulators may have been drinking the same Kool-Aid, or to be precise, vino and the pricy stuff from the vaunted wine country just a short drive from SVB's Menlo Park HQ. In one Zoom meeting during the Covid lockdowns, a senior banker in the company's investment arm was observed literally popping open a bottle with an expensive vintage, bragging about its cost, and that it came from one of the area's best vineyards. The executive sniffed the cork and took a swig before the meeting commenced.

Such bravado isn't really part of the banking culture on the other side of the country, at least not any longer. The wild years of risk taking, of Wall Street leveraging billions of dollars on esoteric investments, are largely a distant memory. The 2008 financial crisis caused every major bank to appreciate the perils of risk and leverage, or the use of borrowing to make outsized bets in far-flung markets. Sources with knowledge of the bank's operations say working at SVB was a throwback to those Wall Street risk-taking days of yore; one person with knowledge of the bank's operations said it was as if he was living through the dotcom bubble and the financial crisis all at once.

Plus, wokeness with diversity training and constant virtue signaling were used to camouflage this problem, the executive said. As SVB embraced woke investment techniques like ESG and touted its compliance with DEI standards, it was pouring its resources into tech companies that weren't making money, and feeding off the irrational exuberance of the Fed's easy-money policies.

As a former executive put it, a huge chunk of its balance sheet involved lending to "VC-backed companies that made no money and lines of credit to PE [private equity] firms."

People close to the management of the bank counter that most of these loans never went into default, and the bank engaged in ESG metrics to lure in European clients that consider the investment process a prerequisite. What they can't deny: More prosaic loans—commercial real estate, mortgages, even car loans—don't have to languish on a bank's books. There is a vibrant secondary market for securitization, where you can sell the loans to a Wall Street firm to package and sell to a pension fund. You can't securitize PE lines of credit and other risky loans to start-ups. That means they just sit there earning interest unless the markets turn negative if the Fed starts raising rates and their market value plummets. Then it really doesn't take much for a bank of this caliber to go the way of Lehman Brothers.

"I couldn't believe the Fed didn't put a stop to what was happening," one former executive tells me. The bank's connection to its frontline regulator is worth noting. Greg Becker, SVB's CEO, was on the San Francisco Fed board (he declined to comment but has reviewed this material). The local Fed had raised some concerns about SVB's business model, but they ultimately went nowhere.

Then came the wokeness.

"We want you to make our annual investment conference a celebration of ESG," was the word that came down from the executive offices to an executive in the firm's investment division in 2020. ESG wasn't a big part of the bank's portfolio, unless you consider investing in woke tech firms a form of ESG. The executive's supervisors did. They also wanted to show off the bank's racial and gender diversity. "I told them, 'Guys, this is a bank of mostly rich white dudes, and some Asians...it's really not that diverse. SVB doesn't have a credible DEI story to tell our investors,'" the former executive said.

It didn't matter; he was on orders to find some diversity, make the conference as woke as possible even if it was, in his words, "window dressing."

What this executive didn't know was that SVB's rock-star status was about to start crashing down. In March 2022, months after he left SVB, the Fed began raising interest rates. The markets corrected, and a shakeout in tech ensued. Those start-ups that were SVB's lifeblood were now looking for cash. The same techies who "tied" all their banking needs with SVB began to pull their deposits from the bank when they saw their own business in peril. A year later, Larry Fink's "rock star" bank was insolvent.

Becker, the former CEO of SBV, in his congressional testimony blamed its demise on an "unprecedented" run on deposits, a magnitude so great that no bank could withstand. The former executive I interviewed agrees, but he can't help but think that the bank's allegiance to woke capitalism played a role in its failure. As its balance sheet was deteriorating, SVB was holding

DEI seminars on the need to end "systemic racism." A top risk management executive who led the firm's diversity training program was quoted in one company brochure stating, "As a queer person of color and a first-generation immigrant from a working-class background, there were not many role models for me to 'see' growing up."

Nice to know, even if SVB is proof there is a huge price paid for embracing woke capitalism. The demise of the San Francisco–based First Republic gives us even more evidence. All these banks, my sources tell me, spent considerable amounts of time and resources praising diversity, etc., when they should have been eyeing their business models for cracks.

Ditto for their regulator. While SVB and First Republic were burning to the ground, San Francisco Federal Reserve president Mary Daly was tweeting about the need to support the Black Lives Matter movement. (She declined comment.) A trendy cultural issue took precedence over the financial nuclear detonation in her own backyard.

Good for "social justice." Terrible for the rest of us.

CHAPTER FOUR

The Summer of Love

The killing of George Floyd by a Minneapolis police officer was a tragedy. Breonna Taylor, a Black woman, was shot dead in her Louisville apartment as police used brute force and bullets to execute a search warrant to apprehend her not-so-innocent boyfriend. Ahmaud Arbery, another Black man, was murdered while out for a jog, mistaken for a burglar in Brunswick, Georgia, by three white men who brutally hunted him down.

This horrible stuff all occurred within weeks during that horrible year known as 2020. It was a bizarre time in American history. The country was in lockdown mode from Covid and on edge.

People were glued to their computers, freaked out by the viral tendencies of social media. Cable news and social media brought the violent reactions to those deaths—nationwide protests, looting, pillaging, and burning of city neighborhoods—into the homes of the country 24/7.

To be sure, the person in the White House didn't help matters, during a period the left oddly described as our "Summer of Love." Donald Trump had spent the past three-plus years tweeting whatever came into his head against enemies real and imagined, saying weird stuff like some "good people" attended a neo-Nazi rally in Charlottesville, Virginia. At least it was a time of relative peace and significant prosperity. Now he faced his first real crisis, the Covid pandemic, the economic tumult it unleashed, and soon the volcanic social unrest that the left spun into some parable about systemic racism throughout the land, illustrated by the fact that Americans had elected an alleged racist to the country's highest office.

The American people are far from racist, of course, most Trump voters included. Majorities voted for a Black president twice, and in 2020 they were on the verge of voting for a VP of color. Trump, meanwhile, is more of a political outlier and certainly was never a member of the KKK. He never fit comfortably into the modern conservative movement, or any coherent political organization for that matter. He was until recently a Democrat. Recall, he supported Bill Clinton back in the day, and loves to spend taxpayer money as much as any Keynesian-oriented social planner; the size of government swelled during his presidency. He once referred to himself as "the king of debt." He railed against free trade, threatened tax increases on big businesses. He also rarely enjoyed significant popularity outside his base of disillusioned, mostly blue-collar voters who saw him as a savior from the ravages of globalism supported by elites in both parties.

Yet he did astutely see a political void, focusing his appeal on a segment of society less animated by various graduations of racism or gender ideology than repulsed by the elites who ran both parties, and big business. That's when Trump, the billionaire of inherited wealth, suddenly became a man of the people. Whether he was earnest or not didn't matter to many average Americans. They elected him president because they despised even more what the elite class stood for: open borders, and the excesses of free trade that hollowed out the industrial heartland and lowered their standards of living.

Helping Trump's cause was the absolute unctuousness of many of his opponents, including the singularly most horrible opponent that the Democrats could muster for the 2016 presidential election, Hillary Clinton. She faced off with The Donald as the front-runner, but with baggage from her husband's own ethically challenged presidency and a lot of her own, she lost.

Trump may win again in 2024, but only if he faces another horrible candidate in Sleepy Joe Biden, if, as expected, he continues to seek reelection. People have a short memory when times are tough. Biden's economy and the inflation he created is a tax on the working class. A possible recession is always knocking on the country's door since the Fed began to raise interest rate to counter the price pressure. With that, it's easy to forget how Trump contributed to the national strife of 2020, his obliviousness to the powder keg enveloping our social order, and the low point of his presidency, the January 6, 2021, Capitol Hill riot.

Biden beat Trump in 2020 promising a return to "normal," but has conducted himself abhorrently abnormally. His presidency is a jambalaya of bad economic policies, underscored by his own inability to utter a sentence that makes sense. Plus, Sleepy Joe Biden has made wokeness the law. You see it in his strict diversity requirements for cabinet positions, and some of the most stringent environmental edicts the country has ever seen. His idiotic racialized demagoguing of a voting law in Georgia, his statements that "systemic racism has plagued our nation," and a lot more. No wonder polls are now showing that the American people loathe Biden more than even Trump. The same polling shows that they may loathe corporate America even more because our titans of finance, as this book will show, followed Biden's lead on progressive policies.

How a bunch of rich dudes became obsessed with the most leftist and radical interpretations of current events is really the central question I try to answer in *Go Woke, Go Broke*. It has no easy answer but try to follow me here.

By 2020, corporate boards leaned increasingly progressive. One explanation is that they were gerrymandered by diversity requirements imposed by stock exchanges like Nasdaq and lefty corporate activists. Another is the progressive politics of the new breed of CEO. ESG and DEI were growing in stature inside every major company, and into a huge and profitable business. Still another explanation is the power of social media to unleash swarms of political provocateurs on anyone or any company that defied the groupthink of the left. Such left-wing trolling was almost encouraged by the people running these powerful companies, who saw themselves increasingly as enforcement arms of the progressive movement.

"I'm cool with that," Mark Zuckerberg said in 2011 during a company-wide Town Hall when asked by the featured guest whether he was in favor of paying more taxes. The guest wasn't just anyone; it was the president, Barack Obama. The "Town Hall" that took place at Facebook's Palo Alto HQ is better described as a love fest between Zuck, the founder and CEO, and Obama. The latter waxed poetically about how his progressive industrial policy of massive new regulations, higher taxes, and subsidizing of progressive fads like green energy was finally starting to bring down unemployment after the worst of the post–financial crisis Great Recession. Zuck kept quiet while nodding in agreement.

Left out from Obama's description of the country's economic "recovery" were some simple and sobering facts; it was statistically the slowest in recent history because all of the above. Lots of blue-collar types voted for Obama, yet wages were declining. The rich were getting richer from a stock market inflated by super-low interest rates and the successful bank bailouts, while the middle got poorer. You couldn't count on Zuck or his lefty minions at Facebook or in C-suites across the tech industry to hold Obama accountable for any of those inconvenient truths.

They were too busy fanboying their progressive messiah.

Tech industry money flowed into Obama's campaign war chest, and the love affair with the progressive left continues to this day. And it goes beyond throwing money at leftist causes and Zuckerberg publicly gushing over Obama that day. His programmers, and those at other major social media platforms—the places where Americans increasingly consume their news—were quietly doing their part to silence of any dissent from left-wing orthodoxy. Their censorship could be described as an in-kind contribution to the Democratic Party and its policy goals.

In 2020 and 2021, questioning BLM, or the deification of George Floyd, or any other lefty cause, like the efficacy of the Covid vaccines, on these platforms meant being "shadow banned" or cancelled from the national discussion that was increasingly occurring on social media. Likewise, questioning the left-wing necessity to dump Donald Trump as president became verboten.

Donald Trump lost to Joe Biden in the 2020 election and took sore losing to new and dangerous levels, concocting a sad spectacle of half-truths to tell his followers he won. Yet his claims of a rigged election aren't all fantasy depending on how you define the rigging. You want proof? For that we turn to the *New York Post*'s October 2020 Hunter Biden laptop story.

The evidence was irrefutable that the future first son was a drug-addicted and—according to a filing in his divorce proceedings—hooker-cavorting DC insider who used his father's name to make millions from foreign corporations. It all appeared on a laptop Hunter left with a computer repairman who turned it over to the FBI. When the feds did nothing, the repairman in

2020 contacted members of the Trump campaign, which began shopping it to various news outlets. The laptop contained emails and evidence of money transfers from China and Ukraine to Hunter, who lobbied on behalf of conflicted companies overseas using his famous last name. It also contained evidence of the old man's knowledge of his son's swampy business dealings. A real debate about what was on Hunter's computer hard drive would certainly make many Americans think twice about voting for Joe Biden even over crazy Donald Trump.

But the lefty programmers at Twitter and Facebook labeled it fake news. They had discussions with the FBI that the computer hard drive was high-level spy craft supplied by the Russians to get Trump elected because the Russians somehow loved Trump. The story was then "throttled" by Facebook—meaning it didn't show up at the top of people's feeds—for months. On Twitter, the reporting was banned for a full two days, allowing a Russia conspiracy theory counternarrative to form. The truth eventually came out, of course, but the American people didn't get to understand the full impact of the story until well into the campaign, and after it was over.

The year 2020 was a horrible time in so many ways. Censorship by social media companies was just one of the tragic events of that year. Covid was a tragedy made worse by the lockdowns imposed by many states, and by Trump's often strange reactions to a seminal event that demanded real leadership. Then there were the worst excesses of progressive politics that had been normalized in the boardroom, with tragic results, as you will soon discover.

On March 24, 2020, Trump and his vice president, Mike Pence, convened a special meeting with some of the nation's biggest investors to discuss how to deal with the Covid epidemic from an economic standpoint. Hospital ICUs were increasingly being overwhelmed; everything from ventilators to masks were in short supply. The initial impulse was to shut down the country—slow the spread by flattening the curve if everyone could just stay indoors long enough. It was costly because businesses would fail. The consumer is the biggest part of the US economy. The government would have to bail out businesses and entire industries during the lockdowns, issuing massive amounts of debt to pay people who weren't working.

Covid's health implications were paramount for policymakers, of course. The pandemic's implications for the economy weren't far behind, which is why the White House was seeking advice from some of the smartest moneymen in the country. The group included hedge fund titans Dan Loeb, Paul Tudor Jones, and Ken Griffin of the Citadel investment empire. Blackstone's Steve Schwarzman and Jeff Sprecher, chairman of the New York Stock Exchange, joined as well.

Trump and Pence were accompanied by Larry Kudlow, chair of his National Economic Council, and his Treasury secretary, Steve Mnuchin.

Noticeably absent from the conference call were CEOs of the nation's biggest banks or major companies, and it spoke volumes about the often tense and fraught relationship between Trump and the corporate powers that be. At best they tolerated Trump for his tax cutting, but for little else because they hated his trade policies and because he made doing business in China more difficult. They also hated the man himself. They mocked Trump as gauche and irrational, a reflection of the belligerence of Middle America to modernism. Trump, they said, represented, the right-wing fringes, working-class white men who don't read their favorite newspaper, the *New York Times*.

They vowed to get him defeated in 2020. Jamie Dimon even suggested as much, at one point remarking that he could beat Trump himself if he gave up his job running the nation's biggest bank to run for president, "because I'm as tough as he is, I'm smarter than he is," Dimon said.

Not all the people at the White House Covid meeting were Republicans, but they weren't of the corporate woke ilk. Sprecher is a traditional conservative and an entrepreneur; his wife, Kelly Loeffler, a former public relations executive, was running to retain her senate seat in Georgia. Griffin took a small hedge fund and created something that rivals Wall Street's biggest investment and trading houses. He's also one of the world's richest men, worth more than $35 billion. Loeb built an $11 billion hedge fund from scratch. He had been known to support Democrats, though he had since soured on the party because of its increasingly progressive agenda.

While not crazy about Trump's Twitter feed, these Wall Street executives liked that he took heterodox stances against China, which was spying on us and ripping off US companies that wanted to do business there. Like Trump they worried about globalism and its impact on the working class.

On this day, they were also worried about how not to destroy the US economy with never-ending lockdowns to flatten the curve of Covid since they believed the cure would be worse than the disease.

The left had been calling for strict lockdowns as Covid infections ramped ever higher. One leftist scientist suggested trillions of dollars in deficit spending to keep people indoors indefinitely. Trump's economic team, as did the bankers who phoned in, worried that such heavy-handed shuttering of business and commerce would spark another Great Depression; spending all that money might bankrupt the country and not make a dent in the Covid-infection "curve."

"We all agreed," one participant told me. "Keep the elderly indoors, same for people with preconditions. Everyone else should live their lives."

News of the meeting filtered back to most C-suites, and an unease set in. Trump and his team didn't seem to be "following the science," the left's favorite phrase to demonize those who questioned Covid orthodoxy on lockdowns and masks and later the vaccine. Big banks told their employees, except for those who were needed to keep the computers running, to work from home. New York City, the financial capital of the world, became a ghost town, inhabited by the homeless who took over blocks of city streets.

That was late March. By early April, the nation remained largely in lockdown mode, and well into early May when another seminal event in the country's history occurred. It was caught on an iPhone camera and broadcast to the world, footage of a Minneapolis police officer, Derek Chauvin, with his knee apparently on the neck of an unarmed Black man named George Floyd, heard pleading that he couldn't breathe while being arrested and handcuffed.

Floyd would later die; the video went viral, and the nation lost its mind. As did corporate America.

George Floyd turned out to be an ex-con with a rather violent record. He had wicked amounts of fentanyl in his system. He was acting strangely in a convenience store that day and tried to pass a counterfeit bill off as real money. The clerk called the cops. Agitated, Floyd then resisted arrest. Subsequent bodycam footage showed that Chauvin may not have had his knee directly on Floyd's neck, as the iPhone footage that went viral suggested. Floyd said he couldn't breathe well before he was on the ground and resisting arrest. The level of drugs in George Floyd's body could have killed him as much as what happened after he resisted arrest. On top of that, Floyd had serious health problems that could have made his heart give out.

He had committed a petty crime and did not deserve the death penalty, to be sure. But even a simple background check would show that George Floyd was no saint; he soon would be for the progressive left and the wokesters who ran our biggest companies.

Being in lockdown mode was a strange experience, and it did very strange things to the American economy and the American psyche. People were out of work and drinking themselves to death; others were working from home and saving lots of money because there was nowhere to spend it. Most socializing was verboten; so was church service. But images of George Floyd's death—filmed by a customer of the convenience store who would go on to win a special citation by the venerable Pulitzer Prize committee—were unrelenting on social media and cable TV. They touched off a spectacle not seen at least since the riots of the 1960s after Martin Luther King Jr.'s assassination. Peaceful protests about alleged police brutality gave way to "largely peaceful protests," and then to full-on insurrections in our major cities. City blocks were being burned and stores looted. Black Live Matter, Antifa, and other assorted radicals ruled the streets in major cities, blasting bullhorns and terrorizing communities.

Covid was everywhere, so the public health bureaucracy told people not to leave their homes, and when they did, to wear a mask. Not so if you were protesting racial injustice. In one of the most absurd public health double standards in modern history, you couldn't hold a wake for a loved one or hug a friend in public without ridicule. But you could rant, rave, and scream, assault and loot away, mask-free, in the name if social justice. You were given a pass from the "following the science" crowd because in the eyes of the elite, the protesters were teaching Americans a valuable lesson; violence was rationalized as a rough form of retribution for the country's systemic racism. Left-wing mobs vandalized monuments of Abraham Lincoln and Ulysses S. Grant—among the most truly progressive leaders in American history—along with those of Confederate leaders in a Stalinist attempt to rewrite American history as purely evil. One particularly lobotomized public official, Mayor Jenny Durkan of Portland, Oregon, referred to this time of mayhem in her city as the "Summer of Love." Protesters literally occupied a police precinct in Minneapolis.

Trump's strong economic policies notwithstanding, his presidency also featured some very low, low points. His threats to shoot rioters in the streets still ring in my ears. He should have demanded that the National Guard be sent to places like Seattle, Portland, and New York to keep the peace, but didn't. Ron DeSantis, the Florida governor, exposed Trump's other weaknesses when it came to Covid. He opened his state for business by June, appointed as his surgeon general a doctor named Joseph Ladapo, who defied the medical establishment, arguing that a virus of this nature couldn't be eradicated through closures; it needed to be managed. The result: Florida's economy soared, and its Covid cases didn't.

Trump, meanwhile, mused about using bleach as a cure, or the effectiveness of quack treatments like hydroxychloroquine. He turned Covid messaging over to Dr. Anthony Fauci, a longtime heath bureaucrat with a mixed record of success addressing other catastrophic diseases. Trump looked past the inconvenient and mounting evidence that Fauci may have had a role in funding gain-of-function research in the Wuhan lab in China, which many believed created Covid. He appeared oblivious to Fauci as one of the top proponents of lockdowns, masks, and later vaccines, "solutions" that worked to varying degrees of ineffectiveness.

Lockdowns on top of the violence and rioting of that summer shook the nation's soul. People were buying guns in record numbers, hoarding food and toilet paper, worried that marauding bands of criminals, under the guise of social justice protesting, would be robbing their homes, which was often the case.

That Trump deserves criticism for his Covid response isn't a radical idea. Big-city mayors and governors who imposed harsh lockdowns and cowered before the mobs should have been impeached. Because of its response to this madness, corporate America deserves a special place in hell as well.

CEOs don't set public policy; they do shape the political and social debate given the very large platform that billions of dollars can buy. When Jamie Dimon, CEO of the nation's biggest bank, talks, people listen. They listen to Mark Zuckerberg and Jack Dorsey when he ran Twitter, as well.

That makes their post–George Floyd posturing so reprehensible because they began framing the debate around George Floyd in ways that would make AOC proud, and probably did.

In the face of unmitigated violence so obviously disguised as social justice, the CEO class began parroting some of the most radical versions of the American experience. America, they said, was systemically racist and the country needed to pay up.

Their words and actions defied a sane reading of our history, the facts about George Floyd, as well as a basic understanding of statistics around policing and race. Heather Mac Donald of the Manhattan Institute argued persuasively in a June 2020 *Wall Street Journal* opinion piece that the police killings I mentioned above were tragic outliers. The stats show no material increase in police shootings of African Americans over the years. According to Mac Donald, "The share of black victims is less than what the black crime rate would predict."

Mac Donald was ignored in favor of racial arsonists who spun modern America into the image of one big slave plantation. All because of a few cops.

On TV, in banal public statements, endless Zoom calls, and in newspaper ads, the CEO and executive class compared America to something like Communist China, an oppressive quasi–slave state, only they did not specifically mention China's transgressions in doing so. That would jeopardize their growing business interests on the mainland.

I would have expected more out of people who deal with numbers and logic every day. They should be assessing these crises in a rational way just as they were taught at Harvard Business School. Why ignore a scholar like Heather Mac Donald on urban issues she's been studying for decades? Why channel the lies of BLM, which has been using imagined racism as a selling point for corporate donations and the purchase of high-end real estate for its leadership?

None of it makes sense unless you understand the arc of corporate wokeness that was building for some time to create the perfect storm at a time when social unrest shook the nation.

Listing all the examples of this mind virus would be a book in of itself, so here's a sampling of the best (or worst): David Solomon, Goldman's CEO, looking to get his woke groove back, stated on his LinkedIn page that he was grieving "for the lives of George Floyd, Ahmaud Arbery, Breonna Taylor, and countless other victims of racism." We're supposed to believe that DJ D-Sol really worries about these poor folks while he spins records in the Hamptons? Was he holding a candlelight vigil for the victims of police brutality? Doubtful.

Not to be outdone by a Wall Street fat cat, the corporate leadership at Starbucks said it "stands in solidarity with our Black partners, community and customers." Really? Did anyone think a company that sells expensive coffee was supporting Jim Crow 2.0?

Brian Moynihan, the CEO of the nation's second-largest bank, Bank of America, or BofA, as it is more widely known, is one of the more reticent top executives in the country. He's an awkward fellow before cameras, which is why he does so few TV interviews. His politics lean significantly left (the Biden administration has him on its short list for Treasury secretary), but there's little in his background that suggests a real heartfelt desire to address social justice issues, per se. Sure, his bank gives to lefty causes to secure brownie points with progressives in Congress and the activist circuit. He also preaches wokeism whenever he can (he's in favor of transwomen using the ladies' room). Yet he spends a lot of time attending Boston Red Sox games in a luxury box.

Now he was joining DJ D-Sol in the sickening bout of CEO virtue signaling as the riots spread. A guy who is tongue-tied in explaining the direction of interest rates found his inner social justice warrior. As he told *Barron's*, "The protests are about not having the equivalent opportunity, criminal justice treatment by authorities, and the serious [Covid-19] infections of communities of color [during the pandemic]. These three coalesced."

Try unpacking that woke gibberish.

Jamie Dimon thought he would let his knee do the talking. In June, just weeks after George Floyd's death and after recovering from heart surgery, he visited a JP Morgan branch in Mount Kisco, a tony suburb of New York City. Posing before the camera with some of the branch's employees, the then sixty-four-year-old CEO of the nation's largest bank dropped to one knee for the photograph.

Was Jamie Dimon now a BLM supporter? A representative declined to answer that question directly at the time, allowing the impression that the CEO of the nation's largest bank, America's banker, was in solidarity with BLM and its brand of social justice. As a JP Morgan executive told me, "Jamie believes the need for social justice is real…the Black community has been ignored for far too long."

George Floyd's death was a tragedy, but it triggered some of the most tragic reactions and follow-on effects. Big companies reached out to BLM and any progressive activist group they could find with copious amounts of corporate donations. CEOs held Town Halls decrying racism seemingly every other day. The aired their wokeness in television interviews. They ramped up race-based hiring and promotions. By doing all the above, they justified the bastardization of our history, the continued balkanization of our common culture, and the looting disguised as social justice protests that created the political momentum for something called the "defund the police" movement—protests and political activism with the goal of weakening police forces across the country. The defund movement believes policing is racist, and to cure that racism, cops need to be taken off the streets. It likens police departments to occupying forces within minority communities, ignoring the obvious reality that many Black and Hispanic families want and need police protection.

The defund movement was (and still is) supported by various Marxist radical organizations, like BLM and far-left pols like AOC. It flourished during the Summer of Love as a new breed of prosecutor, the beneficiary of social justice money, began occupying big-city DA's offices from coast to coast, and simply stopped charging criminals for committing crimes. Whether they knew it or not, the CEOs of our biggest and most prestigious companies, with their social justice preening, helped support one of the most radical and anarchistic social experiments in recent American history.

And self-defeating.

When CEOs took a knee in support of BLM, they created the political cover for the left-wing politicians to put their own employees in harm's way. "Organized retail crime" swept the nation beginning in 2020 as hordes of looters descended upon stores like Target and CVS, emptying them of various goods, putting in physical jeopardy the safety of minimum-wage-earning clerks and overmatched security, while the police did nothing.

"They just come in with bags and steal everything," is how a woman described to me what it's like to shop even to this day at the local CVS in her town near Sacramento, California. The rampant shoplifting began in 2020 and still hasn't stopped because there aren't enough police and because local DAs don't consider such lawlessness criminal enough to prosecute, she said.

Organized retail crime isn't usually deadly, however. The other type of crime resulting from the defund movement often is.

Closer to home for the woke Wall Street CEO class in New York City, a social-activist-obsessed attorney named Alvin Bragg was elected Manhattan district attorney. Bragg has transformed the Big Apple into a criminal's paradise because of his defund policies. His prosecutors won't press charges on anything below a violent felony. Unless, of course, you're Donald Trump; Bragg thought it would be fun to hit Trump with criminal campaign finance violations for paying hush money to the porn star Stormy Daniels during the 2016 election. Likewise for Daniel Penny, a former Marine, who had the unfortunate timing in 2023 of riding a subway while a deranged and violent homeless man was threatening both him and other passengers. Penny stepped in and put the vagrant in a headlock. When the vagrant died, Bragg charged Penny with manslaughter.

The lawlessness combined with the uneven enforcement of the law has made New York a violent cesspool, resulting in a spike in the most violent crimes that inflicts harm on the rich and poor alike. At least the rich can leave, and they did, fleeing to Florida beginning in 2020 in one of the great mass migrations of wealth out the Northeast in history. For New Yorkers like me, it's hard to imagine that not so long ago, people couldn't wait to move to the Big Apple to indulge in its restaurants and cultural institutions in safety. NYC was home of the "broken windows theory" of policing under Mayor Rudy Giuliani and later Mike Bloomberg. Violent offenders were kept off the streets after being busted for less violent offenses and the crime rate plunged. Tax revenues soared. Business flourished.

Those days are long gone, thanks to people like the former leftist mayor, comrade Bill de Blasio, and later Alvin Bragg, and the business community that gave credence to their idiotic social justice posturing.

"Let's give him a chance," Kathryn Wylde, the CEO of a business group called the Partnership for New York City, told some of her members when

Bragg's new approach to law enforcement leaked to the press. In January 2022, Bragg had just taken over as Manhattan DA, a once prestigious post led by nonpartisan prosecutors like the great Robert Morgenthau. Following the playbook financed by George Soros (old George has said he's never met Bragg, but his contributions to outside left-wing political committees helped elect both him and a bunch of progressive big-city DAs), Bragg immediately threw the Morgenthau legacy into the ash heap of history. According to an internal memo, he ordered his prosecutors not to "seek a carceral sentence" except for murders and other extremely violent cases. The memo added that Bragg's new rule "may be excepted only in extraordinary circumstances based on a holistic analysis of the facts, criminal history, victim's input (particularly in cases of violence or trauma), and any other information available."

Writing in coherent English may not be Bragg's strong suit, as the memo demonstrates. But you get its drift: Criminals were given the green light to ply their trade without fear of arrest.

All major cities have business groups like the NYC Partnership, but this one is different, supposedly more powerful. Its members are the CEOs of all the nation's and the world's big banks, real estate companies, and private equity firms; people like Jamie Dimon and Stephen Schwarzman of Blackstone. Alleged titans of high finance. I used the word "alleged" because these powerful dudes were powerless in stopping Alvin Bragg's warped interpretation of law enforcement.

When members of the Partnership initially asked Wylde to investigate what Bragg was up to, her response was that in conversations with Bragg, he seemed more reasonable than the memo suggested. She offered to introduce him to the group so that members could see for themselves that he was not such a lefty monster.

Then bodies started piling up. In early 2022, a recidivist criminal killed Michelle Go, a forty-year-old employee of the consulting firm Deloitte, pushing her onto the subway tracks as she was commuting to work. Weeks later, a homicidal maniac executed a Goldman Sachs employee, forty-eight-year-old Daniel Enriquez, while he was taking the subway from Brooklyn to a Sunday brunch in Manhattan.

The New York City business community suddenly went from woke to very worried. "We need to meet immediately," Wylde told Bragg as the death toll mounted.

About a hundred of the city's top business leaders attended the sit-down. At the time, recently elected NYC mayor Eric Adams was getting increasingly agitated about the city's economy. Even after the worst of Covid had passed, people were still working from home, many in the suburbs, and depriving Adams's budget of tax revenues. He wanted every major firm to get its people back to the office. It was not happening for the simple reason that when given a choice, most people would rather work via Zoom than risk their lives walking from Penn Station to midtown.

Schwarzman told Bragg exactly that during the meeting; people won't return to the office "unless they feel safe. And they don't feel safe." Bragg just sat and listened. One major retailer told Bragg that lawlessness was so bad in Manhattan that he was installing the same type of security used in his stores in the crime-ridden city of Caracas, Venezuela. Bragg seemed unmoved.

Someone else asked Bragg, "If I get hit in the head with a baseball bat, will you prosecute?"

That crossed the line from social justice to assault, Bragg said, so yes, he would.

Bragg did *seem* reasonable, I am told, but he offered no apology or change in how his office would address crime going forward. In fact, he was surprised that the business community didn't know how he would govern. Bragg is a progressive zealot, and deserves scorn for the lawlessness in our streets, but at least he was honest. The business honchos who supported social justice ignored Alvin Bragg's wacko policies—he ran for office in 2021 on a platform of policing equity or "criminal justice reform" without a peep from the city's C-suiters.

Suffice it to say the meeting ended with no resolution other than Bragg's stated intention to meet again if necessary. Crime in NYC continues to soar. Violence and mayhem are now facts of life for millions of American workers, a very steep price paid for "equity."

That's if you made it safely to work; once there you were subjected to more "equity"—DEI sessions that resembled Vietcong reeducation camps.

Particularly after George Floyd's death, HR departments not only forced employees to sit through lectures from experts on critical race theory, but they also imposed what has been described to me as a white-male hiring freeze. To hire a white male, or promote one, HR DEI enforcers demanded so much paperwork, and proof of other diverse hires, that white men for a time literally stopped getting jobs and promotions, my sources at big companies tell me. Corporate boards had long sought diverse candidates; now they sought only diverse candidates.

Next came the DEI-tailored handouts. During the government-mandated shutdowns, people who ran small businesses lost their livelihoods and their dignity, a modern-day *Grapes of Wrath* that Jamie Dimon and Brian Moynihan knew or should have known about because so many small businesses bank with them. Federal government handouts like the so-called PPP, or Paycheck Protection Program, were never enough for many small businesses operating in places where the lockdowns were among the strictest and taxes the highest. The banks certainly had money to provide relief to all, because they were making so much of it themselves; following the various Covid bailouts from DC, and the Fed's pumping of money into the economy, the stock market rallied in ways not seen in years.

But the real economy—not the one taking place on people's Robinhood trading app—was hurting. Small businesses were shuttered; restaurants couldn't open. They all needed help, though after George Floyd, not all small businesses were treated equally. Back at BofA headquarters, Moynihan told his direct reports that because of the need for social justice, they should plan to hand out $1 billion of bank money (in the form of low-interest loans, etc.) only to minority-owned small businesses around the country.

Moynihan, according to my sources, didn't seemed particularly concerned about the fairness of such a program during one of the most difficult times small businesses *owned by all Americans* have ever faced. He also didn't appear particularly concerned about lending terms, my sources at the bank say. He just wanted the money to start flowing based on race. He said regional managers oversaw doling out the money because they were close to the communities they serve. Their guidebook, according to people with direct knowledge of the matter, was in fact several books written by the progressive academic Raj Chetty, whose research obsesses on the lack of economic mobility in the American economy, and how government and big business must step in to right the ship.

Moynihan was a huge fan of the left-wing Harvard professor, who gave lectures at BofA offices. "Raj Chetty was clearly the intellectual foundation of this whole thing," said a former BofA employee with direct knowledge of the matter.

Bank of America declined to comment on the program's success.

When Jamie Dimon got a whiff of what the dude running the nation's No. 2 bank was doing, he doubled down on the woke spending. His stated commitment after George Floyd was to fight racism "wherever and however it exists...This week's terrible events in Minneapolis, together with too many others occurring around our country, are tragic and heartbreaking." Dimon made good on his promise when he pledged $30 billion to close what he called the "racial wealth gap" that allegedly exists between every diverse group and white men. JP Morgan shareholder money was being earmarked to "promote and expand affordable housing and homeownership for underserved communities" and "improve financial health and access to banking in Black and Latinx communities."

"Latinx" is the gender-neutral term for Latino that came into vogue during the craziness of 2020, mainly by woke white people, like Dimon, because many Latinos are culturally conservative and hate it.

A little research by Dimon and Moynihan—again, neither have publicly produced data on their programs' effectiveness—would show that largesse of this nature doesn't work. Scholarship from Abigail and Stephan Thernstrom, in their seminal work *America in Black and White*, is just as easy to find as Chetty's greatest hits. The Thernstroms show that the era of handouts to minorities, particularly to the Black community, hasn't improved poverty rates; they provide evidence that it has made them worse.

In an interview with me a few years back, Abigail Thernstrom, who passed away in 2020, called these corporate-welfare-type programs nothing more than a "way of preventing bad public relations. They think if [social justice activists] wanted to picket major brokerage houses, it would make them look bad. This is a way of buying social peace, and it's not terribly unusual behavior for corporations these days."

A little self-awareness from Dimon and Moynihan and they also might come to realize that the racial wealth gap is also of their own making. In

2020, Dimon's total compensation was $31.7 million, Moynihan's $24.5 million. Take out the richest 1 percent of the richest 1 percent (that is, the white and woke corporate CEOs like Dimon and Moynihan) and you see how working-class people of all ethnicities have been getting crushed in recent years. Don't believe me. A couple of liberal Princeton University economists, Anne Case and Angus Deaton, lay it all out in excruciating detail in their book *Deaths of Despair and the Future of Capitalism*.

They point to the trend, particularly among working-class white men, of people who increasingly can't find work, a wife, or anything fulfilling except a bottle of scotch and some opioids. It's also an increasingly marginalized class in our popular and political culture. Madison Avenue doesn't believe they exist any longer, which is why you barely see a marginalized white guy in a TV commercial these days. There is no affirmative action for these "oppressors," no programs or DEI mandates to hire them.

As Bloomberg reported, after 2020 and through 2021 nearly *all jobs* from S&P 500 companies—the stock market's most powerful corporate entities—went to people of color. Combine already existing affirmative action programs with corporate wokeness on a massive scale, and 94 percent of all hiring went to people who weren't white, Bloomberg said. All things being equal, the plight of *all working-class people* should be top of mind for Dimon and Moynihan, but that's not how corporate wokeness works.

Meanwhile, if George Floyd took out a low-interest mortgage from BofA or JP Morgan, would he really have thought twice about doing what he did in that store? Would the cop have not used excessive force in his arrest? You know the answers. A better use of this shareholder money would be for police training or the opening of drug treatment centers since fentanyl was found in Floyd's bloodstream at the time of his death.

Yes, the summer of 2020 ushered in an era that was an absurd, solipsistic spectacle on many levels. Billionaire CEOs lecturing average Americans about the sins of the past that really don't remain doesn't pass the smell test.

The excesses of the woke corporate cultural change happened so fast, many senior managers didn't know about it until they read it in the paper.

"What the fuck is this about?" a manager in BofA's New York HQ asked his team after reading a *New York Post* story about some weird sensitivity training program going down in the company's massive Charlotte, North Carolina, hub.

Most people don't appreciate the humble roots of the modern Bank of America. It began as NCNB, or North Carolina National Bank, headquartered in Charlotte, a city on the cutting edge of the "New South" and its postwar economic revival. Through a series of acquisitions, the bank grew from a regional powerhouse to a national one when in 1998 it merged with San Francisco–based Bank of America, one of the oldest and most prestigious banks in the country.

And it wasn't done growing. In 2008, at the height of the financial crisis, BofA decided to take the plunge into the world of Wall Street and bought Merrill Lynch, then the largest brokerage firm, while it was teetering on the verge of bankruptcy. With that, it became one of the world's largest financial supermarkets. BofA has multiple corporate offices around the world, but its home is in many ways still in Charlotte, a city the bank dominated for decades economically (BofA employs around ten thousand there), culturally, and even in sports (the NFL's Carolina Panthers play in Bank of America Stadium).

Through it all, the bank had maintained its conservative and business-friendly roots, that is, until Moynihan took over in 2009. He was a top executive at Fleet Financial in Boston (purchased by BofA in 2004), and brought his Massachusetts progressivism to the company, people who know him tell me. They point to his opposition to a 2016 North Carolina law that banned transwomen from using the ladies' room. The law came after reports of sexual assaults committed by men pretending to be women. Moynihan saw his opposition to the so-called bathroom bill as something along the lines of Rosa Parks's efforts to fight bus segregation in the 1950s Jim Crow south. He proudly told shareholders, during an earnings call, no less, "We've been steadfast in our commitment [against] discrimination...We have been a leader in LGBT practices since the '90s."

If you are wondering why the head of the nation's second-largest bank cares so much about public restrooms, you don't know Brian Moynihan, whose zany leftist posturing shows no bounds. In 2020, in the middle of Covid, he thought it would be a smart move to weigh in on the woke controversy involving the Washington Redskins; BofA, a major sponsor of the team, called for a name change amid charges of cultural insensitivity to Native Americans. No surprise that after George Floyd his bank went into woke overdrive, first with the $1 billion race-based lending program, later upped to $1.25 billion, and then with one of the dumbest and most radical diversity programs corporate America has seen during these very radical times.

Chris Rufo, a Manhattan Institute scholar, had been digging into the post–George Floyd corporate woke self-flagellation, and what he found inside BofA's Charlotte headquarters was truly shocking. Senior management teamed up with the United Way for a new way to sensitize employees about racial injustice: "A Racial Equity 21-Day Challenge." Rufo's published research soon went viral and got picked up by the mainstream media. It showed that BofA sent an email to all its Charlotte employees urging them to take part in a type of racial sensitivity training where they would be instructed in the finer points of critical race theory, including "intersectionality, white privilege, white fragility, and systemic racism."

"Intersectionality? I didn't approve of any of this," the manager in New York told his team as they digested the story. "Is any of this garbage true?" he asked. It was. The training manuals for the "challenge" Rufo cited read like they came out of a BLM protest. "Racism in America idolizes white physical features and white values as supreme over those of others," they said. "White people have more limited imagination...experience fear, anxiety, guilt, or shame...contribute to racial tension, hatred, and violence in our homes, communities, and world...react in broken ways as a result."

WTF?! A bank is supposed to be selling financial plans, checking and savings accounts to everyone—Black people, white people, immigrants, you name it. If they have some money (usually above $500,000 in investable assets), they are all eligible to be part of Merrill Lynch's brokerage family. How does teaching intersectionality accomplish that?

During an internal investigation, the people in New York found that the executives in Charlotte gave the woke United Way representative carte blanche to design the program and its format, which included material supplied in an online format since the Covid pandemic was still raging. Management had contracted out sensitivity training to left-wing zealots who urged average people in lockdown and dealing with the nation's disastrous response to Covid to admit to their own systemic racism, as if they were the ones who killed George Floyd. Why did the people BofA go that route? According to my sources, they felt they had no choice given the nature of the country's political debate, and what was being messaged from the top of the bank.

A BofA spokesman confirmed Rufo's reporting but tried to shift blame to the United Way, which put together the program. BofA didn't check what type of woke nonsense was being fed to their employees, he said. Very strange, though not surprising, just another example of major companies willing to do and spend as much as they could to support the notion that America is a racist hellhole.

In the scheme of things for BofA, the 21-Day Racial Equity Challenge controversy turned out to be a relatively minor embarrassment, because going woke was the flavor of the day, and for some very profitable.

Just ask Ibram X. Kendi.

Kendi is no Milton Friedman capitalist according to his writings, but he understands money enough to tap into corporate wokeism. He's a bestselling author on so-called antiracism, or the academic theory involving how best to root out racist thoughts and actions. When you dig deeper into his theories, you discover that Kendi's basic argument is that white racism can be found everywhere—in food, arguments about tax cuts, you name it. And you need a different form of racism to stamp it out by denying opportunities to those who don't fit into his oppressed classifications. Forget the utter unconstitutionality of his remedies and forget about the rise of the Black middle class, affirmative action, and laws that prevent discrimination. In his worldview, the America of today isn't that much different in behavior than the Jim Crow South. The killings of George Floyd and others are proof that Black people are on the receiving end of this racism and in need of reparations.

Kendi gives speeches, collects plenty of grant money, does a lot of MSNBC. He gets paid to spew stuff like, "Since the dawn of racial capitalism, when were markets level playing fields?" Or this deep thought from one of those best-sellers: "When could Black people compete equally with White people?"

Critics, including one writing for the Manhattan Institute's *City Journal*, argue convincingly that Kendi was never much of a scholar, despite his progressive accolades. He "cherry-picks his data when discussing race and health. He laments that blacks are more likely than whites to have Alzheimer's disease, but neglects to mention that whites are more likely to *die* from it, according to the latest mortality data from the Centers for Disease

Control," writes Coleman Hughes in his profile of Kendi titled "How to Be an Anti-Intellectual."

Academia and corporate America ignored Hughes's warnings; after George Floyd, Kendi's star shone even brighter. Our cultural institutions, the media, academia, and business could have turned to accomplished African American academics and authors such as Thomas Sowell, Glenn Loury, Shelby Steele, or civil rights activist Robert Woodson for a more nuanced view of race relations during these fraught times. But they didn't because such free thinkers had the taint of being heterodox and conservative. Instead, they shaped the debate by leaning on leftists like Kendi.

Boston University gave Kendi a new think tank, the Center for Antiracist Research. Money from big companies came flooding in. Twitter CEO Jack Dorsey donated $10 million. "Jack's gift, like the…gifts of so many people and organizations, is essential," Kendi told the university's in-house publication *BU Today*. "But we still need to raise a lot more in order to make the difference that we are striving for. We are going to be engaged for decades in high-quality multidisciplinary research, critical policy and narrative change work, and lending our support to antiracist advocacy. That all necessitates a large staff, a community of well-funded researchers, and a lot of resources."

Decades? Try three short years. By mid-2023, BU was scaling back the antiracism center amid criticism that the center's research output was dismally low despite all those corporate donations. (BU didn't return calls for comment; Kendi, through a spokesman, reviewed this section and declined comment.) Kendi also isn't much of a manager, it turns out. Surprised? You shouldn't be. Kendi was just thirty-seven when he received near-unlimited resources. His résumé contains no significant management experience, but he's woke, and voluble about his leftist beliefs on race on the lecture circuit and in his books. In an era of DEI run amuck during the summer of 2020, why does it matter if Kendi is unqualified for the job? The world's most powerful financiers and businesspeople were too busy expressing their righteous rage, while destroying America's common culture, to use a little common sense.

That common sense would certainly include the funding of charter schools. Helping black children get a quality education denied to them by the teachers' unions, unlike Kendi's research, has an amazing record of accomplishment of lifting people out of poverty. It's also a nonstarter on the left because funding free-market solutions to an urban problem violates the predicates of corporate wokeism.

Corporate wokeness is a lot like other hysterias. The madness of crowds, of course, has been eroding clear thinking since the beginning of time: It created the South Sea Bubble of 1720, the dotcom collapse of 2000, and the 2008 banking meltdown, to name just a few. Religious delirium led to the Inquisition and the Salem witch trials. These were all mass movements that drove far too many people, both in those power and those who weren't, to accept lies as facts, with disastrous results.

It is unsurprising that woke racial insanity at the top of the business food chain would also filter down through the ranks in equally unctuous ways. People felt pressure not just to do their jobs, often via Zoom, but to tell the world how they were fighting racial injustice and the alleged inequalities that exist in a business that has embraced affirmative action, sought out diversity in its ranks, for decades.

"I AM. Not forgetting the PAST. Listening. Bring the Change!!!" read a sign held by a managing director in BlackRock's NYC office during those turbulent months. The man, a white dude, balding and middle-aged, posted the photo and the message on his LinkedIn page. As he looked sheepishly into the camera, it reminded me of those North Vietnamese propaganda spots, where they forced, under the threat of torture, captured US servicemen to denounce America's involvement in the Vietnam War.

There was a Stockholm syndrome quality to it all. During corporate sensitivity sessions in the summer of 2020, employees were encouraged by managers to admit their inner racism. Others, my reporting showed, began believing the nonsense as it was being drilled into their psyches. Being an observer of this weird woke awakening was gut-wrenching, particularly for Wall Street C-suite types who helped expand opportunities to women and minorities during corporate America's alleged dark days.

"I just can't watch the news anymore," John Myers, the retired head of GE Asset Management, snapped in the late summer of 2020 as he saw the riots, followed by reporters justifying them, and people he knew well, CEOs, still falling over themselves to show who wasn't a racist, or who was the most antiracist.

Myers, a Vietnam vet and thirty-year executive at GE, reported to Jack Welch and remembered Welch's push to bring more women and minorities into management positions. Look how far the country has gone off the deep end, he thought one morning as he tuned in to CNBC and listened to CEO after CEO agree with the Kendi and others that corporate America must make amends for the sins of slavery, Jim Crow, and every racial slight perpetrated by people long gone from this world.

Again, the country, and the business Myers worked in and only recently retired from, has strayed far from the days of Welch, who sought out women and minorities rather than push quotas in hiring. Myers called some of his pals still working at big companies to ask: Why are these CEOs doing this? The answer was they felt they needed to go woke, now more than ever before. Society (and their boards) was demanding it.

Well, that's only if you define society as the media, the cultural institutions, and, yes, corporate America, because the American people were becoming horrified by the bizarre spectacle. To engage in such metal gymnastics, I found that wokeness in the boardroom also needed to be nurtured in a way that gives it the aura of credibility.

For that we turn to the classroom of Jeffrey Sonnenfeld.

"You know what's wrong with this country—too many CEOs getting caught up in doing good," snapped a rising star in the corporate ecosystem, guest lecturing a class at the Harvard Business School.

It was sometime around 1981, if Jeff Sonnenfeld's recollection is accurate. He was all of twenty-seven years of age and a newly minted professor at the country's most prestigious business academy. Attending the class were the two men running GE, the iconic industrial company that gave us the light bulb, mass-produced refrigerators, and built jet engines.

One was retiring. He was a tall, courtly, almost regal man named Reg Jones, stepping down any day now to make room for the guy who would run the company for the next three decades and remake GE into something even greater. His name: Jack Welch.

It was Welch, all five foot seven of him, with a thin physique and a nasty gleam in his eye, who quipped during the event—when his boss, Jones, was in the men's room—that he hated the fact that people who ran US corporations were too busy trying to be good corporate citizens to be competitive globally.

Such nonsense had turned what once was a world-dominating corporate America into something like the Spanish Armada—a bulky, clunky, and uncompetitive mess. No match for the lean, mean fighting machine of Japan Inc., Welch said. In making his case, Welch conceded that he sounded a little like Darth Vader. He wasn't much for discussing do-gooderism in the boardroom, or "environmental pollution and educational issues," Sonnenfeld recalls him saying.

It takes some doing to confuse Welch's working-class New England brogue with Vader's modulated intonations as relayed by the great actor James Earl Jones. But you get the drift; Welch can be a tough and often scary character (people who work for him have some stories), and he soon scared a lot of people at GE. Once in the CEO seat, he began wiping out layers of management, laying off thousands of employees. The media called him "Neutron Jack."

Despite the cost cutting, much of Welch's creative destruction worked. Within a few more years, GE was a best-in-class conglomerate, one of the world's most profitable companies. Japan Inc. had been soundly defeated because C-suite executives across the country emulated Welch's management practices and his obsession with the management theory "Six Sigma," where execs focus myopically on problem solving, customer satisfaction, and results.

Do-gooderism, at least for a time, was taking a backseat to profits and enhancing shareholder value.

GE stayed that way nearly to the day evil old Jack Welch retired, and that's when, let's say, things went a little sideways. Do-gooderism was making a comeback; ideas like ESG began percolating at CEO confabs and then the boardroom. Stakeholder capitalism and the relentless search for higher DEI scores from the Human Rights Campaign became fashionable at every major company in the country, if not the world.

Today, Jeff Sonnenfeld is the Senior Associate Dean for Leadership Studies and the Lester Crown Professor in Management Practice at Yale University. The way he describes this turn of events—and he makes a living studying this stuff—the C-suite was merely returning to its roots as a center for social change. "It's part of a tradition. Progressives were always in the business community pushing workplace safety and environmentalism. This is no different."

Welch's replacement, Jeff Immelt, is a thoroughly modernistic CEO of values and nuance and, like Sonnenfeld, a graduate of Harvard Business School. Tall, good-looking, with a full head of hair and a polished tongue, Immelt peppered his language with catchy buzzwords like "imagination" and "innovation." They flowed so eloquently from his lips that even Welch was for a time mesmerized by Immelt's presence, anointing him as his replacement.

This stuff wasn't just rhetoric or symbolism, Immelt assured academics like Sonnenfeld, investors, and employees. They were keys to corporate success.

I bring all this up because the Welch-Immelt dichotomy provides such a vivid lesson in the perils of boardroom wokeness. GE is now a shell of its former self; new management is disentangling its myriad of businesses, selling them off as separately run companies to try to save what is left. Immelt was ousted a few years before the company's wholesale defenestration began.

Again, you can't blame all the company's ills on leftism or Immelt; Welch left him some messes to clean up. Some analysts say Welch's success was manufactured through the financial alchemy of managed earnings, playing fast and loose with accounting. There were circumstances that helped doom GE beyond Immelt's control. The 9/11 terrorist attacks changed air travel and dented a huge part of GE's business, aviation. The 2008 financial crisis brought scrutiny on GE's massive financial unit, GE Capital.

Yet I can't imagine words like "imagination" and "innovation" effortlessly flowing from Jack's lips, and I knew him well (he did use them thirteen times in his books, Sonnenfeld tells me). I can imagine the word "fuck" and "you" being spit out when you got cross with old Jack.

Having a nasty mouth wasn't the reason why GE had such a great run under Welch. Rather, he was an amazing businessman. Did he manage earnings? Probably. He also wasn't alone and did it better than anyone else within the law. He came up through the ranks and ran stuff like factories and knew every detail on GE's balance sheet. He knew how to groom executives for bigger jobs with more responsibility. He had little time for windmills, ESG,

DEI, or stuff that Immelt would later embrace, because none of that stuff contributed significantly to the company's bottom line.

Looking back at the Immelt era at GE, you see that many of his errors were unforced. Massive insurance-related charges appeared out of thin air, catching him off guard even though they were there on the balance sheet in plain sight. There were bad acquisitions and a share price that fell to near penny-stock levels before the GE board said enough and ousted him.

Also, Immelt was tilting at windmills—literally. Amid the various decisional errors, under his watch GE sought to become a huge provider of "green energy" and other woke, inefficient, and dubiously profitable businesses. Immelt served on Barack Obama's CEO Council, a group of C-suiters who gave credibility to a community organizer now president and his quasi-socialist economic agenda.

Immelt declined comment for this book; his press rep reviewed the material, including my contention that his boss would have scored high on the academic woke CEO measuring scale even though he failed as a CEO to keep GE from near destruction.

For his part, Sonnenfeld, back in 2008, said this about Immelt's increasingly uneven performance as a CEO, telling the *New York Times*, "So much of the job of leadership has symbolism intertwined with substance. Immelt has done all the right things, but it doesn't diminish the frustration."

In later years, when Immelt's management problems fully surfaced, Sonnenfeld tells me he did in fact become a critic, "unlike your pals like Nelson Peltz," he said, referring to the high-profile activist investor who bought shares of GE in 2015 to force change in its business model and played a key role in Immelt's eventual ouster two years later.

Peltz, Sonnenfeld says, "endorsed [Immelt's] missteps" by "remaining on his board" and allowing Immelt to stick around as CEO. He adds, "I'm not responsible for Jeff Immelt's missteps and criticized them when they became public."[1]

---

1. Sonnenfeld reviewed all the material in this book that is about him, and I've included his responses. I've never met Nelson Peltz nor spoken to him, though I did break the story that he was looking to oust Immelt from GE. Sonnenfeld declined to produce evidence of our friendship.

Better late than never.

Jack Welch passed in 2020, just days before the Covid lockdowns. In his final years, he confided in more than a few people that his biggest mistake as a CEO was anointing Immelt as his successor.

Immelt in semiretirement wrote a book about his GE experience, aptly titled *Power Failure*. To his credit, he takes some blame for GE's sorry state, but he also blames much of it on what he describes as a mess of a company that Welch left him, his lack of vision about GE as a global company that needed to adapt to new demands placed on the global modern corporation.

Global concerns involve taking bold action to be part of the global community, he said. I guess Welch didn't appreciate GE's need to adapt to the zero-emissions movement, ESG, and windmill business.

That's right: Old Jack wasn't into the woke stuff. Sonnenfeld tells me it was his experience talking to Welch that he was "hostile to CSR," aka corporate social responsibility, which is how he likes to describe what we call corporate wokeism.

As for Immelt, Sonnenfeld says he didn't meet him until later in Immelt's career when he was CEO, even if he once praised his "global vision and large system skills" as among his many attributes before he says the real and ugly truth emerged.

Globalism is a controversial pursuit these days, and for good reason. Average Americans don't see the benefits of corporate elites setting policy on trade, tax policy, or progressive cultural issues. The rise of the populist right—that means Donald Trump, and now politicians like Ron DeSantis and Vivek Ramaswamy—demonstrates that many Americans hate being told they must adapt to living not in their hometown but in a global community of free trade and borderless borders.

Most Americans, it turns out, reside about as far from the Yale School of Management and its globalist business foundations as you can get.

Full disclosure: I like Jeff Sonnenfeld. He is smart, an accomplished academic in the field of management, and well-meaning. He believes in the inherent good of "corporate social responsibility." He also represents a point of view that needs exploring in our discussion of woke capitalism.

Sonnenfeld, 70, has been an academic nearly his entire adult life. As a twenty-five-year-old with an MBA and a PhD in business from Harvard, he was one of the youngest professors at its esteemed business school. He takes pride in his long years as an academic studying C-suite behavior. "I was there before almost all in this field," he tells me. "Environmental issues, corporate governance, global expansion workforce diversity, etcetera, have been our mission since our founding."

Contemporaries agree and credit him with developing a research specialty coupled with roundtables in modern corporate governance and CEO behavior that rivaled the popular Davos gabfest. It was his idea back at Harvard in the 1980s to sit various C-suite executives, other business and even political leaders in a room to think big thoughts.

He called them his "CEO Summits." Later, he took his act to Emory University and then to Yale, where he resides today. He's widely published, has his own column in *Fortune*, and is a go-to dial-a-quote for business reporters (me included).

Even those who don't like Sonnenfeld's act, those who say he's too much of a globalist and doesn't see its corrosive effects on average Americans, concede he's plugged into the CEO circuit better than just about anyone in academia. The big thoughts wafting from his confabs often reflect the politics and culture of the C-suite, such as the type of corporate wokeism that came into full view in 2020.

In the 1960s and 1970s, the Vietnam War and the civil rights movement shaped the values and politics of executives who increasingly occupied the C-suite and were front and center at Sonnenfeld's summits. In the 1980s, it was the movement to force corporations to divest from South Africa as a means of topping the racist apartheid regime. All were discussed at Sonnenfeld's forums.

In the 1990s, Sonnenfeld studied and debated the rise of the imperial CEO like Welch, and how boards need to rein in these all-powerful chief executives. Long before Business Roundtable began embracing "stakeholder capitalism," Sonnenfeld began discussing the need for CEOs to embrace a more comprehensive approach to their jobs.

By 2020, Sonnenfeld and his CEO meetings turned to the social justice movement sweeping the country, and how CEOs were using progressive solutions to increase racial diversity following the death of George Floyd. He made sure to include various GOP figures in finance and politics, including Donald Trump's son-in-law, Jared Kushner, and members of the Trump administration as well, even if the overall progressive tone began to turn off some longtime participants.

One was Harvey Pitt, the former SEC chair, white-collar attorney, and a staunch Republican. Pitt told me that he became uneasy with Sonnenfeld's gatherings during this time because he believed they began to veer too much into progressive politics, as did Sonnenfeld's writings. One example is Sonnenfeld's 2021 guest piece for *Politico* titled "Corporate America Got Woke on Race," in which he cheered corporate America's racial justice moment. "The outrage over George Floyd's murder was a big wake-up call for America's CEOs," he wrote. "An overwhelming majority of the American public wanted executives to speak up and to act on racial inequality in the United States."

Speak up they did, incessantly during our Summer of Love and for most of the following year amid the "largely peaceful protests." Sonnenfeld applauded the CEO class for spending millions of dollars on special programs earmarked for "people of color." The new woke mood of the CEO class manifested itself, Sonnenfeld wrote, into "real efforts with real money behind them" to cure the sins of racism.

It wasn't just social justice that began to catch Sonnenfeld's attention. In June 2022, it was how to employ the collective might of the US CEO class to defeat Russian aggression in Ukraine. Ukrainian prime minister Volodymyr Zelenskyy made a special appearance at one of Sonnenfeld's gatherings. Zelenskyy, of course, enjoys a large degree of bipartisan support in his effort to stave off Russian strongman Vladimir Putin's invasion. He is also an increasingly controversial figure on the right. His demands for higher levels of US aid to fight off Russia's assault, and failure to root out corruption in his government, are at the heart of the conservative critique of US support for Ukraine.

The timing of Zelenskyy's appearance at the CEO powwow was interesting; it coincided with his private meetings with CEOs asking for corporate money to flow into his country. During one meeting, he asked a bewildered Larry Fink for so much free money, the famously garrulous Wall Street CEO was speechless—maybe for the first time in his life. BlackRock is one of the country's financial advisers; such handouts are not what it does. Fink said he had no problem seeking private investment to rebuild Ukraine's economy, I am told.

Sonnenfeld confirms he gave Zelenskyy an open mic to call in to his CEO seminars that were centered on prodding corporate divestiture from Russia. "We hosted President Zelenskyy at our CEO forums…The embrace of Ukraine's plight is hardly outside the pale of the US business community."

Others might disagree. There is a decent argument that US CEOs spend too much time aiding other countries while Middle America is suffering from outsourcing of jobs to India. That progressive politics has created a C-suite zeitgeist that business leaders must see themselves as global citizens first, then American citizens.

In our interview, I asked Sonnenfeld how this type of posturing and progressive politics in general got infused into the executive mindset. A business leader's desire to make the world a better, more inclusive, cleaner, and diverse place spans generations, he tells me. "The notion that CEOs would impact the world through their deeds goes back quite far," he said. At least to the so-called Progressive Era in the late 1800s and early 1900s, he added. CEOs, not just progressively enlightened politicians, were part of a movement to provide basic rights and more humane work conditions for the middle and working class.

"Sadly, academia destroyed the term 'progressive,'" he says, lamenting how it has been hijacked by Bernie Sanders and AOC, who are really "Democratic Socialists"—people who want to redistribute wealth rather than create it. The true progressives are capitalists who support economic growth but also "city beautification, a better environment, and a more egalitarian workplace."

In Sonnenfeld's telling, the CEOs of today who support progressive causes are following that grand tradition. People like Jack Welch, and the notion of shareholder capitalism championed by Milton Friedman, were mere detours in the business community's embrace of righteousness, he explains.

Business Roundtable—the leading business lobbying group—had long embraced social responsibility, through Welch's old boss Reg Jones. Its leaders during the 1970s took the position that "we don't have to be at war with society," he says.

Who can be against that?

Well, there is that slippery slope thing. Totalitarianism often begins with good intentions, the political elite looking to impose necessary order on those unruly masses to make the world a better place. That's before it spirals into repression, because making the world a better place is difficult stuff, people with such utopian ideals are often an uncompromising bunch, and the masses don't like to be told what to do. I'm sure Mao, Marx, Stalin, and Pol Pot really believed that forced collectivization was better for their people. I guarantee they thought they were doing righteous stuff through to the point they began executing people and forcing them into gulags to impose their utopian vision.

I'm not saying that woke CEOs and their HR departments are enforcing wokeism at the point of a gun—though fighting corporate wokeism can get you fired. I'm just saying their groupthink is blinding them to how they're warping the American workplace and our culture.

Their weapons are the forced woke indoctrination sessions, DEI, and ESG. They've joined progressives in this country to try and enact a new American cultural revolution. It leads to some good; learning about the historical struggles of African Americans is a good thing. Ditto for keeping the environment clean. Trans people deserve our respect and companies should consider them viable consumers and employees because they are.

But there's also some really bad stuff when Brian Moynihan's bank doles out a low-interest loan to a rich Black small business owner instead of some working-class white guy on the verge of bankruptcy.

Charles Elson, the founding director of the Center for Corporate Governance at the University of Delaware, has been Sonnenfeld's friend for forty years. Elson and Sonnenfeld are the yin and yang of the academic corporate governance business. Both are academics; both have studied corporate governance for decades; Elson once served on the board of the old Sunbeam corporation, and even took part in the messy firing of its controversial CEO, "Chainsaw Al" Dunlap, back in the 1990s, a time when corporate governance meant axing a lousy CEO, not mandating racial quotas.

Elson, who is retired from the center but still teaches corporate governance at the university level, says he admires Sonnenfeld and his accomplishments, even if he believes Sonnenfeld has helped propel corporate governance into dangerous areas by giving academic credibility to left-wing politics in the boardroom. Once a political moderate, Sonnenfeld has at least in tone "morphed now into, you know, this social justice corporate stuff," Elson says.

Elson attended Sonnenfeld's confabs years ago, and he has read about them, and what Sonnenfeld has written in recent years about social justice and how that reflects the sentiment of the wokeifying CEO class.

"The corporate board and CEO class," Elson says, is now almost uniformly left of center. "They used to be split, Republicans and Democrats," he says. "No longer."

Sonnenfeld, in his research and writing, reflects this "generational" political shift. "It's not like he's convincing them," Elson adds. "It's that they're feeling this way and he's repeating back to them what they'd like to hear."

In our conversations, Sonnenfeld rejects Elson's characterization that he suddenly turned woke; what he does today is no different from what he did when he started the seminars, he tells me. "We did not take a new turn towards social impact...that is where we were from the very start," he said.

Republicans comprise "more than half of our attendees" at his gatherings, he reminds me. They included in the past Donald Trump himself. True, but Sonnenfeld's relationship with Trump has always been fraught. According to a November 2021 piece in *Time* magazine, Sonnenfeld wasn't a big fan of the former president when he was in the private sector as a real estate magnate and reality TV show host. "Sonnenfeld finally gave in to Trump's pestering and invited him to one of his CEO summits," *Time* reported.

Still, Sonnenfeld says, his forums "are truly nonpartisan with no point of view and no woke mission." The topics include "a range of themes" that often deviate from politics, such as "global competition, technological disruption, and supply chain management," and more.

In fact, Sonnenfeld said he has even "critiqued the excesses of woke," including "ESG fads." He refers me to a September 2022 piece he wrote for *The Economist*. "Debate continues over whether ESG metrics lead to superior performance, or whether they are rather associated with well-run companies," he wrote.

Okay, but in the same piece, he also defended C-suite wokeism. In his words: "To those cynics who say, 'stay in your lane' to CEOs they call 'woke,' I ask, 'what lane do you mean? The breakdown lane?'"

Elson tells me, "Jeff wasn't talking about any of these topics twenty years ago," at least not in the same way he does today. Is it a matter of perception? Do Sonnenfeld's political discussions, his aforementioned *Politico* column, and his writings on the virtues of woke corporate solutions to alleged systemic racism generate much more media buzz than his CEO discourses on supply chain management?

Possibly. What's undeniable is that the progressive movement of yesteryear made factories safe for women and children; it brought diversity into the corporation as a worthy goal. Today's corporate progressive movement has pushed us far beyond seeking diversity; we're talking quotas and a lot more. Sonnenfeld's CEO gatherings are a snapshot of this generational shift to the left.

"In my experience CEOs don't relish taking public positions," said Tom Glocer, a veteran of corporate boardrooms as well as the former CEO of Thomson Reuters. "But sometimes politics threaten the very underpinnings of our free-market system, such as the challenge to the rule of law on January 6."

Glocer was explaining his participation in a CEO meeting, convened by Sonnenfeld, to discuss how big business should prepare for further right-wing unrest following the January 6, 2021, Capitol Hill riot.

Those riots, of course, were captured by TV and on iPhone footage in all their gory detail. Flag-waving, tin-hat-wearing morons were defacing the place of government business, the Capitol, hallowed ground of our democracy. That an American president lit the fuse of the insanity, condoned it for hours, made it even more troubling.

Yet this riot was contained to a single horrible day; the madness of one lunatic-fringe crowd. There wasn't the mass and organized looting and violence of the caliber that occurred after George Floyd by BLM, Antifa, and assorted progressive anarchists—the stuff the CEO class said demanded a woke awakening. A few days later, when around forty CEOs and Sonnenfeld held a Zoom call to discuss the riot, there was no right-wing insurrection sweeping the nation. VP Mike Pence had already certified Joe Biden's victory. The worst of the rioters were being identified and arrested, and some thrown in jail. Trump was largely in hiding during the last days of his odd presidency.

But if you believe what the CEOs were saying during the call, it seems like they were living in another country. The public intellectual Jordan Peterson would call it an "asymmetrical application of outrage." The left-wing riots that destroyed cities were a bizarre form of equity, while one day of tin-hat wearing right-wingers are a threat to Democracy.

That's because most CEOs I know see Trump and his supporters through the same prism as the typical progressive journalist: as singularly malevolent characters. The Donald and his peeps do some crazy things, as January 6 showed, but if you know him and the extreme elements of the MAGA crowd, as I do, they're more like cartoon characters than the return of brown-shirted menacing mobs.

Here's proof: Nothing the left and the CEO class fretted about regarding Trump's policies during his four years in office happened. Trump and the mob on that tragic day didn't overthrow the government; not even close (Trump even implored the crowd to protest peacefully). He never finished building that wall cordoning off Mexico that they freaked out over (he should have, or we wouldn't have the migrant crisis we have today). He didn't collude with the Russians; he spoke well of Putin, but multiple investigations show that's where it stopped. I recall how Mark Cuban once said Trump's economic policies—ending NAFTA, going to trade war with China—were going to tank the markets; they didn't. The economy and stocks boomed, in fact.

And for all his nuttiness, he wasn't a warmonger; he kept us out of them.

January 6 was horrible, but it was mostly several hours of horrible idiocy, not the storming of the Bastille that the left and now the CEO class was comparing it to. Several at the meeting said the riot was an indication of more violence to come, that they were preparing for a right-wing civil war. They needed to tighten security and stop making contributions to any Republican who didn't sign a loyalty pledge of sorts and certify that Trump had lost the election. They needed to take a stand against those who sought to upend democracy, which they believed was teetering.

It's hard to justify Trump's actions, and the violence that occurred, but let's unpack the logic here. Why would CEOs think it's okay to frame months and years of real left-wing violence as a cultural awakening while branding a day of mayhem as an existential threat to the nation?

You know the answer.

I raised the issue with Glocer, who contacted me at Sonnenfeld's request to attest to Harvey Pitt's attendance at the CEO summits and how much he enjoyed them, and that he never once complained (as he did to me) that they had gotten too woke. Harvey died, unexpectedly, in the summer of 2023, but Glocer said he remembers "clearly having had a conversation with Harvey during a break at one of the CEO summits in which we each agreed that the content was excellent. He was also engaged and an active participant."

I reiterated what Pitt told me and his perception of the CEO summits going too woke. I also reminded him that opinions like these don't have to be binary. Harvey could have liked some or most of the summits' commentary, but he is also a conservative; he was clearly upset with corporate America's reaction to George Floyd and the social justice movement in general that suggested the country was systemically racist.

Glocer said he understood the world isn't binary and he too isn't a fan of the excesses of woke; for example, he's disgusted with what is happening today on college campuses, how progressive students are responding, many *protesting in favor* of the brutal October 7, 2023, Hamas terrorist murders of innocent Israeli men, women, and children near Gaza.

He's not alone on this front, I must add.

Many progressive CEO types are grappling with sobering reality of left-wing antisemitism—how Israel-hating has been mainstreamed in parts of the Democratic Party, and the Jew-haters in Middle East studies departments and elsewhere in academia normalized a warped interpretation of Israel as a brutal and evil colonialist power.

Look closer and you realize it's another "victory" for corporate wokeness. Who threw money at these schools, funded their billion-dollar endowments? Our progressive C-suite class. Just as the CEO support for racial justice led to the defund movement, the CEO endowment financing of Harvard, Yale, Penn, and MIT, etc., funded campus wokeism and ultimately antisemitism because normalizing progressivism's worst and most destabilizing ideas will always cause a cascading effect. If you can justify riots and looting (renaming them "largely peaceful protests") over the actions of one police officer in Minneapolis, if you can then deem a whole country racist in need of radical reeducation, it isn't that much of a leap to demonize Israel as proxy for America and a racist colonializing power.

I brought up to Sonnenfeld another incident of woke normalizing with similar unintended consequences: his role in protesting a 2021 Georgia voting law, helping to organize a petition, signed by just about every major CEO in the country and advertised in the *New York Times*, alleging that some mild voting inconveniences were tantamount to racial injustice.

The law was the brainchild of Georgia's GOP governor, Brian Kemp, and it appeared innocuous: People had to show proper ID to vote. Mail-in ballots during Covid-19 became a big deal and presented their own unique challenges to the prevention of fraud; the law limits ballot drop boxes so they can be monitored. Political organizers couldn't proselytize voters—handing them water or donuts—while voters waited to cast their ballots.

The media and the lefties in Congress cast all of that as something the KKK would have devised, or, in Sleepy Joe Biden's words, "Jim Crow 2.0."

Sonnenfeld and his CEO pals would soon join the opposition.

In April 2021, Sonnenfeld was hanging in his office at Yale when the call came in, he tells me. Two titans of corporate America, former Amex CEO Ken Chenault and the CEO of Merck, Ken Frazier (neither returned my requests for comment), wanted to do something to make sure the world knew the CEO class was against sending the country back to the dark ages.

"Ken and Ken," as Sonnenfeld called them, are also two of the leading African American executives in the country, so it's assumed they have unique insight into the subject. Glocer said he knew Frazier from Merck, where he had been the pharma giant's lead director. "I was proud to be associated with them in their responses to Charlottesville and I have faith in the bona fides of their interpretation of the Georgia voting law," he told me. In 2017, Frazier famously quit Trump's business advisory council following the former president's creepy remarks on the unrest in the Virginia college town. Trump's infamous words that there were "very fine people on both sides" of the protests that day, including neo-Nazis, prompted such outrage that Frazier publicly bolted from the council. He was subsequently on the receiving end of a mean tweet from The Donald.

Okay, but in Charlottesville Trump was obviously, dangerously, and probably unwittingly being racist (I don't know what's in The Donald's brain cells, nor do I want to). What were the real racial "hardships" imposed in the Georgia voting law? Voter IDs?

Having blind faith in someone, even people as forthright as the two Kens, can lead you down some ludicrous and dangerous alleys. With Sonnenfeld's help—a Zoom call from his office at Yale with his CEO pals—Ken and Ken got more than a hundred CEOs to sign a petition saying a law that restricted drop boxes moved us back to the dark days of racial segregation and lynching.

The CEO names appeared in the ad under the headline "We Stand for Democracy," vowing to defend the right to vote and oppose any "discriminatory legislation or measures that restrict" those cherished rights.

Yes, you read that right: In the warped world of corporate wokeism, democracy is threatened when the law requires a driver's license to vote.

Wasn't this a little overboard? Even Jamie Dimon, people at JP Morgan told me, stayed away from this one. "No," Sonnenfeld tells me, "the law is racist…they reduced the number of drop ballot boxes" from around thirty to just nine. This happened mostly in Fulton County, the home of many African Americans. A bigger concern: Sonnenfeld says the law gave the state legislature "new power to override" elected officials like the secretary of state on election disputes without "required evidence of fraud."

"That makes it racially motivated," Sonnenfeld said.

I guess that's one way of looking at it. Another is that Fulton County is the state's most populous county (home of its largest city and capital, Atlanta). It's not easy to monitor scores of drop boxes for fraud, and drop boxes, for obvious reasons, are particularly susceptible to fraud. Elected representatives of the state legislature having a say over voting irregularities might not be a bad idea as well.

How is that racist?

To listen to Sonnenfeld's explanations, you would think that he and the two Kens were facing off against Bull Connor on the Edmund Pettus Bridge. Dr. King and his freedom marchers faced guns and vicious dogs, water cannons, and bullets; Sonnenfeld and the two Kens enjoyed favorable media coverage from their elegant offices.

And what did they accomplish? More virtue signaling from like-minded CEOs. Delta Air Lines is headquartered in Atlanta. Its CEO, Ed Bastian, made $12 million the same year he told his employees the voting law "is unacceptable and does not match Delta's values." Really? Georgia is in many ways a red state. (Its two US senators are Dems, but its governor is a Republican and the GOP controls the legislature.) Does that mean his employees in Georgia are racist because they voted for the people who passed the law?

The attacks against the law failed the logic test repeatedly. Later that year, Major League Baseball decided to move its All-Star Game that year from Fulton County's Truist Park because of the controversy the law created, which the CEO class, again, gave credence to.

The MLB commissioner, Rob Manfred, cowered as CEOs, joined by civil rights activists like Al Sharpton, Georgia's perennial gubernatorial candidate Stacey Abrams, and basketball star LeBron James, demanded that the league do what the CEOs did and recognize the law as racist with some sort of statement during the game, I am told. To quell the controversy, Manfred just moved the event to Denver in Colorado, a state where the voting laws are even more restrictive, people close to the commissioner tell me.

Little-known fact: Atlanta is also home to the nation's largest concentration of Black-owned businesses. They were deprived of the economic activity the All-Star Game spectacle brings to the host city. An estimated $200 million in spending moved from Atlanta to Denver, all over corporate wokeness.

A better-known fact: In 2022, Abrams, an African American, running against Kemp for governor once again, lost once again and by a substantial margin, even as Black voter turnout soared.

Unfortunately, there will be many more such woke "victories," and the inevitable pushback by Americans who are tired of the endless corporate proselytizing. America is now at war over wokeness and the corporations that are spearheading the charge to remake the American psyche to conform with their leftist beliefs. They see how wokeness justified by the CEO class has led to ever larger lies about the country, and to campus unrest where students at our so-called elite colleges and universities liken Israel to Nazi Germany.

That's right, it's a war, and it's going to get ugly, as you're about to find out.

CHAPTER FIVE

Woke and Broke

There are many rationales for corporate wokeism. One offered by Mark Cuban is worth exploring. It is Cuban's opinion that "no one has gotten crushed by being woke."

Translation: Going woke is good for business.

Cuban's remarks came in a direct message, but his anger was palpable following a column in the *New York Post* I wrote about Budweiser's absurd Dylan Mulvaney ad and how I believed it would lead to a decline in business, and could decimate a once iconic brand.

Cuban is, of course, the voluble billionaire tech entrepreneur, financial TV regular, and until recently an NBA team owner. He's also wickedly woke, and not afraid to offer his perspective on why it's not just good for society to go left (i.e., saving the environment, racial diversity), it's good for business. "How do you reconcile that nine of the ten top market cap companies in the USA are woke?" he asked. The phrase "Go woke, go broke" is part of the "conservative echo chamber," Cuban assured me. "You have to look at the real results. Gen Z and young Millennials laugh at all of that."

Okay, let's explore.

At six foot three, broad-shouldered and fit, Cuban is both physically imposing and imposingly opinionated. He grew up as a working-class Jewish kid outside Pittsburgh and made his fortune because he's a great salesman who saw an opening in selling technology during the early stages of the internet boom three decades ago.

His enormous wealth is a product of starting something that eventually became something that he sold to Yahoo, the early pioneer in internet search. It was called Broadcast.com, a website that streamed audio from sporting events and talk radio. Cuban unloaded the website for $5.7 billion. Wall Street tech analysts regard it as among the worst deals ever consummated by a big publicly traded company. Yahoo paid a ton for something it could never make work, and eventually shut it down.

It was a great deal for Cuban, however. It made him a billionaire several times over. Money brought Cuban fame and freedom—hanging out at Dallas Mavericks basketball games (he bought the team in 2000 for $285 million and announced the sale of it in 2023 for $3.5 billion), host of the popular *Shark Tank* franchise, one of the so-called sharks who uses his entrepreneurial acumen to judge start-ups on the television show.

Cuban's stature is well earned, which means he should understand a thing or two about what sells and what doesn't unless his progressive politics are blinding his business judgment. Those "real results" that woke produces in a business environment that Cuban is pointing to include the enormous profits being cranked out by Big Tech, companies like Google and Apple, which preach diversity at every turn, support left-wing causes, and make big donations to Dem pols.

They have also created some of the best businesses in America. It's Ben & Jerry's ice cream, which hasn't found a woke ideal it doesn't support. It's also Nike, the legendary woke sneaker company, which resurrected the career of Colin Kaepernick, the former NFL QB. Kaepernick was once a player with some potential. As his career fizzled, he started protesting alleged police brutality against African Americans by taking a knee during the national anthem. Nike, as Cuban pointed out, played into that theme, tapped into the left-wing passion that Kaepernick generated on and off the field with a new ad campaign: a black-and-white close-up of Kaepernick letting his freak flag fly with the caption "Believe in something. Even if it means sacrificing everything. #JustDoIt."

Sales soared.

Stirring stuff, and in Cuban's view, another victory for the business model of wokeness. "Young people are making buying decisions that will stick with them forever," he tells me. "Like which phone, which sneaker is woke."

These young consumers "are the most desirable demographic to advertisers...this is why the platforms that generate the most ad revenue and product sales are woke and geared toward young audiences."

As Cuban explains it, the NBA, the league he knows well, gets it. See the NBA owners' so-called Social Justice Coalition, which throws money at stuff euphemistically termed "police reform" (aka defunding the police). It supports overt acts of virtue signaling by players such as LeBron James donning a hoodie after the controversial 2012 shooting death of Trayvon Martin—one of several flashpoints in the social justice movement.

The story of Trayvon Martin is indeed tragic. The African American teenager was shot by George Zimmerman, a mixed-race man serving as a neighborhood watch captain. Zimmerman thought Martin was a criminal, not some kid out for a walk. LeBron made him a martyr even if his social justice meme leaves out some key facts. Zimmerman was cleared by a Florida jury because evidence shows the shooting was done in self-defense. Martin was hardly any innocent kid who happened to be wearing a hoodie, but a troubled teen. He was beating Zimmerman bloody before he was shot.

The hoodie meme might be a distortion of the truth, but apparently it sells NBA tickets, at least according to Cuban. So do other overt displays of social justice posturing after another social justice flashpoint—the death of George Floyd. Cuban says Major League Soccer gets it as well. Soccer, he said, saw its popularity rise when it mixed in some social justice with its games, earmarking money to minority businesses and embracing other social justice initiatives.

These fan bases are "young and connect with woke programs," Cuban assures me.

On the other hand, maybe not so much. Nike's customer base isn't exactly representative of Middle America. Moreover, are kids in red America, say, in Mississippi, really buying Air Jordans to embrace their inner AOC? In addition, what's to say Gen-Alphas and Gen-Zers will remain woke as they experience the world for the first time outside the confines of being brainwashed in the college classroom?

"Republicans buy sneakers, too," remarked a smart businessman in explaining why social justice/politics and business mix worse than oil and water.

It is fashionable to mock jocks as dummies; some are. Some understand business better than the typical corporate CEO. One of those is basketball icon Michael Jordan, the name behind those vary popular sneakers I just mentioned known as the Air Jordan.

It was 1990 and Jordan had just signed his big Nike endorsement deal. There was pressure on him to delve into politics in his home state of North Carolina. At the University of North Carolina, Jordan majored in something called cultural geography, where he also must have developed some good business skills. He chose to stay in his lane, not get on any customer's bad side, and it paid off. Air Jordans remained wildly popular, as did Jordan himself.

Woke CEOs might want to follow his example; despite Cuban's assertions, research by professors David McLennan and Whitney Ross Manzo of Meredith College shows that younger generations are hardly a woke monolith. "The results from our work suggest there is a strong conservative element within Gen Z on policy issues and the role of women in politics—a shift to more traditional views among the male population," they wrote in a 2022 opinion piece for *The Hill*. "Coupled with the fact President Biden's approval among Gen Z has dropped precipitously from the highs enjoyed by former President Obama, it is apparent both sides have mischaracterized this generation greatly."

A more representative sample of Middle America is the NFL fan base, something that closely resembles a broader demographic of the American population: working class and professionals with disposable income and not necessarily woke.

Cuban says football fans are too old and too non-woke to really matter to advertisers. They're not where the money is and will be. "The average age is fifty-five," he says. "Baby Boomers went from sex, drugs, and rock and roll to sit-ins and protests to now 'shut up and dribble,'" a reference to now famous comments made by Fox News host Laura Ingraham about LeBron James attacking conservatives like Donald Trump.

A couple things. People are living longer; fifty-five is the new forty-five. An average age of fifty-five is a demo with *a lot* of disposable income compared to student-debt-heavy Millennials and after. It's the reason the NFL cranks out $18 billion annually in revenues compared to the more woke NBA, which comes in around $10 billion. (Major League Soccer is a paltry $200 million.) Nike may have sold some sneakers using Kaepernick as a symbol of rebellion, but the NFL demo was repulsed by his antics, according to my reporting and the league's own internal surveys I was briefed on. Fans thought he was a washed-up player; they believed he started the one-knee protest after the Ferguson riots from the bench, literally, looking for some cheap publicity.

They hated that he sullied their game with politics during the national anthem, no less. They hated that the increasingly progressive suits who run the NFL thought it was just swell—a moment in social justice history—to have a protest before every kickoff. They began to boycott games. NFL TV ratings declined—until they stopped the nonsense and got back to playing football without the woke politicking.

The NFL and its politically correct commissioner, Roger Goodell, routinely ignore data that football's fan base doesn't appreciate player or league wokeness, my NFL sources tell me. Goodell's obsession with embracing wokeness is something owners hate as much as the fans do. The owners have accepted it because Goodell runs a hugely profitable organization for them. It's the-devil-you-know in this fraught relationship. In fact, their allegiance was tested during the Kaepernick-inspired one-knee debacle; a group of owners would later unsuccessfully try to get him removed.

One of those, Jerry Jones, the owner of the Dallas Cowboys, is hardly a right-wing culture warrior. But he knows something about business, having turned the Cowboys into the most valuable franchise in sports. He filled the leadership void left by Goodell, demanding that his team start standing during the anthem because the players were pissing off the people who pay their salaries—average NFL fans. Other owners soon followed his example.

Jones may have stopped the bleeding, but NFL TV viewership is fickle, Nielsen data shows. In 2023, NFL viewership soared, but cord cutting, where younger generations consume less programming on TV and more on their tablets, is always lurking, as is fan aversion to the league's wokeness.

Also, football fans are plain tired of the racial politics that Goodell has made part of the sport. After George Floyd's death, Goodell ordered the playing of what's known as the Black National Anthem before games. Pregame ceremonies and commercials were endless in their racial sermonizing.

Did some people turn the channel? They sure did, and they will continue unless there is an intervention to stop the NFL's woke insanity. "I was at a recent ownership meeting," an attorney from a white-shoe law firm told me. "You almost forgot that they were debating the sale of the Commanders; 90 percent of the discussion centered on the diversity of coaches, team executives. It was mind numbing."

Like most corporate boards and C-suites, white males make up the majority of those on the coaching and management side of the NFL. Approaching 60 percent of NFL players are Black. Still, the NFL isn't slave labor. Its players are well paid. The number of minority coaches and football executives is starting to grow, and oddly, you don't really hear how great players are being turned away from coaching jobs, probably because many of them want to do something else in retirement, like sports broadcasting.

Once again, I'm withholding this source's name because he needs his day job. He attended the May 2023 meeting of the NFL's thirty-one "principal" owners as a rep for an owner who couldn't make it. The meeting was supposed to focus on the recent sale of the Washington Commanders to an investment group led by private equity executive Josh Harris.

Selling a team is a complicated matter. League rules demand that the principal owner maintain a certain equity stake. The league requires background checks of new owners and management because the NFL is an exclusive club, a multibillion-dollar business built on an image of integrity and symbolized by the so-called shield in its logo. You really want to know who you're letting into the proverbial tent.

The sale, according to his account, took a backseat to multiple other discussions: how to get more minorities in management, coaching, and owning teams. "It was crazy," he told me. "Every discussion with the league involved diversity. You almost forgot we were there to debate the sale of a team."

The tortured history of how the Commanders became the Commanders is worth mentioning here as well; it is another example of how corporate wokeness can lead to the destruction of a once great franchise, and how it threatens the business of the NFL.

For decades, the Commanders were known as the Washington Redskins. A proud Native American emblazoned on their helmets signified the warrior spirit of the team.

The 'Skins were the winners of Super Bowls, the home of the "Hogs," proudly rotund offensive linemen, and the "Smurfs," super-fast undersized receivers. The team featured both huge and smallish players who congealed to make magic on the field.

The team's rousing battle song was "Hail to the Redskins." It was all defenestrated because being a Redskin became construed as an evil form of cultural appropriation, a mocking of Native American culture that can't be tolerated. (The team is looking to revise the song, but with new, more woke lyrics.)

Fans had no say in the name change; social activist groups, whose members probably never watch football, did. The team's then owner, Dan Snyder, after years of fighting off the PC police, eventually couldn't withstand the pressure, including now from Goodell following the death of George Floyd and the riots that followed. The Redskins soon became the more PC Washington Commanders. The team now regularly ranks at or near the bottom in attendance.

The Redskins—I mean the Commanders—haven't won a Super Bowl in years, so part of the fan erosion is based on performance. Still, the Redskins meant something to Washington's longtime fans. Like the Stalinist rewrite of the history books, there isn't much talk at the stadium about the Redskins and their storied history, the original fight song, and more.

Fans are mad for many reasons, including the simple fact that woke doesn't sell, no matter what Mark Cuban tells you.

But let's get back to Cuban's initial premise that the biggest, most successful companies in the world are woke, so it must be good for something in business.

Cuban fails the test of logic. First, his definition of wokeness—being a CEO who cares about preserving the environment and hiring a more diverse workforce—is benign and not reflective of what wokeness is in practice: the radicalized agenda of diversity training, quotas, and DEI. His argument is also a non sequitur. He wants you to believe that by using your Apple iPhone or the Google search engine, sitting through an NFL pregame ceremony preaching social justice, you're personally affirming the woke cause. Every time you download a song on iTunes, listen to a decidedly unwoke Joe Rogan episode on Spotify, or catch an episode of *Yellowstone* on Netflix, you're throwing your hat in with the lefty virtue signalers.

You're not, of course. These companies make superior products, and their stock price reflects that. When their products get stale or face competition, the stock price reflects the decline in sales and profits. In 2022, tech stocks corrected, violently in some cases, as earnings faltered. I didn't hear Cuban blame that on the growing anti-woke backlash in conservative politics.

Yes, it takes some twisting of logic to accept corporate wokeness as anything but a house of lies, and more often than not, a business disaster.

It also takes some pressure.

"Congrats, you won...so you're done, right?" Jay Clayton told yet another representative from the burgeoning social activist movement who got an appointment to meet him at the Securities and Exchange Commission's offices in Washington.

In 2017, Clayton became Donald Trump's SEC chief, head of the federal agency that regulates both the markets and, by extension, every public company where shares are held by American investors.

The win Clayton was referring to was the general acceptance of the "G" in ESG, the governance part of the investment approach. Most large corporations have taken major steps to improve their governance through the hiring of independent audit committees to look at corporate conduct, and board membership that is "staggered," where directors' terms run out at different times to prevent groupthink.

Who can be against any of that?

When he took at the job, Clayton was in his early fifties, though he doesn't look his age. In fact, with a thick mop of dark hair, parted to the side, he looks like a gracefully aging fraternity dude. But make no mistake, Clayton is no "dude." He spent three decades in the corporate law circuit, working and advising big US companies like Google, Apple, and Amazon on how best to finance IPOs, etcetera. He's an expert at guiding big companies through the complex scripture that is the US securities laws, which is enforced by the SEC, the agency he now leads.

Politically, Clayton is a fiscal conservative. He also considered himself a progressive in an old-fashioned way. As a top partner at Sullivan & Cromwell, he sought out women and minorities for key roles. He believed in the benefits of diversity, having established the SEC's first diversity and inclusion strategic plan. He also believed in merit. The last thing he ever wanted was to stigmatize someone as an affirmative action hire, as he has seen so many times in his career. Being an expert in securities laws doesn't necessarily make you an expert in the social justice movement. Clayton had no idea how far left the notion of governance had become.

He was about to find out.

"No, we're not done," his guest replied ominously, "we've just begun." Independent audits committees were so yesterday, Clayton was finding out from his guest. The new breed of corporate activists wanted something more and ambitious out of the G in ESG: mandatory race- and gender-based board composition. Prohibitions on political spending that prevented companies from supporting free-market groups, and limits on corporate use of fossil fuels were all on the guest's agenda for SEC action.

As I mentioned earlier, activist groups like the Human Rights Campaign and the Center for American Progress play a key role in the nurturing of woke capitalism, observers tell me. (Reps for both groups received source material for this book; HRC didn't comment.) Among their tools of the trade: They publish reports on corporate behavior even as they receive money from big business. A rep for CAP says its corporate donations represent less than 1 percent of its budget. Yet the group "proudly" displays its business-community partners on its website, which only further burnishes its ability to extend to get buy-in from powerful government agencies in pursuit of their cause, critics say. According to Clayton, they wanted his buy-in to take corporate America to a whole new woke level.

HRC, as I pointed out in prior chapters, is run by a former Obama campaign aide, Kelley Robinson, with a stated goal of ensuring that "all LGBTQ+ people, and particularly those of us who are trans, people of color and HIV+, are treated as full equal citizens" as if they're not already.

CAP was started by a man named John Podesta to improve "the lives of all Americans through bold, progressive ideas...Our aim is not just to change the conversation, but to change the country."

Pretty radical stuff coming from people you wouldn't expect to be seated in the SEC chairman's office, unless woke capitalism is the flavor of the day.

You might know Podesta as the reason why there was a Hillary Clinton email scandal. The longtime Dem consultant, aide to Bill Clinton, then Barack Obama, and now Joe Biden, was working on Hillary's 2016 campaign when he idiotically opened a phishing email sent by some hackers. Within no time, WikiLeaks began posting communications from the former First Lady that showed she was cavalier with classified documents on her own personal server—kind of like the stuff getting Trump in trouble for today—and nearly led to Clinton's indictment.

Okay, that was dumb, but don't underestimate Podesta's broader intelligence, Beltway clout, and, by extension, his influence in corporate America. He created CAP in 2003; it touts a "non-partisan" mission as a think tank, but its real power is the ability to set a progressive agenda with Democrats in Congress and the White House on policy matters that include the economy and business. Yet its policy goals are anything but nonpartisan. They include stuff like "economic justice," "employment diversity," and "climate change" among its many leftist shibboleths. CAP's political power comes from seeding Democratic administrations and congressional staff with its associates—a type of woke regulatory capture. CAP, for instance, doesn't get directly involved in the so-called proxy voting process like other such groups. Rather, its market power comes from helping shape public policy on business issues through research and working with members of Congress. It's notable that big blue state and city pension funds in places like New York State, New York City, and California push a similar progressive boardroom behavior. As such CAP's overall agenda becomes an important touchstone for the big private asset managers—places like Vanguard, BlackRock, and State Street—and others that want to manage the billions in blue-state and city government pension money.

It's a woke power lunch, so to speak.

If you want further proof of CAP's corporate power, check the list of its contributors. *Politico* once called it a "fundraising juggernaut" thanks to Podesta's high-profile connections to the Democratic elite. Other CAP honchos bring political influence as well. CAP's longtime president, Neera Tanden, left the organization in 2021 to work in the Biden White House. The organization's revolving door with left-wing bureaucrats only enhances its power—and ability to raise what it argues is de minimis corporate money. Yet, running CAP can pay as well as many private-sector jobs because of its high-powered donor list. It has included in recent years mainstream companies as diverse as the philanthropic arm of Bloomberg L.P., the big financial data and news organization created by the billionaire centrist and former New York mayor Michael Bloomberg, as well as Amazon, JP Morgan, Microsoft, the Charles Schwab Corporation, Bank of America, Levi Strauss & Co., Verizon, Wells Fargo, Apple, Google, and Walmart. (A CAP spokeswoman points out that JP Morgan and Apple didn't donate in the latest reporting period, but investment powerhouses like Fidelity Investments and PE behemoth KKR did.)

CAP and its fellow travelers wanted vast identity-based corporate disclosures on employment and salaries, separated by race and gender, Clayton recalls. CAP says it is simply asking for rules that prod companies to disclose if they have a process of building more diversity; the info on employment breakdown is no different than what companies give the government. Clayton didn't see it that way. The activists explained that corporate America was still way too white, male, and straight, he recalls. Disclosures were needed to include hiring from the LGBTQ+ community, all enforced by SEC rulemaking. These disclosures could lead to diversity quotas enforced by SEC regulatory fiat.

"I can't support that," Clayton responded when the matter was presented to him several times, in fact, during his four years running the commission. "What you call 'equity' is really compensating people for the sins of the past. That's an issue for Congress, not a regulator."

Their answers, ominously and almost uniformly, were something along the lines of try harder, he says.

The ominous day is now upon us. Clayton went back to private practice after the 2020 election. Gary Gensler, a lefty former Goldman banker, now heads the SEC. He has made codifying corporate wokeness into law a priority of the agency.

Gensler was appointed SEC chair in 2021 by Joe Biden, but he doesn't really answer to our brain-addled president. My sources tell me he's a product of the super-progressive senator from Massachusetts, Elizabeth Warren, who supported him for the SEC job and, if Biden wins a second term, possibly Treasury secretary.

Warren is powerful because she's on various Senate committees that oversee finance and because she has the ear of Sleepy Joe on economic issues. Bankers like Jamie Dimon and Larry Fink fear and loathe her because she's off the deep end in terms of leftism and nasty about it. One of her star pupils happens to be Gensler; he's a male version of Warren, among the most woke, annoying, and, according to some of the people he regulates, dangerous bureaucrats in government.

It's been an interesting journey for Gensler to the left. He began his career in finance as a moderate and liberal on social issues, people who know him tell me. He worked at Goldman as a banker, then went into the Clinton administration and seemed to fit right in with the middle-of-road economic team led by Treasury Secretary Robert Rubin, another Goldman alum, and economist Larry Summers.

Something changed along the way. One explanation according to these people is the tragic death of his wife from cancer and the experience of being a single dad raising his children. It led to a woke awakening, they said. Slowly, Gensler began to preach big government solutions. During this time, he also aligned himself with Warren, and his move to the left was complete.

These days, he is widely reviled on Wall Street for channeling Warren's anti-business politics through intense regulation, and enforcement actions even for petty crimes. The crazy Nasdaq race-based listing rules have his fingerprints on them, my sources say. He has largely ignored real pump and dumps in so-called meme stock—the trading in money-losing penny stocks hyped by fraudsters—while focusing on making companies disclose how their operations impact the environment. And he doesn't take criticism very well, I am told. "He's always got to be the smartest guy in the room, and he leaves no room for disagreement," is how the late Harvey Pitt, himself a former SEC chair, described Gensler. An indication of just how much Gensler is reviled on Wall Street: A meme being emailed around various trading desks shows his angular face on the contorted body of the plotting and diabolical Mr. Burns from *The Simpsons*.

Gensler's tenure has also been marred by several big blunders that critics say also underscore his woke blind spots. One of the biggest: He cozied up to

Sam Bankman-Fried, the progressive mega-donor and later crypto fraudster, just before SBF's crypto exchange, FTX, imploded and SBF was busted for stealing customer money to gamble in the markets.

Gensler saw none of this coming despite significant warnings from people like hedge fund trader Marc Cohodes, who called out SBF's fantastical claims of his wealth and business acumen. Instead, like dozens of Democratic pols seeking access to SBF's large kitty for political contributions, Gensler met with the former crypto wunderkind twice and was on the verge of approving SBF's dream of an SEC-approved crypto exchange, just before FTX collapsed.

The SEC may soon roll the dice again. Gensler is pushing through the commission new rules forcing companies to disclose how they will reduce their carbon footprint well into the future. What company can reliably estimate what its carbon footprint will look like in the coming years? How do you even reliably measure a carbon footprint? No one really knows, but Gensler doesn't care.

Mandating other progressive edicts won't be far behind if Biden gets another term. My sources close to the commission say Gensler is already weighing codifying DEI into the securities laws, the same stuff Clayton passed on (an SEC spokesman declined comment on what I'm reporting in this book about the chairman). In April 2023, Gensler said as much during an online chat with Lloyd M. Johnson Jr., publisher of something called the *Black In-House Counsel Annual Report*, which describes itself as the "premier source of information and engagement for Black attorneys across the legal industry."

Asked about the SEC's enforcement of DEI more broadly as part of its embrace of ESG, Gensler said the SEC is traditionally an agency dedicated to investor protection and enhancing capital formation, but times are changing. Companies must adhere to a new type of disclosure that alerts investors on subjects that go beyond profits and losses.

"What does change over time is what information investors look at, and over the decades, this has shifted," he said. "What does this mean for the 2020s? There are tens of trillions of dollars of assets under management and investors are looking to companies to disclose information about climate risks and about cyber risk. Building from predecessors in this job, we're also looking at workforce or what one might call 'human capital disclosures.'"

Corporate wokeness comes in many forms. It is possible SEC-mandated DEI. It is stakeholder capitalism and ESG, leftist activist groups overriding shareholder concerns in making demands on public companies or demanding disclosures to satisfy their progressive agenda. It's Nasdaq's listing rules that don't apply to China Inc. It's shareholder money flowing to the financially suspect Black Lives Matter movement. It's the imposition of racial quotas on management or forcing oil companies to cut back on drilling when gas prices are soaring.

It's saving the environment even if it bankrupts the working class with inflation.

It's the celebration of everything trans by Target and Budweiser. It's the Walt Disney Company normalizing same-sex kissing scenes in cartoons made for children and opposing a law that prevents the teaching of sex ed to toddlers.

Disney's embrace of wokeness is both scary and amusing, as I will be explaining in the coming pages, but here's a little taste. Disney's annual report grades managers on wokeness—literally. C-suite performance includes measuring an executive's diversity and experience in the field of ESG.

No surprise that Bob Chapek, its now former CEO, scored low on the diversity metric because, guess what? He's a white dude.

Yes, it's all very chilling, sickening, and sometimes amusing. So, grab your popcorn, sit down, and try to enjoy the horror movie about to unfold.

CHAPTER SIX

The Fight Begins

"Are you kidding me?" Ed Rensi muttered in anger, bewilderment, and some shame as he watched on his TV the business world devolving before his very eyes. Rensi is the retired CEO of McDonald's USA, and lives in Sarasota, Florida. These days, he works as a consultant in the fast-food business. He "loves" watching cable news, particularly Fox News, "24/7," he tells me, for the latest reporting on stocks or politics because, let's face it, that is what semiretired executives like him do before a round of golf.

Lately, it's been more of a love-hate relationship with the news, Rensi would admit. First the pandemic, then the civil unrest, and then corporate America's bewildering and idiotic response embracing wokeism as the cure for what ailed a divided nation.

Sometime in March 2022, he saw the news of the day take an even more sinister turn. Yes, he had witnessed years of heightened corporate wokeism, and it bothered him, but not like what he had just heard. The Walt Disney Company, right here in his home state, announced something he believed was 100 percent anathema for any business.

The newish (soon to be ex-) CEO of Disney, Bob Chapek, was diving headfirst into the hyper-partisan world of politics. Chapek announced that Disney would use its corporate resources to overturn the will of the people and do whatever it could to kill legislation in Florida that prevented the teaching of sex ed to children.

"I'm sitting in my office," Rensi recalls. "I see this report about this Disney CEO getting into social engineering and using corporate money to do so. Now this is totally nuts. This guy is literally threatening to use shareholder money for social engineering!"

The "guy" he's talking about, Chapek, had a lot on his plate as a CEO. He had just been selected to replace longtime CEO Bob Iger, and business was off. Disney's woke movies were floundering, and a once great American franchise was being branded as an arm of the progressive left.

Chapek knew Disney needed a lot of fixing. Maybe his most difficult task, unbeknownst to Rensi: Chapek wanted to move Disney to where he saw the customer base as being, somewhere closer to the political center.

Iger, of course, was a Hollywood icon, his tenure at Disney regarded as an amazing success: hit programs, soaring theme park attendance, and a best-in-breed stock price—even if, just before he left, he saddled the company and now Chapek with a mountain of debt buying 21st Century Fox from media mogul Rupert Murdoch.

With a soaring stock price, investors seemed to overlook Iger's other indulgences: He used his corporate platform to tout progressivism throughout the House of Mouse, whether it was in programming or the parks and their endless diversity celebrations. Iger told people once he left Disney, he was thinking about running for office, as a Democrat, of course. Hardly shocking. He could finally put to good use his record as one of the wokest CEOs in America.

Chapek, meanwhile, had no political ambitions. Politically he was a moderate Republican, and he wanted to channel his more culturally conservative Indiana roots in managing a company that appealed to Middle America. Most of all, he wanted to run Disney like a business, not an arm of the DNC, he told his direct reports once he took over as CEO in February 2020.

It was an uncomfortable marriage from the beginning because Chapek was not a Hollywood insider, but an operations guy and not a great manager, as we will discuss later in this book. After he took over for Iger, Disney's finances began to slide; Covid obviously hurt park attendance, but the movie slate remained weak. Chapek was diving into streaming, but that proved costly and initially unprofitable. The cultural differences between Chapek and the company's infrastructure also added to the tension. Disney is a blue company, but it is operating largely in a red state. One reason its workforce leans heavily left is because during his fifteen years as CEO, Iger instilled progressivism in all aspects of Disney—movies constantly featuring gay characters even in children's programming, theme park experiences that celebrated gay pride seemingly almost every other day, and stringent diversity mandates in hiring.

Behind the scenes, Chapek fought this peer pressure the best he could. It was a constant battle, his supporters say. In late February 2022, it reached a crescendo when Florida governor Ron DeSantis did something sure to enrage wokesters across the country and at Disney: A new law that said public schools in the state couldn't teach sex education to children.

Initially, Chapek wanted to lay low. He announced in a firm-wide memo that the law would be for the people of Florida and the politicians to decide. He was too busy running a company and paying down all that debt from the Murdoch deal.

Makes sense, right? Then he heard from his employees. They revolted. Protests, emails, threats, all the stuff that the old mean non-woke Jack Welch would laugh at, but stuff that sends the new breed of CEO like Chapek into woke anaphylaxis fits. No one in Hollywood would want to produce or direct a Disney movie again if he didn't take on DeSantis, Chapek was told.

The media and its bedfellows on the left had successfully panned the Parental Rights in Education Act as the "Don't Say Gay" law. It was a clever but slanderous interpretation since the law never mentioned the word "gay." His board began to feel the heat; Disney chair Susan Arnold urged Chapek to announce his opposition, someone with direct knowledge of their conversations told me. Iger, in retirement and still considered a demigod of the CEO class, chimed in with a tweet attacking the law, adding to the pressure on Chapek.

In a few weeks, the midwestern Republican caved.

"Our employees see the power of this great company as an opportunity to do good. I agree," Chapek stated in a memo announcing his opposition to the legislation. "Yes, we need to use our influence to promote that good by telling inclusive stories, but also by standing up for the rights of all."

Telling inclusive stories sounds so quaint. Mandates to teach gender pronouns while sexualizing children through content in cartoons might be a tougher sell when you consider that most people who watch Disney programs or attend its parks aren't leftists wearing pronouns on their sleeves. No matter. Chapek said he was doing good by defeating something that was the brainchild of the state's popular GOP governor and about to be put into law by the popularly elected state legislature.

"This is insane," Rensi recalls thinking, unaware of the full backstory of Chapek's one-eighty, though it doesn't really matter. Chapek sounded just as woke as Iger, even more so. And "he's using corporate and shareholder money to send a political message. He's not supposed to do that," Rensi said.

During his years in corporate America, Rensi had fought too hard for diversity and equal opportunity to allow his record to be hijacked by CEOs posing as social justice warriors, using the boardroom to support leftist political causes that much of the country opposes.

Someone needed to step in and scream, "Enough!"

Rensi was going to be that someone.

Let me give you a little background on what makes Ed Rensi a real social justice warrior, as opposed to the woke types you see so much on TV. For most of his professional life, he worked at McDonald's, one of the nation's iconic fast-food restaurant chains. Rensi spent forty years there, including seven of which he was the guy in the CEO suite of its US operations, which means he knows a thing or two about which battles CEOs should fight and which they should stay away from.

Woke politics, and politics in general, all his experience told him, should be avoided like the plague, because you want to sell to everyone. Playing politics is a surefire way of appealing to no one, or Larry Fink wouldn't be feeling like such a punching bag these days, as we will explore in the next chapter.

And it's not because Rensi is some heartless capitalist. Far from it. He grew up in a small town in rural Ohio, the son of a cop and a bookkeeper. He worked his way through Ohio State, flipping burgers in a local grill room. He's a second-generation Italian American. His grandparents came here as poor farmers who lived off the land in a house without running water. He proudly recalled to me that their bathroom wasn't in their house. It was the "*bacouz*"—Italian slang for "backhouse."

From those humble beginnings, Rensi went on to do great things in business. And give back. "At McDonald's we believed in charity, I helped start Ronald McDonald House," the company's nonprofit to support children with cancer and their families.

And he wasn't afraid to argue for his version of social justice with just about anyone, including Milton Friedman. Yes, that Milton Friedman.

It was sometime in the early 1980s in San Diego at the Torrey Pines resort overlooking the Pacific Ocean and a five-star gold course. McDonald's teamed up with Coca-Cola for a conference where executives met and discussed big thoughts in between rounds of golf.

Their guest speaker was Uncle Milton, whose economic model was then being embraced by the Reagan administration as it attempted to reverse the malaise of the 1970s. Friedman didn't disappoint the crowd, arguing how they must put aside their private opinions, their noblesse oblige, and focus on enhancing shareholder value.

The crowd ate it up, but not Rensi. At a private lunch, he confronted Friedman, told him how McDonald's was giving back, how it made the strides it made in minority communities, how it created a charity for children with cancer, the Ronald McDonald House.

"Young man," Friedman, then in his sixties, told the forty-something Rensi, "it's not the role of corporations to take shareholder money and spend it on charities."

"Mr. Friedman, it's not called charity; it's called marketing. Being concerned about the community, about our customers, is marketing our brand."

Friedman sat and listened. He was "shocked," Rensi remembers, and so were the other executives at the table; he had just jousted with the Great One by explaining succinctly that there is a capitalist rationale for corporations to help people beyond their shareholders.

There still is, Rensi tells me during our interview, though not the type being preached by Disney, or scores of other US companies these days. McDonald's is a big company, but Rensi says it's the sum of its parts that gives McDonald's its special sauce. It operates as a franchise business; entrepreneurs own their own stores, tens of thousands of them. It is one of America's remarkable success stories, a business that can be found in the suburbs and tough inner-city neighborhoods, owned by a cross section of people from all races.

Ray Kroc, the founder of modern-day McDonald's, is often described as a ruthless capitalist in the business of mass-producing crappy food. Rensi describes him as a man who believed in making money, but also charity and diversity—bringing African Americans into the franchise business was part of Kroc's vision for the modern McDonald's. It's why Rensi says he loved working for him. Like most business types, Rensi is fiscally conservative and socially moderate. Sure, he believes in limited government, but he also takes pride in McDonald's and Kroc's egalitarian bent—the way he describes it, a type of non-woke wokeism, if there can be such a thing.

It's in his DNA. When he was in college, Rensi tells me he grew to hate the Vietnam War that was raging because of the injustices it exposed: "White college kids were getting deferments and Black kids were getting assassinated by the Vietnamese." That experience left its mark on him, and for the better, when he became a manager.

His trek up the McDonald's corporate ladder began after graduation during the turbulent 1960s, when he noticed something about the company. Many of its customers and employees in the inner cities were Black. The stores were mostly white-owned. He and Kroc knew that needed to change if McDonald's was to grow and thrive. Management needed a stake in the communities they serve. He made it a priority to bring on Black-owned McDonald's franchises, particularly in the inner city. Kroc hired a man named Robert Beavers to bring African Americans into the franchise business. Herman Petty became the first Black franchisee in 1968. By 2008, there would be more than three hundred.

"Inclusion is good for society. Inclusion is good for business," Rensi says. "In fact, I worked my ass off bringing Black people into franchisee positions. We wanted to build in the Black community and for it to have a stake in McDonald's because it was common sense, good business, and sociologically, philosophically, and spiritually the right thing to do."

What he was watching unfold on TV was altogether different. It was an absurd spectacle on many levels. Billionaire CEOs had joined the left's warped version of George Floyd's killing. A simple examination of facts about police killings, or corporate hiring polices, or corporate America's strong record on the environment, or Americans' attitudes toward everything from race to broad acceptance of gay marriage would easily debunk the progressive myth making.

But the CEO class gave credence to the lie that America was an evil, xenophobic monarchy of white oppressors. It was such a strange time, because these CEOs were supposed to be good at selling things—iPhones, movies, credit cards, computers, and, in the case of Disney, movies—yet they were indulging in stuff that they had no real expertise in. Even worse, they were pissing off at least half of their customers who were not woke and certainly not racist and evil.

What consumer wants to hear he or she is racist because they support Donald Trump, Rensi began asking friends and business associates. The consensus was uniform: not many, which is why he knew he had to act.

Disney operates six theme parks in Florida. The House of Mouse is among the state's largest employers, and very powerful in state politics. So powerful, in fact, that decades ago the company created its own governing quasi-city, the Reedy Creek Improvement District, a twenty-five-thousand-acre plot of land around several of its Orlando theme parks, including the big one at Disney World.

Reedy Creek dates to the days of old man Walt Disney and his plans to design a futuristic "planned city that would consist of residential and commercial areas as well as attractions," according to a 2023 report commissioned by the state legislature on the district's creation and years of corporate welfare benefits.

As the report pointed out, Disney's "bold concept was given a name: EPCOT," or Experimental Prototype Community of Tomorrow. Reedy Creek was the conduit for Walt's ambitious plans to take Disney to new levels, expand out of its corporate headquarters in Burbank, California, and its first theme park, Disneyland. Florida, with its vast spaces, would become the company's future and effective HQ. He picked the thirty-nine-square-mile plot of land near Orlando in central Florida because the area was a backwater and the state offered tax incentives that could not be seen anywhere else in the country. Plus, it was Florida, a burgeoning tourist destination.

Old Walt died before the state legislature officially established Reedy Creek in 1967, but he set the political wheels in motion for the windfall of benefits the state bestowed upon what would become one of its largest employers. Florida granted Disney what is essentially its own city, with its own taxing authority and government structure.

Walt's plans for a futuristic city never materialized; EPCOT is, for all intents and purposes, a mere theme park. No one really lives within Reedy Creek's boundaries. What did materialize was the Disney empire in central Florida: the expansion of Disney World and other theme parks, much of it on the backs of the state's taxpayers. Reedy Creek maintained its self-governance status and special taxing status that included the issuance of municipal bonds, like the state or any city in the state. The district, if it wanted, could build its own nuclear plant.

For years, governors and state politicians didn't question these perks because it was Disney, and taking on the company's lobbying was political suicide.

Yes, Florida had been very good to Disney; it's a business-friendly place, unless, of course, you bite the hand that feeds you.

Rensi tells me Chapek did just that when he announced he would take on DeSantis and a law curtailing teaching sex to minors that most Floridians supported. A public company, he says, was essentially endorsing a political movement that said refraining from instructing preteens in the proper way to perform fellatio would lead to LGBTQ+ discrimination. Chapek said Disney was planning to use its lobby power and shareholder money to finance the progressive culture-war machine.

It all made Rensi's blood boil. "CEOs and companies have no business getting involved in social engineering, and that's what the guy was doing."

Bernie Marcus thought so as well.

Marcus is a great American executive, one of the founders of the Home Depot franchise, a man who worked his way out of poverty, growing up in a fourth-floor tenement in Newark, New Jersey, to become a billionaire several times over. Marcus's story is an amazing one: After graduating from college, he worked in sales and soon was named CEO of a company called Handy Dan, a midsized chain of hardware stores, only to be fired in the mid-1970s with no place to turn.

Sheepishly, he asked his friend, the financier Ken Langone, for career advice. Langone, a Wall Street legend, had brought Ross Perot's Electronic Data Systems public a few years earlier, then one of the most sought-after deals. He helped create one of the nation's largest computer companies and made Perot a billionaire.

Langone was ready to do it all again.

Like Marcus, Langone came from humble roots. He's the son of a Long Island plumber, and isn't afraid to explain himself in a typical New York way. "You just got hit in the ass with a golden horseshoe," he told Marcus, imploring him to start that idea for a massive, nationwide store not just for hardware, but all home furnishings.

Langone offered to raise money, essentially putting Marcus in business. Home Depot was born and has grown into a $300 billion market value company.

Handy Dan closed its doors more than thirty years ago.

Now both in their nineties, Langone and Marcus remain close friends. Both dedicate themselves to philanthropy; Langone built one of the nation's great medical centers in New York, NYU Langone. He financed the reconstruction of St. Patrick's Cathedral after it fell into disrepair.

Marcus's charitable giving is equally formidable. In recent years, he has become more active in politics, starting something called the Job Creators Network, an advocacy group to promote free-market solutions to economic problems.

Free-market types like Marcus or Rensi traditionally believed the government shouldn't be meddling with corporate affairs. Let the markets work their magic even at the Magic Kingdom. But this wasn't pure government meddling. There was little free-market about what Disney was doing. It was using its own legislative might, shareholder money no less, to thwart the will of the people of Florida on an issue that doesn't impact Disney's bottom line. It was looking to fuck with the state's governor duly elected by voters who support his political vision.

And where was the shareholder proxy vote for all of this?

Rensi had been involved with Marcus's Job Creators project for the past few years, and one afternoon in the middle of the Disney-DeSantis throwdown, Marcus had one of his people call Rensi with a proposal: Let's start something new to fight Disney and the entire corporate wokeness machine. A new "Boardroom Initiative" to convince the CEO class of the pitfalls of mixing leftist politics with their businesses, the destruction it will cause corporate America and American society.

"They said to me, 'Hey, we're really upset about all of this stuff. What do you think?'"

Rensi said he was too and couldn't wait to get started.

CHAPTER SEVEN

"Who the Fuck Are These People?!?!"

A reckoning for one of the nation's top executives begins with a strange vehicle parked outside the opulent midtown Manhattan home of BlackRock, the world's largest money manager. Larry Fink, the company's founder and CEO, and long considered the world's most powerful investor, was peering out the window of his office when he noticed something a bit odd: a truck containing a billboard featuring the image of an ominous-looking executive in a dark suit.

Scary-looking shit, so Fink looked closer. What he saw shocked him. *He* was the ominous-looking executive, situated next to the caption "Who Is Larry Fink?" and a website address of some organization he had never heard of.

The signage was dramatic in a creepy way. Fink, dressed in a dark suit, looked like he had just ordered a hit on someone. His silhouette was placed in a darkened background, which heightened his faux sinister features. The words "Paid for By Consumers' Research" appeared at the bottom of the billboard, with a website address, WhoIsLarryFink.com, that led you to a page that cited some of Fink's greatest woke hits.

Go to the website and you can find interviews quoting Fink stating unequivocally that he said he is "a globalist and proud of it," links to his comments about how CEOs need to save the environment through ESG investing, and how it was their duty to bring about "racial equity." There were his boasts about expanding BlackRock in Communist China, stuff about Fink's early career as a bond trader when he lost a ton of money speculating in esoteric markets. For extra measure, it threw in some #MeToo incidents involving top BlackRock executives.

"Who the fuck are these people?!?!" Fink shrieked, ordering his staff to do a deep dive into whatever the hell is this Consumers' Research thing. In short order, Fink's minions reported back the following: The group, for lack of a better set of words, is a right-wing trolling organization, albeit an effective one in recent years. Its stated purpose as "an independent 501(c)(3) nonprofit…is to increase the knowledge and understanding of issues, policies, products, and services of concerns to promote the freedom to act on that knowledge and understanding."

Its unstated goal is to fuck with people like Larry Fink. For the past three years or so, Consumers' Research has been attacking various targets in government and the private sector it considers responsible for the ongoing woke destruction of the US economy and our common culture.

Fink was now high on its target list, which, if you know anything about these people, ain't no fun.

Starting in late 2021, signage, lots of it on trucks, was starting to appear all over midtown Manhattan displaying the group's handiwork. For a time, Larry Fink's face was nearly as ubiquitous as ads for Broadway shows. Fink might be rich and powerful, and famous on Wall Street, but he wasn't anything close to a household name. Now plenty of households, at least those in Manhattan and a lot more given the media coverage that came next, were getting to know Larry Fink.

Ed Rensi, the former McDonald's CEO, hated corporate wokeness. His approach to combating it involved private meetings with CEOs explaining the dangers of alienating large swaths of customers with excessively left-wing politics. Consumers' Research got down and dirty. Its modus operandi was to engage in a nasty Wall Street "street fight" with BlackRock, and Fink, the prominent forces in corporate wokeism.

Like Fink, I had never heard of Consumers' Research until I witnessed its handiwork firsthand. I asked Fink who was behind plastering his face literally all over midtown Manhattan. "Fucking Leonard Leo," he tells me. Fink believes Leo, a prominent conservative activist, is playing a key role in making him the Dr. Evil of corporate wokeness.

I also didn't know much about Leonard Leo either, other than that he is a right-winger with a substantial bank account. With a little digging, I found out that his conservative street cred is substantial: He is a key member of the Federalist Society, the influential organization of lawyers, which helps steer GOP presidents on appointments to the federal judiciary and the Supreme Court. More recently, he has funded the sharp-elbowed conservative assault against stuff like ESG investing. He's considered reclusive but has enough dough to fund various groups, like Consumers' Research, in the anti-woke counterattack that we've seen increasingly in recent years.

Enter a dude named Will Hild. Leo may be lurking in the background of Consumers' Research, but Hild does the day-to-day grunt work. He's a thirty-something conservative political activist, a graduate of Georgetown Law School. He works mostly from his home in Bethesda, Maryland, but that hasn't stopped him from making Fink's life a living hell in New York City.

Hild tells me Consumers' Research is the oldest consumer advocacy organization in the country. In the 1930s, the organization exposed defective and unsafe appliances and products, stuff like electric blankets that burned people to death. It went dormant for decades, and somehow found another life in the 2000s when right-wingers snatched up the trademark and began using it to attack what they argued were business-killing environmental laws.

Its attacks against Fink, he says, is keeping in that tradition. Hild has added a decidedly Millennial twist to the group's activism: social media attacks, blast emails, and the type of trolling that Fink is the target of.

None of which is cheap, and that's where it appears Leo comes in. An October 2022 *New York Times* piece on Consumers' Research showed that some of the group's donors have ties to Leo. So does Hild, who says he met Leo more than a decade ago in the conservative-activist biosphere and later at the Federalist Society. They're so close, Hild tells me, that he considers Leo a "mentor." Asked if Leo is a major donor to Consumers' Research, Hild says he "never discusses where we get our money from. It opens up the people to too much abuse from the very same woke activists we are fighting." Leo declined repeated requests for comment.

The Consumers' Research money trail has certainly raised more than a few eyebrows in the mainstream media. It is often referred to as a "dark money" organization; because of its structure, it doesn't have to disclose a donor list. News reports state that the group has attracted millions of dollars from various sources, a testament to the appetite on the right to fight back against corporate progressive policies. Most of it obviously goes into the product: ads, billboards, and marketing. Hild has a small staff, and, as I stated earlier, his office is his house.

Hild tells me he joined Consumers' Research at Leo's behest during the dark days of Covid. It was immediately following George Floyd when he, like most of the country, witnessed the gross spectacle of corporate virtue signaling. Angered by big companies funneling shareholder money to left-wing organizations like BLM and other forms of CEO virtue signaling, Hild decided to fight back.

Consumers' Research certainly has other targets. It took out national ads lampooning the wokeness of Bank of America chief Brian Moynihan, and its "ideologically driven agenda on the American people," some of which this book covered in previous chapters. Yet Hild and the organization hold a special contempt for Fink and BlackRock, because of their financial power and desire, Hild says, to launch a left-wing "cultural revolution."

Either way, Hild says it is his job, not Leo's, to provide the counternarrative to Fink's devotion to ESG since BlackRock is the investing movement's standard-bearer. Oil companies aren't drilling because of ESG and Fink's push to spread it throughout corporate America; globalists like Fink spread progressivism but invest in one of the least progressive places in the world, Communist China. DEI enforced through ESG metrics is depriving white men of work.

Hild likened Fink to a five-star general, directing the forces of corporate wokeness against a besieged American public.

Hild wouldn't provide me with exact numbers, but he confirmed he spent more on his BlackRock campaign than any other target, "a bit over $4.5 million." And, he says, it's money well spent. Fink and BlackRock's prominence in the progressive-corporate infrastructure demands such attention.

Hang a bit with Hild, as I did, and you come away with two impressions. First, he's a true believer in the cause of anti-wokeness, but he's also having a lot of fun. He brags about all the different ways he trolls Fink. In addition to the mobile signage in Manhattan, he created a special ad, a "Wanted" sign, a goofy meme of Fink in a black cowboy hat. Fink was wanted, it read, for "Attacking American Energy Production."

Cute. Even cuter: It was his idea to have the truck parked across the street from BlackRock's midtown offices so Fink could see it every day he came and left the office, he said.

"After he saw the truck, I heard Larry 'Keith-Mooned' his office," Hild tells me with a laugh. Keith Moon was the famous drummer for the Who, the rock band known for trashing its hotel rooms after every performance. Hild says his sources inside BlackRock said Fink was so angry "they heard stuff breaking" from the executive floor.

Fink adamantly denies the office incident as another example of Hild's smear campaign. Hild, of course, would describe what he's doing as something closer to God's work. In his telling, ESG puts money in Fink's pocket—he earned $25 million in 2022—but average Americans are paying the price. He's exposing the very scary truth about the how one very powerful firm and man is responsible for taking the country down the road to progressive serfdom.

Yes, serious stuff, though I also can't help but chuckle imagining an unshaven Hild in his shorts and sneakers nipple-twisting one of the most powerful financiers in the world. It is no fun if you are Fink. The Consumers' Research anti-Fink jihad has received significant business media coverage, in places that BlackRock clients pay attention to, like Bloomberg, the *Wall Street Journal*, the *New York Times*, and the *New York Post*. As Hild has made Fink the poster child for ESG excess throughout red-state America, BlackRock's has lost public pension-fund business in Red States. The attacks also took a personal toll on Fink. One afternoon some rando accosted him on the street, I am told. "Those crazy right-wingers made this happen," Fink told an associate, who told me. The incident forced Fink to hire 24/7 security.

Is Hild making his crusade against Fink too personal? Absolutely. Does Fink really need to be trolled outside his office, 24/7? Of course not.

That said, you could see how Fink was ripe for the group's anti-woke ESG trolling. By controlling so much money, BlackRock will always get a lot of attention. Its size allows it to control global markets, set interest rates, bail out countries if need be. Then there's Fink—maybe the most voluble executive in the financial business—particularly on the issue of ESG.

Fink's yearly annual report missives—his so-called CEO letters fashioned as think pieces on everything from investing to public policy—have in recent years taken a more progressive tone, dedicated to the benefits of woke matters including ESG and corporate diversity. They're also impactful. CEOs follow his every move because they need to know what the guy holding their stock thinks. Fink has so much market power that he regularly consults with top economic officials in the Biden administration, members of the European Union, the Saudi royal family, and with top Chinese financial officials. You can make the case that Larry Fink, from his office in Manhattan, very much controls the US economy at least as much as the Fed does with interest rates, or the Treasury secretary does when he or she implements fiscal policy.

Fink built his career on hard work and incredible thirst for success, all of it well earned. He was the King of Wall Street for decades before he became the face of progressive investing that Hild and the American right say they fear and loathe.

The loathing part has shaken Fink and BlackRock's business model, as you will soon discover. Wall Street types who dive headfirst into the country's toxic political climate are taking on much more than market risk, which they understand. Political risk is a danger on another level. The markets, even when they crater, often do so at least semi-predictably. Politics, particularly today's brand, are Hobbesian—nasty and brutal. The political process turns men and women into primates throwing shit at each other to get ahead.

That's if you go there, which Fink did. Attacking Larry Fink as Mr. ESG has become a rallying cry on the populist right, up there with migrant bashing and same-sex bathrooms. Fink often gets angry letters from Congress demanding to know why BlackRock is aiding and abetting the left. Popular governors like Florida's Ron DeSantis have held Fink as the embodiment of corporate wokeness run amok. In the December 2023 GOP presidential debate, BlackRock and Fink were attacked by the candidates for using this economic "power" to enforce various forms of leftism.

As I write this, the bad publicity is showing some signs of letting up, but only as BlackRock and its CEO have moved away from woke capitalism as fast as they once embraced it. Still, it's impossible for BlackRock's PR spin machine to undo Fink's status as a woke political symbol, a crude one at that and often devoid of reality, as most political symbols are. Based on my reporting, Hild has played a key role in this demonization, something that the people at BlackRock would concede as well since they've spent the past two years looking to control the damage of Hild's character assault.

In our conversations, I remind Hild it is dangerous to look at Fink through rigid ideological lenses. People are complicated, including Wall Street fat cats. One reason, probably the primary reason, Fink has gone all in on ESG is not politics but because it's a huge moneymaker. Fink also sees what's going on today in the renewable energy business as the early stages of a transformational business, a lot like tech was after the initial dotcom bubble burst, with tremendous societal benefits because cleaning the environment isn't all bad. Hiring a diverse workforce sounds like the right thing to do. And there is demand for sustainable investing. BlackRock at its height amassed around $1 trillion in assets tied directly to ESG, producing countless billions in profits because of the high fees charged for these specialized investments. BlackRock shareholders have done well.

Plus, Fink has been a moderating force on policy issues pushed by all those leftists who run key regulatory agencies in the Biden administration. Just one example: In 2023, he played a role in convincing SEC chair Gary Gensler to pull back on some of the most onerous aspects of his new rules that would force companies to make costly, and dubiously legal, climate disclosures to investors. Yes, the man reviled on the right as the king of ESG-led corporate leftism told Gensler some of the stuff he was proposing was bonkers, too costly for smaller companies and a waste of time.

Hild isn't buying it. ESG at BlackRock, he reminds me, goes far beyond a few specialized funds that Fink is offering to a few woke clients. The methodology until very recently had encompassed all its investing decisions, as you will see. Hild points out that I may not fully appreciate BlackRock's enormous power—that is, Fink's enormous power—to influence corporate behavior. Because of BlackRock's size and scale, and Fink's constant messaging of its benefits, ESG has been institutionalized throughout the money management business, Wall Street, and by extension corporate America. Companies adopt plans for so-called zero-emissions standards or quotas to meet ESG diversity metrics in anticipation that BlackRock might start a proxy campaign or force a shareholder vote on these issues. That's what happens when you own so many stocks of the world's biggest companies; you get to tell the CEOs of those companies what to do.

"Larry literally said that at BlackRock, they believe behaviors must change, and they're going to force them to change," Hild reminds me, citing something Fink said in 2017 at a *New York Times* "DealBook" conference. Fink's exact words: "Behaviors are going to have to change. This is one thing we're asking companies. You have to force behaviors. At BlackRock we are forcing behaviors."

Even with all of that, I find it sad that Fink is at the center of this shit storm, because I know him better than Hild's manufactured parody. ESG should be an asterisk on Larry Fink's amazing career as an entrepreneur, investor, and government adviser, not its defining moment. His embrace of progressive capitalism is a more complicated story than you see on those billboards, motivated in part by a noblesse oblige, the accompanying desire to make enormous money, plus the human flaw of seeking the accolades that often comes from corporate virtue signaling.

I see Fink's role in corporate wokeness as something close to Icarus—flying too close to the proverbial woke sun for your own good.

Corporate wokesters take note.

So, who really is Larry Fink?

Fink is well past retirement age, in his seventies, and showed no signs of stepping down until recently when he became Public Enemy No. 1 for the right. His No. 2, and possible successor, Rob Kapito, is in his mid-sixties and expected to be around for a while as well. They're both BlackRock lifers—founders, in fact. And despite its image as the Death Star in the woke universe, BlackRock is run "like a family business, kind of like a bagel shop," one former executive tells me.

I'm fully aware of the antisemitic overtones of the statement, but it wasn't meant as such. It also wasn't meant as a criticism. Fink started the firm with a handful of people who left First Boston with him back in 1980s, and many remain. Many of them chose to stay because it's more appealing than the stifling bureaucracy at most Wall Street firms.

Fink is a tall man, about six foot two, and fit for a person who makes a living sitting behind computer screens all day. Far from the Dr. Evil type portrayed on those Will Hild billboards, he looks more like a college professor. He's bald and wears wire-rimmed glasses, and occasionally can be seen around the office donning a cardigan. He's rich, of course, worth well north of $1 billion, but is also funny and self-deprecating and refreshingly candid. He refers to himself as "the Jew from Los Angeles," the proud middle-class son of a college professor mother and shoe store owner dad. His sentences are strewn with the word "fuck," or when something goes bad, the term "shit show." It's almost endearing unless you're on the other end of one of his infamous tirades.

True, Fink never gave up the rough edges he developed while he was on the trading desk for the first part of his career. He also never gave up another traders' habit: the love of gossip. Wall Street trading desks, where Fink cut his teeth before starting BlackRock, run on information and gossip on where the markets are going, what companies are merging, which CEO is getting the boot. Traders feast on "intel," using so-called actionable information to gain an edge on the other side of the buy or sell order.

Fink runs BlackRock in the same way, always looking for some edge, but also, I think, because he just loves to show he's in the know. He holds court in places like San Pietro, Wall Street's very expensive cafeteria in midtown Manhattan, seated along "chairman's row," the restaurant's most exclusive tables, talking, laughing about competitors, sharing stories about top politicians and how they're running and ruining the world.

There is a downside to being so verbose. A bank CEO told me Fink's relentless gift for gab is what kept him from achieving one of his dreams: being nominated as Treasury secretary. Fink thought he had a real chance during the Obama years, but ultimately he didn't get it because "Larry can't keep his fucking mouth shut," the CEO said.

Okay, you don't want the Treasury secretary leaking the nuclear codes, but Fink's network of contacts in global finance isn't a bad thing—and it's served both Wall Street and Washington well. He knows where markets are heading, the inner workings of corporate America. He isn't afraid to chat up CEOs on various issues, or to lend a hand in a time of crisis. When in 2023, David Solomon, the embattled Goldman CEO, appeared almost daily in the pages of the *New York Post* for his missteps, competitors at JP Morgan danced in the hallways. Fink called him and offered both condolences and advice on how to ride out the storm.

"David, I know how it feels, just hang in there," Fink said. Solomon thanked him.

Another of his underappreciated qualities: Fink is among the best risk managers on Wall Street. When he started BlackRock more than thirty years ago, he created an entire subsidiary for investors who want to manage risk. Those investors include the US government, which after the 2008 financial crisis turned to Fink to manage the risk assets it acquired during the bank bailouts. He was the go-to guy for Hank Paulson, the Bush Treasury secretary, and Tim Geithner, the New York Fed chief and later Obama Treasury secretary, as they worked to save the big banks in the aftermath of the 2008 financial crash. It didn't hurt that BlackRock was subsequently awarded a huge government contract to manage the government's bailout-related portfolio.

As Fink would concede, being a risk manager didn't come easy or cheap. He is also considered one of the founding fathers of something known as securitization—the packaging of various forms of debt into a bond that became one of Wall Street's most profitable businesses beginning in the mid-1980s. There's a do-gooder side to the business that Fink takes pride in, not much different than his rationalization of ESG. Securitization is why banks still make thirty-year mortgages to average Americans and people with modest incomes can buy a home. Wall Street offloads the interest rate and default risk of a mortgage in the form of a bond sold to a third party. A pension fund or asset manager purchases the packaged or "securitized" mortgages because, the theory of securitization posits, not all of them could default at once. Plus, the return on the bond compensates for the risk. It's a win-win for everyone involved: If banks can keep the loans off their books, they can keep lending money, and interest rates will fall. Middle America has access to affordable housing. Wall Street firms like First Boston earn a profit by doing good.

Fink's first brush with media attention came during these years. His team was making such huge profits at First Boston underwriting and trading this stuff, that Fink was on the short list to be CEO. Those profits translated into something that is good for society, Fink liked to think. "Market supporters, such as Laurence D. Fink, a managing director of the First Boston Corporation, argue that mortgage rates have been lowered by as much as one and a half percentage points because of the secondary market," the *New York Times* reported in 1984.

Like ESG, securitization has a downside that its math often fails to appreciate. Allowing everyone to own a home by diversifying risk never really works out as planned because banks will inevitably lend to riskier and riskier borrowers to turn a profit. See the 2008 financial crisis when banks held securitized bonds based on flimsy lending standards of the underlying mortgages, which defaulted in droves. The banking system crashed, as did the US economy.

You could say a dry run of the 2008 collapse occurred just after Fink extolled the market's virtues in that *New York Times* piece. In 1986, just before the infamous stock market crash, interest rates unexpectedly fell, and the mortgage bond market suffered a similar upheaval because many traders were betting on just the opposite scenario. Their "hedges," or trading positions to mitigate risk, turned into massive losses. Fink's losses totaled $100 million in just one quarter. Even now, that would be a staggering amount of money. First Boston was heading for insolvency; it was later renamed Credit Suisse First Boston because the big Swiss bank took a majority stake to save what was left.

All that led to an ignominious exit from the firm and forced Fink to do a little soul-searching. He decided a career change was in order. No longer would he be a Wall Street gunslinger; he would be an investor.

And it paid off even more than Fink could imagine. He didn't just save his career; within a few short years Larry Fink would emerge as the most powerful force in the investing world.

"The biggest mistake I've made was letting Larry go," Stephen Schwarzman once said when looking back at his own long career on Wall Street. That's saying something, because Schwarzman has certainly seen a thing or two during his forty years in banking. Schwarzman is the cofounder of the Blackstone Group, which dominates a $4.4 trillion business known as private equity. If Blackstone sounds a little like BlackRock, it isn't a coincidence. BlackRock got its start as a subsidiary of Blackstone, and the fact that they're no longer under the same corporate umbrella haunts Schwarzman to this day.

Schwarzman began his career at Lehman Brothers a few years before Fink started on Wall Street. He was a key player in the firm's famous civil war of the 1980s, chronicled by Ken Auletta in his book *Greed and Glory on Wall Street*. Schwarzman was an ally of Peter Peterson, a former Nixon commerce secretary who as CEO ran investment banking at the firm.

Peterson found himself on the losing end of the struggle between bankers and traders. In the crass language of 1980s finance, he was "blown out" of the company. A year and change later, in 1985, Schwarzman joined him and they decided to start something still pretty novel at the time—a private equity firm.

PE, as it is known, is now a huge business; back then, it was a backwater. Schwarzman and Peterson saw growth in buying decent companies in need of fixing and taking them private, while often dumping management so they could fix things without shareholders demanding results each quarter. Profits come later when the company is sold to the public. There is even a nifty tax break to the whole scheme, known as "carried interest," which means money made from the sale is taxed at a lower rate.

The companies in Schwarzman's portfolio became some of the most profitable in the world. Blackstone was the first PE firm to surpass $1 trillion in assets. It did so in 2023 and now has a capitalization surpassing even Goldman Sachs in stock market value.

Peterson has long retired from the business (he died in 2018), but Schwarzman, at seventy-six years of age, is still going strong despite persistent rumors of retirement. First, he likes to work, and the money is good. He is worth $41 billion and one of the richest men in the world. He is a Republican, though he hires people who give tons of money to Democrats, which helps Blackstone keep in the good graces of the White House no matter who is in power. His longtime top lieutenant, Tony James, has been frequently mentioned as a possible Treasury secretary whenever the Dems take the White House. (James left the firm in 2021; Jon Gray, also a Democrat, is now Schwarzman's heir apparent.)

Wall Street CEOs thrive on power. They seek it and luxuriate in the reality of being able to sway markets and opinion and shower themselves in all the power that money affords. It is why they work so hard, all the long hours, the days and weeks away from family. They envy those with more of it. It's the reason "letting Larry go" still haunts Schwarzman. From its humble beginnings as Blackstone Financial, the modern BlackRock has become a behemoth in size and profitability.

And Schwarzman may have sold out cheap. His $5 million investment in Fink's new firm (a line of credit as it turns out) seemed like a lot back then. By 1994, Blackstone Financial was renamed BlackRock and its business was gaining significant critical mass selling mutual funds, the go-to investment of small investors who flocked to Wall Street to save for retirement. Fink decided he wanted to break free from Schwarzman. Their relationship had grown fraught (it still is today) over strategic direction and their rapidly growing egos. Fink found an outside investor, PNC bank, to buy Schwarzman's stake, and offered Schwarzman $250 million to go away. That type of return on his investment was a deal Schwarzman couldn't refuse.

Oh, how he wished he had. At the time of the divorce, the renamed BlackRock had a market value of $240 million. Over time, success and size allowed Fink to buy his independence. PNC is no longer involved. BlackRock's market value stands at above $100 billion and it holds $10 trillion in investable assets, everything from stocks to bonds to currencies, real estate, and crypto. While Blackstone is the largest owner of commercial real estate in the world and has branched out to other businesses (attaining a market value of $150 billion), Fink has his hand in every major public company in the world.

Yes, two different firms, but some things never change. The Fink-Schwarzman rivalry lives on as they gauge each other's stock price, which firm is bigger on a market basis on any given day, and who makes it into the gossip pages for ostentatious displays of wealth and power. "Steve's ego is too big," is how Fink once described his old boss after seeing press on one of Schwarzman's swanky birthday parties, a who's who gathering of the Wall Street and Washington power elite with a few celebs thrown in for good measure. Schwarzman, unsurprisingly, thinks Fink spends too much time blabbing, particularly on the woke ESG stuff.

They also share plenty of the same traits. Schwarzman knows how to sniff out a great deal, as he did taking Hilton Hotels private in 2007 and then spinning it out to investors in 2013, making $14 billion in the process, considered the most successful PE turnaround of all time. Fink's dealmaking has been equally astute. He sold a chunk of BlackRock to the brokerage firm Merrill Lynch in 2007 to take advantage of its vast army of salesmen or financial advisers. Merrill Lynch brokers sold BlackRock funds to small investors, and Fink's assets under management, or AUM, soared.

Fink bought back that stake after Merrill nearly succumbed during the 2008 financial crisis, and for the first time in decades, he achieved full independence. And he was now free to do some deals. In 2009, he purchased Barclays Global Investors, which catapulted BlackRock into the stratosphere of money management.

It also underscored Fink's ability to snoop out trends. So-called passive investing—or investing that involves buying indices and baskets of stocks as opposed to stock picking—had grown in leaps and bounds with stocks on a secular bull run and investors tired of paying management fees for active management. In one swoop, BlackRock became among the biggest sellers of a passive investment vehicle that would exploit this trend, the so-called exchange-traded fund, or ETF. These are mutual fund-like products that "passively" follow indices, the S&P, Nasdaq, or a market sector. They revolutionized investing because they also allowed small investors to trade popular indices and other baskets of stocks on major exchanges.

As passive investing began to explode—$11 trillion flowed into such funds by 2023—Fink wanted every dollar going to BlackRock. He came pretty close. Just before BlackRock purchased Barclays, its AUM was just $1.3 trillion. In about ten years, its AUM would grow nearly 700 percent.

The passive investing revolution also gave BlackRock its boardroom clout, even if it wasn't really designed to do so. You see, most people buy index funds and ETFs simply to invest, not to vote on shareholder measures during the proxy process. That's why the funds themselves merely mirror a basket of stocks. Passive management is the task of a functionary that takes money in, buys a group of stocks, and pays out money when people withdraw their investments. Active funds and activist investors, meanwhile, do the stock picking and the shareholder politicking.

BlackRock took passive investing a step further. By owning so many different stocks, and in such quantities, it could and did use passive investing to shape boardroom behavior.

Enter ESG.

ESG was a mere pimple on the ass of the emerging BlackRock empire when the firm offered its first sustainable fund in 2005. The pimple would grow to a tumor in the coming years, thanks to a woke perfect storm. It began with BlackRock's growth, coinciding with the rise in the so-called green economy pushed by big government.

A demand from tree-hugging rich investors and lefty politicians who run blue-state pension funds gave it another push. Climate obsession in Europe represented another untapped market for BlackRock's ESG fund business. Stakeholder capitalism also mainstreamed ESG in corporate America. Soon, Fink's marketing team figured you could create ESG portfolios, convert them into ETFs, and sell them to the small investor clients of Merrill's brokerage department. Because these portfolios were so specialized, you could also charge more for them. It is no accident that BlackRock's stock price appreciated more than 500 percent since it offered its first ESG fund, compared to a 272 percent rise in the S&P.

The forces pushing corporate wokeness and ESG would continue for the next fifteen years, and you can't separate the political climate from ESG's growth. One reason CEOs caved to BlackRock's ESG edicts was because they weren't in a very good place. The Great Recession had set in after the 2008 financial collapse. There was serious talk from both parties about nationalizing the banking system. Bipartisan populism was rampant. Excessive CEO pay while people were losing their homes during the mortgage crisis struck a nerve on both the right and left.

Fink was said to be shaken, particularly by the Occupy Wall Street movement—the left-wing populist protests that began to swell in cities, including in BlackRock's home, New York. These protests took a decidedly anti–Wall Street tone, as the name suggests. Fink witnessed politicians tapping into this angry populism and attacking his friends. Congressional committees hauled in bankers like Goldman Sachs CEO Lloyd Blankfein, demanding to know details about their compensation, well into the millions of dollars, even after the financial crisis bank bailouts. A former academic turned Democratic senator from Massachusetts named Elizabeth Warren made a name for herself by attacking the leaders of the financial system. It was only a matter of time before Fink would be next, unless, of course, he changed the narrative. ESG wasn't just a moneymaker but a necessity, a survival mechanism, as the angry populist hordes began to form.

If you ask Fink about his politics, he will describe himself as a liberal in the old-school sense. He believes in big government to address social ills, and he believes that free markets create societal wealth. He's pretty Clintonian in that regard. He also bet big beginning in 2007 on a first-term woke US senator from Illinois named Barack Obama to beat Hillary Clinton, the heavy favorite for the Democratic nomination for the 2008 presidential race. Fink had traders' intuition that Obama could win, and Clinton, with the baggage of her husband still fresh, and a lot more, couldn't. He was right, of course. When I asked Fink if he was concerned about Obama's lack of experience and dalliances with left-wingers in the Chicago political machine (the radical Reverend Jeremiah Wright and former Weather Underground radical and political activist Bill Ayers), he assured me Obama "is going to win and he's a moderate."

Obama did win the nomination and the presidency that year. Fink's support may have saved him the ignominy of a congressional inquisition, but it certainly helped BlackRock secure government business and make a lot of money managing the Treasury's and the Fed's large portfolio of assets it bought from banks during the 2008 bailouts.

Whether Obama governed like a moderate isn't a matter of debate. But give Fink credit for seeing the future clearly—a new progressive industrial policy forged and forced on the business community by the White House and the political left. One difference between him and, say, Jeff Immelt at GE, is that Fink figured out how to make money from going woke; he could charge top dollar to offer ESG investments as the White House was incentivizing through tax credits and other measures a new green economy.

That's why ESG was becoming not just a backwater business at BlackRock, but a way of life.

"The environment is a huge risk factor that needs to be considered in *all our investment decisions*," Fink announced one afternoon sometime in 2016, the last year of the Obama presidency, as the country prepared for a showdown between Hillary Clinton and Donald Trump.

Fink convened a "global conference call" with all of BlackRock's nineteen thousand employees to announce the big news. He said he had spoken with the BlackRock board, and they had agreed that the firm would use ESG as part of its entire investment process along with traditional metrics. ESG would go beyond sustainable investing funds; it would be woven into the DNA of BlackRock's investing models.

What this meant in practice is a matter of debate. Portfolio managers, or BlackRock's PMs, had some latitude to ignore ESG when necessary, a BlackRock spokesman tells me. Yet Fink's messaging during those early years was adamant. Ignore ESG at your own risk, which is why his PMs didn't, as other people at the firm say.

Fink believed that a new ESG economy was about to emerge, the second coming of tech, and BlackRock needed to get in front of it. Pension funds loomed large in Fink's thinking since so many were run by progressive pols who embraced all things green. The company already had a burgeoning business investing money for government retirement funds both here and abroad; by mainstreaming ESG into BlackRock's investment formulas, the company would earn points with so-called blue-state fund managers (run by Dems), who control nearly $3 trillion in investable assets. That's nearly twice as much as those funds run by Republicans, who hate ESG. On top of that, there's more than $10 trillion in foreign state-owned, so-called sovereign wealth funds, particularly in Europe, where progressive finance bureaucrats also love woke investing.

By going all in on ESG, BlackRock's assets under management (and profits) would soar.

To bolster his push in ESG, BlackRock soon provided all employees with an ESG cheat sheet—a memo that explained the finer points of their new investing regime, which they should even memorize. Titled "ESG Pillars," it contained a graph explaining the factors that go into the clunky acronym. Another internal memo described "ESG Integration" as a "priority for our clients."

Fink loves to use the word "alpha," an investment term that describes returns that exceed expectations, or real money. In one meeting, Fink said that because of ESG, BlackRock's alpha was about to grow on trees. The beauty of it, he postulated, was that while eliminating climate risks from corporate balance sheets, BlackRock would also lead the effort to de-risk American business and investing. Alpha was created even for its portfolio companies, because these businesses would grow and expand while eliminating all the costs associated with global warming, flooding, weird weather patterns, pollution, sickness, and disease. All that takes money to address—and getting rid of them through sustainable investing created a huge business opportunity. There were other alleged benefits: ESG edicts on diversity and stakeholder capitalism would settle a divisive and restless nation, which is always good for profits.

The real ESG scorecard is far less sanguine. Years of ESG haven't stopped climate change. China and India don't buy the ESG mantra, and the asset managers in this space have stopped trying to get their buy-in; those two enormous nations are exempt from ESG mandates.

ESG-specific funds are expensive; they rarely beat market averages. In fact, they're some of the worst investments in an era where you can make real money—Fink's alpha—by purchasing a mutual fund that simply follows the S&P.

Fink's support for ESG may have been motivated by presidential politics, as well. Fink's long-held dream was for his name to be on the US currency as Treasury secretary. People at BlackRock tell me it's no coincidence that BlackRock's ESG obsession grew when it looked like Fink once again had a real shot at Treasury secretary if Hillary Clinton could beat Donald Trump in 2016, as most Washington and Wall Street insiders (wrongly) predicted. Lesser financial figures had done so (Jack Lew, a midlevel Citigroup executive, was Obama's Treasury chief), so why shouldn't he have his turn? With the Democratic Party turning left, particularly on the environment, making BlackRock the epicenter of ESG revolution could mollify power lefties like Elizabeth Warren who hate bankers in such jobs.

And if the Treasury thing didn't work out, so what? Fink and BlackRock were too busy ringing the ESG cash register to really care.

BlackRock's success in ESG can be found in its stock price, which nearly doubled over the next two years—and how its success led to imitation. Copycat ESG investments cropped up seemingly by the day. Other big asset managers began using ESG, like BlackRock, as a universal investment technique to "force behaviors" and make money.

"We're big and loud and that's why people listen," is how one BlackRock portfolio manager put it to me as the firm made ESG its central mission. Seeing BlackRock's ESG-powered profitability and size soar, State Street and Fidelity were jumping on the ESG gravy train, as well.

As did Vanguard, the second-largest money manager after BlackRock. It is the company of the legendary Jack Bogle, who before his retirement evangelized and popularized apolitical, plain vanilla index investing for decades. He had long relinquished his management role (Bogle retired in 1999 and died in 2019), and good thing, because ESG was about as far from Bogle's passive-investing mission as you could get.

New management at Vanguard couldn't just let BlackRock have all the fun—and make all the ESG profits—though playing catch-up wasn't easy. By now, Fink had become the Chuck Schumer of ESG investing; like the chatterbox senator from New York, he never met a camera he didn't love when it came to singing the praises of sustainable investing, and the money particularly from government pension funds obsessed with sustainable investing began to flood into BlackRock.

Clinton, of course, didn't make it in 2016, and Fink never made it to Treasury. The fact decidedly non-woke dude, Donald Trump, was in the White House, appointing non-woke regulators to key positions, did nothing to deter BlackRock's ESG push, or Fink's desire to talk it up as the money kept coming. He ramped up his ESG roadshow at conferences, on financial TV, and elsewhere, probably because he could without regulatory reprisal from the alleged right-wingers running DC now.

Fink wasn't Trump's Treasury secretary, but he was something possibly better—Donald Trump's money manager. BlackRock had handled Trump's investment portfolio for years. When Trump invited Fink to the White House with a contingent of CEOs, he said, "Larry did a great job for me. He managed a lot of my money. I have to tell you, he got me great returns."

Perhaps because of Fink's relationship with Trump, BlackRock's biggest critics initially came from the left over ESG. Environmentalists claimed that you could buy your way into the ESG club through a practice known as "greenwashing," and BlackRock was among the biggest greenwashers of them all.

All you need to do is snap up tech companies with low carbon footprints that preach green and diversity, and presto, you have an ESG fund. In one jarring example of the practice, a company called Hartford Funds put the word "sustainable" on a bond portfolio to gin up woke investor interest. It worked. The fund grew to over $100 million in assets, even though the intricacies of the bond market make it difficult to enact ESG mandates on portfolio companies.

Another sticking point for the left: BlackRock was still the largest investor in energy and gas companies worldwide—more than $200 billion in oil patch and energy stocks held in its portfolios—no matter how much Fink touted himself as Mr. Sustainability. Elizabeth Warren saw him as a foe, publishing open letters demanding that Fink begin divesting all BlackRock money in energy companies. Climate activists frequently held rallies outside Fink's office in midtown.

BlackRock responded to the attacks by throwing the left a bone: It would no longer invest in a carbon-intensive segment of the coal business, known as thermal coal production. With the left-wing criticism somewhat muted, BlackRock went back to work marketing ESG as the future of investing. The firm won lucrative ESG investing assignments from companies and in places as diverse as the sovereign wealth fund of Finland and the New York State Common Retirement pension fund. Within a few years, BlackRock's "pure" ESG footprint expanded first to $500 billion, then eventually to nearly $1 trillion. Multiply that by the ESG fees—about five times higher than those that track regular stock indices—and you really have that alpha Fink loves to jerk off about.

BlackRock was indeed swimming in ESG alpha; its share price soared 135 percent between 2017 and 2022, compared to a 60 percent increase in the S&P. The firm was easily earning close to around $5 billion a year in pure profits.

Not bad for a guy who was fired from First Boston for losing $100 million.

"Our flows continue to grow and dominate," Fink bragged to Wall Street analysts around this time. "BlackRock is a leader in [ESG], and we are seeing the flows, and I continue to see this big shift in investor portfolios."

Fink couldn't have done it alone, of course. To execute the big investment-cultural shift that he envisioned, he needed a wingman, someone to work the phones daily with middle management. His choice: Brian Deese, a former senior adviser to President Obama, who was said to have played a key role in negotiating the Paris Agreement, a UN-sponsored treaty among the world's largest nations to reduce their carbon footprint. In 2017, Deese became Fink's ESG internal disciplinarian.

Here was the Trump administration on the verge of bolting the climate accord, while the dude who negotiated the treaty was hired by the world's largest asset manager to enforce it on American business (Deese declined to comment).

In 2020, Donald Trump would lose the White House to Joe Biden, and then Democrats once again controlled the White House plus Congress. Deese with a handful of other BlackRock executives unsurprisingly joined the Biden administration in 2021.

Not Fink. He chose to stay and make money. The three years Deese spent at the firm preaching the gospel of ESG clearly made a difference in making ESG BlackRock's thing and the company uber-wealthy, my sources there tell me. Deese was Mr. Inside, while Fink relished being Mr. Outside preaching the virtues of ESG and collecting those high-fee assets from people who didn't seem to notice the expense and the lack of performance.

"Larry loves to be a celebrity CEO and the press loved to hear him spout about everything from ESG to stakeholder capitalism," one BlackRock executive told me.

Fink even started to tweak his ESG messaging; it was no longer just about a clean environment. It was about civil rights. Corporate America was still too white and male. BlackRock wanted to change that.

"We have engaged companies on board diversity for many years," Fink announced one afternoon. "That engagement informs our voting guidelines for 2022. For example, in the U.S., we believe boards should aspire to 30% diversity of membership and encourage companies to have at least two directors on their board who identify as female and at least one who identifies as a member of an underrepresented group."

What Fink is alluding to is DEI, a key component of the "G" in ESG. BlackRock demanded it from its portfolio companies. Give the firm credit for practicing what it preached. According to people inside the firm, Fink instituted a new policy in which managers would be docked pay if they didn't meet the same ESG/DEI hiring goals it imposed on companies in its various funds.

"What we're doing internally is if you don't achieve these levels of impact, your compensation could be impacted," according to one internal memo. BlackRock managers provided me with another memo they said underscored Fink's diversity commitment. It informed staff how best "To celebrate International Women's Day." The firm, it said, "will house pop-up pledge stations in many offices around the world, asking BlackRock citizens: what's *one thing you commit to doing differently to advance gender parity at BlackRock.*"

The emphasis is not mine—it is BlackRock's. This is from a 2019 communiqué authored by Rachel Lord, then head of BlackRock's Asia business. Today Lord remains one of the most powerful people at the firm, a member of its executive committee and a close associate of CEO Larry Fink.

During the pandemic, like most C-suite execs, she conducted company business on conference calls, which she held from her home office. On one, you can't help but notice a large replica of a North Korean propaganda mural in the background. It depicts a missile, crushing something that looks like a cartoon of Donald Trump. The caption below, translated from Korean into English, reads: "Let's crush the US nuclear war scheme with our whole nation's unified power." (A BlackRock representative told me that the mural is nothing more than a comical memento a relative of Lord's smuggled out of the country and declined further comment on it.)

Most Wall Street CEOs are, at bottom, selling a product. Fink, because he loves to talk and talk and talk, was particularly gifted at selling ESG when the investing zeitgeist was all about sustainability. He wasn't merely a businessman now; he was becoming the conscience of Wall Street, its philosopher king. Competitors immediately noticed the change, including Jamie Dimon. They were envious of Fink's emerging status.

Dimon and Fink have an interesting rivalry. They run the nation's largest bank, JP Morgan, and largest asset manager, respectively. That gives them clout with the media, which means they also compete for attention. When Dimon took a knee during the George Floyd craziness, people who know Fink tell me he couldn't help but snicker at such a crass display of virtue signaling. As Fink was doing his version of taking a knee with his yearly CEO letters on ESG, sustainability, and DEI, Dimon told colleagues that Fink was playing with fire, too much sermonizing that was bound to cause blowback. Fink's increasingly preachy tone was going to lead to trouble because most Americans just aren't that liberal. "There are a lot of investors in Texas," an associate of Dimon told me in summing up his boss's thinking about Fink.

If word of Dimon's criticism made it back to Fink, he didn't seem to care. "As we enter 2018," Fink wrote in his CEO letter, "BlackRock is eager to participate in discussions about long-term value creation and work to build a better framework for serving all your stakeholders. Today, our clients—who are your company's owners—are asking you to demonstrate the leadership and clarity that will drive not only their own investment returns, but also the prosperity and security of their fellow citizens. We look forward to engaging with you on these issues...Companies must ask themselves: What role do we play in the community? How are we managing our impact on the environment? Are we working to create a diverse workforce? Are we adapting to technological change? Are we providing the retraining and opportunities that our employees and our business will need to adjust to an increasingly automated world? Are we using behavioral finance and other tools to prepare workers for retirement, so that they invest in a way that will help them achieve their goals?"

The closest example I have found of corporate leadership of this type was embodied in a man name Henry Luce, who created *Time* magazine and built it into a vast, culturally and politically important media empire known as Time Inc. It's hard to believe *Time* magazine, now largely a website, was a thing back in the day, but it was. Its power to influence public opinion can be best described as Fox News, CNN, and MSNBC rolled into one. During the Luce years, from the 1930s to the late 1960s, *Time* was hardly woke. It was staunchly anti-Communist. It portrayed America as the world leader, capitalism as the creator of immense wealth, and applauded the nation's gambits like the Vietnam War as world-saving gestures to fight off the Communist threat.

Doesn't sound like Luce and Fink have much in common, but here's where they might. According to the veteran journalist Lance Morrow, writing in his fabulous book about Time Inc., *The Noise of Typewriters*, Luce always wanted to be president. He couldn't bring himself to run because being "president was a comparative transient. Luce by then had been in the office at Time Inc. for 28 years, the length of seven presidential terms. Over so many years his influence over the American people and the world as editor and chief had become enormous."

Likewise, Fink had always wanted to be Treasury secretary, a position denied to him probably for good when Trump became president. He was said to bet so big on Hillary Clinton winning in 2016 and him getting the cherished cabinet post that BlackRock bought a huge new $183 million office in Washington so presumably Fink could watch over stuff when he wasn't hanging in the West Wing. After Clinton lost, Fink told people at BlackRock he was actually better off (ESG was making him a billionaire)—and so was the country. He too had Lucean visions, remarking to one associate that he would "have more impact from his desk at BlackRock than he could in the White House."

It's hard to fault Fink for wanting to do good or using his perch at the top of American finance to make the world a better place. Utopian aspirations and finance also can mix like oil and water. The boardroom wasn't designed to enact social change; people get elected to do that, and no one elected Larry Fink, which means he better watch out. Dave Komansky was the longtime CEO of Merrill Lynch, and suggested as much, my sources say.

In semiretirement, and until his health went south, Komansky was a member of the BlackRock board of directors. He and Fink went back for years; they were close friends and could be honest with each other. Komansky had been growing anxious about all of Fink's virtue signaling. One day he called one of his former Merrill underlings, now a top executive at another bank, and relayed his concerns that while his friend Larry was "one of the best CEOs he ever met," he was also "getting too political" and that's dangerous territory.

Komansky died in 2021, and I don't know if he made any of those concerns to Fink directly, but BlackRock was making too much money and Fink was having too much impact to slow down now. He was also the toast of the investment world. Plaudits flooded into BlackRock about Fink's ESG evangelizing. In 2018, a company called American Water, the largest water provider in the country, and a BlackRock portfolio company, congratulated Fink for being the conscience of the investing world.

"Larry again, we at American Water applaud the actions of BlackRock and you as the leader in challenging corporations to be successful financially, socially and ethically," the company wrote in a letter I obtained, boasting about its commitment to ESG, diversity, and how it was inspired by BlackRock mandates. "We take these values as well as all ESG principles very seriously and continue to challenge ourselves to be even better in the future."

BlackRock didn't invent ESG, of course, but a good case could be made that the firm institutionalized it. Companies like American Water may really love socially motivated investing. They also may have fallen in line with ESG because they felt they had to, to keep BlackRock from selling their stock. Competitors chased BlackRock's tail not just because they believed environmental Armageddon was around the corner; they saw from BlackRock how much money could be made on ESG.

"If you ask Larry if ESG increased his AUM, he would say of course and point to all the government pension-fund money at BlackRock, all those high ESG fees the company made," said one former high-ranking SEC official and observer of the ESG movement. "ESG has been very good for Larry Fink."

That would soon change.

CHAPTER EIGHT

The Boys from Brazil (and Belgium)

For most of his life, Daniel Blake had never heard of Dylan Mulvaney.

Oh, how he wished that were still the case.

It wasn't so long ago, about a year to be exact, in May 2022, that Blake landed his dream job: overseeing all of marketing for Anheuser-Busch, the company that makes two of the nation's most popular beers, Budweiser and Bud Light. It took nearly ten years of marketing crap brands and taking every shitty assignment, but he was now playing in the big leagues, promoting "the King of Beers," the brew of the construction worker, the jock, and the cowboy. The beer of Super Bowl ads, Spuds MacKenzie, the Clydesdales, family cookouts, and watching baseball with the crew.

That masculine—some would say "fratty," others would say all-American—image of Budweiser worked for years. So why change now?

Blake was asking the same question. In early 2023, someone in his department reckoned that the brand needed an image makeover to be less masculine with a new social media campaign featuring Dylan Mulvaney, a flamboyant transwoman influencer. That someone believed it would be great to have Mulvaney appear in some Budweiser ads to widen the brand's appeal away from cowboys and construction workers. Weird spots began featuring Mulvaney that ran on social media then went viral, and not in a good way. Let's just say Bud's loyal customers were more than a little perturbed at being associated with a biological man masquerading as a woman.

A nationwide boycott was on. The beer of cute little Spuds MacKenzie and hot babes in bikinis found itself in the middle of the nation's culture wars.

The company's phones were flooded with nasty calls complaining that the beer and brand they loved had gone utterly and insanely woke. The volume of calls nearly broke the system, such that operators were replaced by answering machines. Fights were breaking out in bars if someone ordered any type of beer with the word "Budweiser" on it. Distributors were getting death threats. Kid Rock was shooting Bud Light cans and filming it to create another viral moment on social media of non-woke backlash. Conservative media was having a field day.

Worst of all, Bud Light was the top-selling beer in the country before anyone heard of Dylan Mulvaney. Not any longer. Sales tanked and showed no signs of reversing; the fallout began affecting sales of Budweiser, not just the low-cal version. The stock of Anheuser-Busch's parent company, AB InBev, was in free fall.

And that's why Blake's career suddenly took a nosedive. The ads appeared without his knowledge, he told people. Initially, he was assigned to a team trying to stop the bleeding. As they began to unpack the situation, what they discovered was possibly the biggest marketing fuckup in the history of such fuckups. A personalized can of Bud Light featuring Mulvaney's beaming smile was created. She featured it in one spot celebrating her new "partnership" with one of America's iconic brands. In another, Mulvaney was giggling and drinking beer in a bubble bath, of all things. Some genius thought Dylan Mulvaney, a man transitioning to a woman, should be the face of Bud Light!

Again, all news to Blake. Mulvaney was chosen as one of 150 so-called influencers used by the company's marketing department for social media promotions without much input from anyone in management, it appeared. A brand team run by Alissa Heinerscheid, the first woman to manage the marketing of the nation's most popular beer, made the move to hire Mulvaney as a company-paid influencer. From a marketing perspective, you can see why Bud Light went there. Sales had peaked years earlier. Competition from craft beers, spiked seltzers, and spirits had squeezed sales further. Heinerscheid concluded that Budweiser had an image problem—it was too macho. In the era of corporate wokeness, the way to reverse that tide is to appeal to a woker demo, like urban hipsters with disposable income. Management wouldn't object; actually it would applaud the move. AB InBev had gone all in on left-wing business practices. DEI was big in hiring and in brand influencers.

With that as a backdrop, it becomes clear why Heinerscheid decided to change Bud's macho image to something "less fratty" and more "inclusive" (her words), and how a transwoman influencer might just do the trick. Mulvaney could appeal to the DEI desires of management. Major brands have been leaning on influencers—people with social media followings for one reason or another—as a cheap and effective way to build a brand in the new world of Twitter, Instagram, and TikTok. Bud was also leaning on them heavily in recent years because the suits who run AB InBev aren't just woke, they're also cheap. People who know the company say they take an almost sadistic glee in cost cutting, making influencers a key part of the marketing strategy.

Except in the beer business, skimping can get you in real trouble. Not just because you might end up with someone like Mulvaney. You also might be breaking the law.

Lawyers at the company are supposed to vet everything for "suitability." It is illegal to sell beer to anyone under the age of twenty-one. Mulvaney has a huge presence on Instagram and a bigger one on TikTok, the popular and controversial China-owned short-video app where the demographic is decidedly young, much of it below the age of nineteen, and clearly below the drinking age.

Saying TikTok is also controversial is no understatement. Members of both political parties want it removed from various app stores, because it is credibly accused of stealing user data for Chinese espionage purposes, and its videos brainwash America's youth with everything from porn to anti-American propaganda.

Consider: Around ten million people follow Mulvaney on TikTok. That's far bigger than the daily circulation of any newspaper, far more people than watch the most popular cable TV news show. With masses of American youths obsessed with TikTok and its stars, Bud Light was, albeit unwittingly, advertising the sale of beer to millions of minors.

And Mulvaney was indeed a star in the world of social media influencing. She did work for other big companies, such as Nike and Walmart. She's repped by the big talent agency CAA, which has lots of access to major corporations. She had appeared on red carpets and on popular podcasts and talk shows.

In October 2022, Mulvaney managed to score a sit-down interview with the most powerful man in the world, President Joe Biden, as she celebrated her transition from man to woman. Just before her Bud ads became famous, she was famously chronicling her yearlong transition in a series of short social media videos titled "365 Days of Girlhood." In these spots, she discussed the bodily changes that accrue from surgeries and hormone treatments. Instagram videos showed her fiddling with a tampon, doing girly yoga poses.

"This is my 221st day of publicly transitioning," Mulvaney told Biden during their chat that appeared on the lefty news site NowThis News.

"God love you," Biden said before extolling the virtues of gender-affirming care for kids.

You see, Mulvaney got her meeting with the president because she's among the most famous trans influencers in the country, yet no one at the top of AB InBev's management knew she had joined the company—at least that was their story and they are still sticking with it. Not Brendan Whitworth, the CEO of AB InBev's Anheuser-Busch division, who said he found out the company had a contract with Mulvaney from news reports; ditto for AB InBev's CEO, Michel Doukeris. If you listened to the company's spin doctors, Mulvaney was some sort of bizarre apparition who came out of nowhere. Strange since someone in legal must have vetted her contract. Didn't someone from payroll cut Mulvaney a check, because presumably she doesn't work for free?

Yes, very odd, because this unknown was well known by the most powerful man in the world.

One reason to be dubious of these weird semi-denials is that in the world of woke capitalism, Mulvaney does seem like a real catch. That "halo effect" explained earlier suggests that younger demos will buy products with an image that attaches itself to diversity, and increasingly gender diversity. She checked most if not all the DEI boxes imposed well above Heinerscheid's and Blake's pay grade. Given where business has been heading, you could see how the woke suits may want to position Bud as the official beer of the trans community.

That's the reality distortion field version of hiring Mulvaney and woke capitalism in general. The undistorted reality, of course, is far different. Most people are increasingly repulsed by companies channeling leftism when they sell stuff, or Target wouldn't be in such hot water with its customers. The same could be said for Disney, BlackRock, and, yes, Budweiser. People don't want to be hit over the head with messaging that men can be women and vice versa every time they shop or drink a beer.

By mid-April, weeks after the first Mulvaney spot ran, AB InBev management got the memo that the company was in really deep doo-doo; sales were still tanking, and internally the company realized that its most popular brand faced its first existential threat in its 150-plus-year history (it still is, as we will discuss later).

Whitworth, a former US Marine who did a stint in the CIA, was put in charge to get Bud's macho groove back. He seemed like the perfect vessel to reestablish Bud's street cred. He donated to GOP candidates. He was friends with Donald Trump Jr. He even looks like a typical Bud drinker, with noticeable stubble on his chiseled face.

Then he began opening his mouth. Disaster! Budweiser, he said in one of his bizarrely fatuous statements, has "thousands of partners, millions of fans and a proud history supporting our communities, military, first responders, sports fans and hard-working Americans everywhere. We never intended to be part of a discussion that divides people. We are in the business of bringing people together over a beer."

Where did Mulvaney come from and why? Whitworth didn't say, and still hasn't. How about a simple apology? He didn't and still hasn't. Sales fell further; distributors were now threatening to boycott Bud.

That's when management went looking for scapegoats.

An obvious one, my sources there tell me, was Heinerscheid, given her past comments about the need to move away from Bud's traditional customer base. In late April 2023, she was placed on involuntary leave.

The other scapegoat was Blake.

"You got to be fucking kidding me," Blake snapped after he was told he would be joining Heinerscheid in taking a compulsory leave from the company.

AB InBev still refuses to answer very simple questions about the Mulvaney interlude even after reviewing material in this book, including if

Heinerscheid and Blake remain at the firm (their LinkedIn profiles say they left in November 2023 and December 2023, respectively). The company is also refusing to provide their contact information despite various meetings with reporters blaming the Mulvaney fiasco on the marketing department.

What we do know from various sources inside and outside AB InBev is that new brand managers were being brought in. The marketing department was restructured to prevent influencers like Mulvaney from appearing allegedly out of nowhere. And Budweiser, if you believe its new ads, is back trying to appeal to fratty, macho dudes.

I'm skeptical of Budweiser's re-rebranding given the wokeness of its corporate masters at AB InBev, people who remained aligned with progressive corporate policies.

Further proof of the company's entrenched wokeness comes from a person close to Blake. This person tells me that when managers at AB InBev informed Blake he was heading out the door with Heinerscheid, he was told the company needed a fall guy—literally. They couldn't just oust the first woman brand manager of Bud Light, they needed to whack a white dude.

If they didn't, it might destroy the company's DEI rating.

Daniel Blake's LinkedIn profile describes the veteran marketing executive thusly: "Passionate marketing executive with...years building and growing brands. Vast experience crafting and executing long and short-term portfolio strategy. Proven track record of delivering top and bottom-line growth among large legacy brands and new-to-world brands alike. Thoughtful leader and proud developer of talented, collaborative, and high-achieving teams."

If anything, people who worked with Blake say that description undersells his talent. He understands better than most people in the company what the typical beer drinker likes and does not like.

And he's aware that woke doesn't sell to this customer base.

When the Mulvaney mess hit, Blake had been with Anheuser-Busch for the past decade, his first job out of the Darden School of Business at the University of Virginia. Management handed him "every crappy assignment," an associate told me, before he made it to the big leagues of beer marketing, running marketing for all of AB InBev's brands, including its biggest and most iconic, Budweiser. A life's dream for someone working in the beer industry given Bud's history of famous promotions, the Clydesdales, Spuds MacKenzie, and all those amazing Super Bowl ads.

That said, the job isn't exactly a layup. The competition is fierce, and beer doesn't sell well to younger demos these days. At Budweiser, you're also not really selling taste. "Piss water" is how a friend who fancies himself a beer connoisseur once described the tasteless carbonated stuff that we call Budweiser. He reserved even harsher descriptions for its evil stepchild, the lower-calorie and less tasty Bud Light.

Okay, you get the point. In terms of taste, Bud isn't the king of beers, or the queen, or even the duke. Probably some low-level servant. So why do people drink the stuff? First, it's pretty cheap compared to other brands (a six-pack might set you back about $7 depending on the state). You also drink it because it stands for something. Bud has an image developed by smart branding experts like Blake, and yes, Alissa Heinerscheid, and many others over the years. It's masculine, blue-collar, and American, which might be a curse on a woke college campus, but Bud's loyal customers would say with a smile it's why Spuds MacKenzie picks up the girls in bikinis, and why you can imagine yourself downing a cold one while seated in a wagon pulled by the majestic Clydesdales.

It's why until recently, for all the demographic shifts in the spirits industry, this piss water retained its No. 1 status as the top US beer.

As Blake told *Adweek* back in 2018, the classic beer drinker is "loyal, hard-working and dedicated to his family." He was describing a Father's Day ad campaign involving someone named Joe Gray, from Cherry Hill, New York. The ad included interviews with his three children, who are discussing what to buy Dad. He has enough socks, so one of the kids comes up with the idea to buy him what he loves—not a tampon, or a bra, or a yoga mat, but a cold six-pack of beer.

"Fathers like Joe deserve the best possible gift on their special day," Blake said. "We just wanted to point his family in the right direction so that they could show Joe how much he means to them."

Blake came up with ad gimmicks like paying for a couple's marriage, with a rep from Anheuser-Busch officiating the wedding. A great gift for working-class newlyweds. Anheuser-Busch later threw him a marketing curveball with Kirin beer, which AB bought from a Japanese company in 2008. Someone who worked with Blake called it a "shit brand" that Blake saved, and it was not easy. You associate beer with the Germans, not the Japanese, which made Blake's job getting broader traction outside the Asian market an uphill battle. By most accounts, he succeeded because he didn't disrespect existing customers with an ad featuring a Japanese transwoman.

"I'm a businesswoman. I had a really clear job to do when I took over Bud Light, and it was this brand is in decline...We need to evolve and elevate this incredibly iconic brand. What does evolve and elevate mean? It means inclusivity. It means shifting the tone. It means having a campaign that's truly inclusive and feels lighter and brighter and different. And appeals to women and to men."

And the kicker: "You've got to see people who reflect you in the work. And we had this hangover—I mean, Bud Light had been kind of a brand of fratty, kind of out-of-touch humor, and it was really important that we had another approach."

Alissa Heinerscheid made those unfortunate comments (calling customers demeaning names isn't how you sell stuff) in a March 2023 interview on something called *Make Yourself at Home*, a podcast that "takes you into the homes of people you admire, to give you a window into who they are."

Based on my reporting, Heinerscheid would be someone worthy of that description before she became known as the person behind Dylan Mulvaney at Bud Light. Despite her strange choice of words, attracting new customers—a younger, possibly more progressive, college-educated customer that populates the 25–54 age demo—is the heart of marketing because they have purchasing power and years left to spend what they have. The trick for people like Heinerscheid is taking a mature brand like Bud and making it appeal to new groups without alienating traditional customers.

Under the best of circumstances, it's a balancing act. AB InBev's obsession with woke capitalism made it nearly impossible, my reporting indicates. As one of her former colleagues told me, "Alissa was stretching with Mulvaney, because there was a top-down edict to follow DEI guidelines in the hiring of influencers. In my view, that's how she got to Dylan Mulvaney. Corporate wanted all departments to be 'purpose driven,' as they put it."

A little background on Heinerscheid: She is a Harvard graduate with an MBA from Wharton. She worked at Johnson & Johnson and General Mills. People who know her say she's not particularly woke, possibly a Republican. She's married to a partner at an investment firm she met at Harvard. They have two kids and live in Manhattan—not exactly workers-of-the-world-unite stuff.

In July 2022, management of AB InBev made her the first woman brand manager of Bud Light—Budweiser's No. 1–selling brew—because her ads were, put simply, really good. They won awards and appeared during the Super Bowl. One of her best was a 2023 Super Bowl ad that featured the thirty-six-year-old actor Miles Teller and his young wife dancing while they crack open a couple of Bud Lights and their French bulldog looks on. Cool stuff, certainly not something objectionable to a construction worker downing some Buds with his pals after work. Something a young professional Millennial or Gen-Xer might respond to.

She's also responsible for something more artful and creative: a medieval-themed *Game of Thrones* ad that aired during the Super Bowl in 2019. Critics called it an advertising tour de force, featuring many of the characters of the popular HBO series. According to *Forbes*, "The king and queen cheer for the 'Bud Knight' as the joust begins, but that happiness turns to shock as the Bud Knight is unhorsed, then to horror as his opponent strides over to him and crushes his skull. And their shock becomes ours when it turns out that the Bud Knight's opponent was none other than Gregor Clegane, the so-called Mountain from *Game of Thrones*. If that isn't enough, one of Daenerys's dragons then shows up and burns the crowd to a crisp…It's a minute of TV that entertains and intrigues, but it also does something more. But if we read a little deeper, there's a fascinating tension in the ad, a maybe unintentional battle between two very common understandings of the Middle Ages that tells us something really interesting about how we think about the medieval in the modern world."

Quite a contrast from Dylan Mulvaney's shtick, which is why in understanding how wokeness came to Bud Light you first have to understand the progressive leanings of its corporate parent, AB InBev.

Some dudes out of Brazil and a few from Belgium run the company. Beer business executives describe them as unimaginative globalist financial types with hedge-fund backgrounds who enjoy cost cutting to make their numbers work and keep Wall Street happy. They were never particularly good at creating stuff, just buying shit, squeezing it together, and turning it over to the bean counters. InBev is known pejoratively on Wall Street as a "roll-up," a mishmash of companies, in this case unrelated beer brands, acquired through highly leveraged acquisitions.

Anheuser-Busch, then owned by the iconic beer-making Busch clan out of St. Louis, was its biggest acquisition. In 2008, InBev paid $52 billion for the company, $48 billion of which came in the form of debt. Low interest rates around the time of the financial crisis made such leverage palatable. The InBev people renamed the company AB InBev, and their debt-fueled acquisition binge would continue for nearly a decade until the conglomerate achieved pre-breakup GE-level scale. By the time they finished around 2018, $100 billion in debt sat on AB InBev's balance sheet.

The cost-cutting fanatics at AB InBev certainly had their work cut out for them, and marketing, despite its traditional importance at Anheuser-Busch, took some of the biggest hits, former executives tell me. Immediately after the merger, top marketing people left. Oddly—or not so oddly for some Belgian-Brazilian corporate drones—no one seemed to stop and consider that branding was the key to Budweiser's success; "piss water" doesn't sell well unless you're drinking it for something other than the taste.

Papering over these missteps, at least for a time, was the company's stock price. Wall Street loves it when companies slash jobs and costs. AB InBev's stock, trading under the symbol BUD, would soar around 200 percent in the eight years after the Anheuser-Busch deal.

It was also classic short termism, however. As the old saying, often attributed to Jack Welch, goes, any moron can raise prices or lay people off. That's what AB InBev did, and it set the stage for the company's eventual decline. The Budweiser brand, known for its innovative ads, now seemed like an afterthought as part of the growing, increasingly faceless conglomerate. Marketing relocated from St. Louis to New York's Flatiron District to be close to the Madison Avenue ad business. Management teams were quickly jettisoned out of St. Louis as well.

The new Budweiser was in the sterile offices in New York and across the world, and, strategically speaking, a million miles away from places in Middle America and people who drink a lot of beer.

The real home of old Bud is, of course, Anheuser-Busch's original headquarters not far from the original brewery in south St. Louis, a working-class enclave in the city. Visitors can tour the giant brew kettles, get a glimpse of how beer was made back in the day, and taste the product. There was something majestic and American about the place. It reeked of nostalgia of a product that might have been invented in Germany but is as American as hot dogs and apple pie, and a perfect complement to a warm summer day.

If you tour the 155-year-old brewery (as I have), you can see the same red Budweiser wagons featured in all those commercials being pulled by those amazing Clydesdales. People who lived in the neighborhood worked at the plant, and they hung out after a long day at the local pub to down a cold one, fittingly, I might add, because Budweiser was an American success story. Its founders, German immigrants Eberhard Anheuser and Adolphus Busch, handed leadership down to family members for decades. The company remained in the family through 2002 when August Busch III—aka "Auggie Three Sticks," the great-grandson of Adolphus—named Patrick Stokes as CEO. A Busch may not have been officially in charge, but based on my reporting, they still kept a keen eye on the family business.

The so-called outsider didn't change much, and before long another Busch, Augustus IV, took over. Number IV certainly understood marketing, and he made sure that Bud's brand still stood for something the founders cherished—friends, family, country, leisure, and of course, no politics—thanks to some of the most memorable TV commercials in history. The Clydesdales, majestically beautiful, stomping through the snow, roaming the American landscape pulling the red wagon, spoke to people's desire for community as opposed to division. In one ad, just after the 9/11 terrorist attacks, the great horses are seen taking a knee as they overlooked a twin-tower-less skyline of Manhattan. I still get goose bumps from it.

The crazy dog Spuds MacKenzie catching the eye of bikini-clad women sounds sexist in the dominant woke culture, but it was cute and funny, and most Americans would say it still is. It also worked. Bud became the No. 1 beer, only to be surpassed by its low-cal alternative, Bud Light, sometime around 2001, mostly because of this image. Dudes who like dogs and pretty women in bikinis also like beer.

What a concept!

"When you say Budweiser, you've said it all" became the brand's slogan in the 1970s. It was unveiled in a TV spot featuring a multicultural cast, an African American woman as the lead singer of a chorus of singers in front of a map of the USA. Bud knew its customers, and the Busch family got to know the people who sold their product because 155 years of selling stuff successfully teaches that.

"Remember the Bud ad campaign 'Frankie and Louie'?" Scott Matagrano asks me one afternoon. Matagrano works on Wall Street, a partner at a hedge fund. He grew up in the Bay Area. His dad, Louis Matagrano, and uncle Frank ran one of the largest Bud distributors in the San Francisco area. The Frankie and Louie ad featured two reptilian creatures hanging in a swamp outside what looks like a bar croaking the word "Budweiser."

As with most Bud ads, distributors get a sneak peek of them at their annual conference in January. In 1999, Auggie III did the honors, Matagrano tells me. "As the lights go out, my father notices something weird. It's his face—his real face—on Louie the lizard, my uncle Frank's face on Frankie the lizard. Both are croaking out the word 'Budweiser.' The place filled with distributors from across the country went nuts."

"Bud was close to its distributors, particularly the big ones, so Auggie the third knew my dad and uncle pretty well. It was kind of family," Matagrano says. "That's the type of company Budweiser was."

The Busches may have been good at selling beer, but they were a complicated bunch. "Auggie Three Sticks" was considered a brilliant executive, having expanded Anheuser-Busch's US operations to nearly two dozen separate breweries, but he had a frosty relationship with his son, Auggie IV. Still, revenues topped $17 billion by 2007—Budweiser plus another dozen brands and the family cemented AB's prominence in the American beer market. When Auggie Busch IV took over in 2006, he wanted his own legacy and purchased the naming rights for the next two decades for the new Cardinals stadium in downtown St. Louis. Despite his reputation for having a wild streak in his private life, AB appeared invincible, until it wasn't.

By the mid- to late 2000s secular changes in the beer business started to shake the empire. Craft brews were becoming a thing; so were spiked seltzers and spirits like bourbon. All became more popular with the target audience known as the "25–54 demo." I've covered Wall Street for three decades. The combination of a strong brand but declining sales and management stagnation is usually a recipe for a hostile takeover.

That's when InBev, owners of Stella Artois and other foreign brands, swooped in with increasingly enticing offers that the family eventually couldn't refuse: a $52 billion price tag for the entire Budweiser franchise. InBev's offer was about $20 above AB's recent average stock price of about $50. The deal would make the Busch family one of the wealthiest in the country.

InBev bought something special, even if it needed some fine-tuning. According to *BusinessWeek*, around the time of the sale, one of every two beers that someone drank came from Anheuser-Busch. The company had twelve breweries in the United States and now synergies with a global franchise.

InBev, however, wasn't finished. It saw itself building a beer empire through acquisition. Management's calculation was that InBev—now AB InBev—should prioritize growth through acquisitions and squeeze every cost imaginable to pay for its buying spree. This age-old corporate trap usually leads to disaster because cutting your way to earnings growth never ends well. "The minute InBev got in there you saw a difference," said one distributor. "I used to go to the stadium [Candlestick and later Oracle] to watch the Giants play all the time. There used to be Bud signs everywhere. Then suddenly you saw Coors signs everywhere, and no Bud signage."

The architect of InBev's corporate expansion and the cost cutting that followed was the Brazilian financial executive, InBev CEO Carlos Brito. *Barron's* named him in 2010 to its list of the thirty best CEOs. The financial publication credited him for the bull run in the company's stock price and increased profits in the first few years after the 2008 Anheuser-Busch purchase.

What the financial press didn't appreciate is just how unimaginative the new owners were.

"InBev let it be known to the street and its distributors that they'd rather lose market share to increase profitability," the Budweiser distributor added. "That went against the ethos of the 'old' Bud and the Busches. Nothing has ever been the same. They reduced their marketing spend in major metros. That opened the door to Coors taking over sponsorships of pro sports stadiums—which are extremely lucrative for beer sales—concerts too. Even though the market is saturated with all kinds of gimmicky beers now, this would not be happening if the Busches were still running the company."

Bud's numbers were signaling trouble. Sales of Bud Light, then America's top-selling beer, hit their all-time high in 2008, forty million barrels a day. They would decline 40 percent by 2020.

Called in now was Michel Doukeris as AB InBev's new CEO. On paper, he looked like a winner. Doukeris joined InBev in 1996 and worked his way through the ranks to take the top job when Brito retired in July 2021. He has degrees in chemical engineering; he did postgraduate work at the prestigious Wharton business school. But he was also fully versed in the InBev business model of cost cutting, and, even worse, according to company executives, he would soon exhibit a significant appetite for corporate wokeness that he probably picked up at a place known as "Davos."

Davos, of course, is that Swiss mountain hamlet and home of the high-profile confab of globalist CEOs and world leaders, also known as the World Economic Forum. "The World Economic Forum brings together government, businesses and civil society to improve the state of the world" is its lofty mandate found on the front page of its website. The get-together occurs once a year in this ski village. I've been there, and it's quite a spectacle. You get to drink real hot chocolate (not the crappy Swiss Miss stuff), surrounded by lots of armed guards at checkpoints to protect the various billionaires, CEOs, diplomats, prime ministers, and presidents as they arrive.

Guests fly in on their gas-guzzling private jets to listen to themselves and various speakers yammer away about interest rates, inflation, global poverty, global warming, and lots and lots of global stuff. It's a Sonnenfeld CEO conference on steroids. Sheryl Sandberg promotes her books there. Bono shows up to alert the crowd that "capitalism is a wild beast." I hung with Kevin

Spacey at a bar one year before he was cancelled. Al Gore caused a stir one year as speculation swirled that he was flying in on his private jet to talk about...global warming (a Gore press rep later denied that he flew in on a private jet).

That's the public spectacle; the private spectacle is where deals get done during private dinners and receptions and wherever the wine flows. Bankers swarm like bees on honey to pitch the heads of sovereign wealth funds (the Saudis are omnipresent) and global mega-companies. Jamie Dimon, the head of JP Morgan, is there, of course, holding a private party with clients. Larry Fink attends and does the same with his peeps.

The emcee of all this madness is Klaus Schwab. I've never met Schwab, though I know people who have. (A spokeswoman has declined comment.) Let's just say he's not the type of guy you want to have a Bud with. He's a globalist's globalist, loves to spew about big weighty and woke issues, probably even while he's on the toilet. He started the forum in the early 1970s after a brief career as an academic (he is said to have befriended Henry Kissinger and the economist John Kenneth Galbraith while studying at Harvard), using his network of contacts to make the confab a big deal among the business and academic elite. Though he's of Swiss descent he grew up in Germany during World War II and witnessed its ravages, so I'm sure he sees the conference as doing something good for the world. Davos is where regulators from the International Monetary Fund, the World Bank, and just about every powerful global government enterprise meet with the global CEO class to figure out the world's manifold problems: global warning, hunger, poverty and armed conflict, and more. Schwab is at the center of this power lunch that sets the agenda of global economic governance given the power of the people who attend.

Of course, economic issues are a top priority at the WEF. Longtime IMF chief (and now European Central Bank president) Christine Lagarde never seemed to miss a Davos date as she doled out money to countries in economic need. She's setting the parameters for these countries' future fiscal policy that often includes high levels of debt and high taxes, so that the executives from BlackRock, also in attendance, can stuff their funds with sovereign IOUs without fear of default.

Critics of the Davos form of globalism contend that for all the crowd's good intentions, the results are heinously bad. The economic growth of countries in the middle of such global bailouts stalls because Davos's trained bureaucrats demand higher taxes and regulation. The working class is decimated, as it was in Greece before the country began to reject the Davos formula for free-market capitalism.

Another criticism comes from my more cynical Wall Street banker sources: They say Schwab provides an overly friendly venue to anyone who espouses progressive globalist bromides while kissing his king. Just before the 2020 Covid lockdowns, President Donald Trump—yes, the very non-globalist Donald Trump—went to Davos to get stroked by Schwab in one of the most bizarrely gratuitous exchanges at an event usually replete with fatuous ass kissing.

"Congratulations," Schwab gushed as he introduced Trump to the crowd, "for what you have achieved for your economy, but also for your society. We discuss here very intensively the question of inclusiveness, but all your politics certainly are aiming to create better inclusiveness for the American people."

Trump ate up the affection because, well, he's Trump.

Aside from the inane side of the WEF, the conference does have influence. When I ask my CEO sources who came up with the notion of stakeholder capitalism, ESG, and the rest, they say Schwab and the WEF had a big hand. "Davos Man" represents the ultimate marriage of the progressive globalist corporate citizen with the globalist progressive regulatory bureaucrat.

It's unclear when Doukeris transformed himself into one of Schwab's star pupils—a so-called Davos Man, according to former Bud executives. But when he did buy in, he did it with gusto, these people say. His first conference appearance can be traced to 2022, according to a conference agenda. He told *Forbes* in 2022 that AB InBev subscribes to the so-called Davos Manifesto, the confab's pledge for corporate wokeism that states, "The purpose of a company is to engage all its stakeholders in shared and sustained value creation. In creating such value, a company serves not only its shareholders, but all its stakeholders—employees, customers, suppliers, local communities and society at large."

That year, his "chief sustainability officer," Ezgi Barcenas, updated the crowd during one presentation about the company's progress in meeting its ESG goals. Doukeris had just implemented the company's latest ESG plan, outlined in something Schwab would have undoubtedly applauded. The AB InBev "Environmental Social Governance Report" unveiled its "ESG strategies" that will help the company meet its utopian corporate goal of a "future of more cheers."

Those cheers would be met by creating "a sustainable, equitable future for all" by promoting "inclusive growth and sustainable livelihoods...We believe that the future of business and of the planet is inclusive...a future with more cheers."

A spokesman for Doukeris declined comment other than to push back on the "Davos Man" label. It does not fit, he tells me, because "Michel is a tough businessman." Being a ruthless cost cutter doesn't preclude him from adopting the woke Davos mindset, or I wouldn't have so much material for this book. So I did a little research, and it's fair to say that over time the ethos of Davos—ESG and globalism—was clearly growing on Doukeris. Attending the conference in 2023, with the Swiss Alps in the background, he explained to reporters from Yahoo Finance how he had just got done chatting with some people from the very woke United Nations. Davos, he said, is the "best place to meet people. I was just telling you that I met one of our colleagues from the United Nations on the streets. And, they had like a 10-minute conversation walking. Good learnings and great experiences so far."

In the same interview he bragged that that ESG is "part of everything we do" at AB InBev, adding, "because beer is inclusive, natural, but most of all is very local. So, if our communities are not thriving, our business is not doing well."

One former company executive puts an even finer point on Doukeris's woke Davos allegiance. He refers me to one of AB InBev's recent annual reports. "This thing dedicates like a hundred pages discussing DEI or how we were meeting the UN's human rights index. Marketing teams were no longer measured on merit but increasingly how diverse the teams were and how we could increase our ESG scores."

Unsurprisingly, this executive says, that woke mantra from Doukeris and his senior management team filtered down through the ranks of the company, and particularly marketing, as will become painfully obvious. Even worse, meeting woke ESG standards, he says, was used to paper over the company's floundering growth.

To get a sense of the increasingly dire situation facing AB InBev, by early 2022 its stock hovered at around $40, a 70 percent decline from its highs in just four years. AB InBev's revenues stood at $57 billion at the end of 2022, which is just about where they were in 2017. Since the 2008 Anheuser-Busch acquisition and as this book goes to press, shares are up, but not enough, according to Wall Street analysts. They are underperforming various benchmarks, like the S&P, and by a lot.

An April 2021 report from Krause Fund Research summed up AB InBev's plight as a "mature company who has already reached its peak…They follow trends rather than creating them and rely heavily on their brand name to stay relevant.…Anheuser-Busch's cash flows are being allocated to debt repayments, thus leaving less capital for them to create new products from scratch."

"Investors were showing up asking managers about organic growth, and what they were doing with DEI to meet ESG metrics, and being more woke was something they could more easily control than producing a new product. We were covering up for our poor core finances with ESG," the former senior executive tells me.

What would Jack Welch do in a similar situation? Innovate, lop off layers of bad managers, and throw money at creative. Stay out of Davos and worry about the shareholder.

Stay away from corporate wokeness.

Doukeris appears to have done just the opposite. He kept cutting costs, his marketers sought cheaper ways to sell stuff using social media, and he was looking to score big on ESG.

They were setting the stage for Dylan Mulvaney and one of the largest consumer backlashes in American history.

CHAPTER NINE

This Bud Is Not for You

In 1979, Anheuser-Busch unveiled one of Budweiser's signature, and inclusive, slogans (of the non-woke variety): "This Bud's for You." The words would appear in TV commercials for decades. During this time, Bud would eventually capture 51 percent of the beer-drinking market in the United States because most people can relate to commercials featuring men and women hanging at bars, downing a few cold ones after a long day at work.

Bud was about community, commonality.

And it sold.

In 2016, with beer sales slipping, AB InBev used a transgender comic, Ian Harvey, in an ad with Seth Rogan and Amy Schumer. The ad ran during the 2016 Super Bowl. In 2021, with sales slipping even more, the company featured a transgender male-to-female athlete to support "gender equity" in sports in one of its beer ads. A year later, sales still sliding downward, AB InBev celebrated Pride Month, adorning cans of Bud Light sold in Canada with pronouns and the words "Celebrate everyone's identity."

Was there some marketing data to show that these ads appealed to the typical beer drinker? Only the warped data of ESG, DEI, and woke capitalism. No wonder sales kept slipping. How does telling your audience it's fair that biological men compete with women in sporting events lead them to buy more of what you're selling? Why would someone want to buy a product from a company that says it is "progress" to undo Title IX, which bans discrimination based on gender in sports? Who wants to be bombarded with gender-identity slogans when downing a cold one?

Not many people, of course.

So, what does all of the above accomplish? It explains how the inevitability of Dylan Mulvaney was just a few ads away, and with it the desecration of a great American brand.

Every year in January, AB InBev puts on a big shindig with its distributors and wholesalers. It's a convention of beer sellers, so there's lots of partying, of course, and some business. The business often consists of previews of the upcoming ads to get their feedback on what might or might not work. That's why the distributors get a special screening; there are still people even at a woke company like AB InBev who want to make the distributors' jobs easier so they can sell more beer.

Back in the Anheuser-Busch days, one of the Busches usually addressed the troops. In January 2023, Daniel Blake and Alissa Heinerscheid previewed the upcoming ad schedule, including those that would be aired during the Super Bowl a few weeks later in February, the biggest ad spend of the year.

If Dylan Mulvaney was on anyone's mind at that year's event, held in Anaheim, California, no one could tell. The duo brought up the upcoming Miles Teller ad for the Super Bowl. The company was trying to position itself for a future where possibly fewer people might go to bars because of Covid. That's why Teller and his wife were drinking beer in their living room with their dog.

But that doesn't mean Mulvaney wasn't lurking somewhere over the festivities. By February, she was onboarded as a Bud influencer by the Heinerscheid team, people close to the company tell me. The decision was made to make Mulvaney a voice in Bud Light's "March Madness" social media promotion. The big college hoops tournament is also a big beer-drinking event as people watch and place wagers on games in homes, bars, in Las Vegas, and, despite what Heinerscheid said, in frat houses.

Based on my reporting, AB InBev's recruitment of Mulvaney involved several corporate imperatives that coalesced into one imperfect shit storm.

First, there would have been no Dylan Mulvaney beer ad unless Budweiser management—the people who run AB InBev—forced middle management to embrace diversity, including the LGBTQ+ variety, in the company's marketing plans, former executives of the company say.

Heinerscheid clearly saw success defined as moving Bud's beer-drinking demo beyond older, non-woke cowboys and construction workers, I am also told by former executives. Lastly comes the issue of money, or lack of it. AB InBev's cost controls meant marketers like Heinerscheid had to be more creative to get out their message, these people add. Social media ads are cheap, and if they go viral, they are highly effective. They also appeal to that younger demo she was seeking that gets its info and entertainment from their iPhones as opposed to TV.

Social media, however, comes with lots of landmines. It's a window into the American psyche, amplifying national trends and fears. Opposition to the trans movement—the politicization of gender and its implications for children and society as a whole—is something that had been slowly galvanizing lots of Americans for the past few years on Twitter, Instagram, and even on TikTok, as the popular right-wing "Libs of TikTok" account demonstrates with its mocking displays of progressive overreach.

Calls to boycott Target and later Disney's woke programming began on social media. And so would calls to boycott Bud Light. The left has used the power of Facebook, Twitter, and Instagram to enhance its power for years now. Middle America has also learned to use the internet to its advantage. Go woke and you might just go broke.

Not that the peeps at Budweiser noticed any of this. On February 11, 2023, in an Instagram post and using the hashtag "#budlightpartner," Mulvaney got things rolling. She appeared in a bubble bath drinking a beer, with cans of Bud Light displayed in the background. There was a split screen with her in the bathtub and the Super Bowl ad showing Miles Teller dancing with his girlfriend.

As Mulvaney shimmied in her bath, a caption read, "Only Bud Light would have a commercial so catchy it makes you want to dance in the tub."

The post garnered tens of thousands of views.

With the February test run deemed a success (that is, no significant controversy), the company went out on a limb even further with Mulvaney for its March Madness promotion. Budweiser, as you might know, has offered a Sergeant Schultz defense on the Mulvaney meltdown. The idiot German prison guard in the 1970s sitcom *Hogan's Heroes* was known for knowing "nothing" as his excuse for American GIs continuing to escape from the fake prison camp. AB InBev continues to channel the fictitious dimwit only in real life in trying to explain how it came to work with Mulvaney.

Except, for a bunch of know-nothings, Bud certainly made Mulvaney feel part of the team. The company created a special, personalized can displaying Mulvaney's likeness, a present that she said commemorated the one-year anniversary of her transition to "womanhood."

"The best gift ever," Mulvaney gushed as she sipped her beer in front of a six-pack of Bud Light in her next social media spot. She was seated at a table with cans of beer all around; her dark hair was tied in a bun. She wore a black dress, with black elbow-length gloves. Her neck was adorned with what look like pearls.

It was an imitation of Audrey Hepburn's Holly Golightly character in the movie *Breakfast at Tiffany's*, and it failed miserably. First, Mulvaney looks nothing like Audrey Hepburn, and her imitation of a ditzy woman wasn't funny. It was demeaning to any real woman who likes sports.

"Happy March Madness!! Just found out this had to do with sports and not just saying it's a crazy month!" read a caption. "In celebration of this sports thing, Bud Light is giving you the chance to win $15,000. Share a video with #easycarrycontest for a chance to win good luck. #budlightlightpartner."

On April 1, 2023, Mulvaney uploaded her March Madness video. Maybe it was the fake Audrey Hepburn look that got under people's skin, but seemingly within minutes, the beer-drinking world erupted in disbelief and then anger as the spot was retweeted millions of times, shared many more times, with commentary from a consumer base rebelling against wokeness and calls for a boycott. Mulvaney's older spot in the bubble bath was unearthed as well. It was equally retweeted and vilified. People filmed themselves throwing Bud in the garbage, expressing outrage in ways the company had never experienced. Celebs soon joined the backlash. "I will be deleting all Anheuser-Busch products from my tour hospitality rider," Travis Tritt, the country music star, tweeted just after getting wind of the Mulvaney promotion. "I know many other artists who are doing the same."

Kid Rock took the social media outrage to another level.

I'm pretty certain Kid doesn't spend much time following Dylan Mulvaney on social media, but once he saw Bud's relationship with the lefty trans influencer go viral, he decided to do a little viral influencing of his own. Sporting a hoodie and a baseball cap turned backward, Kid is near a lake looking like he's doing a little duck hunting. Instead, he approaches the camera and says, "Grandpa is feeling a little cheeky today. Let me say something as clearly and concisely as possible." He then pulls out a semiautomatic rifle, aims it at a table stacked with cases of Bud Light, and starts blowing them away. The camera cuts back to Kid. "Fuck Bud Light and Fuck Anheuser-Busch. Have a great day."

The Instagram video was seen by millions of people and proved that Kid Rock understood Bud's customers better than Budweiser.

Inside AB InBev, the initial response was to ride out the storm. By doing that, management unwittingly allowed a rumor to spread that Bud Light had introduced a special Mulvaney-branded beer for wider distribution. It didn't; the can was a one-off gift, though a weird one for any company worried about maintaining its brand identity.

No wonder the crisis kept building; the alienation of traditional customers was growing more serious. "Get my beer out of that glass," a fifty-something general contractor—someone right in the middle of Bud's demo—demanded after ordering a Coors Light that the bartender poured in a glass with a Bud Light logo on it.

"It's just a glass," the bartender responded.

"No, it's not, and I can't be seen holding anything to do with Bud Light," the man said. "Put my beer in something different."

The man, a lifelong Republican, said that he was doing what he did after a typical day working his jobs in northern New Jersey: having a beer at a local bar. He used to settle into his seat with a cold Bud Light in his hand. Not anymore after the knuckleheads at AB InBev thought it was smart to throw in his face the likeness of Dylan Mulvaney.

The bartender found a plastic cup and, at least for this bartender, the crisis was averted. Not for AB InBev. In fact, it kept getting bigger. About two weeks into the meltdown, AB InBev was forced, finally, into damage control mode, and it issued its first statement on the matter as sales of Bud Light tanked, along with the company's stock-market value: "Anheuser-Busch works with hundreds of influencers across our brands as one of many ways to authentically connect with audiences across various demographics. From time to time, we produce unique commemorative cans for fans and for brand influencers, like Dylan Mulvaney. This commemorative can was a gift to celebrate a personal milestone and is not for sale to the general public," an Anheuser-Busch spokesperson told Fox News.

Management also assigned Daniel Blake and his team to counter-program the damage Mulvaney had caused. They released several real television spots, including one featuring Bud's iconic Clydesdale horses, and a lot—and I mean a lot—of American flags in the background. Then came the men—the real men: an advertisement featuring football star Travis Kelce titled "Backyard Grunts." As if a bunch of straight dudes in their backyard drinking Bud and grunting would make people forget about Dylan Mulvaney.

It didn't, of course. Behind the scenes, flacks worked the phones with selected reporters arguing that the marketers were largely, if not solely, to blame; management had no clue about their strategy. To this day, that's largely the company's position, and it fails the smell test. Official influencers don't appear out of thin air; as I pointed out earlier, lawyers approve contracts. Someone in payroll had to have cut Mulvaney a check.

The "lone wolf" scenario made no logical sense to Bud's once loyal customers either, which is why the boycott kept gaining momentum. Brendan Whitworth, Anheuser-Busch's CEO, finally stepped in. But his public statement as damage control was as bland as the taste of one of his beers. With tensions running this high you would think the AB flacks could come up with an apology and something better than "We never intended to be part of a discussion that divides people. We are in the business of bringing people together over a beer."

Unbelievably, a lot of thought was put into Whitworth's trite response. Don't say anything to piss off anyone—the trans community, the frat community, conservatives, or anyone else. But the opposite occurred. By opening his mouth yet saying nothing substantive about how Mulvaney made it to influencer status, Whitworth managed to piss off everyone.

Scrambling to stop the bleeding, Whitworth sought help from some of his conservative friends, including Donald Trump Jr., the former president's son and his father's right hand in the populist MAGA movement.

"So, here's the deal. Anheuser-Busch totally shit the bed with this Dylan Mulvaney thing. I'm not, though, for destroying an iconic company for something like this," said the former president's eldest son on his *Triggered* podcast. The decidedly unwoke Don Jr. brought up Anheuser-Busch's political donations, which lean significantly Republican, a reflection that Whitworth's politics were in line with the MAGA movement, he said.

"When I actually look into it, I'm not gonna blame the whole company for the inaction or the stupidity of someone in a marketing campaign that got woke as hell."

Nice try. Don Jr.'s support fell as flat as the bromides offered by Whitworth. Inexplicably, Whitworth next appeared on the very woke morning show *CBS Mornings*. It was a head-scratching display of corporate messaging and incompetence. Instead of disavowing the decision to hire Mulvaney, he assured anchor Gayle King that "Bud Light has supported LGBTQ since 1998, so that's twenty-five years. As we said from the beginning, we'll continue to support communities and organizations that we've supported for decades."

The "support" Whitworth referenced was not just the hiring of Mulvaney, but the millions of dollars AB InBev spends on causes like the National LGBT Chamber of Commerce.

AB InBev had hired the crisis PR firm Mercury Public Affairs, known for its high-level clients in politics and business and a team of flacks with sharp elbows. What have they brought to the table in terms of new messaging to change the narrative? Nothing as far as I can tell (people there didn't return calls for comment). The messaging stayed the same and it wasn't working. Sales continued to crater—and the virus spread to other AB InBev brands.

The bitterest pill for the company? Sales of rival beers exploded.

By the middle of May, AB InBev shares were still tanking, and Wall Street was panicking. Heinerscheid and Blake were now out of the mix, on leave and nervously awaiting their fate. Doukeris tried his hand to right the ship. In a conference call with analysts, he blamed the Mulvaney backlash on the ills of social media that distorted the facts. As Doukeris tried spinning the narrative, he framed the Mulvaney fuckup as a one-off in the scheme of things at a massive global company. "We need to clarify the facts that this was one can, one influencer, one post and not a campaign," Doukeris said.

The statement was somewhat inaccurate as Republican senator Ted Cruz and his staff easily discovered when they unearthed an earlier social media spot involving Mulvaney. Cruz and his staff began investigating the mess not long after the Kid Rock video went viral. Their focus wasn't the absurdly woke rationale for Mulvaney that Heinerscheid alluded to in that podcast but something more serious: that AB InBev may have violated the law by marketing alcohol to people under the drinking age of twenty-one.

There was strong evidence, according to Cruz's staff, that Mulvaney and by extension, AB InBev, targeted children in social media ads. TikTok was one of Mulvaney's top tools as an influencer, and its audience is generally on the young side; 25 percent are between ten years old and nineteen. Staffers found one social media post where Mulvaney was shopping for Barbie dolls. In another, she's lip-syncing "I am Eloise, I am six" while dressed as a small child. Eloise, of course, is the main character in one of the most popular children's books ever created.

"The woke ideology has so permeated corporate America and there has been an attitude that whatever they do, it's just fine and their customers will endure it," Cruz told me in an interview. "I mean, it really is frightening. I cannot think of another example of a company that's demonstrated such manifest contempt for its customers, and such lack of basic understanding of who they are."

The more the right started looking into Mulvaney's social media feed, the more they found stuff that you can reasonably say should have cancelled Mulvaney from any mainstream ad, not just one for beer. Still, I have to admit that part of me feels sorry for Mulvaney. She received death threats throughout the summer of 2023. She was relentlessly hounded whenever in public by reporters and wannabe reporters with iPhones looking for a viral moment. She was the target of an insane amount of social media abuse. Meanwhile, AB InBev acted as if she didn't exist once the you-know-what started hitting even though the company hired her for her ability to influence.

How could they not know her various antics since they're all over the internet? How could they not know she was controversial? That was the point in hiring her: She gets lots of eyeballs wherever on the internet she goes. They were now treating her like she was a rounding error on AB InBev's balance sheet that needed to be written off as fast as possible.

That's one way to look at this sordid drama. Another, of course, is that Mulvaney is much more than a private person coping with a lifestyle choice and online bullying. She is an activist, who seeks publicity as part of a political movement to take the country in directions that most people want to avoid (her reps didn't return emails and calls for comment).

Listen to the leaders of the trans movement, people like Dylan Mulvaney, and you also discover that they often compare themselves to those who led the civil rights movement of the 1960s. But Dr. King fought for equal access to public accommodations, voting rights, equal access to housing and education. Trans people have all of that and more—their right to transition is covered by many if not most insurance plans.

Sorry, what the trans movement really wants is America's total buy-in to celebrate and legitimize this lifestyle right down to legitimizing it with their kids. One of the means to create this "acceptance" is through the coercion that is at the center of corporate wokeness. They are demanding a cultural revolution enforced by every company these days in the form of DEI, ESG, and woke advertising.

Yet increasingly, average Americans see the trans movement and corporations sponsoring their efforts for what it is: a political movement they vehemently oppose. They're incensed that corporate America has joined that fight, and they are fighting back, both at the ballot box with politicians who push gender ideology on their kids, and at big companies that do the same.

And they're also using the power of their purses and wallets to revolt.

"Let's face it, Dylan Mulvaney is too political, and that was the basic mistake these guys made," said a former AB InBev marketing executive who spoke to me on the condition of anonymity because he has signed a confidentiality agreement with the company. "This was like putting Joe Biden or Donald Trump on a can. You're bound to piss off at least half the country."

CHAPTER TEN

The Not So Wonderful World of Woke Disney

There is, unfortunately, no shortage of examples that underscore the evils of woke capitalism. Those corporate indoctrination sessions foisted upon law-abiding Americans to atone for sins for which they aren't even remotely responsible immediately come to mind. Parents having to deal with companies like Target normalizing gender reassignment when they go shopping there with their children is another level of evil. Watching Dylan Mulvaney squeal in a bubble bath is a form of evil because it makes beer drinkers sick.

It didn't take me long to find possibly the ultimate example of woke excess attempting to destroy innocent lives; all I had to do was tune in one morning and listen to Megyn Kelly, the former Fox anchor, now podcaster, interview someone named Sage Steele.

Until recently, Steele was a popular ESPN anchor. In late 2021, she apparently forgot the national freakout that was going on over race. Defying the insane etiquette of her woke supervisors, she stated during an interview how proud she is to have a white mother and a Black father. She considers herself biracial, as if that is something bad. Her other hearsays that day included questioning ESPN's Covid vaccine mandate at a time (imposed by its parent company, the Walt Disney Company) when the vaccine was particularly ineffective against the emerging omicron variant. As she explained to Kelly, all that marked the beginning of the end of her career at ESPN.

I spent some time interviewing the people at ESPN about the strange case of Sage Steele, and from their end, the exact cause of her contretemps remains a bit murky. Steele, they say, was at times a difficult employee; she rubbed her colleagues the wrong way because she was opinionated. She pissed off Disney, ESPN's corporate parent, for various reasons that we will soon discuss.

I also spent some time interviewing Steele, who offers me a more cogent view on her eventual defenestration from ESPN. Put simply, she was an opinionated conservative outsider at a network that is decidedly woke; she wasn't afraid to tell her bosses that on more than one occasion. When she appeared to step over the woke line, she was toast.

Again, there are at least two sides to any story, so I attempted to present both of them here. Even doing so, I came away with something pretty concrete, and hard to dispute: Sage Steele's career began to take an immediate Orwellian turn south the minute she started throwing some verbal brushback pitches at the woke powers that be that ran ESPN.

There is, of course, no First Amendment right to a job. I get that. At the same time, I can safely posit that the circumstances surrounding Steele's unfortunate last years at ESPN sum up the evil that is woke capitalism and how the people at the top of corporate America have normalized this cruelty. It also demonstrates why ESPN's and Disney's unflinching dedication to wokeness is a business disaster. It should be terrifying for Disney shareholders, at least those who aren't obsessed with ESG scores.

Full disclosure: I'm not a regular viewer of the network that bills itself the "Worldwide Leader in Sports" and I didn't know much about Steele until I heard her discussing her bizarre and Kafkaesque experience on *The Megyn Kelly Show*. Because I cover business, and the business of media, I'm better acquainted with ESPN's balance sheet and contribution to Disney's bottom line.

ESPN, of course, is a very big business. It's the ratings leader in cable sports programming. Its hosts are considered a big deal in the community of sports-addicted watchers, and that's a lot of people: ESPN's top shows bring in about one million viewers, and not surprisingly they are mostly men.

I saw one stat that said almost half of all Americans (again mostly men) between 30 and 49 watch the channel. That's firmly in the sweet spot of the so-called demo—the 25-to-54 age bracket that most broadcasters look for in an audience to sell stuff to. No wonder ESPN still touts about $2 billion to $3 billion a year in profits.

According to one Wall Street narrative, ESPN is such a cash cow that Disney could monetize it at any time at a huge profit through a sale or a spin-off as a stand-alone public company. By the time this book goes to press, Disney may have already done so. Either way, ESPN is a golden child in its corporate universe, this theory holds. If Disney keeps it, Jimmy Pitaro, the network's longtime chairman, is a possible successor to Disney boss Bob Iger.

The counter-narrative is that ESPN's best days are behind it. It's starting to bleed viewers, yet another victim in the cord-cutting death march that has besieged cable TV. Buying the rights to sporting events is expensive and getting more so. ESPN+, its so-called over-the-top streaming service, is considered the future as cord cutting fully disintermediates the cable business. But depending on the quarter, it's either losing subscribers or not gaining them fast enough. All this bleeding comes even before ESPN hits the inevitable ratings cliff when consumers entirely ditch cable. The cash cow becomes a cow.

With a fragile business model, it would make sense for ESPN to go out of its way to appeal to its customer base. That's not happening. If anything, ESPN and its anchors go out of their way to preach woke politics that turns off at least half of America, probably even more.

Yes, ESPN is indeed a weird place, an enigma from a programming standpoint. Its viewership skews men who like sports and obsess over scores, highlights, commentary about top stars, and more. Not the type of demo you would think is comfortable hanging out at a lefty college safe space. Nonetheless, the network's programming is often almost indistinguishable from MSNBC, except for the sports ticker at the bottom of the screen.

Again, I'm not sure who exactly ESPN programs to since sports viewers aren't the most politically correct bunch. An ESPN insider once told me part of the move to left-wing propagandizing at the network was the success of the sports website Deadspin, a property inside the now-defunct Gawker media empire. Also very bizarre when you consider what happened to Gawker and, by extension, Deadspin. Sure, it employed some talented reporters who broke a lot of stories. It also had a nice swagger and a well-known animus for anything it deemed right-wing and unwoke (my employer, Fox News, was at the top of its target list).

Its antics did attract a lot of eyeballs. Stories about CEOs screwing around, gay sports figures created a lot of buzz, those very valuable "eyeballs," but also plenty of headaches. The entire edifice came crashing down when Gawker ran a video showing Terry Gene Bollea, better known as the wrestler Hulk Hogan, having sex with a woman who happened to be a friend's wife. The Hulk sued for invasion of privacy and was backed, stealthily at first, by well-known conservative tech titan Peter Thiel. Thiel hated Gawker because he's gay and wanted to remain private about it. Gawker outed him and Thiel never forgot or forgave the place. With endless cash from Thiel, Hogan hired good lawyers and won a huge jury award, $140 million in damages. Gawker declared bankruptcy; its properties were sold off in Chapter 11.

In other words, copying Deadspin's approach to sports coverage is like trying to create wealth by copying the old Soviet Union's economic system. It's dumb, and yet the clowns at ESPN went there.

The question is, why?

Based on my reporting, it's not that much different from what happened at Anheuser-Busch following the InBev deal. ESPN's de-evolution to the Worldwide Leader in Woke Sports began with a corporate takeover, in this case, its 1996 purchase by the Walt Disney Company.

Since then, there's been no turning back from the wokeness.

It didn't have to end up with the woke shit show that best describes the modern ESPN, and for that matter, Disney's current and sorry state. Disney of the mid-1990s—as it was poised to buy ESPN—was all about *The Lion King* and *Pocahontas.* Mickey and Minnie were still around. The values of its founders, the legendary Walt Disney and his brother Roy, were still held in high regard, and Disney's programming was culturally relevant. A trek to Disney World in Orlando was an American family tradition. Children grew up learning the parables of *Beauty and the Beast*, *Snow White*, *Peter Pan*. The list is endless.

The pre-Disney ESPN was the home of Chris Berman's booming voice, and inside baseball about sports. Big personalities debating college hoops, the Super Bowl, the next big contract in baseball.

Those days are over, for both ESPN and Disney, and you will soon discover why. To say both ESPN and Disney are swirling down the same woke drain is no overstatement. Disney earned $3.3 billion in 2023, but that's significantly less than its profits in 2022, and the year before that, and before that. Billions of dollars in revenue disappear each quarter as more and more families shun the company's wokeness, as we will explore later in this chapter.

Its stock price has fallen so much that it has wiped out nearly $50 billion in market value between 2020 and early 2024. Likewise, the more political ESPN gets, the fewer people watch. ESPN was in a hundred million homes in 2016, and now it's in just seventy-four million.

ESPN's wokeness went into overdrive after George Floyd, with programming featuring subjects as removed from sports as police brutality, and the celebration of transwomen competing against real women in sporting events. ESPN promptly lost more than a million viewers.

Coincidence? I'll let you decide.

If you're over, say, fifty years old, you probably remember children's programming like *The Wonderful World of Disney.* The show, which aired from the late 1960s through the 1970s, was must-watch TV in my house. It ran on network TV, so you didn't have to go to the movies to get a taste of Disney's iconic programming. Michael Eisner, then the Disney CEO, remembered the show. He reprised it in 1986 (under the name *The Magical World of Disney*) and became its host. It was a ratings success not because Eisner was good in front of a camera. In fact, he sucked at it. It worked because the programming—Peter Pan, Mickey Mouse, and so on—and new stuff followed in Disney's tradition of culturally iconic, teachable moments for kids, and we're not talking about teaching kids how women kiss.

That would come later.

The dimensions of the modern Walt Disney Company owe much to Eisner's vision for the company. He brought in talented people like filmmaker Jeffrey Katzenberg to run his studios. A string of box-office hits followed: *Who Framed Roger Rabbit*, *The Little Mermaid*, and many more. He purchased Miramax, also an incubator of iconic movies. Disney was killing it; the theme parks expanded and pulled in more traffic than ever. Shares had increased ninefold from the time Eisner took over until the mid-1990s.

But Eisner wanted more. It was his vision to create a massive entertainment conglomerate, along the lines of GE, various businesses that shielded one another for the inevitable ebbing and flowing of profits. In 1995, he spent $19 billion to purchase Capital Cities/ABC, then one of the largest corporate acquisitions in history. Eisner's transformation of Disney was in motion.

His plan was for Disney to retain its place as an incubator of culturally relevant programming, much of it aimed at children, with sports, and national and local news. Mickey and Minnie were going to be collaborating with the highest-rated TV network, ABC. Throw in, as the *Wall Street Journal* pointed out, "10 owned-and-operated TV stations, 21 radio stations, interests in several cable networks and publications from Women's Wear Daily to Institutional Investor," and you get one hell of a powerful entertainment product.

One of those cable outfits, ESPN, loomed large in Eisner's plans, I am told, since he was looking for diverse revenue streams, and we're not talking about the woke-diverse variety here. It was Eisner's bet that the whole of Disney would be more valuable than the sum of its parts, the exact mantra of Jack Welch at GE. Instead of mixing finance and light bulbs with pet insurance (yeah, Jack had a pet insurer nestled inside GE), Eisner envisioned a business model where declines in theme park attendance are offset by *Monday Night Football* eventually airing on ESPN.

Eisner was a tough businessman, not woke, and in many ways Machiavellian (he declined comment through a spokesman). He ultimately fired Katzenberg; he hired super-agent Michael Ovitz as Disney president, only to fire him a year later. He would earn the enmity of the increasingly progressive Disney family, namely Roy E. Disney, who was on the board and had a say in corporate affairs well after the death of Walt and his father, Roy O. Disney. Eisner is a Democrat, but people who knew him say he made a point of creating a programming and entertainment product that was nonpolitical.

Those days ended in 2005 when he was ousted and Disney started being run by Bob Iger, who, as you will see, is among the most politically progressive men ever to run a major company.

Eisner's vision of an entertainment conglomerate worked for years, but less and less so now. And not just because Disney is big and at times difficult to manage no matter who is in charge. Rather, the company's leftist politicization is killing it; ESPN is a casualty of this bizarre woke logic. So is Disney, of course, and so is Sage Steele.

I once asked Alan "Ace" Greenberg the secret to his success as possibly the best speculator to have ever graced a Wall Street trading floor. Ace was the former chairman of Bear Stearns. He was a Wall Street legend for many reasons (his quirky side hustles performing magic tricks among them).

Bear imploded not coincidentally after he was sidelined from management. Ace, meanwhile, managed money successfully for nearly fifty years, right up until his death in 2014 at the age of eighty-six. It's not that he didn't lose money, because he did. But his real skill was in not losing a lot of money so that his winning trades always kept him flush. Kenny Rogers would say Ace knew when to hold 'em and knew when to fold 'em. Ace told me it was a lesson he learned from his dad, who ran a profitable clothing store in Oklahoma City. "If you got bad inventory, mark it down and sell it quickly."

Degenerate gamblers have a habit of doubling down on their bad bets until they're living on the sidewalk. As do woke corporations. Disney's post-Eisner bet on a progressive entertainment experience, and of course, the rigid conformity it enforces against dissenting voices, has hurt its bottom line, as we will explore shortly. It has also hurt people, real people, who dare to speak their minds.

One of those is Sage Steele.

A point should be made that ousting Steele for defying corporate leftism's marching orders, humiliating her in front of her colleagues and fans, along with the rest of the Disney/ESPN woke infrastructure, has done nothing to reverse Disney's or ESPN's decline. In fact, I know people who since hearing her story won't ever watch a football game televised on that channel again.

This might be a suitable time to explain what it's like working at ESPN if you're someone like Sage Steele, now a fifty-something mixed-race woman who is not afraid to express her heterodox political views. To begin with, management isn't exactly the nurturing type. There's also navigating the minefield of the network's woke politics.

As she moved up the ranks, Steele tells me she mostly kept her politics to herself. Her strategy worked, at least for a time. Steele made it through her ESPN hazing, first as a fill-in studio host on a variety of shows. Ultimately, she achieved ESPN royalty, becoming the anchor of *SportsCenter*, the network's premier program.

All that and she couldn't survive ESPN's corporate Stalinism once she began doing what her colleagues were doing—airing her political beliefs. Unlike her colleagues, Steele mostly confined politics to social media and not on the network, she tells me. But even that ran counter to the network's left-wing mandates when she spoke up against multiculturalism dividing the country along racial lines or criticized transwomen competing in women's sports as patently unfair. Then she was branded a conservative and "a Trump supporter," which is the ultimate scarlet letter in mainstream media, even though Steele says she never publicly stated who she voted for.

"Not everyone was a fan," was how one ESPN executive described Steele's relationship with many of her broadcast colleagues as her political views became more known inside the network. Some key players in management weren't happy with her either, my sources say. One reason might have been the progressive marching orders from above.

Jason Whitlock, a longtime sports journalist and a former ESPN personality, is a Black conservative. He once described ESPN's lurch to the left (again on Kelly's podcast) this way: "Disney has gone about the business of feminizing and wokefying sports."

Don't believe him? Go back as I did and listen to ESPN's anchors endlessly politicizing everything from Donald Trump and George Floyd to Ron DeSantis that mirrored the politics of its corporate parent.

Sorry, politics front and center on a sports network is more than a bit off-putting. Even more so when it's some of the most progressively leftist proselytizing on broadcast television. Even worse when voices like Sage Steele's are cancelled by the people running the network who care less about their viewers than they do about pushing their left-wing agenda.

"Looking back, that was the beginning of the end for me, though I didn't know it at the time," Steele remarked as she tried to attach some context to how her career at ESPN ended. The "it" she's referring to is the ESPN coverage of the racial justice movement in 2020, something she said she was purposely kept out of. After George Floyd's death, ESPN's top personality, Stephen A. Smith, did a two-hour special as if it were a defining moment in sports. Yes, Floyd's death was a tragedy, but was it really something as important to ESPN's core viewers as the World Series? The network provided full coverage of the verdict, as the police officer Derek Chauvin was found guilty of second-degree murder of Floyd. It aired an interview with Keith Ellison, the leftist attorney general of Minnesota, who brought the charges against the cops arrested in Floyd's death.

Not exactly your typical sports programming, but if you're going to do it, do it right. Include some voices of Black conservatives to provide an interesting take on the issue and the social upheaval that followed. That's what Steele told management after they broke the news to her that her voice wasn't going to be included in the network's official Floyd special.

The Undefeated Presents Time for Change: We Won't Be Defeated was a special program that purported to "feature a roster of thoughtful and respected ESPN anchors, analysts and contributors, high-profile athletes, authors and psychologists exploring Black athletes' experiences with injustice."

A full "roster," but no room for Sage Steele, because, Steele says, some of the talent involved in the special told management her conservatism put her "Blackness" into question. Steele was hurt and let her managers know, and eventually her exclusion was leaked to the media. ESPN's defense was that it didn't have enough time to include her; Steele's response: "Trying to define who is and isn't Black enough goes against everything we are fighting for in this country, and only creates more of a divide."

It's hard to take ESPN's comments seriously given the political trajectory of its programming during this fraught time. This is, after all, the sports network that held a moment of silence when Ron DeSantis and the Florida legislature passed the law ending sex ed for toddlers in his state. "They also had their lead NBA host nearly in tears on the air the day of the NBA draft—talking about *Roe v. Wade* being overturned," Steele recalls. Anchor Jemele Hill called Donald Trump a "white supremacist who has largely surrounded himself with other white supremacists." Management barely noticed until the remark started to go viral on social media, prompting a typical response from Trump that for a change wasn't an exaggeration: "ESPN is paying a really big price for its politics (and bad programming). People are dumping it in RECORD numbers. Apologize for untruth!" he tweeted.

In the end, ESPN did apologize to The Donald, or kinda. "The comments on Twitter from Jemele Hill regarding the president do not represent the position of ESPN. We have addressed this with Jemele, and she recognizes her actions were inappropriate."

Yet Hill remained at the network; she wasn't taken off air or made to grovel for her job or denied assignments.

That special type of torture is reserved for conservatives like Sage Steele, who, as she puts it, was increasingly "being forced to choose between my job and standing up for myself."

Given her anti-woke history, it's hard to imagine Steele wasn't near the top of ESPN's shit list when she appeared on the now defunct podcast *Uncut with Jay Cutler* in September 2021. Just a few months earlier another ESPN reporter named Rachel Nichols was fired for being secretly recorded during an off-air open mic moment complaining that she had to give up her role as the lead NBA reporter to a Black woman because of ESPN's DEI policies. The recording was leaked, and Nichols was gone.

A case could be made that Steele should have thought twice about going near any such woke sacred cows. Or maybe she thought free speech still means something in the profession of journalism.

Uncut with Jay Cutler was a podcast anchored by a former Chicago Bears QB that attracted a niche audience of athletes, agents, and sports journalists. Lots of chitchat about sports and cultural issues. Unlike Colin Kaepernick, Cutler had a real career in the NFL: twelve seasons. He made All-Pro and played in the Super Bowl. He retired in 2017 and remains in the news because he was the husband (now ex) of reality TV star Kristin Cavallari and, most recently, for hosting the podcast that doomed Sage Steele's ESPN career.

Like Steele, Cutler is a right-winger (he voted for Trump), so you can almost understand why the woke gentle souls at ESPN were listening intently to see if she would violate some woke orthodoxy, which she did not just once or twice, but three whole times, including the deadliest of them all, involving race.

That came when she explained her racial identity. Steele told Cutler she was proudly biracial. Her dad, a strict disciplinarian, was the first African American to play varsity football for West Point. He went on to be an All-American and achieved the rank of colonel in the Army. Her mom is of Italian and Irish descent who defied her parents when she married a Black man. She spoke about how many biracial people, including former president Obama, chose to identify as Black, despite, as in Obama's case, being raised by a white mother and white grandparents.

"You do you. I'm going to do me," she told Cutler. She found Obama's choice "fascinating," because his biological father, after getting divorced from his mom, "was nowhere to be found." Remember that this was just a year after George Floyd, and corporate DEI departments were monitoring unwoke speech like the old KGB.

She then questioned women dressing provocatively at work, stating that men shouldn't be let off the hook for being pigs, but women are almost asking for offensive comments if they're going to wear provocative clothing. Woke hysterics had moved a bit past their height during the #MeToo movement, but not much. The lefties found that offensive as well.

The third tripwire was hit during a discussion on Covid vaccines, and in particular mandates by companies to force employees to get the jab, a huge trend early in the pandemic when the vaxxes were considered "safe and effective" and companies used them to compel workers to get back to the office. In the fall of 2021, questioning them or the attempt by big government and big business to compel people to take them was like questioning the sanctity of Mother Teresa.

Yet Steele went there, calling ESPN's vax mandate "sick and scary," adding, "I didn't want to do it. But I work for a company that mandates it and I had until September 30 to get it done or I'm out." She further explained why she ultimately got the jab: "I have a job, a job I love, and frankly a job that I need," adding that such corporate totalitarianism is hardly surprising, "especially with Disney."

What followed was immediate condemnation not just from the usual woke suspects but from her colleagues, much of it on social media. Steele complained to her bosses. If ESPN didn't allow people pissing in the proverbial tent, why was it different for her? "They ignored me and allowed it," she said. Instead, ESPN launched an investigation of her conduct and then issued a statement setting the stage for disciplinary action against their onetime star who dared to do something that might lower Disney's DEI ranking.

Was it the Obama statement, the vaccine stuff, or her comments about women dressing provocatively that got her in trouble? Was it all three? To this day, ESPN hasn't said anything other than to confirm that Steele crossed the woke line and would have to pay for it. "At ESPN, we embrace different points of view—dialogue and discussion make this place great. That said, we expect that those points of view be expressed respectfully, in a manner consistent with our values, and in line with our internal policies," the network told Fox News at the time. "We are having direct conversations with Sage, and those conversations will remain private."

People at ESPN don't dispute that Steele faced some disciplinary action, mostly for her comments calling Disney's vax mandate "sick." Steele tells me, "It was all three...my boss specifically told me on the phone that my vax mandate comments were number one, followed by race, followed by women."

To keep her job, Steele said she was then given an ultimatum—publicly apologize or leave. And she couldn't use the word "Disney" in her apology; that's how paranoid the ESPN brass was about offending their lefty corporate masters. Steele said she relented because she would have lost her job, her career, and everything she had worked for over the years. She was now a single mom, recently divorced from a stay-at-home dad, and raising three kids. She needed the paycheck. "I know my recent comments created controversy for the company, and I apologize. We are in the midst of an extremely challenging time that impacts all of us, and it's more critical than ever that we communicate constructively and thoughtfully."

When I think of someone like Sage Steele putting out drivel like that, I can't help but think of those hostage videos, where under the threat of torture people will say anything their captors demand. They do that to survive. Steele wasn't really given the dignity to survive at ESPN.

She was immediately "suspended with pay," she said. And when she returned, she says, she was denied key assignments. One hit her hard: She was told she could not appear as a host for the V Foundation cancer research fundraiser that ESPN jointly operates with the charity. Stuart Scott, an ESPN anchor who died of cancer in 2015, and Steele were tight. She began hosting the foundation's dinner in his memory, she said. A rep for ESPN says the V Foundation wanted Steele off the program that year because of her vaccine comments. As for being suspended, the rep says Steele "was with us for two years after the issue and on air every day."

Steele says ESPN's actions speak louder than its banal explanations, as she went through the assignments she was denied and the ostracism she endured. With the controversy swirling, fully vaxxed, she contracted Covid—not that her supervisors cared that it made their mandates look idiotic.

It's not all bad for Steele. As ESPN and Disney were playing their woke games, she sued. "After I was suspended with pay, I filed my lawsuit in April 2022," she said. "Definitely an interesting dynamic for those sixteen months while the lawsuit was pending." She charged the company with violating a Connecticut state law (the network is based in Bristol, Connecticut) that prohibits corporations from disciplining employees for exercising constitutionally protected free speech. After hiring bulldog attorney Bryan Freedman, she announced that she was parting ways with ESPN and had settled the case in August 2023. The settlement numbers are confidential, though I'm sure she got a good chunk of change. If you know Bryan Freedman, you also know he doesn't settle cheaply.

As for her career, Steele tells me she's enjoying her freedom to speak her mind. She gave a blow-by-blow account of her travails to Megyn Kelly. She occasionally appears on Fox News. From time to time I see her posting stuff on Instagram with her family.

"The freedom has been incredible," Steele says. It's "helping me realize how much fear had been instilled in me and others while at ESPN and Disney."

Welcome to the wonderful world of woke Disney.

In the summer of 2018, Disney issued a press release to make an important announcement in the increasingly woke world of corporate America. It would be the latest big company to join the righteous cause of…banning plastic straws.

Yes, an unbelievably momentous decision made by the House of Mouse, or so top executives wanted everyone to believe. Lots of stuff was going on in the world back then. Terrorism, Iran coming close to getting nukes, China's imperialism, and, according to Disney, the great scourge known as too many plastic straws.

Not long ago, top executives wouldn't be bothered by outlawing plastic straws. They were too busy trying to sell stuff, improve their company's stock price, and make money. A win-win-win for everyone, including employees, who get raises and promotions when their employer is doing well. They didn't have time for abstract worries about carbon footprints or finding the next LGBTQ+ influencer for their social media ads.

Oh, how far we have come. The woke devolution of Disney is a case study in how progressivism seeped into corporate decision making, and how this mind virus is threatening to destroy its host.

Disney's announcement came in a florid statement that suggested that fewer plastic straws would save the planet. Under the headline "Disney Expands Environmental Commitment by Reducing Plastic Waste," the company said it would eliminate "single use plastic straws" in its theme parks and corporate locations. According to various environmental studies, plastic straws were killing marine life and wildlife by the bundles. People throw them on the ground or in the ocean while they are sipping a soft drink. They end up as a poisonous snack for deer or dinner for sea turtles.

Unveiling the grand plan to make the world safer for turtles was a man named Bob Chapek, chairman of Disney "Parks, Experiences and Consumer Products," and a rising star inside the company. "These new global efforts help reduce our environmental footprint and advance our long-term sustainability goals," Chapek announced in a press release. To put an even finer point on his move, Chapek and Disney said fewer plastic straws combined with other environmental efforts would "reverse the decline of wildlife around the world" because plastic is made from petroleum and, you know, fossil fuels are next-level evil.

Or as Chapek put it: Getting rid of plastic straws "and other plastic items are meaningful steps in our long-standing commitment to environmental stewardship." By mid-2019, "The Walt Disney Company will eliminate... more than 175 million straws and 13 million stirrers annually."

Wowza. Seems like a lot of work went into this analysis from old Bob and his team of flacks and number crunchers. On one level it worked; the PR gimmick garnered lots of press about how Disney took a giant step for mankind in joining the great plastic straw ban even if the science behind the entire effort was largely BS. Plastic straws account for a small percentage of the global garbage problem, and let's be clear, the actual number of plastic straws being thrown in the ocean or anywhere near any wildlife is impossible to measure, as a few skeptical and real scientists said at the time. How many animals died from eating them? Unknown, and probably de minimis compared to the other stuff that's killing the spotted owl.

The kicker, of course, is that like most ESG-driven woke efforts there is a downside for average people, the folks who consume Disney's entertainment and pay a lot of money to hang out at Disney World. Replacing plastic straws with the paper variety is expensive. Those costs are passed on to consumers, families already stretching to afford Disney's overpriced theme parks. Disney World may think it's the happiest place on earth, but not for people who pay for the trip. Based on what I have seen cited, a no-frills excursion to Disney World for a family of four costs anywhere from $5,000 to $6,300, not exactly affordable for working-class families on a budget.

How much value this stunt produced for Disney shareholders is also very debatable. Unless you can find some value in woke capitalism and its manifestation in ESG.

Bob Chapek obviously did in his quest to be Disney's next CEO, a job he got over a heavily favored Kevin Mayer, who was running Disney's streaming business. Bob Iger, the icon of the Hollywood establishment and a Wall Street darling, had indicated that his days as CEO were over and he set up a beauty contest between his two most senior executives, though I doubt the plastic straw gimmick is what put Chapek over the top. In any event, Chapek was named CEO in 2020, fired two years later, and replaced by Iger, another casualty of corporate wokeness gone wild, as you will soon find out.

My guess is that Chapek's edge in getting the top job at Disney came in part from running a profitable balance sheet as head of parks, while Mayer was trying to figure how to make streaming profitable. It's also likely he and his team came up with numerous other woke gimmicks for Disney's board and Iger to chew on, which is why most people don't know Chapek is a

Republican. They assume that he's even more of a lefty than Iger given his uneven record running the House of Mouse during this brief and disastrous time in Disney's corporate history.

Still, Chapek is an unusual type of executive to champion corporate wokeism. He's got an MBA and a degree in microbiology, not exactly gender studies. He's not a Disney lifer and excelled at the operations side of the business, as opposed to the studio stuff that past CEOs focused on. His first big job was running Disney's Buena Vista Worldwide Home Entertainment, selling Disney movies, its huge library of classic films and newish cartoons, on DVD. He made the company a fortune. Next, he ran Disney's theme parks, which put him in line to be Iger's eventual successor.

But there were always gaps in his C-suite experience. People who know him say he's cold and often aloof. He has "no EQ," one rival entertainment CEO told me, referring to the term known as "emotional quotient," a form of intelligence good managers use to relate to people and sell a certain vision of the company to the rank and file. "Bob hated small talk and never asked how you were doing," is how one associate described Chapek. "I don't think he really had any friends at work. He preferred to hang out at his house in the Florida Keys with his family rather than dine with board members."

And he wasn't woke, at least not on a personal level, which made him an even stranger fit given what Disney's corporate culture had become. "In his heart, Chapek hated the left-wing stuff always pushed by Iger, and vowed to end it once Iger was out," the associate added. "If Iger would have three same-sex kissing scenes in a movie, Chapek if he had his way, would cut it down to one," the associate added.

Iger is, of course, the other Bob in the Disney drama. Bob Iger was Disney's longtime CEO, who by the time of his retirement in 2020 (he remained as chairman until 2021) was considered among the best in the world. During the Iger years, top-rated shows flowed from Disney's various platforms and its nascent streaming service. Its stock price soared. One major status symbol came in 2011 when the legendary Steve Jobs appointed Iger to serve on the board of mega-company Apple.

Disney shareholders weren't eager for him to leave as he approached retirement age even if they didn't appreciate the other side of the Iger record, the one that imperils Disney to this day. Disney's stock was pumped by the irrational exuberance of the bull market. He overpaid for his key acquisitions. His deal-making chops were earned through a series of acquisitions—Pixar, Marvel Studios, and Lucasfilm, and the big one in 2017, buying 21st Century Fox's entertainment assets for $71 billion. The acquisitions saddled the company with billions in debt, and that would be a huge problem when the market cycle turned. Iger got into streaming with Disney+ because he saw how streaming would disintermediate Disney's business model of theatrical releases and wanted to get ahead of it. It was all very expensive and still doesn't turn a real profit.

Moreover, Iger was among the most woke CEOs in America, and with an ego to match. From his C-suite, he butted heads with Donald Trump, abruptly resigning from one of the former president's advisory panels after Trump pulled the United States out of the Paris climate accords. He threatened to stop filming movies in Georgia over the state's abortion restrictions. It seemed that Iger did not think conservatives owned Disney's stock or took their kids to Disney movies, or he didn't care. Increasingly under Iger, same-sex characters were being introduced to Disney movies and cartoons aimed at children. *Toy Story 4*, remakes of *Beauty and the Beast*, and *Jungle Cruise* all had gay characters. Disney executives defended such content based on their brevity. "You could blink and miss it," one told me. Still parents became increasingly concerned that Disney—the Disney of Walt and Roy, the Mouseketeers—wanted to indoctrinate their children to the LGBTQ+ lifestyle through what should be entertainment. Transgender greeters began appearing at its theme parks. Employees no longer used the words "boys and girls" at Disney World when talking to children to spare any potentially trans child the horror of hearing that there are two genders.

Inside the company, executives began enforcing diversity mandates to make Snow White non-white. A photo of the Seven Dwarfs looked like they grew seven inches. Disney scrubbed rides of anything decreed non-woke and offensive; the popular Jungle Cruise was updated to remove references to indigenous people, who of course live in the jungle.

Old movies and cartoons included trigger warnings; *Dumbo*, *The Jungle Book*, and *Aladdin* contain "negative depictions and or mistreatment of people or cultures. These stereotypes were wrong then and wrong now."

The company's "Reimagine Tomorrow" initiative set racial quotas for Disney characters: 50 percent from "underrepresented groups." An internal document explaining the initiative lays out the extent that Disney has embraced quotas throughout its businesses. According to the document, "50% or more of regular and recurring written characters" must come from so-called "Underrepresented Groups." This standard is applied, the document says, in "on screen representation [and] creative leadership" all the way down the corporate food chain to "line producer and/or production department heads (i.e.: DP, composer, costume designer, editor, production designer, music supervisor…)." The document states that "paid employment opportunities such as apprenticeships, internships, expert advisers to facilitate union eligibility" must meet the same criteria.

Beginning with Eisner, Disney began a tradition openly celebrating homosexuality at its theme parks with so-called Gay Days. But what began as an event for a few hundred people grew to a party of tens of thousands during the Iger years. A theme park made for children took an overtly sexual turn. Signage at Disney World directed people to parties such as "lesbo-a-go-go" and "Muscle Beach." Disney World seemed to be covered with Pride-colored flags, clothing, and Pride-oriented merchandise. In fact, the festivities took over the whole town of Orlando, with various events Disney also accommodated. So disturbed were families who happened to show up to Disney World during the bacchanalia that Disney began issuing warnings about when Gay Day commenced and ended.

Inclusiveness is a worthy goal, and Disney was all about inclusion. But there was also a smarmy hypocrisy to the way Disney practiced it. As management was telling families they needed to be accepting of alternative lifestyles, it was also groveling to the leaders of the oppressive Chinese government and the Chinese Communist Party. The CCP isn't known for its acceptance of the gay community, or any community that defies its rigid philosophy. And yet Disney has made no secret of its lust for the Chinese markets both to sell movies and to expand its theme parks. This as the Chinese government continues to openly oppress everyone from gays to the Uyghur Muslim minority. The most disgusting example of this hypocrisy occurred in 2020 during the airing of the film *Mulan*, where credits gave kudos to the very Chinese government entities leading what some have called the genocide of the Uyghur people.

Chapek's defenders tell me that he was no fan of this type of woke hypocrisy but that he was powerless to scale it back.

And why would he try if he had his eyes on Iger's job?

Exactly why Iger chose Chapek as his successor is a mystery to most people in and around the Disney orbit (company officials, major shareholders, analysts, bankers), because they're so different. Iger looks Hollywood, like he actually appeared in a Disney movie back in the day. He's fit even as he passed seventy years of age. He knows all his direct reports' spouses by name; he knows how to control a room. Chapek is in his mid-sixties, and for most of his time at Disney proudly sported a shaven bald head; it literally gleams in front of the cameras. He looks like a guy who could be a member of the Hells Angels motorcycle gang if he weren't wearing a suit. Bikers are at least interesting; Chapek is the last guy you want to have a beer with.

So how did Chapek become CEO?

One explanation offered to me by a Chapek crony was that "Iger killed everyone else," and one legitimate potential successor, John Lasseter, the guy who created some of Disney's most successful animated movies—*Toy Story*, *Cars*, and *Frozen*—left amid allegations of sexual harassment. Unwanted hugging can get you bounced at the woke House of Mouse, as it did Lasseter.

Chapek, in other words, was the last man standing. He ran a huge chunk of the company's balance sheet successfully, something the board demanded from Iger's successor. He understood programming enough because of his stewardship of the DVD business.

That still didn't fully explain how Chapek, who had no experience in the creative part of entertainment, found himself running what's at bottom a creative entertainment company. According to one CEO who knows both Chapek and Iger well, the decision wasn't made purely on the merits.

Iger, this CEO said, wanted someone in that job who would never do it as well as he did. "Bob Chapek was set up to fail," this CEO said. "Everyone knew he didn't have the chops to run Disney, and Iger did as well. That's why he chose him."

Chapek did fail, as we will explore in a bit, though his biggest failure may have been his ultimate refusal to follow his gut and fully remove wokeness from Disney. For all Chapek's managerial flaws, he really believed the boardroom of Disney should be a place that stayed mostly out of politics, and that Disney needed to dial down the wokeness, people who worked with him tell me. He lacked the intestinal fortitude to get that done.

Not that exorcising the woke demons would be easy, but Chapek made it exponentially more difficult with a series of managerial blunders and missteps that ironically forced him back into the progressive trap he was trying to escape.

In 2020, not long after Chapek became CEO of Disney, he began a series of meetings with various key executives at the company. According to people who know Chapek, he felt the creative types who develop programming were too over-the-top woke. He acknowledged that politics was something Iger indulged in, probably too much, and he thought it took the company in some very dark places, the people add. Disney's customers were far less political, less progressive than the company's corporate culture. These people also say Chapek remarked that he had a good working relationship with the conservative governor of Florida, Ron DeSantis, an important ally for an executive whose operations are largely located in the state. Chapek, they said, had wanted to move more employees to Florida, expand its operations in a business-friendly state with no income tax. You can't do that if the company appears to be the entertainment arm of the left.

Chapek's challenge was enormous. On top of depoliticizing a company that had been thoroughly politicized, he needed to reopen the parks after Covid. There was the enormous task of making streaming profitable, or at least not losing so much money without Mayer, who left when he didn't get the top job. (Mayer became CEO of the short-video app TikTok; he now runs a portfolio company owned by Blackstone and has returned as an adviser at Disney.) Money was increasingly tight, the stock off its Iger highs, and he had to grow his business so he could pay down all that debt Iger left him with the 21st Century Fox deal.

Chapek certainly inherited a heavy load. And that was before he got into a legal pissing match with America's sweetheart.

In July 2021, the actress Scarlett Johansson filed a lawsuit against Disney alleging that the company screwed her out of millions of dollars over her role in the prequel to the Marvel franchise *Black Widow.*

Disney released the movie simultaneously in the box office and on its streaming platforms. Part of Johansson's total payout for the movie was based on theater ticket sales; that's why most blockbusters all have some theatrical window. Thus Disney's actions cost her money.

It was the first major test of Chapek's management skills as CEO, and it would be the first of many failures.

Chapek was unmoved by Johansson's arguments that Disney breached her contract. One reason, I am told, is that Disney was starting to bleed big-time. There was too much debt and not enough money coming in. Johansson would have to get with the belt-tightening program. Her contract guaranteed a "wide theatrical release" window, but that could include all the streaming services under the Disney umbrella to meet that requirement. There was not an exclusive *theater* guarantee, Chapek's people argued. Meanwhile, such windows were getting smaller with the advent of streaming, which at the behest of Iger was now corporate priority.

His plan was not just to fight her in court, but according to company insiders, to embarrass Johansson in the court of public opinion before getting to the real courts. He had his staff draft a particularly nasty press release. Disney called her lawsuit "especially sad and distressing in its callous disregard for the horrific and prolonged global effects of the Covid-19 pandemic." It included this zinger: "Disney has fully complied with Ms. Johansson's contract and furthermore, the release of Black Widow on Disney+ with Premier Access has significantly enhanced her ability to earn additional compensations *on top of the $20 million she has received to date*" (emphasis mine).

The bitter feud between a studio and one of the biggest stars, almost unheard of in the movie industry, continued for several months. The first thing to know about legal pissing matches like this one is that nearly all of them get settled. It's why you say something bland and boilerplate, that the charges have no merit, and so on. You want to keep the avenues of communication open and make a deal.

Second, it's not smart for a fat-cat executive who earned $14 million in 2020 when small businesses were forced to shut down to take on a celebrity that most people like. Johansson might be a lefty, or she might not be; what is clear is that she doesn't wear her politics on her sleeve.

Alan Horn told Chapek as much, my sources tell me. Horn is a long-time entertainment executive who has been at Disney for decades, highly respected for his sense of what sells and doesn't sell in Disney movies. Horn was chairman of Disney studios until 2020, when at seventy-seven, looking for more free time, he semiretired to the position of chief creative officer.

Horn wasn't running the show anymore, but Chapek presumably kept him around because he knew what he was talking about. Horn heard what was in the press release and didn't like it. It was too personal. He didn't need to release Johansson's salary to the world. It went further than merely raising the issue that she was well paid. Plus, you never win taking on America's sweetheart.

Chapek was unmoved; according to people with knowledge of the matter, he thought he had the upper hand exposing a greedy Hollywood type as America was still reeling from Covid. Chapek couldn't have been more wrong, and Horn more right.

As the case moved through the courts, both sides slinging mud, Disney, and Chapek specifically, ended up with most of it. Instead of receiving accolades for beating on a greedy actress, Chapek received scorn as a bad manager who can't handle talent. At one point, to gain a PR advantage, Chapek tried to appeal to Wall Street; he attended analyst conferences explaining how in the new world of streaming, talent will need to adjust their ambitions on money. To make streaming profitable, to pay for the Fox deal and more, Disney had to find money somewhere. Collapsing the theater window might finally help put streaming in the black.

The argument made conceptual sense, but Chapek could not make the sale. The bad press over the case continued, as did a downward trajectory in Disney shares. In September 2021, the two sides reached an undisclosed settlement, with $40 million going to Johansson, according to Dominic Patten of *Deadline*.

I am told that Chapek tried to shift the blame to his old boss, and increasingly his new nemesis. Iger had launched Disney's ambitious and costly streaming strategy that Chapek was trying to fix. In Alex Sherman's masterful tick-tock of the Chapek-Iger feud, the CNBC reporter details how Chapek told the board that he wanted a bigger seat at their table, fearing Iger was taking shots at him in private meetings with directors. He also couldn't wait for him to be out of the company, when he would have to relinquish his job as chairman.

In late 2021, Iger's retirement was complete. He left the top spot in Disney's board for a $10 million consultant gig, which meant he wasn't totally out, as Chapek was about to discover.

Picking a fight with Scarlett Johansson was dumb, but picking a fight with Bob Iger was a high-stakes move by someone as politically obtuse as Chapek. The CEO of a large entertainment company once described Iger's power in the entertainment business this way: "He's the guy that holds court with everyone once a week in the back room of some restaurant. When I say 'everyone,' I mean every major Hollywood CEO, producer, agent, you name it. The dinner is private, and they set the agenda for the business."

I couldn't confirm whether any of this is literally true, but Iger's *macher* status among the Hollywood elite is both legendary and definitely true. Chapek, in his desire to set himself apart from Iger, in his anger about dealing with Iger's leftovers, from debt to fixing streaming and overt wokeism, went to war with a skilled and determined enemy.

In fact, not long after the Johansson mess ended, Iger went to work on Chapek, Chapek's people at Disney tell me. A person close to Iger denies this; Iger, this person says, had no contact with board members until the moment they called to offer him Chapek's job. Yet no one is denying the obvious: that Chapek and Iger were at odds, and at times bitterly so. Was it Chapek's less woke agenda, or did he think he was a lousy CEO? He also could have been pissed over what he thought was Chapek trying to shift blame to him on the company's tenuous financial condition or the Johansson mess. No one really knew. (Iger and Chapek declined to comment; a Disney spokesman and a spokeswoman for Chapek have reviewed the material from this book but didn't provide further comment.)

The exact cause of the Chapek-Iger clash doesn't matter because Chapek may have survived it if he didn't pick a fight with someone even more powerful in his ability to publicly humiliate him.

That someone was Ron DeSantis.

In early 2022, DeSantis was on the verge of being reelected Florida governor and by a landslide. He had made defeating wokeism wherever it existed a key part of his political appeal. His latest assault on the woke: a law curtailing sexual education for children in the state.

The bill, presented to the Florida legislature in March 2022, prohibited public schools in the state from teaching sex ed to children in kindergarten through third grade, including "classroom instruction by school personnel or third parties on sexual orientation or gender identity." Sex instruction of increasingly younger children had been building for years, and it had been infused with the politics of the LGBTQ+ movement, including normalizing gender reassignment therapies for kids.

Progressives in the teaching establishment were now pushing research purporting to show that children were increasingly questioning their gender as early as kindergarten. To emotionally handle the trauma, they needed support with sex education starting as early as possible. Such classroom instruction prevents "child sex abuse and intimate partner violence," but also "increase[s] appreciation for sexual diversity and improve environments for LGBTQ students, among other benefits," according to a piece in Montclair State University's in-house magazine that describes research done by two of its top professors.

There was a dubious nature to these "studies." Most were research-infused opinion pieces produced without control groups, margins of error, or real statistical findings. Real studies show that as many as 80 to 90 percent or more of children who suffer from gender confusion get unconfused within a few years. The debilitating effects of coaching them into a trans lifestyle and then giving them puberty blockers and gender reassignment surgery, however, cannot be reversed.

Parents began noticing the political side of the gender debate and fought back. So did public officials like Virginia governor Glenn Youngkin, and now DeSantis. The new Florida bill channeled those concerns of parents and the broader conservative movement; it was one of several lines in the sand drawn by right-leaning pols that reflected the growing unease with the American family being force-fed the left's value system.

Chapek sensed that getting involved in an issue so toxic was bad for business. In March 2022, as news of the law started circulating inside Disney, he told his board and his direct reports that Disney would sit this one out, according to people with direct knowledge of the matter. They say he recognized that there would be some heat from within; anyone could see how progressives in the company, in Hollywood, etc., would be upset with DeSantis's gaslighting the LGBTQ+ community with a law that essentially said their lifestyle was verboten in the classroom.

The flip side: DeSantis was popular, and most Floridians voted for laws like this one. Most Americans don't want their kids learning about all the pluses in LGBTQ until later in life. There was a growing danger in going woke. Preaching progressive values directly after George Floyd might have been tolerated by an American public inundated by footage of the ex-con screaming, "I can't breathe." It had since lost lots of its luster, and the right increasingly saw Disney as a target-rich environment for attack. If conservative talk show hosts began to target Disney with their vitriol, that's tens of millions of people who might decide a trip to Disney World wasn't worth it. Disney could be in for the same treatment that has caused so much agita for BlackRock, Budweiser, and Target.

And it wouldn't take much to get the vast right-wing spin machine moving. Conservatives were still steaming over Disney's treatment of the actress Gina Carano being fired from a starring role in the popular *Mandalorian* films less than a year earlier. Carano was a well-known conservative in Hollywood. She's against preferred pronouns, and questioned mask mandates during Covid, which had already put her on the Disney shit list.

Her tweet that likened vax mandates to the hysteria of Jew-hating during the Holocaust ultimately got her the boot. Okay, it was awkward and, obviously, historically inaccurate. But a firing offense? Conservatives saw it as a double standard given all the dumb and insane stuff that comes out of the mouths of lefty Hollywood types. How many Hollywood types openly supported the BLM movement without similar recriminations?

I could not determine whether Chapek had the final say in Carano's ouster. It should be noted that Iger was still at the company as chairman while Chapek clearly indicated he wanted to wean Disney off wokeness, people with knowledge of the matter say.

Ron DeSantis presented Chapek with a significant test in that regard.

Chapek had a difficult balancing act to perform, made more difficult by his own management blind spots, and soon Bob Iger. In early March, just after his "retirement," Iger tweeted about the DeSantis legislation. It's what you might expect from someone who wore woke on his sleeve: "If passed, this bill will put vulnerable, young LGBTQ people in jeopardy." The tweet further inflamed the Disney rank and file, which began to talk about protesting the law at the theme parks and a lot more.

Whether Chapek knew it or not, he was sitting on a powder keg. Iger ran what was considered among the most LGBTQ+-friendly companies in America, and it hadn't changed much since Chapek took the job. The law was now being dubbed smartly in a propaganda sense by a coalition of left-wing activists and celebrities (yes, I know that's redundant) as the "Don't Say Gay" bill, and it worked. Opposition was growing in all the familiar places: the media, Hollywood, academia, and in the Disney rank and file.

Chapek in a very Bob Chapek way didn't understand the unrest inside his company. His outside PR advisers at the Brunswick Group were worried that any public statement would draw too much attention and possibly start a civil war inside Disney that was already brewing following Iger's tweet. If you want to stay out of this thing, do so with silence, they recommended at one point.

Apparently they didn't push hard enough. In the final product, Chapek's memo said taking a stance on the law would further "divide and inflame" the people of Florida and the country. Such corporate virtue signaling "can be counterproductive and undermine more effective ways to achieve change."

Chapek appears to have forgotten just who works for Disney. People like Latoya Raveneau, executive producer for Disney Television Animation, who was caught around this very same time admitting in a Zoom call with employees that part of her job was to "add queerness" to children's programming.

The video was leaked to the inimitable non-woke muckraker Chris Rufo, who posted it on his Twitter feed. "SCOOP," Rufo tweeted. "I've obtained video from inside Disney's all-hands meeting about the Florida parental rights bill." In the video referenced by Rufo, Raveneau said Disney's management was welcoming of her "not-at-all-secret gay agenda." She added, "I was wherever I could just basically adding queerness" to programming. "No one would stop me, no one was trying to stop me."

She wasn't alone, of course; in fact, she speaks for many of the people who occupy key jobs inside Disney, my reporting shows. No wonder that despite a few hits, so many Disney movies are now bombing at the box office.

Who in Middle America wants to sit through two hours of this stuff with their kids?

Suffice to say, Disney isn't Middle America even if its Florida theme parks are in the middle of Florida. The Hollywood crowd occupying its Burbank, California, headquarters went nuts after Chapek's memo went public. Disney faced a walkout by employees. There was an explosion of social media hashtags bemoaning Chapek's neutrality because in the progressive mindset, life isn't neutral, it's binary and Manichean. Depriving a five-year-old education in gender fluidity is pure evil in their worldview.

The vitriol of a very loud minority began to rattle Chapek and his team. They never saw such anger and protesting. Susan Arnold, who took over as board chair once Iger vacated the seat, is openly gay, and she got an earful from the LGBTQ+ community. She relayed all of this to Chapek, who now had a choice to make: Would he stand up to the woke crowd or cave?

He chose the latter.

The best source for what occurred next is from DeSantis's own political memoir, *The Courage to Be Free: Florida's Blueprint for America's Revival.* In it, he recounts the conversation he had with Chapek, who explained that while Disney gets "pressured all the time" from various interest groups, "this time is different. I haven't seen anything like this before."

DeSantis's response: "Do not get involved with this legislation." Disney, like BlackRock, Nasdaq, and every woke company in the world, was expanding in the country of intolerance and slave labor, China, yet it was complaining about intolerance in Florida over forbidding the teaching of sexual acts to minors. "You will end up putting yourself in an untenable position," DeSantis said. "People like me will say, 'Gee, how come Disney has never said anything about China, where they make a fortune?'"

Chapek ignored the warning. He reiterated that he had no choice; a civil war had broken out inside the company. Thus began Bob Chapek's walk into total wokeness, issuing a memo stating emphatically that Disney was ready to use its corporate resources—the shareholder money that Ed Rensi believed was sacrosanct from politics—to defeat the guy he considered a business partner just days earlier.

"The biggest impact we can have in creating a more inclusive world is through the inspiring content we produce, the welcoming culture we create here and the diverse community organizations we support, including those representing the LGBTQ+ community," read Chapek's one-eighty.

"I want to be crystal clear: I and the entire leadership team unequivocally stand in support of our LGBTQ+ employees, their families, and their communities. And, we are committed to creating a more inclusive company—and world," he stated. "We all share the same goal of a more tolerant, respectful world. Where we may differ is in the tactics to get there. And because this struggle is much bigger than any one bill in any one state, I believe the best way for our company to bring about lasting change is through the inspiring content we produce, the welcoming culture we create, and the diverse community organizations we support."

Chapek then pointed to Disney's high DEI ranking from the leftist Human Rights Campaign, no less. "In 2021, we provided nearly $3 million to support the work of LGBTQ+ organizations. And we have a long history of supporting important events like Pride parades, and for being there in times of need…All this is why we have earned a 100% rating from the Human Rights Campaign for 16 years in a row."

In subsequent remarks Chapek went further in genuflecting to the woke. He said he called DeSantis "to express our disappointment and concern that if legislation becomes law, it could be used to unfairly target gay, lesbian, non-binary and transgender kids and families," adding, "The governor heard our concerns and agreed to meet with me and L.G.B.T.Q.+ members of our senior team in Florida to discuss the ways to address them."

Chapek then told investors at the company's annual meeting that he always was against the law, and just wanted to work privately to kill it. The statement further enraged DeSantis and the Republicans in the state legislature, people close to the matter tell me. Disney became that target of the right that Chapek initially feared but was too weak to prevent.

Meanwhile, the so-called Don't Say Gay bill passed with flying colors.

Richard Bates, the longtime Disney lobbyist, died unexpectedly in December 2020 of a heart attack. He was a former Democratic Party man, but certainly not woke, extremely bipartisan, and influential with every CEO since Eisner. He met with members of both parties regularly. Iger may have been a lefty, but Bates sold right-wingers on Capitol Hill that they had a voice at Disney through him. In 2017, when conservative groups tried to mount a boycott over what it believed was Iger's initial forays into progressive programming, Bates defused the situation. He made sure that Iger knew what more than half the country wanted in children's programming.

"If Bates were alive, he would have convinced Chapek not to oppose DeSantis," said one longtime media lawyer who also served as a top regulator in the Trump administration. The former Trump official said Bates would have argued to ignore the noise inside the company and just reiterate his record with supporting LGBTQ+ causes.

Without Bates to provide support, Chapek's sounding board was Arnold, for obvious reasons: She knew the LGBTQ+ activist circuit well. People close to Arnold say she was navigating a sensitive situation; angry calls came from various political groups and her email inbox was jammed with complaints. She found herself in the middle of the storm as well and was looking to help Chapek quell the controversy the best way she knew how. Her advice to Chapek: Explicitly say he was sorry. That's right: Apologize for not wanting to teach toddlers their gender pronouns.

Chapek agreed. The apology was made, as was a pledge to use shareholder money to support LGBTQ+ charities.

In the summer of 2022, Chapek somehow got a contract extension. In return, he appeared not just to give up on his plan to de-woke Disney, but to take progressive messaging in its programming and at the parks to new, more dangerous levels. One media industry CEO, knowing what he knew about Chapek—his lack of EQ, etc., his management flaws, and his knack for ignoring advice—summed it up this way: "It's totally fitting that Chapek would totally overcorrect on wokeness."

Chapek personally intervened to reinstall an unnecessary and contrived same-sex kissing scene initially removed from the latest Buzz Lightyear animated film, a move that was destined to further strain his relationship with DeSantis and make him a target of every conservative commentator in the country. He released another children's movie with an openly gay character, this one titled *Strange World*. Very strange, because the parental rebellion over sexualizing children was a very real phenomenon. Not so strange that the movie lost tens of millions of dollars at the box office.

Chapek, my sources say, told some people inside the company who cautioned him on the move that he had no choice but to go woke. Yes, he might further anger DeSantis. He may have gotten a new contract with his board, but his standing with Disney's employees was still tenuous.

And as predicted, DeSantis pounced. DeSantis wanted to hit Disney in the pocketbook. He began pushing legislation to end its special tax status known as Reedy Creek; he wanted state employees to be looking over Disney's corporate governance shoulders.

Chapek was fighting a two-front war: DeSantis for being too woke and Iger, who didn't like even the most feeble and non-woke changes that Chapek tried (and failed) to enact. Iger's intentions couldn't have been made clearer during a CNN interview that spring. When asked about Chapek's response to the Florida law, Iger said, "A lot of these issues are not necessarily political. It's about right and wrong. So, I happened to feel, and I tweeted an opinion about the 'Don't Say Gay' bill in Florida. It seemed potentially harmful to kids."

I have an additional call in to Iger for an explanation of how refraining from instructing third graders in various forms of gender preferences is "potentially harmful to kids." His handlers have yet to respond. But Iger wasn't just delivering an opinion; he was delivering a message to Chapek, people close to the matter say. He wanted Chapek out, and possibly his job back. Retired CEOs rarely publicly rebuke their successors; when they do, as Jack Welch once did to Jeff Immelt, it means they want change.

Chapek was clearly scrambling to survive. He changed flacks and grew a beard to strike a softer appearance, and started meeting with employees to show he wasn't some hard-ass corporate bureaucrat.

Imagine if Chapek took on the woke masses, told Iger publicly to fuck off, and stood up for parents and families. Imagine if he dared his board to fire him if they didn't like his push to de-wokeify Disney. Chapek was becoming a corporate casualty because he did none of that. Picking political fights with people who do politics for a living is dumb; failing to see the righteousness of his new more formidable non-woke opposition might be his dumbest mistake of all.

If you look at a stock chart for the Walt Disney Company for the first half of 2022, you will see lots of red. If you looked more closely you would notice something even more terrible: Disney was one of the worst-performing stocks during the first half in the entire Standard & Poor's index of the market's 500 largest stocks.

It reflected a grim reality for Chapek: Wall Street was pricing in the disaster.

Was it inflation squeezing profit margins? A trip to the happiest place on earth is expensive. Yet Americans were spending a lot of money on a lot of things, so why weren't they spending more of it on Disney?

It's equally plausible that the great corporate conglomerate envisioned by Eisner wasn't working as planned because wokeness permeated its entire being.

Before the end of 2022, Chapek was indeed ousted, despite his new contract. There was some drama around fourth-quarter earnings; Disney's financial and management problems were worse than the board was led to believe by Chapek and his team. His CFO gave a last-minute briefing that revenues were $1 billion lower than anticipated, and well below Wall Street estimates.

Iger was back as CEO, unsurprisingly, and also unsurprisingly, he's facing some of the same issues and pressures that doomed Chapek: a struggling streaming business, not enough theme park attendance to make up for the difference, a wonky stock price, calls to spin off ESPN because of cord-cutting issues, and an American consumer tired of having progressive cultural change shoved in their face.

Plus, some real activist investors, not the woke type, were demanding results.

Nelson Peltz and Dan Loeb, two of the toughest activists in the business, were in the stock and pounding the proverbial table for earnings and an improved share price, even if that meant no more transgender greeters of children at the parks. They wanted Disney to start appealing to preferences of Americans who missed Disney's traditional programming. They wanted a possible sale of ESPN. They wanted the place to start worrying about shareholders instead of stakeholders.

Iger is not only dealing with Loeb and Peltz, but the raging conservative commentators and his non-woke customers, who appear to be the majority.

Disney has become the latest BlackRock, Target, or Budweiser, a corporate punching bag for an energized un-woke America.

Iger is woke, but unlike Chapek, he is also known to be able to read the room. In September 2023 he told shareholders that he's looking to tone down the company's woke agenda, or in his words, "Our primary mission needs to be to entertain…and to have a positive impact on the world. I'm very serious about that. It should not be agenda-driven."

That's right. Go woke, go broke.

CHAPTER ELEVEN

The Biggest Woke Target in the World

"I don't believe any of this transitory inflation garbage," James Gorman told me one night over dinner. We were discussing a spike in consumer prices that the Federal Reserve and the Biden White House brushed off as temporary, or in the lingo of economics, "transitory."

It was the summer of 2021. The Covid lockdowns were largely over. The Biden administration was spending money like crazy and would have spent even more to "stimulate" the economy were it not for Joe Manchin's veto in a 50-50 split Senate. Fed chair Jerome Powell was also printing money premised on the need for "monetary" stimulus a full year after the economic lockdowns had ended and with the economy doing just fine.

Sleepy Joe and Jerome Powell made quite a disastrous duo; both should have stopped spending money months earlier when it was clear the economy was in Covid recovery mode. They didn't, of course. It was one of the biggest economic mistakes in recent history and the American people will be paying the price for years to come through higher inflation that was anything but transitory. Powell finally came to understand the policy error and stopped the monetary printing press. Sleepy Joe on the other hand remained oblivious and kept spending. His latest boondoggle: something called "Inflation Reduction Act."

The name of the $9 trillion blowout was an insult to every man, woman, and transgender person on earth because there was nothing in that pile of pork that would reduce inflation, unless you consider tax credits for EVs as anti-inflationary.

Gorman is easily one of the smartest CEOs on Wall Street because he must be. Morgan Stanley is one of the firms that brings Wall Street to Main Street. As CEO, he serves millions of individual investors through Morgan's brokerage department. That means he and his team need to see through government spin on economic data. Gorman saw the orgy of spending for what it was: an idiotic cure looking for an economic problem that didn't exist. A convenient excuse to further the expansion of government to meet the left's political agenda of endless transfer payments, an EV in every garage, less oil exploration, tons more government spending, and of course, too much money chasing much fewer goods.

"I can guarantee you that inflation is real and it's going to be an issue," I recall him telling me. "This isn't going away."

It didn't and still (as we go to press) hasn't. From early 2022 and through much of 2023, the Fed raised interest rates eleven times and yet inflation remains at stubborn levels. Sure, we're not in a recession, for the moment. But the base interest rate that the Fed controls—known as the federal funds rate—has gone from zero to 5.5 percent. Those moves filter through the banking system; it means borrowing becomes more expensive, people cut back on credit card use, and home prices decline because mortgage rates are too high. The Fed has currently paused the rate hike machinery, but more rate increases are possible even after it starts cutting them to avoid a recession, which is the current plan for 2024. If history is any guide, inflation never dies an easy death.

How did the Fed get this so wrong? One explanation: Our policymakers' knowledge of financial history has been shaped in a pre-ESG environment. Under normal circumstances, you could accurately blame inflation as the by-product of loose monetary policy, plus government spending also infusing the system with too much liquidity and not enough supply to sop it all up. A few rate hikes, a mild recession, and, presto, inflation would normally be vanquished.

But these are anything but normal times; the fiscal and monetary spending experiment was unprecedented; US debt grew to 129 percent of GDP by

2022—a dangerous level of inflation-inducing stimulus. Then came ESG. The folly of needless conservation reduced the supply of goods and services, particularly in the energy sector, and pushed inflation to a whole other level (9 percent at its peak). ESG's imperatives gave energy companies the economic incentive—that is, more people buying their stock—to stop drilling oil, which translated to higher gas prices. ESG was literally demanding that oil companies invest in windmills and renewables just as Russia was about to invade Ukraine and upend the global oil markets.

All this came as the US economy was back open for business, people had stimmy checks ready to spend, and families needed to put food on the table and gas in their tanks.

By December 2021, on the eve of the invasion, a move that would send gas prices soaring here in the United States, ESG was one of the biggest sectors in the US economy when you combine all the asset managers and the various lecherous consultants working the ESG economy. Wall Street was making a lot of money from it, the stock market was booming because of the cheap money hangover courtesy of the Fed, and yet increasingly construction workers and other middle- and lower-class people couldn't afford the basics. ESG provided economic incentives to hire people based not on merit but on color and gender, which is never good for productivity and price stability. ESG incentivized companies to make average shareholders and Americans second-class citizens because they were obligated to serve the "global community" before thinking about profits, losses, and expanding employment. Again, how does that lead to an efficient US economy? Milton Friedman must be rolling in his grave.

Do a little research and you quickly discover that inflation has destabilized societies throughout history. It's essentially a regressive tax that the rich can overcome by speculating in the stock market to make up for their decline in purchasing power (when money and borrowing is cheap, speculators will speculate and drive up stock prices). Working-class people can't do any of that.

Granted, ESG wasn't the sole reason for inflation during the Biden years, but it helped make it increasingly difficult to eradicate using normal policy tools. Let's hope there will be political, economic, and reputational implications for the responsible parties. Joe Biden loves to talk a good game about the headline economic numbers—low unemployment, job creation, a roaring stock market, and so on. They're all doing so well. Superficially, the economy is great. I say superficially because most Americans don't feel that it is. Because of stubbornly high prices for the basics—food, gas, energy—they believe the country is in a dark place.

You can see it in the vitriol displayed on social media, and the anger now being vented at wokeness, and at Biden himself. The president's approval ratings, particularly on the economy, still suck because of inflation even as its rate continues to fall. Dirty little secret: While the *rate* of inflation is coming down, prices are still outrageously elevated. Depending on the poll, Biden is losing to Trump, the same Trump who's been indicted not once, not twice, but five times, and that on top of instigating a violent, treasonous riot. The reason goes beyond the very real possibility that a vote for the feeble Biden for a second term is actually a vote for his deeply regrettable VP, Kamala Harris. It's also because people look back on the Trump years as a time when they could afford taking the family to Applebee's for dinner.

True, Biden, along with the money-printing Jerome Powell, deserves scorn for making inflation the monster that it is. Political forces unleashed by Will Hild and his Consumers' Research attack ads have convinced plenty of people that ESG and Larry Fink deserve a place in this hall of shame as well. In making his case over the past three-plus years, Hild may have stepped over the line more than a little (the billboard trucks stalked Fink even as BlackRock moved its offices to the Hudson Yards on the western edge of midtown Manhattan). It's always dangerous personalizing so much of Fink's role in ESG, or he wouldn't need constant security.

That said, the overreach achieved its crude goals. Larry Fink became the public face of something many Americans despise because they've been convinced it costs them more to live.

As his assault gained momentum, Hild was no longer satisfied with tarring Fink just with ESG; he also began harping on his business in China, and how Fink was kissing up to Public Enemy No. 1 of the right: China's Xi Jinping. ESG depriving Americans of food and energy, while BlackRock splurges in China, or so a new set of Will Hild attack ads began pointing out.

BlackRock does have a small money management business in China. But why let facts get in the way of effective propaganda? By highlighting the connection, Hild knew he would get even more anti-BlackRock traction in red states, where China's military ambitions, use of slave labor, and responsibility for Covid deeply resonate.

He wrote the governors of ten states, both blue and red, people like Ron DeSantis of Florida and Kathy Hochul of New York, to drive this home even further. "Starting today, Consumers' Research, the nation's oldest consumer advocacy organization, will issue a Consumer Warning focused on the world's largest money management firm, BlackRock. The warning is meant to raise awareness among American consumers that BlackRock is taking their money and betting on China. In so doing they are putting American security at risk, along with billions of dollars from U.S. investors, including many state-run pension plans."

Kathy Hochul, a Democrat, wasn't really listening, but Ron DeSantis and Greg Abbott, the governor of Texas, were. So were Henry McMaster, the GOP governor of South Carolina; Jim Justice, the governor of West Virginia; Kevin Stitt of Oklahoma, and Greg Gianforte of Montana. They all had money with BlackRock, lots of it. No longer. Each of these states announced that they were reconsidering their relationship with BlackRock, and in some cases, Fink & co. got the boot altogether. In December 2023, the Tennessee attorney general went even further. He sued BlackRock for misleading "consumers about the scope and effects of its widespread ESG activity" as it "downplayed the extent to which ESG considerations drive its investment strategies across all holdings even in non-ESG funds."

Even mild-mannered Mike Pence decided to join the Fink-bashing fun. The former Trump VP, who defied his old boss and certified Trump's 2020 loss to Biden, was running for president. What better way to appeal to red-blooded red-state voters than to take a shot at BlackRock?

"Activist investors in the private sector are all too happy to play along. In one recent instance, an insurgent shareholder, backed by BlackRock, the world's largest asset manager, forced Exxon Mobil to put three environmentalists on its corporate board," Pence wrote in a *Wall Street Journal* op-ed. "States with large employee pension funds invested in the stock market would be well advised to rein in massive investment firms like BlackRock, State Street and Vanguard, which manage a combined $22 trillion in assets and are pushing a radical ESG agenda."

Pence was referring to what some consider the high point in Fink's ESG strategy. In 2021, BlackRock, along with Vanguard and State Street, used the investment might Pence referred to and pushed on the board of ExxonMobil an activist investor, Engine No. 1. Most so-called activists buy stock, push for board seats, and demand changes to increase share price. Engine No. 1 is a bit different; it also looks to advocate a green agenda on its target companies, including oil companies.

It did so against Exxon management's best efforts, and it would have had no shot unless a bunch of allegedly passive investors came to its rescue. They were essentially forcing the nation's largest oil producer to scale back on doing what it does best: drill for oil.

With that type of support, Engine No. 1 got three seats on the Exxon board, almost unheard of in the activist investment realm. Fink even took a victory lap; that year he used the word "climate" twenty-one times in his CEO letter. He said he was "concerned about Exxon's strategic direction," and that it needed board members like the people Engine No. 1 added with "diverse energy experience to augment existing skillsets." Engine No. 1 would make sure Exxon knew Larry Fink was constantly looking over its shoulder.

The Engine No. 1 gambit underscored BlackRock's strength to "force change." The *New York Times*, one of Fink's go-to reads, said the firm "wouldn't have had a chance were it not for an unusual twist: the support of some of Exxon's biggest institutional investors...Climate activists declared a major triumph, and a blindsided Exxon was left to ponder its defeat."

The high didn't last, however. By 2022, Hild had thoroughly achieved his goal of making Fink the biggest woke target in the world. And aside from the stinging agitprop, he was mostly using Fink's own words against him.

All those years where Fink wouldn't stop yapping about the benefits of ESG, or doing business with China and other progressive corporate mandates, left an enormous woke paper trail. Hild had tons of material to work with, and he relished doing so. He placed more of his signature mobile billboards strategically throughout the country. One replicated a hundred-dollar bill and Benjamin Franklin's likeness colored red, stating, "BlackRock: Taking Your Money and Betting on China." Fink's head shot was placed on another, also colored in red. Still another depicted him, in a black suit, towering over a miniature cartoon of Uncle Sam. He was holding a wad of cash, waving it in his face. In the background appeared the faces of a smiling Xi Jinping and Vladimir Putin.

These were all Will Hild "specials," and they continued to drive Fink crazy. "I've never met Putin; I've never been to Russia," Fink fumed. "I have a tiny business in China," he snapped.

All true, but those facts were no match for Hild's interpretation of them—and the spin was catching on. The *Wall Street Journal*'s editorial page had long criticized Fink's role as an ESG apostle, stoking inflation and woke corporate policies through investing. Now those critiques could be found on straight-news pages.

Fink and his inner circle were facing up to a grim reality: ESG used to be something to brag about and a moneymaker, but it was becoming a PR nightmare and costing the company money. Years earlier, Fink had taken red-state pension funds, and the politics of their fiduciaries, for granted; he went all in on ESG because the big pension money was woke in lefty California, New York and Europe. He now discovered just how much the recent economic growth of the more conservative South and Midwest had caused their pension assets to explode—people were leaving the progressive hellscapes in New York and California for lower taxes and law and order in Florida and Texas. As much as $5 billion in such assets from these places disappeared from BlackRock's books in less than a year.

"Did Larry go too far in pushing ESG and corporate progressivism over the years?" I asked one BlackRock PR official in the middle of Hild's campaign. "Don't get me started," was his answer.

As the pressure built on BlackRock in 2022, and into 2023, Fink initially showed defiance. "I'm the same turd I've always been," he said with a slight laugh one afternoon as he discussed his growing PR problem. He also wanted me to know he's not a zealot on sustainability. "We are fiduciaries for clients of all types who pay us for this stuff. You want a portfolio of sin stocks; we will get you one.

"Check my speeches and letters," he added. I did, and found one from 2021, the same year BlackRock was supposedly all in on ESG. It does in fact read like it was written by a political moderate. "A successful transition—one that is just, equitable, and protects people's livelihoods—will require both technological innovation and planning over decades," Fink wrote. "And it can only be accomplished with leadership, coordination, and support at every level of government, working in partnership with the private sector to maximize prosperity."

Fink also reminds me that he famously railed against Modern Monetary Theory, an economic model infused with some of the most zealous ESG attributes and touted as gospel by leftists Elizabeth Warren, Bernie Sanders, Alexandria Ocasio-Cortez, and others. It postulates one of the least historically accurate accounts of monetary policy, namely that governments will face no consequences spending whatever they need to keep the welfare state up and running.

Fink has called it "garbage."

All true, but it was no match for Hild's exposé of Fink's virtue signaling. Fink was at the pinnacle of high finance for so many years that his words do matter, of course. Which is why his miscalculation on ESG messaging continues to haunt him to this day. Fink's PR handlers desperately tried to stop the bleeding as Hild's assaults continued to generate copy for reporters, and more assets to flee from BlackRock. They began frantically calling contacts in the business media to plead a type of revisionist history that is hard to sell even to journalists, like me, who like Fink and respect most of what he's done in his long career. "There are funds worse than BlackRock on ESG!...BlackRock owns billions in oil company stocks!...There are companies—Tesla and Apple—doing more business with China than BlackRock!...Vanguard does ESG!" they argued.

BlackRock is part of the Net Zero Asset Managers initiative, a group of asset managers that vowed to use ESG to push the country to reach net-zero carbon emissions by 2050. There are bigger lefties on Wall Street than Larry Fink. Until recently Elon Musk was one, and he still does a lot more business with China, and he receives a hell of a lot more government EV subsidies to produce green electric cars that aren't so green. Apple doesn't need such corporate welfare, but its headquarters might as well be in China; about 40 percent of its production capabilities reside there.

Fink's flacks couldn't change some pretty woke facts. Vanguard quit the Net Zero Asset Managers in late 2022, amid the growing ESG uproar that spread beyond red-state politicians to include average investors who didn't like their money being used for a political cause that produced lower returns.

Apple CEO Tim Cook keeps his politicking to a minimum. Sure, Musk does business in China where some Tesla factories operate. He has also become a hero to the right, having vocally attacked the progressive movement and its warped ideological bias that permeates culture and business. He spent $44 billion of his own money to buy the social media platform Twitter, renamed it "X," and began un-cancelling right-wing voices.

Fink's allegiance to ESG and its progressive urges is still hot and fresh. Most of the red-state officials angered about ESG don't even know the name of Vanguard's quietly woke CEO; yet they know Larry Fink.

With the 2024 presidential election approaching, could Larry Fink himself be a political issue? ESG hatred might even resonate with independents who also had grown tired of corporate leftism that was being woven into Fink's image.

Increasingly it had become a tough time to be Larry Fink. The pressure from the right was obvious, but then came pressure from the left, which never quite liked the fact that a Wall Street fat cat was stealing its thunder on the climate issue and making a lot of money doing so.

"Brad, I can't do that," Fink pleaded one afternoon, during a tense telephone conversation with Brad Lander, New York City's comptroller, an elected official who serves as the city's de facto chief financial officer. Lander is a former community organizer from Missouri, who somehow became a Big Apple politician. As comptroller, he's supposed to be the guy who makes sure NYC's bills are paid, its pension obligations met. Given the size of the city's retired workforce, and the exodus of taxpayers to the tax-friendlier confines of Florida, you would think any convo with Fink would be to figure out a way to keep money flowing to the pensions of all those retired cops and firefighters. Fink is, after all, very good at understanding markets.

Lander had other things on his mind. He wanted BlackRock to begin phasing out what the left calls "high-emitting assets" from its portfolios of oil and gas stocks.

Embracing wokeness in corporate affairs is risky business, as Fink is discovering. You anger red-state pols, but no amount of corporate virtue signaling will satisfy the woke lust of progressive looney toons like Lander or Elizabeth Warren and her gang. Fink can afford to ignore Warren a little; she's just a politician, one of a hundred in the Senate. Her oversight of his business is basically thirty thousand feet.

Not so with Lander, who plays a leading role in managing more than $20 trillion in pension money. Fink's firm manages some of it and gets paid handsomely to do so. That means he can't just hang up the phone on this raging idiot. Instead, he tried to talk some reason. BlackRock holds $260 billion in energy stocks. If Fink sold everything, it would crash the stock market, possibly the global economy. Gas prices would certainly soar; inflation would skyrocket even more. In NYC, Lander's working-class teachers, bus drivers, cops, and firemen would feel immediate pain for some possible—not guaranteed—environmental benefits given the mixed science on the subject.

Plus, what he was asking was kind of impractical. New York can't dictate the portfolio we manage for Texas, I am told Fink shot back as Lander kept pushing his grandiose visions of windmills and waterfalls supplying all the world's energy needs. (Fink would not confirm this conversation; Lander didn't dispute its substance.)

Suffice to say, "Brad" wasn't impressed or convinced, my sources tell me. Radical ideologues don't respond well to common sense.

One day it was Lander taking his shots at Fink; the next it was DeSantis or some dude from Tennessee he had never heard of. Fink had become a bipartisan punching bag. Even George Soros took a swing at him, criticizing BlackRock's business interests in China. In an editorial featured on the pages of the right-leaning *Wall Street Journal* opinion page, the lefty investor turned activist said BlackRock's work in the mainland to offer money management services to millions of Chinese was potentially damaging to "the national security interests of the U.S. and other democracies."

The attacks got to the point that Fink held a company-wide Town Hall to explain why his employees were reading about BlackRock so much. "We're hated by both sides...In the middle is where we want to be."

His public posturing, however, masked his true moods, which started shifting from furious to melancholy, people who know Fink tell me. Presented with a positive mention in the media, he lamented, "I certainly suck less." When he saw coverage of the Consumers' Research propaganda, he exploded. "This is so un-American!"

Fink desperately sought allies. There would be pushback in states boycotting BlackRock from moderates; teachers' unions, among others, liked BlackRock and ESG. "The unions will hate what these guys are doing, and they will fight back," Fink told his people. The pushback never came, at least not with any degree of significance.

There was proverbial blood in the water, and conservative advocacy groups, their fellow travelers in politics and the media, circled like sharks. The *Washington Post* reported that Consumers' Research had some Fink-bashing support from a group called the American Legislative Exchange Council.

"Just after Thanksgiving, dozens of state lawmakers packed into a hotel ballroom in downtown Washington to plan their next assault on a movement that pushes companies to confront global warming and social injustice," the *Post* reported. The article quoted an anonymous speaker at the event: "Every big problem needs a face and a name. The worst offender out there is BlackRock and Larry Fink."

That speaker, my reporting confirms, was Will Hild.

Fink at seventy was planning for retirement in a few years and dreaded ending his career this way. As much as they tried, his flacks couldn't change the perception that Fink was Mr. ESG. Again, Fink would say he was merely responding to demand; investors and pension funds, here and abroad, wanted their portfolio companies to be diverse, carbon neutral, or at least planning to get there someday. The planet is worth saving.

Okay, but plenty of people also hate corporate wokeness, and for better or worse, ESG was now his baby. He owned it and the trouble it now brought because for far too long, that's all he seemed to be talking about. The firm wasn't in the red (it earned nearly $6 billion in 2022), but AUM was off 15 percent that year, falling from $10 trillion to $8.5 trillion. Some of it was the result of a declining stock market, inflation-induced market volatility. But the stench of ESG also turned off many customers.

Traders appeared to be pricing in something bad. Shares of BlackRock topped out at $955 in November 2021. They fell 37 percent to around $600 by the fall of 2023, while the S&P declined just 9 percent. The company kicked off the New Year in 2024 with layoffs, after seeing its assets under management decline more than $1 trillion during the height of the ESG backlash.

The hits just kept coming. Fink and Blackstone founder Steve Schwarzman were once business partners, friends, and now, quietly, rivals. People who know them tell me they have personally kept score on who is doing better ever since the time Fink bought out Schwarzman's share of his business thirty years earlier. In a moment of weakness, Schwarzman famously stated the biggest mistake he had made was letting Fink leave Blackstone to start BlackRock, given the enormous power the firm has accumulated.

Now, with the redolence of ESG all over BlackRock, that power seemed to be in retreat with investors. By early 2023, Blackstone's stock value easily surpassed BlackRock's by tens of billions of dollars.

That's when BlackRock's senior management, board, and Fink himself made the decision to move away from ESG both in practice and in messaging. First came the spin on BlackRock's business model. "We don't make people do anything. We invest," Fink began telling people. Then came an attempt to cancel the term "ESG" from the vocabulary of every BlackRock employee. ESG had become so toxic that Fink said you wouldn't ever hear the letters come out of his mouth again.

"You can say it," he tells me during one of our chats, "but I won't anymore."

The firm's one-eighty on ESG continued with its Washington, DC, lobbying department bringing on board GOP types, even some who worked for the Trump administration and its former SEC chair, Jay Clayton.

Republicans working at BlackRock—what a concept!

It was a corporate necessity now. The Senate remained in Dem control, but Republicans took the House after the 2022 midterms. Right-wingers saw how DeSantis used ESG-bashing to score political points and easily win reelection, so why shouldn't they? That meant ESG hearings could be coming, featuring Larry Fink as the star witness. Yikes! Fink dreaded the thought of being cross-examined as so many CEOs were in the aftermath of the financial crisis, straining and sweating to give answers in front of cameras that would make him look far worse than any Will Hild billboard.

Next, the firm-wide edict to consider ESG in all investment decisions was amended. It would be used for European clients where the demand remained strong, preserved for blue-state US pension fund officials who wanted it, and sustainable funds. But in the United States, PMs and analysts could just do what they were trained to do and invest without obsessing about DEI scores and carbon footprints in managing most BlackRock portfolios.

"ESG is essentially window dressing now," a BlackRock portfolio manager told a top Wall Street broker who sold the companies funds. "If you're not managing a sustainable fund, you're not using it."

BlackRock also wanted to make sure to tell the public that it really loved America. It wasn't some sort of Maoist front operation depriving them of gasoline or forcing DEI standards that hurt working-class, binary white men. During its forty years in business, BlackRock didn't do much TV advertising; it really didn't need to because BlackRock products sold seamlessly through brokers. That was before its brand had been hijacked by what Fink called "the radical right."

Beginning in mid-2022, BlackRock unveiled the "About BlackRock" ad campaign to get some of those right-wingers to back off. One ad featured real firemen (finally an ad where all the actors are real dudes) extolling the virtues of hard work and financial planning. Very American! Another BlackRock ad could have been produced by a GOP political operative: lots of construction and factory workers, more real dudes on Harleys, real women in the kitchen, and the actors didn't appear to meet DEI standards.

"From the plains to the coasts, we help Americans invest in the future… BlackRock."

Oh, and by the way, not a windmill in sight!

The PR staff at BlackRock would tell you monitoring Fink is a singularly impossible effort. He's the boss, and he loves to talk and talk and talk (far too much, they would say in moments of candor), whether it's at conferences or with the media. He still does some—Fink made an appearance at the COP28 climate summit in Dubai in 2023, an occasional appearance on financial TV. But clearly, he was now receding a bit into the background. His client letters were now less preachy, not a lot of chest-pounding about changing the world.

New voices then began channeling BlackRock's less woke messaging. Suddenly, BlackRock's share price has been improving; assets began returning as it moved away from ESG messaging. AUM is back at $10 trillion as ESG began to recede as a company talking point. Fink also did his part to change the subject from ESG. Once a skeptic of the burgeoning crypto business, he pushed for the adoption of a Bitcoin ETF, and became an emerging hero to crypto lovers.

It wasn't all smooth sailing, thanks to Hild. The task of this re-messaging BlackRock fell in part to Rob Kapito, Fink's longtime No. 2. He was considered a perfect choice because he had almost no progressive political footprint.

In a 2022 speech he opined on how Millennials and Gen-Zers are so pampered they may not be able to handle inflation like the Boomers did back in the 1970s. "For the first time, this generation is going to go into a store and not be able to get what they want…And we have a very entitled generation that has never had to sacrifice."

He began targeting the oil and gas industry in meetings and at conferences, to make sure they knew BlackRock was on their side. His underlying message: BlackRock really wanted them to drill, baby, drill. Amid the changing tone, climate activists were targeting BlackRock and Kapito at industry conferences. Right before one event, Hild heard through his sources that Kapito was speaking at an oil and gas conference in Austin, Texas, and made sure Kapito was greeted on arrival with those zany billboards asking: "Who Is Larry Fink?"

At least it wasn't Kapito's face on the billboard, he must have thought (he declined comment).

Kapito is on the short list to replace Fink as CEO when he retires in the next few years, possibly sooner rather than later given the pressure Fink is under. So is a man named Mark Wiedman, who runs BlackRock's so-called client business—the very important function of trying to get the company's funds into the hands of more consumers.

He too joined the media tour. In October 2023, speaking at a conference sponsored by the media company Semafor, Wiedman showed just how difficult it was for BlackRock to put the ESG genie back in the bottle when he was asked by conference moderator Liz Hoffman about the unrelenting conservative attacks on BlackRock and how ESG is now something of a controversial subject.

Wiedman said ESG is a "capitalist impulse…a demand from clients." Really? Pushing DEI and racial hiring quotas and sustainability seems about as capitalist as Joseph Stalin. Wiedman then said something he probably wished he hadn't. BlackRock's problem, he suggested, could be traced to *someone* talking too much about ESG. He didn't mention who that someone was and he didn't have to; everyone in the audience knew why BlackRock was persona non grata in red-state America.

"Speak softly and invest money," Wiedman said. "We don't need as much talk, so we've been a little quieter because actually, that's what our clients are looking for."

As word of Wiedman's dig at Fink made its way back to BlackRock's offices, the consensus was that Wiedman had just talked himself out of CEO competition.

CHAPTER TWELVE

Woke Is Finally Broken

I want you to know that there is no bias at Twitter; we are open to all points of view," Jack Dorsey explained to a group of right-leaning and skeptical journalists one night in May 2018. The hastily arranged meeting took place at the Norwood Club's townhouse in lower Manhattan. It's a discreet venue in the fashionable Chelsea neighborhood that caters to an artsy crowd, perfect for someone like Dorsey, who despite running one of the most important tech companies, mostly shuns the limelight and is known for his devotion to meditation. The email invitation was equally discreet. It said Jack had asked the attendee to show up at 8 p.m. sharp "to discuss social media, Twitter and anything else on your mind with him." No other details were provided, including why the king of all media wanted to hear from a bunch of ink-stained wretches he has almost nothing in common with.

Twitter was, of course, the ubiquitous and, back then, woke social media site. Dorsey was its cofounder and now CEO. The company had gone public about five years earlier, with shares trading as high as around $70, and a valuation of around $60 billion. Dorsey had become a billionaire and a modern-day Henry Luce since the platform has two hundred million active daily users—many more readers than *Time* ever had.

Yet Dorsey and Twitter couldn't figure out a way to consistently make money and investors were losing their patience. Bots and fake users flourished on Twitter, and they are hard to monetize. So is political bias. Plenty of conservative politicians, opinion makers, and journalists—as it turned out, rightfully—believed the company had been systematically silencing them. There were calls for boycotts; the need to create Twitter alternatives. In Congress, an effort was under way to end social media's quirky regulatory status. Politicians on the left and the right started to agree that Twitter should be run more like a public utility.

That regulatory quirk I mentioned involves something known as Section 230 of the Communications Act, a law that shields social media platforms from lawsuits for publishing problematic content on their sites. It's a big deal to get that shield. Conventional news organizations can get sued for libel on their pages; Twitter can't. It was granted because lawmakers envisioned social media as the ultimate free-expression venue. Its alleged open architecture is designed to allow all voices and opinions to be heard.

I say "alleged" because the reality was far different. Twitter employs teams of content moderators to sift through postings that may violate its so-called terms of service. Some violations are obvious: threats of violence, rape, and calls to commit blatant illegality—though a lot falls through the cracks or Twitter wouldn't be such a cesspool of outrage and hate. What doesn't get a pass: conservative opinions that were almost always swept up in the moderators' desire to make Twitter a safer and, as it turns out, more woke space.

Right-wingers in Congress who weren't on Twitter's campaign contribution gift list (for obvious reasons) were talking about revoking all its Section 230 privileges. Given Twitter's tenuous finances, such a move would make its insolvency a foregone conclusion since snark and vitriol bordering on slander is how it attracted users and of course advertisers.

That's why Dorsey needed to get the word out to conservative media types that Twitter was a force for good, not censorship.

Dorsey had a tough sell that night. A few weeks earlier he had retweeted an article from left-leaning political consultants saying that the Democratic Party should forget about bipartisanship and do whatever it could to defeat the Trump-led GOP. Dorsey labeled it a "great read." The conservative blogosphere lit up, as did a few right-of-center Twitter employees who said he was creating a hostile work environment by being so partisan.

I am told that experience and the growing right-wing discontent in Congress was enough for Dorsey to come out of his man cave and start meeting with conservative opinion makers, first in DC and then New York. It was an awkward experience; Dorsey seemed friendly enough, but he also seemed clueless to even the basics of the conservative movement. He was in his early forties at the time, had attended New York University—not exactly an ashram—but he appeared stumped that night in New York when someone brought up the name William F. Buckley, the father of modern conservatism.

After some blank stares, one by one the attendees began counting the ways Twitter engages in overt and dangerous left-wing bias. The group told him that conservative voices were being "shadow banned," or throttled, while left-wingers can say almost anything. Dorsey politely contended that no such efforts were taking place. It would make no sense from a business standpoint to do so; Twitter ad rates are contingent on user growth and engagement. The more the merrier for everyone.

Again, Dorsey seemed honest and forthcoming. I'll be generous and say he was clueless to the politicization of thought inside his company. Proof came about four years later, on October 27, 2022, to be exact, when Twitter changed hands, changed its name, and the left-wing bias of the platform was exposed like a festering sore by Elon Musk.

Musk is the volatile but brilliant CEO of electric carmaker Tesla. He was also the world's richest man, worth more than $200 billion, and just used a chunk of his enormous wealth to purchase Twitter, and promptly renamed it "X." His mission: to remove the platform's wokeness and transform it into a real "digital town square."

Of course, nothing is ever easy with "Crazy Elon." It was a wild ride from Musk's announced "best and final" offer of $44 billion to buy Twitter in April of that year to the scene months later walking through the front door of the company's San Francisco headquarters holding a sink. Ever the showman, Musk filmed his grand entrance, posting the spectacle on his own feed with the caption "Let that sink in."

The statement underscored the tense and fraught negotiations between Twitter and Musk leading up to his arrival that day—and his plans to remake the place against the wishes of most of the company's woke employees. Dorsey had since retired from day-to-day management. The new CEO, Parag Agrawal, initially rebuffed Musk's overtures, and not because the money wasn't good. Musk in recent years was a far different political animal from the guy running Tesla to clean up the environment. He had become somewhat conservative and definitely not woke. He railed against the progressivism of the Democratic Party, its obsession with race and gender, its stifling of free speech.

He often targeted Twitter in his assaults of leftism in popular culture, the media, and business, venting obsessively on Twitter about Twitter's role in it. He believed, like many conservatives, that the platform was cancelling, sometimes quietly and sometimes not (in the case of Donald Trump, and Covid-vax skeptic Alex Berenson), voices dissenting from progressive orthodoxy.

But he had money, and he was willing to do what others wouldn't and pay top dollar for this POS of a business. Agrawal's initial inclination to reject Musk's money and preserve Twitter's woke business model was quickly overruled by his bankers at JP Morgan, and his major shareholders, who finally saw a big payday for holding the stock, my sources at the bank tell me. They said he had a fiduciary responsibility to ignore Musk's wonky politics but not his money. Musk was widely overpaying for something that could soon be worth closer to $4 billion. There was no better deal in the wings. Twitter had no choice but to take the offer, and if Musk tried to weasel out, Agrawal needed to sue him.

Which Musk did, not long after signing on the dotted line when he realized the truly fucked condition of Twitter's balance sheet. Musk, if you know his management style, isn't a conventional CEO—that's why he's known as "Crazy Elon" by bankers who cover him. At Tesla, he has no chain of command; he thumbs his nose at his board and has no problem telling the SEC to fuck off, which he has done repeatedly after the commission tried to force him to stop tweeting after he posted fake news about taking the EV maker private that moved Tesla shares. He manages by instinct, and that instinct told him to buy Twitter and then try to get out of the deal when he saw how the thing is a money sinkhole.

The SEC largely gives Musk a get-out-of-jail free card because they're afraid banning him as CEO would rattle the markets. At one point Tesla had the market value of the next seven of the biggest automakers combined. It's in every index and every stock portfolio. Who wants to be responsible for the decimation of 401(k)s across the planet?

Twitter isn't Tesla, however, and the Delaware Court of Chancery isn't the SEC. It's the place where business disputes of this nature have been adjudicated for decades, mostly without fear or favor. After Twitter had sued Musk in Chancery, the judge made it clear she didn't care for Musk's antics. He was about to be called to testify, to explain the meaning of his last and final offer, and why for such a smart guy he didn't do his homework before signing the deal papers. That's when Musk finally became a conventional CEO, for a moment, and paid the money.

Give Musk credit. Sure, he engaged in horrible dealmaking, but he did keep his word on stripping the woke from Twitter—and its name. He fired Agrawal and most of the company's woke workforce. He re-platformed conservatives banned for various reasons, including questioning Covid. He reinstated Donald Trump's account, suspended since the January 6 riot.

He then released what he called "The Twitter Files."

Musk commissioned a handful of non-woke journalists to sift through Twitter emails surrounding major and controversial events: Covid, the *New York Post*'s Hunter Biden laptop story, the 2020 election, the January 6 Capitol Hill riot. Their goal: Disclose to the world the lefty bias of one of the world's most important receptacles of information and opinion.

Silicon Valley, the epicenter of alleged anti-establishment wealth, was quite establishment, the Twitter Files showed. Twitter had conspired with various levels of government to stifle speech of any kind that somehow deviated from establishment thought on Covid, banning journalists and academics who said vaccines were suspect and the lockdowns foolish.

Twitter was also playing footsie with the FBI and other governmental bodies investigating the 2020 election because the feds were obsessed with the idea that Russian disinformation was being used to elect Donald Trump once again. There wasn't much evidence that the Russians were successful at electing Trump president in 2016, but the FBI didn't care; it was monitoring Twitter with the help of management, proceeding as if Putin himself was mean-tweeting stuff about Sleepy Joe from his many troll accounts. Because of pressure from the feds, the Hunter Biden laptop story was initially banned from the platform, the Twitter Files showed.

Woke stakeholder capitalism at work and exposed by the onetime woke CEO of an EV maker was poetic justice. Musk for all his craziness showed brilliantly how Twitter's management was taking orders not from shareholders, who held stock in a company that was perpetually losing money, but from "stakeholders" known as government bureaucrats and the progressive left to shape opinion.

But that might be changing.

You might say what we are experiencing because of Musk and others is a great unwoke awakening. Twitter might still resemble a cesspool of snark and trolling, but it is no longer a place of right-wing censorship. Boycotts of lefty brands—Budweiser, Target, Disney, BlackRock—all find resonance on the platform now known as "X," and woke is breaking. Even better, across corporate America, finally, many of the elites that supported wokeism for so long have woken up and realized the monster they created.

They're cutting off endowment funding for the elite colleges they graduated from because wokeness resulted in antisemitism both tolerated and celebrated on campus. As we will soon discuss, Budweiser is trying to go unwoke in its messaging. BlackRock is running from ESG. Disney says it's deemphasizing politics.

It's finally dawned on our corporate masters that they're not our masters; American workers don't see the benefits of ESG; they see inflation. They're tired of being called racists in corporate diversity training sessions and are letting their supervisors know about it. They're suing their employers because aspects of progressive boardroom behavior are clearly illegal. After a recent SCOTUS ruling outlawing affirmative action in college admissions, many companies suddenly realized their diversity mandates resulted in illegal quotas.

The American people are embracing unwoke entertainment. The most popular comedians—Bill Burr, Dave Chappelle, Joe Rogan, Whitney Cummings—are unwoke and proud of it; they fill arenas bashing the progressive norms with humor. Consider: Spotify stood by Rogan when the left attacked him for being skeptical of Covid vaccines. Chappelle's Netflix comedy special *The Closer* was deemed transphobic because he made a few jokes about this protected class. A "team trans" employee walkout ensued to get Netflix to deplatform Chappelle. Unlike Disney's Bob Chapek, who caved to wokesters, the people running Netflix, its co-CEO Ted Sarandos, didn't buckle in the face of the mob. He called Chappelle's jokes "artistic expression." The crisis passed because customers were happy with the unwoke outcome.

A new unwoke coalition is forming: Middle America and increasingly some rich and powerful business elites. Some of the business types are doing it out of necessity, of course. Go woke, go broke is more than the title of this book; it's a business reality.

"Well, we woke up a lot of corporate executives to the fact that they don't have to do what Disney did. They don't have to do what Budweiser did. Budweiser and Disney did corporate America a big favor, because they just showed how stupid all this woke stuff was."

In late 2023, Ed Rensi was giving me a status report on his effort to end corporate wokeness and doing a victory lap at the same time. It was Rensi, the former CEO of McDonald's USA, who witnessed and recoiled from the wokeness at Disney and the rest of corporate America, and how it was rotting the soul of capitalism. He decided to fight back, with an assist from Bernie Marcus of Home Depot fame, and Marcus's Job Creators Network.

Rensi started an offshoot organization called the Boardroom Initiative and spent about three years alerting CEOs that woke boardroom behavior should be anathema; using shareholder money to support left-wing politics was immoral, probably illegal, and definitely idiotic, because they would be pissing off most of their customers.

When Rensi officially began his counteroffensive in April 2022 with an appearance on Fox Business, no one gave him much of a chance. Somehow, his nascent effort gained traction. A big assist came via the genius of Alfredo Ortiz, a longtime marketing executive who is the president of the Job Creators Network. It was Ortiz's idea to start the initiative, with Rensi at the helm. Ortiz has a particularly sharp eye for catchy billboard ads that mock left-wing excess. His latest campaign was dubbed "Rock the Woke," and he envisioned a billboard in Times Square displaying the Disney mascot Mickey Mouse in some unflattering way. There was just one problem, Ortiz was told when he had his legal team investigate the matter; Disney had copyrighted nearly all the body parts of the world's most famous rodent.

Except one. Mickey's rear end.

"Perfect," Ortiz snapped. The billboard would show Mickey's ass being kicked by a woman's black high heel with the words "No Mouse in My House" displayed in the background.

The ad ran in June 2022, and Rensi was off and running even if the woke headwinds were still strong. The Summer of Love hadn't quite faded. CEOs were still hugging it out, though not so obviously, with the left's version of America as a thoroughly racist, damaged and in need of radical change nation of bigots. The challenge to the Florida law for depriving minors of lessons in gender fluidity was still seen as a corporate necessity at Disney, albeit a quieter one. Executives were still explaining why they had to oppose the Georgia voting law as racist, but less so when Black voter turnout surged in its aftermath.

Diversity training to rid employees of racist thoughts remained in force, though HR managers were now reevaluating the extent. A new documentary began making the rounds. *The Fall of Minneapolis* provided evidence that George Floyd's murder might not have been one. Derek Chauvin, the police officer in a federal penitentiary for the next two decades, might not have had his knee on Floyd's neck; the film depicted Floyd as a drugged-up ex-con who doesn't deserve his lofty status in the civil rights movement.

So compelling was the film's message that Black scholars Glenn Loury and John McWhorter are now skeptical that Chauvin got a fair trial and Floyd was deserving of sainthood.

Can we now get Jamie Dimon, Brian Moynihan, and David Solomon to reassess their views on "Saint George" (hat tip for the name to the great Gerald Baker), and apologize to the country for joining the left in their past gaslighting of America as a racist hellhole during our Summer of Love?

Doubtful. But change is in the air. Corporate America may have lost its mind after Floyd's death. Thank God that the rest of the country didn't. The man who pushed the Georgia voting legislation through the state's legislature, Governor Brian Kemp, easily won a second term against his longtime nemesis, Stacey Abrams, the left-wing political activist. Abrams's career appears in tatters these days and she's getting what she deserves. A case can be made that she took food out of the mouths of Black-owned businesspeople in Atlanta by making the political environment so toxic that MLB was forced to move the All-Star Game in 2021 out of the city to somewhere less volatile.

Here's the good news for *all* of Atlanta's business community: The 2025 All-Star Game is heading back to Atlanta without a peep from the left.

Rensi was also noticing something else that made him smile from ear to ear: Increasingly he was preaching to the converted. C-suiters who for so long embraced the left were running in the opposite direction. "This stuff is just so bad for society and business," Rensi said his CEO pals came to realize.

Even the clueless execs behind the infamous Dylan Mulvaney Bud Light commercials began seeing the light.

"It was only one social media spot and we're much bigger than just one brand," Cesar Vargas, AB InBev's chief of government affairs, sheepishly explained to a group of reporters one morning in late September 2023.

Vargas was accompanied by the company's outside PR team, Mercury Public Affairs. It was one of several meetings Vargas was doing with the media to get reporters to change the subject from his marketing nightmare and show that AB InBev is a real business, not a woke arm of the Democratic Party, sources tell me. During the powwow, I am told that Vargas never mentioned the name Dylan Mulvaney once, or terms like DEI, ESG, or any of the corporate mind fucks that led to a transwoman joining team Budweiser. He spoke about the size and scale of AB InBev's businesses. Also, how the company really cares about its customers, even those "fratty" real male types.

It's time to move on, he said.

Good luck with that. In late 2023, a marketing and branding company called Publishers Clearinghouse Consumer Insights surveyed five thousand people and came up with the following bad news for Bud. First, "54 percent of all beer drinking Americans are aware of the Mulvaney campaign." Not a great sign if you're trying to get people to forget about Dylan Mulvaney. Even worse for AB InBev, the group's research shows Budweiser has lost nearly half its customer base.

Yes, stuff not easy to move on from. Which is why more than a year after Dylan Mulvaney, AB InBev is still being asked the same questions: Why did the company think it was smart to attach a beer brand to a transwoman? How is the company planning to dig itself out from the branding disaster? How long before your customers return? When will you simply apologize?

I am told Vargas and other AB InBev executives still don't have good answers—and still have offered no apology—just platitudes that attempt to downplay the entire sordid affair that can't really be downplayed. The cold, hard facts showed that Bud's adventures in wokeness were a disaster. Its share price remains flat; it would be lower without plans for a buyback. Bud Light sales remain weak. No surprise that an overcorrection in its marketing efforts is in the works. Anheuser-Busch in late 2023 inked a $125 million branding partnership with some decidedly macho people, namely Dana White and his mixed martial arts sports platform, UFC, to repair Bud's relationship with its still pissed customer base.

The deal was costly and underscores the broke nature of going woke. Anheuser-Busch CEO Brendan Whitworth had to pay White about five times more than the people who own the beer Modelo did for the same cross-branding deal, marketing sources tell me. And to show those customers that this isn't Dylan Mulvaney's beer company anymore, Whitworth agreed that part of the promotion is for Anheuser-Busch to sponsor something really, totally non-woke (some might say insane): a new competition called "Power Slap," where men literally slap one another in the face until one can't take it anymore or gets knocked out.

No joke. One dude stands with his hands behind his back, while the other full-on slaps him. Then it is the other guy's turn. Not sure how that squares with Alissa Heinerscheid's stated game plan to transform Bud's brand to something "truly inclusive," but as I've reported, she's no longer running Bud Light's marketing.[1]

Will stuff like mixed martial arts and Power Slap work for Bud? The geniuses at AB InBev better hope so. US beer sales fell 13.5 percent in the quarter ending in September 2023, nearly six months after the world could not unsee Mulvaney giggling in a bubble bath while sipping from a can of Bud Light. Adding insult to injury, rival Modelo has become the nation's No. 1 beer.

In November 2023, Whitworth was seen at a UFC fight groveling to Kid Rock, possibly to get him to say something nice after literally blowing up Bud Light's brand on his Instagram page back in April. He did, sort of. In a

---

1. AB InBev CEO Doukeris and Whitworth declined to speak directly to me, though I've reviewed material with press reps. I've tried to reach out to Heinerscheid, and she hasn't returned my calls. I have asked AB InBev's media team to share with her the same book material I shared with them and provide me with a contact for her lawyer because they had made her the scapegoat for the Mulvaney fuckup, and they have declined. Another low for corporate wokeness.

December 2023 interview with journalist Tucker Carlson, Rock stated, "Bud Light deserved a black eye, and they got one...Do I want to hold their head underwater and drown them because they made a mistake? No, I think they got the message."

Or maybe not. Year-over-year sales for Bud Light are down 30 percent for the final weeks of January 2024, showing the brand damage continues, and still no apology for Dylan Mulvaney. For the 2024 Super Bowl, Anheuser-Busch splurged, spending another $21 million on ads featuring the Clydesdales, macho dudes, old mascots, and new influencers (Dana White) who aren't Dylan Mulvaney.

Memo to Brendan Whitworth: An apology for mixing wokeism with beer would be a lot cheaper and probably more effective in repairing the brand damage than expensive ad spends and Power Slap deals.

Like the people who run Bud, the folks at Disney aren't too keen on explaining their adventures in wokeness, and the brand damage that ensued. Both the new CEO, Bob Iger, and the old one, Bob Chapek, declined requests to sit down with me.

Iger is the man who made Disney the woke monstrosity it has become. Fitting that he is grappling with the same type of anti-woke consumer backlash that is crushing companies like Target, Budweiser, BlackRock, and a lot more.

Wokeness is so bad for business that Disney has been forced to admit as much. In a November 2023 "10-K" filing to investors, the company disclosed that its progressive stances are taking a chunk out of its bottom line because "consumer perception of our position on matters of public interest, including our efforts to achieve our environmental and social goals, often differ widely and present risks to our reputation and brands."

It must be scary for Iger and his team to concede how their adherence to some of the zaniest far-left cultural principles is destroying a once great household name. It's one reason why Iger, in his second tour of duty, is having second thoughts about how progressivism has progressed at Disney with each movie flop, and about his stuttering attempts to sell woke programming on its streaming channel.

People who know Iger say the backlash to the company's wokeness is jarring. Disney used to receive accolades for going left at its parks and movies. No longer. It's the reason Iger in late 2023 announced that he wants to take the politics out of Disney's programming and theme parks. In March 2024 he abruptly settled with Ron DeSantis and is no longer fighting the governor's plan to place the Reedy Creek district where Disney operates largely in state hands. I don't remember the last time Disney flicked in an obvious same-sex kissing scene into one of its new animated movies.

The great Bernie Marcus told me that companies dumb enough to squander their brand to go woke set themselves up for eventual failure; they were just too blinded by the lefty accolades from the cultural czars in the media, the ESG enforcers, to know what was in store for them. "The American people remember; their sales are going to stay down," he said.

Bernie was talking specifically about Budweiser, but he could have been talking about Disney, Target, BlackRock, or any company that thought being politically progressive wouldn't end up in disaster. The stench of wokeness is like skunk piss. It takes a lot of work to wash off.

Iger, I'm sure, expected a hero's welcome when he came back to Disney in November 2022, because he received nothing less during Disney's boom times. He got just the opposite as soon as his buddies on Wall Street began to dissect his growth plans, which are pretty much devoid of growth. Disney shares declined 10 percent in his first year back on the job compared to a 19 percent rise in the S&P. Things are getting better for Iger in 2024—his stock is up, as are profits—but only through insane cost cutting and turning away from the overt wokeness he instilled in Disney's culture and programming.

What I could never understand about Iger, or any liberal C-suite type, is just how little they knew about the progressive movement when they were preaching all that left-wing dogma for all those years.

In the hierarchy of the progressive left, the C-suite liberals are also the enemy because they make money and run businesses. The left looks at people like Bob Iger, Michel Doukeris, or Brian Cornell as nothing more than useful idiots in the cause of progressivism. The progressives don't care if these companies become uncompetitive and file for Chapter 11 bankruptcy as long as the welfare state is big enough to dole out checks to the unemployed.

And the real leftists are now in charge; President Sleepy Joe Biden has appointed more hard-core progressives in key regulatory posts than even Obama. Iger hated Trump, but Trump was good for his business. If he wanted to buy or sell a division, Trump's DOJ would give it the green light. Not Sleepy Joe's. My sources close to the company say the lefties in the Biden administration continue to thwart sensible dealmaking across corporate America, but also most of all in media, where these anti-trust bureaucrats are particularly sensitive to possible concentration of power. What the Bidenistas don't get is how much media power is dispersed these days by new media—the internet. Disney can't control thought any more than my employer, Fox News, because there is robust competition for ideas and information. The market, meanwhile, is saying Disney needs to become smaller, nimbler, more shareholder-friendly (as opposed to the idiotic stakeholder type) by selling ESPN, ABC, its theme parks—or even the whole company to Apple, which has the cash and is looking to extend it into entertainment.

But the left doesn't like deals that make shareholders happy—or Apple bigger even if being big means relatively little in an era where technology creatively destroys behemoths overnight. They'd rather Disney die a slow, excruciating death and watch shareholders suffer (even if those shareholders are lefty teachers in public pension funds that hold the stock). They would love nothing more than to watch Iger squirm as he tries to manage something burdened by the costs of streaming, a secular decline in movie attendance, and a stale product than allow him to rejuvenate Disney with a sale to a cash-rich tech firm. That's why as one longtime (and left-of-center) media CEO told me he can't bring himself to vote for Biden. "Communists run all his major economic departments and they're destroying the economy," he said.

That's the logic behind woke capitalism; there is no real logic.

Like Iger and Disney, other woke companies are also running away from leftism as fast as they once embraced it. They too saw how woke leads to going broke. As red-state officials keep in place their bans on BlackRock, Larry Fink and his team have announced that they will be shutting down ESG funds; they've scaled back support on ESG measures during proxy battles, and affiliation with environmental organizations.

BlackRock isn't alone among top asset managers shuttering ESG funds because the demand is drying up but also because ESG strictly enforced could be illegal. The big asset managers have largely stopped using their "passive" investment clout to support ESG proxy proposals, fearing anti-trust violations being raised by Republicans in Congress, I am told. It took a while, but one smart guy (Ohio congressman Jim Jordan) figured out that by joining all these eco-alliances, the big asset managers were pooling their investment power not just to clean up the environment, but to make a lot of money; they were, in Jordan's words, "a cartel," which is what the anti-trust laws were supposed to prevent.

They were also reneging on their legal responsibility to their clients, their fiduciary duty to do what's in investors' best interests, because ESG is such a boondoggle for investors. In late 2023, data from Morningstar showed just how far the ESG movement has fallen from its once lofty height because of its lousy returns. Investors yanked $14 billion from ESG funds over the first nine months of the year when it was clear that plain vanilla index funds cost less and always outperform those that virtue signal with their money.

Funds that once strategically placed the word "sustainable" in their names to drum up investor interest are taking the word out. ESG was never a match for the markets, and now the evidence is as plain as the decline in Disney's stock price, or BlackRock's loss of business. As reported by CNN in late 2023, "The iShares Global Clean Energy exchange-traded fund, which tracks the performance of sectors from renewable electricity to semiconductors to solar energy, has slumped 27% this year, underperforming the MSCI All-Country World index's 15% gain. The fund is on pace for its third straight annual loss."

Investors also might have realized that woke investing doesn't accomplish much. The *Harvard Business Review* released a report aptly titled "ESG Investing Isn't Designed to Save the Planet," pointing out the obvious: ESG is a farce. Its metrics are non-standardized, there is no proof ESG is making the world greener or societies more inclusive and the returns stink.

You see, throwing investors' money at windmills, or electric cars, or whatever else the ESG crowd dreamed up may help you appeal to the left and get you kudos in Davos. But if the technology doesn't work, or people won't buy an EV because it's too expensive, you're screwed. Markets sniff out inefficacies, and ESG has become one big inefficient mess. So inefficient that Hertz, the big rental car company, is getting rid of much of its EV fleet and buying gas guzzlers. As Allysia Finley, writing in the *Wall Street Journal*, so eloquently put it, "Americans don't want to plan trips around the locations of electric-vehicle charging stations—often to discover later that the chargers are broken. Nor do they want to download multiple apps to charge at different stations or worry about their battery range degrading in cold temperatures."

ESG made Wall Street a lot of money. For average people, it's all pain and hard to find gain. If you're a blue-collar worker and can't afford heating oil, an electric vehicle, or a sunroof, it's hard to appreciate a future with a cleaner environment.

I suspect that's why Larry Fink is rediscovering the political moderate he always was and why BlackRock has plans to expand everywhere but in its ESG business. In 2024 it bought an infrastructure firm for $12 billion and began redeploying resources away from ESG and into non-woke areas such as alternative investments (funds that invest in everything from art to currencies to private equity) and technology. BlackRock became one of the first firms to issue an ETF based on the "spot" price of Bitcoin, the controversial cryptocurrency embraced by libertarians wary of government spending debasing the US dollar. Fink referred to Bitcoin as a "store of value." The libertarian icon and former congressman Ron Paul would be proud.

And guess what happened? The bleeding began to stop! BlackRock's assets under management grew in 2023 and into 2024. Fink even made some friends among red-state pols; he and Texas lieutenant governor Dan Patrick—hardly a wokester—joined forces to create an investment fund to support the state's electric grid. Patrick was so giddy about doing business with the new Larry Fink that he referred to the BlackRock CEO as the "king of Wall Street."

Nice.

Fink's foray into wokeism was a heuristic adventure, on-the-job training in how playing with progressive politics in business is like playing with proverbial fire. "I'm far from woke," he tells me when we discuss the past couple of years of him being in the line of fire. He reminds me of the fossil fuel investments BlackRock has, his ties to oil company CEOs ("I talk to them all the time"), and his politically moderate position on various issues. He's a proponent now of nuclear energy to provide that transition to an eventual green economy so people can afford electricity and don't have to starve to meet strict ESG metrics. He sees merit in the Supreme Court ruling banning affirmative action in colleges that had prevented Asian students from gaining admission to Harvard ("I think the ruling was a good thing"). He tells me he met with GOP presidential candidate Nikki Haley because he likes her positions on supporting Israel and Ukraine in foreign policy and the need to balance the budget.

He also concedes his mistakes in his messaging on woke capitalism, which is why there is hope for those who seek its end. Fink tells me it was never his intention to delve into the politically toxic part of "the other letters," the social and governance stuff that gives fuel to DEI, and corporate donations to Black Lives Matter.

"I believe I could have been more literate when I was talking about ESG because I was really talking about sustainability," Fink tells me. "I should have been more focused."

Fink still believes ESG can lead to something big; advances in sustainability might create the next internet. He says it can be done methodically, without caving to the demands of the environmental left that will lead to fuel shortages and social upheaval. It's why he says BlackRock will never divest from the oil and gas industry.

Critics would say Fink's moderate transformation is out of necessity. He has always been somewhat of an escape artist, the risk-taking trader who transformed himself into risk-managing asset gatherer. I take Fink at his word because what he did next became an important marker in the battle against the excesses of woke ideology. Some top CEOs initially remained silent following the October 7, 2023, Hamas massacre near Gaza, fearing backlash from the progressive anti-Israel left. Fink released among the most forceful and certainly non-woke condemnations yet. "I'm absolutely devastated by the horrific acts of terrorism committed in Israel," he wrote on his LinkedIn page. "There are no words for the kidnapping and the murder of so many innocent people... We also know that the impact of this tragedy is being felt far beyond the borders of Israel. Many of our colleagues have family and friends in the region. Some have lost loved ones or fear gravely for their safety."

Good for him.

Wokeness isn't dead, but increasingly it's in retreat. States are outlawing DEI in public schools and accommodations. Texas is demanding that underwriters of its municipal debt take an oath that they do no business that curtails the sale of firearms, impedes oil drilling, or threatens Israel's right to exist. Businesses are running to places like Texas and away from blue states where woke politics rules. David Solomon, the woke CEO of Goldman, is eyeing the low taxes of Texas as a hub for his asset management unit. Almost simultaneously, Goldman began ending some of its "diversity programs" in recruitment and investing. Ken Griffin's Citadel has moved out of the crime-ridden, high-tax confines of Chicago for sunny, safe, low-tax Florida after a colleague was robbed at gunpoint going out for a cup of coffee.

Bud Light went back to the old formula of featuring real men and women in its ads. BLM is losing its corporate support. The Coca-Cola Company removed any reference to the group from its targeted charities list after one of its chapters demonstrated the true evil of wokeness and celebrated the Hamas terrorist attacks.

Target is weighing how to handle Pride Month without sparking a boycott. Meanwhile, its DEI-loving CEO, Brian Cornell, announced that he is being forced to close nearly a dozen stores in urban areas because of "organized retail crime." Cornell, you might recall, said DEI is good for business. He must not have understood that the same activists pushing DEI also pushed the "defund the police" movement, which has been bad for his business.

American Express, which indulged in wokeness by subjecting employees to the nonsense of critical race theory, changed its diversity training, people there tell me. No more CRT lectures, I hear. A spokesman assures me hiring and promotion isn't done based on race, sex, or gender despite its website citing the company's commitment to DEI standards. DEI doesn't prevent the company from hiring the best people regardless of race, he says. Good to hear. Another good thing to hear: CEO Stephen Squeri was smart enough to appoint to his board Jay Clayton, the former SEC chair who told activists to pound sand when they wanted the SEC to adopt what he viewed as race-based reparations. It was Clayton, my sources said, who made sure Amex and other companies scrubbed from their HR seminars the racist antiracism promoted by the high priests of CRT.

As for stakeholder capitalism, its utter uselessness and corruption was demonstrated by crypto bro Sam Bankman-Fried. The notorious SBF, before he was sent to jail in a multibillion-dollar crypto scam, said he dedicated his entire crypto empire to something called "effective altruism," the latest iteration of lefty boardroom politics that involves making money and then donating it to various lefty charities. There was just one problem: SBF was also stealing money to make the world a better place, gambling and losing in the crypto markets, then financing his lavish lifestyle and virtue signaling by pilfering the accounts of people who had money in his other business venture.

SBF may be an extreme example of the hypocrisy of woke capitalism, but he's not totally an outlier. Rather, he's just another example of how our social-justice-obsessed CEO class uses wokeness as cover for their slimy dealings, such as all the business they lust for with the oppressive regime in Communist China.

Ed Rensi predicted it all. As he met with more than two dozen CEOs, he explained that corporate wokeness might sound good on paper or in the media, but it's a loser with the American public.

"I told them they're going to get their ass handed to them," he said. "How can you cater to just 15 percent of your customers and piss off 85 percent of your customers? You gotta stop and think about what you're doing, the impact, and think about the unintended consequences.

"I told them they will pay the price because there's nothing good going to come of this. You're artificially promoting people, just because of their skin color and their ideology or their haircut.

"I told them you're out of your fucking minds."

Average Americans are paying a different price. Wokeness in business is dying, but diversity training remains; ESG is limping along, but in the words of one BlackRock senior executive, it's still "a real business." Every blue-state pension manager still demands it, and many corporations adopt its business metrics. DEI officers are losing their jobs, but not fast enough. The progressive playbook remains in place; George Soros is in his nineties, but he's handed his son the progressive infrastructure he created to dole out his billions. HRC, CAP, soft-on-crime Manhattan DA Alvin Bragg, and leftist regulators aren't just going to give up and go home because they lost a few battles. It won't be long before the left pushes another major company to use its lobbying power, its cultural importance, to try and force behaviors. It will take a degree of vigilance from the non-woke media, parents, elected officials, and the American public to expose, condemn, and fight this type of totalitarianism.

That's why now is not the time to let those CEOs who went woke off the hook. When Jamie Dimon was photographed on one knee in 2020 seemingly in solidarity with BLM, he was giving credibility to a lie that America was inherently racist and needed radical reform. That radical reform led to the defund movement, and lawlessness in the streets in major American cities.

That said, it's good to see woke dying little by little. Davos in 2024 had a decidedly non-woke theme: "Rebuilding Trust." It seems the globalist crowd is coming to realize that the woke agenda of ESG, DEI, and the rest just rubs the hoi polloi the wrong way. Jamie Dimon suggested as much in an interview with CNBC from the Swiss ski resort. The JP Morgan CEO who thought he was smarter and tougher than the populist former (and maybe next) president said the following about Donald Trump: He's "kind of right about immigration. He grew the economy quite well. Tax reform worked. He was right about China."

A spokesman for Dimon explains his apparent conversion to non-woke this way: "Jamie is on-record saying he's the least woke person you'll ever meet. Just recently, he said he's a red-blooded, full-throated patriotic capitalist." That's when I bring up a few things; first Dimon's love affair of stakeholder capitalism, his ditching of Milton Friedman and shareholder capitalism with the Business Roundtable, and how it has led to the woke overreach he now bemoans. "He said that in order to get great results for shareholders, you have to focus on your other main stakeholders as well—your customers, your employees, and your communities. This is totally logical and has nothing to do with wokeism."

Really? Dimon's $30 billion splurge of *shareholder money* to close "the racial wealth gap" during the Floyd riots isn't wokeism? And where are the results aside from earning JP Morgan some DEI points from activists like the Human Rights Campaign?

I then asked about Dimon's little one-knee episode during the height of the BLM riots. After allowing the Dimon-knee incident to stand as a BLM-inspired statement, people in JP Morgan's PR department now say this about their boss's posture that day: It was misinterpreted. Jamie isn't a BLM supporter. The boss was merely kneeling to fit into the photo so he wouldn't block the camera from the people behind him.

It took him three years and probably pressure from clients in red-state America to come up with that one.

Tragedy, unfortunately, has also been a catalyst for further positive change away from wokeness in the boardroom. As if the woke ideology didn't need any more evidence of its depravity, the October 7, 2023, terrorist attack and the woke reaction to it shocked much of the civilized world. Including some top Wall Street executives who not so long ago saw progressivism as a corporate necessity and helped nurture it through the college endowment system.

What these financiers failed to understand, possibly until now, is that when you invite into your culture the notion that America is evil and capitalism is a form of oppression, and reparations and recriminations for the sins of the past are necessary, everything is on the table. Israel, America's most trusted ally, also becomes a colonialist oppressor. Terrorists like Hamas "justifiably" seek its destruction because Israel is associated with the evil that is the United States. It's the only way for the Palestinian people to gain their freedom.

All historically inaccurate, of course. Israel has long supported a two-state solution that has been rejected by the Palestinians for decades in favor of complete Jewish annihilation. The very fact that this warped version of reality is considered settled science at our top schools is further evidence of how wokeness, whether it's in the boardroom or the classroom, is both pervasive in our culture and evil at its core.

The business community is getting a real education in this evil. Its top members have watched in horror as the elite colleges they attended and endowed condone nihilistic and disgusting displays of anti-Jew bigotry from students following the largest mass murders of innocents in recent history.

They've also come to believe that the academics and administrators running major universities have allowed an inaccurate history of the Middle East and the Jewish state to fester and grow into a leviathan that has spilled into open harassment of Jewish students at Harvard, MIT, and Penn. College administrators, it seemed, feared the rebuke of the leftists that fill many of their departments and the students brainwashed with left-wing dogma.

One such academic on the receiving end of the backlash against campus unrest is a banker named Scott Bok. He is the CEO of Greenhill & Co., a boutique investment bank, and *was* chairman of the board of trustees of the University of Pennsylvania, his alma mater. Critics say he ignored pleas from alumni about a controversial Palestinian literary event on campus during Yom Kippur. Some of the so-called literary experts preached vile Jew hatred of the type you would find at a neo-Nazi rally. After the Gaza massacre he and the university's president, Liz Magill, critics contend, put out tepid denunciations about the orgy of killing (that included beheadings, rapes, and burning of infants), and the orgiastic celebrations of it by some of their students.

Magill and Bok, to be fair, did condemn the October 7 attacks, but not enough for Marc Rowan. Rowan is the CEO of private equity firm Apollo Global Management. He's rich, worth about $6 billion. He's also a UPenn graduate of its elite business school, Wharton. He wrote an open letter to Magill and Bok, demanding their resignations, and began to call like-minded graduates to stop giving money to the school.

Magill and Bok later resigned after Magill's disastrous appearance before Congress. The campus unrest, and the displays of open hostility toward Jewish students after the attack, provoked House hearings in December 2023. Under questioning mainly from New York representative Elise Stefanik, Magill and other university leaders at Harvard and MIT stated that disciplining open bigotry, hatred, and threats against Jewish students on campus is a "context-dependent" matter.

Disgusting, which is why after Magill got the boot, Harvard's president, Claudine Gay, was ousted next. She too flunked answering the same simple question by Stefanik, and in January 2024, months after her disastrous hearing performance, Gay announced her resignation.

Magill hasn't said much since her defenestration. Gay, however, offered a decidedly different rationale for hers. It wasn't because of her initial weak condemnation of the October 7 massacre or her odd rationalization of it in front of Congress. Or the multiple instances of copied material found in her research that came to light.

Gay was the first African American leader of the prestigious school. In her telling, she had to step down because she was tired of being "subjected to personal attacks and threats fueled by racial animus."

Sorry, it was not racism that caused Claudine Gay to call it quits (or for Harvard to allow her to quit), but the so-called antiracism of DEI that exposed her real liabilities. Yes, she was the first African American (and the second woman) to serve at the top of the university. A real get, it first appeared. Then little by little, credible evidence kept emerging that that's about all she brought to the job. Hedge fund titan Bill Ackman, a Harvard graduate and political centrist, took to social media to expose Gay's academic and other shortcomings. Not only was her scholarship ridiculed as weak (and some copied), but details also began to leak that her tenure at the top of Harvard has seen free speech muzzled.

Soon, many graduates and then administrators concluded for her to remain running Harvard is to degrade the value of their diploma.

Rowan and Ackman, of course, deserve credit for trying to bring some sanity to academia. My question is: Why did they wait so long?

Rowan had been a donor to UPenn during that time, giving $50 million of his own money and leading a fundraising drive that brought to the school's endowment another $1 billion. There were no real strings attached to that money, I am told. That means Rowan's money was used to finance woke educational courses that teach students about the evils of Israel as an oppressor of millions of Arabs; how America is racist; how capitalism is evil; how men can be women. And let's not forget how white men need not apply for any job, to atone for the past sins of people they didn't know and have no relation to other than the color of their skin.

Ackman is a graduate of Harvard's elite business school. After Gay's resignation he ominously posted on X, "Et tu Sally?" It was a reference to MIT's Sally Kornbluth, another university president who waffled before the nation during the congressional hearings on the need to condemn antisemitism.

Like Rowan, Ackman has given millions to his alma mater. And again like Rowan, where was he when the pedagogy of hate was spreading in the classroom years earlier? When Harvard was cancelling classes in Western civilization while teaching the made-up evils of US capitalism and fabulist tales of Israeli aggression, his money flowed into the school. I know he wrote a four-thousand-word essay on X where he attacked Gay as a DEI hire, and that DEI institutionalizes racism. But why only now?

The turning point on their condemnation of the woke shouldn't have been the ultimate by-product of this disgusting theology: overt racist nihilism.

As much as corporate wokeness is in retreat, I do wonder whether the forces of sanity started too late, and that some level of the mind virus is forever baked into American culture. For answers, I turned to the great Bernie Marcus.

We last spoke in late 2023, and at ninety-four years of age, Bernie tells me he doesn't have a lot of time left. He's done many remarkable things during his long life and career: He rose from an impoverished youth to become a billionaire several times over. He overcame antisemitism in the boardroom and created one of the great American companies, Home Depot. He's given millions away to charity and his philanthropic efforts include making sure capitalism survives. His Job Creators Network and Boardroom Initiative continue to expose how corporate wokeism will be the death of our once great economic system.

I'm seated in Bernie's spacious home in Boca Raton; he was once an imposing man, over six feet tall with broad shoulders, even just a year ago. He's a frail man now; the ravages of age do that to you, sometimes overnight. But his mind is quick. "Charlie, I'm ninety-four years old. Unfortunately, I have a sixty-year-old brain, a ninety-four-year-old body," he says with a smile.

Then he explains why he's worried about the future and why he's so "pissed off." He rattles off the examples of corporate wokeism—Disney, BlackRock, Target, and Budweiser—and how much damage the woke mindset has caused to the economy and country. Corporate money—woke corporate money—flooded into the coffers of BLM, for instance, and into major colleges and universities, the same campuses that now condone Jew hatred.

The same colleges, he said, are also being influenced by their foreign donors to warp the minds of students. "Are you watching where the money is coming from?" Bernie mentions Qatar, the country that is home base for much of Hamas's leadership, which has been a major donor to elite schools in recent years. "All these countries are throwing money at the universities, developing these studies in the Middle East that are biased that teach kids Israel is a form of apartheid."

Marcus is referring to the racist regime of South Africa pre–Nelson Mandela that the left loves to compare to Israel over its fraught relations with the Palestinians. On college campuses these days, students receive one-sided propaganda about the Arab-Israeli conflict: alleged Israeli occupation of Arab lands that leaves out the real facts. Israel is a tiny country that has given up territory it seized in battle for years to appease its Arab neighbors. Gaza was self-governing before October 7. The West Bank still is. The Palestinians have rejected peace overture after peace overture for a two-state solution. Instead, they want Israel eradicated. The colleges, endowed by Wall Street money and money from places like Qatar, have promoted that propaganda, Marcus points out.

It's why, he says, college kids rejoice in screaming, "Kill the Jews."

"And I tell you something," Bernie recalls. "I grew up during the Holocaust and this is no different."

I bring up the justifiable anger of Marc Rowan and Bill Ackman over the campus Jew-hating, and that while they're making a lot of noise, they seem to be in the minority among our corporate elite. Even with wokeness in retreat, where are the nation's CEO class protesting antisemitism in the way that they virtue signaled over George Floyd?

Where's the CEO petition in the *New York Times*?

Bernie's answer: "When I was coming up, the guys who ran businesses, they were courageous. They didn't give a crap about anyone; they did the best for their business, their associates, their employees and shareholders."

As for the modern CEO, "They're fearful; they're cowards and they're still afraid of the woke mob."

It's why the fight isn't over.

Notes

Chapter One: The Great Goldman Chick-fil-A Debate

Reporting for this section is derived from author interviews as well as Charles Gasparino and Lydia Moynihan, "Goldman Sachs CEO Hit with Cultural Revolution, Overworked Millennials and Chick-fil-A debates," Fox Business, March 23, 2021.

Background on the Cathy family and the founding of Chick-fil-A comes from author interviews and various public sources, including the company website and Hillary Hoffower and Nancy Luna, "Meet the Cathys, Heirs to the Chick-fil-A Empire, Who Have a Fortune of More Than $29 Billion and Are One of America's Wealthiest Family 'Dynasties,'" *Business Insider*, October 2, 2023.

The quote from Gerard Baker comes from Gerard Baker, "How American Institutions Went from Trust to Bust," *Wall Street Journal*, September 8, 2023.

For Goldman Sachs's history, including John Whitehead's military service, see various public sources, author interviews, and Lloyd C. Blankfein and Gary D. Cohn, "Memorandum to All Goldman Sachs Employees on John C. Whitehead," Goldman Sachs website, February 8, 2015.

On David Solomon and his management style, see various public sources, including William D. Cohan, "The Next Goldman C.E.O. Is One Woke Dude," *Vanity Fair*, March 12, 2018.

Bari Weiss's comments on DEI are from *The Megyn Kelly Show*, Episode 687, December 15, 2023.

Reporting for Goldman Sachs's pronoun guide comes from author interviews and Lydia Moynihan, "Goldman Sachs Hands Out 'Pronoun' Pamphlets as It Fights Sex Harass Suits," *New York Post*, April 13, 2023.

The definition of CRT comes from author interviews and Jacey Fortin, "Critical Race Theory; A Brief History," *New York Times*, November 8, 2021.

The CRT lectures at major companies are from author interviews and confirmed by the companies themselves.

Additional reporting on the debate over ESG and DEI is from various public sources, author interviews, and Robert Maranto and James D. Paul, "Other than Merit: The Prevalence of Diversity, Equity and Inclusion Statements in University Hirting," American Enterprise Institute, November 8, 2021; James Surowiecki, "The Hottest Trend in Investing Is Mostly a

Sham," *The Atlantic*, May 26, 2023; Mike Edleson and Andy Puzder, "Is ESG Profitable? The Numbers Don't Lie," *Wall Street Journal*, March 10, 2023.

Information on how corporate wokeism and ESG were influenced by Occupy Wall Street and the 2008 bailouts comes from author interviews and Jonathan Younger, "Occupy Wall Street's Influence on Corporate Purpose," Ketchum, October 6, 2021.

The desire to win business from blue-state pension funds propelling ESG comes from author interviews; on the size of blue-state pension funds compared to those in red states, see Ross Kerber, "Blue State Pension Funds Invest More Money," Yahoo News, September 20, 2023.

Reporting on David Solomon's problems at Goldman Sachs comes from author interviews and Lydia Moynihan, "Goldman Sachs Bankers 'Really Bummed' over Loss of Free Coffee Perk," *New York Post*, January 6, 2023; Jen Wieczner, "Is David Solomon Too Big a Jerk to Run Goldman Sachs?," *New York Magazine*, August 11, 2023.

On Dan Cathy's shoe shining, see various public sources and Ariel Zilber, "Former Chick-fil-A Boss Dan Cathy Suggests White People Shine Black People's Shoes in Resurfaced Video," *New York Post*, May 31, 2023.

Chapter Two: The Wokening of Corporate America

On the history of the word "woke," see various public sources, including Aja Romano, "A History of 'Wokeness,'" *Vox*, October 9, 2020.

On the growth of the Black Lives Matter movement and Colin Kaepernick's social justice protesting from the Ferguson, Missouri, riots, see various public sources, including Zack Stanton, "How Ferguson and Baltimore Explain Why It's Different This Time," *Politico*, June 11, 2020; Rory Carroll, "NFL: Protesting Players 'On the Right Side of History,' Union Says," Reuters, February 5, 2021; Patrick Hruby, "Three Years in the NFL Wilderness: What Colin Kaepernick Lost—and Won," *The Guardian*, August 19, 2019. A BLM press representative did not return a request for comment.

On Kamala Harris's support of BLM, see Sam Dorman, "Kamala Harris Praises BLM; Says Ongoing Protests Are 'Essential' for Change in US," Fox News, September 25, 2020.

Reporting on major companies giving to BLM comes from author interviews and various news sources, including Mercey Livingston, "These Are the Major Brands Donating to the Black Lives Matter Movement," CNET, December 11, 2023; Tatum Hunter, "25 Companies That Support Black Lives Matter (BLM)," Built In, September 21, 2023.

Background on the history of BLM and the Marxism of its founders comes from author interviews and Mike Gonzalez, "Marxism Underpins Black Lives Matter Agenda," Heritage Foundation, September 8, 2021.

On the lavish lifestyle of BLM's founders, see Joshua Rhett Miller, "Black Lives Matter Used Donations to Buy $6 Million Southern California Home: Report," *New York Post*, April 4, 2022.

Information on the Navy SEAL Foundation being deprived of contributions because of corporate donations to BLM comes from author interviews with Wall Street executives involved in the fundraising.

On Black athletes making the billionaires' club, see Jen Omowale, "8 Athletes Who Reached Billionaire Status," Revolt, November 13, 2023.

Reporting on BLM's opposition to Israel, pro-Palestinian support, and reaction to the October 7, 2023, Hamas terrorist attack comes from author interviews and published reports and Jason Riley, "Black Lives Matter and the World's Oldest Hatred," *Wall Street Journal*, October 31, 2023; Hansi Lo Wang, "The Complicated History Behind BLM's Solidarity with the Pro-Palestinian Movement," NPR, June 12, 2021.

Information on diversity training comes from author interviews of people inside such meetings and Barton Swain, "How 'Antiracism' Becomes Antisemitism; Demonizing People in Racial Terms Because They're Successful Turns Out to Have Consequences," *Wall Street Journal*, December 29, 2023.

Reporting on the theory of intersectionality used in critical race theory and corporate diversity training derives from author interviews and various public sources, including "Kimberlé Crenshaw on Intersectionality, More Than Two Decades Later," Columbia Law School, June 8, 2017; Jane Coaston, "The Intersectionality Wars," *Vox*, May 28, 2019.

On the racial rationing of Covid vaccines, see Harald Schmidt, Lawrence O. Gostin, and Michelle A. Williams, "Is It Lawful and Ethical to Prioritize Racial Minorities for COVID-19 Vaccines?," *JAMA Network*, October 14, 2020.

On the Veterans Administration rationing Covid vaccines based on race, see Nikki Wentling, "Minority Veterans to Receive Priority for Corona Virus Vaccines," *Stars and Stripes*, December 10, 2020.

Reporting on NextEra comes from author interviews; information on American Express's CRT training and the alleged firing of Brian Netzel comes from author interviews and Jon Brown, "3 More Plaintiffs Join Class Action Against American Express Alleging Discrimination Toward White Employees," Fox Business, September 25, 2022; "American Express Slapped with Lawsuit Alleging Discrimination Against White Employees," Fox Business, August 24, 2022. American Express provided background on the lawsuit and said CRT sessions were not mandatory.

Reporting on Business Roundtable ditching shareholder capitalism for stakeholder capitalism and Jamie Dimon's statement comes from author interviews and "Business Roundtable Redefines the Purpose of a Corporation to Promote 'An Economy That Serves All Americans,'" Business Roundtable website, August 19, 2019, and "Business Roundtable Redefines the Purpose of a Corporation to Promote 'An Economy That Serves All Americans,'" Business Roundtable, August 19, 2019.

On Gillette's toxic masculinity ads, see various news reports and Charles Taylor, "Why Gillette's New Ad Campaign Is Toxic," *Forbes*, January 15, 2019.

Reporting on Milton Friedman and shareholder capitalism derives from author interviews and Justin Fox, "The Social Responsibility of Business Is to Increase...What Exactly?," *Harvard Business Review*, April 18, 2012.

Background on Milton Friedman and his support for shareholder capitalism comes from various public sources, including Milton Friedman, "The Social Responsibility of Business Is to Increase Its Profits," *New York Times*, September 13, 1970.

Information on Jamie Dimon's long history of staff cuts despite his claim to stakeholder capitalism comes from author interviews and various public sources, including Sandra Ward, "Primerica to Cut Work Force at Smith Barney by 3%," Dow Jones, October 2, 1990.

Reporting on US productivity stalling out since 2005 comes from author interviews and various public sources, including Charles Atkins, Olivia White, Asutosh Padhi, Kweilin Ellingrud, Anu Madgavkar, and Michael Neary, "Rekindling US Productivity for a New Era," McKinsey Global Institute, February 16, 2023.

Reporting on the beginning of socially responsible investing is from public sources and various author interviews, including Yale University's Jeff Sonnenfeld and the University of Pittsburgh's Vanitha Swaminathan.

Information on corporate donations to the Center for American Progress and the Human Rights Campaign is from author interviews and the organizations' websites.

Reporting on the Human Rights Campaign, its connections to George Soros, the DEI ranking of companies, and its leadership comes from author interviews and various public sources, including the Human Rights Campaign's website; Samantha Riedel, "Trying to Drag Us Back: HRC President Kelley Robinson on the Push Against Trans People," Them, March 20, 2023; Dana Kennedy, "Inside the CEI System Pushing Brands to Endorse Celebs Like Dylan Mulvaney," *New York Post*, April 8, 2023. HRC was given material from this book and did not respond to a request for comment.

Details of the HRC's "Corporate Equity Index" and JP Morgan's support come from author interviews and the organization's website.

Background on the United Nations' role in ESG comes from author interviews and Qayyum Rajan, "Where Did the Term ESG Come from Anyway?," ESG Analytics website, March 29, 2022, and Elliot Wilson, "United Nations' Free Thinker Who Coined the Term 'ESG'—and Changed the World," *Euromoney*, October 1, 2021.

On ESG growing to a $50 trillion business, see "ESG Assets Rising to $50 Trillion Will Reshape $140.5 Trillion of Global AUM by 2025," Bloomberg Intelligence, July 21, 2021.

Information on how BlackRock, Vanguard, and State Street use their size of $22 trillion in combined assets to push ESG comes from author interviews and Farhad Manjoo, "What BlackRock, Vanguard and State Street Are Doing to the Economy," *New York Times*, May 12, 2022.

Reporting on conflicts involving the proxy advisers and ESG, how former SEC chair Jay Clayton sought to address them, and how Biden SEC chair Gary Gensler reversed Clayton comes from author interviews with Clayton and others and "SEC Adopts Rule Amendments to Provide Investors Using Proxy Voting Advice More Transparent, Accurate and Complete Information," Securities and Exchange Commission website, July 22, 2020; Lawrence A. Cunningham, "Commentary: Gensler Should Keep Clayton's Pragmatic Proxy Adviser Rules," *Pensions & Investments*, February 24, 2021; Nicolas Grabar and Shuangjun Wang, "The SEC Backs Off on Proxy Advisory Firms," Harvard Law School Forum on Corporate Governance, December 19, 2021. Proxy advisers did respond to request for comment.

On BlackRock, Vanguard, and State Street joining the Net Zero Alliance, see "The Net Zero Asset Managers Initiative," April 20, 2021.

The description of ESG-specific funds is from Jeffrey R. Bohna, Lisa R. Goldberg, and Simage Ulucam, "Sustainable Investing from a Practitioner's Viewpoint: What's in Your ESG Portfolio," *Journal of Investing* 20, no. 2 (2022).

Information on corporations embracing diversity as a mandate that's good for business, and the controversy of that approach, comes from author interviews and Kim Elsesser, "The Business Case for Diversity May Be Backfiring, a New Study Shows," *Forbes*, June 20, 2022.

Reporting on Nasdaq's diversity rules comes from author interviews, including with Nasdaq CEO Adena Friedman, SEC filings, and Charles Gasparino, "Why Nasdaq's Latest Diversity Plan Is Hypocritical," *New York Post*, December 5, 2020; Alexander Osipovich and Akane Otani, "Nasdaq Seeks Board-Diversity Rule That Most Listed Firms Don't Meet," *Wall Street Journal*, December 1, 2020.

Information on BlackRock's and JP Morgan's business dealings in China comes from author interviews and various public sources, including Richard Henderson, "BlackRock, Schroders Hunt China Deals in Growing Private Markets," Bloomberg, June 29, 2023; Clay Chandler and Nicholas Gordon, "BlackRock Is 'Blundering' in China—All the Way to the Bank," *Fortune*, September 9, 2021; Thomas Hale, "BlackRock Wins Approval to Run Wealth Business in China," *Financial Times*, May 12, 2021; Li Yuan, "China Is Rocked by Uncertainty. Why Is Wall Street Bullish?," *New York Times*, October 6, 2021.

Reporting on NBA attendance growing comes from author interviews and Mike Vorkunov, "NBA Sets New League Attendance Record in 2022–23," *The Athletic*, April 10, 2023.

Information on the controversy surrounding NBA business in China comes from author interviews and Sopan Deb, "After a Boycott, Chinese Television Is Again Airing N.B.A. Games," *New York Times*, March 31, 2022.

On McKinsey's data on the racial/gender makeup of boards and corporate use of ESG and DEI, see "Woke and Broke," *The Economist*, September 30, 2023.

Research on the growing wealth gap as companies embrace ESG comes from author interviews and "Aggregated CEO-to-Worker Compensation Ratio for the 350 Largest Publicly Owned Companies in the United States from 1965 to 2022," Statista website.

Chapter Three: DEI or DIE?

Reporting on how and why CEOs began to embrace corporate wokeness comes from author interview with retired McDonald's USA CEO Ed Rensi.

Reporting on the Biden administration's strict DEI standards in appointments to major cabinet positions and to the Supreme Court comes from administration officials who spoke to me on background.

Information on the influence of activists groups pressuring business to adopt progressive policies (i.e., the Center for American Progress and the Human Rights Campaign) as described in this section comes from former White House officials who interacted with members of both groups.

For the DEI explosion following George Floyd's death, see "Woke and Broke," *The Economist*, September 30, 2023.

On the corporate use of "racial equity audits" and the outcome of their implementation, see "Why DEI Won't Die," *The Economist*, October 7, 2023.

Information on United Airlines' and Boeing's adherence to DEI comes from author interviews and Brian Flood, "Former FAA Safety Expert Addresses Airline DEI Controversy, Viral United Comments," Fox Business, January 17, 2024; Shannon Thaler, "Boeing Prioritizing Diversity and Inclusion over Flier Safety, Elon Musk Says After Near-Catastrophic Alaska Airlines Mishap," *New York Post*, January 11, 2024.

Reporting on DEI's transition into racial quotas comes from author interviews and published reports, including Jeff Green, David Ingold, Raeedah Wahid, Cedric Sam, and Daniela Sirtori-Cortina, "Corporate America Promised to Hire a Lot More People of Color. It Actually Did," Bloomberg, September 25, 2023.

More background on corporate America's embrace of DEI standards comes from author interviews and various public sources, including Robin J. Ely and David A. Thomas, "Getting Serious About Diversity: Enough Already with the Business Case," *Harvard Business Review*, November–December 2020; Caroline Colvin, "Once Neglected, DEI Initiatives Now Present at All Fortune 100 Companies," HR Dive, July 20, 2022; Andrew Ross Sorkin, Ravi Mattu, Bernhard Warner, Michael J. de la Merced, and Lauren Hirsch, "Why Corporate America Is Worried About Affirmative Action," *New York Times*, June 30, 2023.

The information on "diversity statements" and the research on them by author Andrew Gillen comes from author interviews and public sources, including Robert Maranto and James D. Paul, "Other Than Merit: The Prevalence of Diversity, Equity, and Inclusion Statements in University Hiring," American Enterprise Institute, November 8, 2021.

Information on McKinsey & Company's support for DEI comes from various public sources, author interviews, and the "Diversity, Equity & Inclusion" page on McKinsey's website.

Reporting on the SCOTUS affirmative action decision impacting DEI comes from Charles Gasparino, "What SCOTUS Affirmative Action Ruling Could Mean for DEI and the Business of Corporate Wokeness," *New York Post*, July 1, 2023.

Reporting on "microaggressions" comes from author interview with the executive in the meeting and public sources, including Kalia Simms, "Microaggressions in the Workplace: How to Identify & Respond to Them," Great Place to Work, March 27, 2023.

Information on Dylan Mulvaney and Budweiser comes from author interviews and various public sources.

Information on using marketing to achieve DEI in the workplace comes from author interviews with academic Vanitha Swaminathan at the University of Pittsburgh and practitioner David Evans of the Collage Group, and fact-checked with both.

BlackRock's sales pitch to diverse investors comes from documents obtained by the author.

On information regarding DEI in marketing on gender fluidity, see various public sources, including Jose Criales-Unzueta, "What Is Queer Fashion, Anyway?," Them, October 11, 2021.

An example of LGBTQ+ literature targeting children is Kyle Lukoff, *When Aidan Became a Brother* (New York: Lee & Low Books, 2019).

Reporting on Target CEO Brian Cornell's statements on DEI and examples of LGBTQ+ displays at Target and the controversy it started comes from author interviews and various public sources, including Yael Halon, "Target CEO Says Woke Capitalism 'Great' for Their Brand and 'the Right Thing for Society,'" Fox News, May 23, 2023.

Information on Cornell's background and political beliefs comes from author interviews with people who have direct knowledge of the matter.

Reporting on PepsiCo's wokeness comes from author interviews and the blog *Starkman Approved*, March 26, 2023.

Details of the Kendall Jenner Pepsi ad and how much she makes per social media promotion are from former PepsiCo employees and various public sources, including Daniel Victor, "Pepsi Pulls Ad Accused of Trivializing Black Lives Matter," *New York Times*, April 5, 2017; Rachel Togerson, "Kendall Jenner, Gigi Hadid Earn $300,000 Per Instagram Post," *Us Weekly*, December 18, 2015.

Details of Target's Pride Month celebrations, types of merchandise, and retailers' target demo come from author interviews and various public sources, including Dominick Reuter, "Meet the Typical Target Shopper, a Millennial Suburban Mom with a Household Income of $80,000," *Business Insider*, February 4, 2023; Siddharth Cavale, "Target Removing Some LGBTQ Merchandise Following Customer Backlash," Reuters, May 24, 2023.

Information on the HRC pressuring corporations to carry out its agenda and appointing former Obama aide Kelley Robinson as its president comes from author interviews and Elizabeth Bibi, "Kelley Robinson to Serve as President of the Human Rights Campaign," Human Rights Campaign, September 20, 2022.

Reporting on the Center for American Progress and its connections to George Soros comes from author interviews and Center for American Progress, "Activist Facts" website. On Soros's contributions to left-wing causes and politicians, see author interviews and public sources, including Brian Schwartz, "Nonprofit Financed by Billionaire George Soros Quietly Donated $140 Million to Political Causes in 2021," CNBC, January 4, 2023.

Information on the customer boycotting of Target and the social media backlash comes from author interviews with marketing executives and people close to the company, and public reports such as Jordyn Holman, "Target's Sales Hit by Pride Month Merchandise Backlash," *New York Times*, August 16, 2023.

Reporting on how marketing is cancelling white men in TV commercials and the prevalence of DEI in advertising comes from author interviews with marketing executives and public reports, such as Teresa Hopke, "White Men Are Feeling Left Out of Diversity, Equity, & Inclusion. Why Should We Care and What Should We Do?," *Forbes*, March 30, 2022; "Let's Talk About Forced Diversity in TV Commercials," *The Cranky Creative Blog*, January 5, 2022.

Reporting on Silicon Valley Bank's collapse and the embrace of progressivism comes from author interviews with former employees, and public sources, including Katherine Donlevy, "While Silicon Valley Bank Collapsed, Top Executive Pushed 'Woke' Programs," *New York Post*, March 13, 2023.

Details on risk taking at SVB and the embrace of DEI and ESG come from author interviews with former employees and reps for Greg Becker, and from Douglas Landy and Chanté Eliaszadeh, "Tying Deposit Insurance Reform to Reform of the Tying of Deposits," White & Case website, October 3, 2023.

On SVB's CEO Greg Becker on the board of the San Francisco Fed and the board's mulling of ditching him at one point, see public reports, including Kyle Campbell, "Report: SF Fed Mulled Removing SVB's Becker from Board Before Failure," American Banker, September 28, 2023.

Reporting on the San Francisco Fed chief's support of BLM comes from author interviews and public sources, including Paul Sperry, "Why Woke 'Frisco Fed Chief Missed Silicon Valley Bank's Warning Signs," *New York Post*, March 17, 2023.

Chapter Four: The Summer of Love

Details on the spending habits of Trump and the rise in the national debt during his presidency come from author interviews and various public sources, including Allan Sloan and Cezary Podkul, "Donald Trump Built a National Debt So Big (Even Before the Pandemic) That It'll Weigh Down the Economy for Years," ProPublica, January 14, 2021.

On Mark Zuckerberg's meeting with former president Obama, see various news accounts and "Remarks by the President at a Facebook Town Hall," Obama White House website, April 20, 2011.

Reporting on the "shadow banning" of Covid skeptics and conservatives comes from author interviews and public sources, including Justin Hart, "The Twitter Blacklisting of Jay Bhattacharya," *Wall Street Journal*, December 9, 2022; New York Post Editorial Board, "Twitter's Secret Shadow Bans Are Why the Public Has Turned Against 'Experts,'" *New York Post*, December 9, 2022.

Details of the meeting between the Trump White House and major Wall Street executives to discuss economic dislocations around Covid and lockdowns come from author interviews and various news accountings, including Charles Gasparino and Lydia Moynihan, "Trump, White House Tell Wall Street Execs Lockdown May Last Beyond Easter: Sources," Fox Business, March 24, 2020.

Jamie Dimon's remarks about beating Trump in a presidential race come from various public sources, including Brett Michaels, "Jamie Dimon Says He Could Beat Trump: 'I'm Smarter Than He Is,'" *The Hill*, September 12, 2018.

For details of George Floyd's death, his prison record, his arrest, and his use of fentanyl, see published reports, including Matt Walsh, "New Revelation Prove Yet Again That Derek Chauvin Was an Innocent Man Railroaded in the Name of 'Racial Justice,'" *The Matt Walsh Show*, Episode 1248; Amy Forliti, "Lawyers for Ex-cops Raise Floyd's History of Crime, Drug Use," Associated Press, September 10, 2020; Evan Hill, Ainara Tiefenthaler, Chrisiaan Triebert, Drew Jordan, Haley Willis, and Robin Stein, "How George Floyd Was Killed in Police Custody," *New York Times*, May 31, 2020.

Following the death of George Floyd, protests turned violent, and the term "largely peaceful protests" was used by media to describe the increasingly chaotic situation, according to author interviews and various public reports, including Derrick Bryson Taylor, "George Floyd Protests: A Timeline," *New York Times*, November 5, 2021; Brakkton Booker, Bill Chappell, David Schaper, Danielle Kurtzleben, and Joseph Shapiro, "Violence Erupts as Outrage over George Floyd's Death Spills into a New Week," NPR, June 1, 2020; Steven Sloan, "Largely Peaceful Protests Against Police Brutality March On," Associated Press, June 7, 2020; Laura Kelly, "US Image Takes a Hit as World Reacts to Floyd Protests," *The Hill*, June 6, 2020.

On the defacing of statues of Lincoln and Grant, see public sources and Henry Olsen, "The Anti-statue Movement Has Taken a Turn into Absurdity," *Washington Post*, June 22, 2020.

The contrast between Trump's handling of Covid and that of Florida governor Ron DeSantis, who opened the state largely by June 2020, is documented by multiple public sources, including Dylan Scott, "How Ron DeSantis Transformed into an Anti–Public Health Crusader," *Vox*, April 27, 2023.

For details of Dr. Anthony Fauci and his alleged role in funding gain-of-function research, see public reports, including Sharon Lerner, Mara Hvistendahl, and Maia Hibbett, "NIH Documents Provide New Evidence U.S. Funded Gain-of-Function Research in Wuhan," *The Intercept*, September 9, 2021; Katherine Eban, "In Major Shift, NIH Admits Funding Risky Virus Research in Wuhan," *Vanity Fair*, October 22, 2021.

The statistical fallacy of police brutality targeting African Americans is documented by various public sources and reports, including Heather Mac Donald, "The Myth of Systemic Police Racism," *Wall Street Journal*, June 2, 2020.

Goldman CEO David Solomon's statement on George Floyd's death is from David Solomon, "My Message on Inclusion," LinkedIn, May 30, 2020.

For the statement by Starbucks on alleged police brutality, see "Black Lives Matter: Starbucks Update on Standing Against Racial Injustice," *Starbucks Stories*, June 12, 2020.

For Bank of America CEO Brian Moynihan on alleged police brutality and social justice protests, see Beverly Goodman, Reshma Kapadia, and Leslie P. Norton, "These CEOs Are Speaking Out Against Racism. What They Say They Can Do Better," *Barron's*, June 5, 2020; Charles Gasparino, "Where Is the CEO Outrage During the Ongoing War Between Israel and Palestine?," *New York Post*, October 14, 2023.

Information on Moynihan attending Red Sox games at Fenway in box seats comes from author interviews and Gayle Fee, Laura Raposa, and Erin Hayes, "Inside Track; Hub's Movers & Shakers Make Sox Scene," *Boston Herald*, April 12, 2006.

Reporting on Jamie Dimon taking a knee in apparent support of BLM while visiting a branch office comes from author interviews and various public sources, including Thornton McEnery, "Jamie Dimon Drops into Mt. Kisco Chase Branch, Takes a Knee with Staff," *New York Post*, June 5, 2020.

The reaction to Manhattan DA Alvin Bragg's policing by the Partnership for New York City comes from author interview with the group's president, Kathryn Wylde.

Soros's statement that he never met Alvin Bragg is from Ty Rousch, "George Soros Denies GOP Conspiracy He Backed DA Bragg," *Forbes*, March 31, 2023.

Information on the growth of the "defund the police" movement following George Floyd's death, its impact on crime, and the business community's reaction to Manhattan DA Alvin Bragg's soft-on-crime policies comes from author interviews and various news accounts, including Charles Gasparino, "Eric, It's Safety First! Adams' Loud Promises to

NYC Businesses Not Kept," *New York Post*, May 28, 2022; "Angry Biz Leaders to Meet with New DA Alvin Bragg, Discuss Recall Efforts over Soft-on-Crime Agenda," *New York Post*, January 10, 2022.

Reporting on Bank of America's $1 billion commitment to expand opportunities in Black communities and Brian Moynihan asking managers to read author Raj Chetty's work for guidance on how to spend money comes from author interviews as well as news accounts, including "Bank of America Announces $1 Billion/4-Year Commitment to Support Economic Opportunity Initiatives," Bank of America Newsroom, June 2, 2020.

Information on Jamie Dimon's $30 billion pledge to fix racial inequity comes from author interviews and public sources such as "JPMorgan Chase Commits $30 Billion to Advance Racial Equity," JPMorgan Newsroom, October 8, 2020.

Information on Dimon, Moynihan, and corporate America's use of welfare-state capitalism in the aftermath of George Floyd comes from author interviews and Emily Rosenman, "From the Racialization of Finance to the Financing of Anti-racism: Tracing the US Financial Industry's Investments in Closing the Racial Wealth Gap," *Environment and Planning A: Economy and Space*, December 12, 2023.

For Abigail and Stephen Thornstrom's work on targeted programs for minorities and her quote to me, see Charles Gasparino and Joseph N. Boyce, "Jackson, Wall Street Have Their Big Day, but Will It Fuel Minority Opportunities?," *Wall Street Journal*, January 16, 1998.

For Thornstrom's stats on Black poverty rates, see Barton Swaim, "How 'Antiracism' Becomes Antisemitism; Demonizing People in Racial Terms Because They're Successful Turns Out to Have Consequences," *Wall Street Journal*, December 29, 2023.

Reporting on corporate America's hiring of nonwhite employees comes from author interviews and Jeff Green, David Ingold, Raeedah Wahid, Cedric Sam, and Daniela Sirtori-Cortina, "Corporate America Promised to Hire a Lot More People of Color. It Actually Did," Bloomberg, September 25, 2023.

Information on Bank of America's CRT program in its Charlotte office comes from author interviews with BofA executives, Manhattan Institute scholar Chris Rufo, and published reports, including Christopher F. Rufo, "Bank of Amerika," *City Journal*, August 18, 2021.

Reporting on Ibram X. Kendi and his Boston University antiracism think tank and its corporate funding comes from various public sources, including Elizabeth Lukehart, "If It Ain't Broke, Don't Fix It. Smash It, and Build Something Else," Medium, May 30, 2020; Coleman Hughes, "How to Be an Anti-intellectual," *City Journal*, October 27, 2019; Sara Rimer, "Jack Dorsey, Twitter and Square Cofounder, Donates $10 Million to BU Center for Antiracist Research," *BU Today*, August 20, 2020.

Information on the troubles with the Kendi think tank, including scaling back its operations, comes from author interviews and a report from Stephanie Saul, "An Ambitious Antiracism Center Scales Back amid Allegations of Poor Management," *New York Times*, September 23, 2023. Kendi declined to comment.

The BlackRock managing director posting racial justice messaging on social media comes from the LinkedIn page of the executive.

Reporting on Jeffrey Sonnenfeld's "CEO Summits" and interactions with people like Jack Welch, Ken Frazier, Ken Chennault, and other CEOs comes from author interviews with Sonnenfeld, and subjects themselves, as well as various public reports, including Jeffrey A. Sonnenfeld, "The Jack Welch That I Knew," Yale Insights, March 2, 2020; Jeffrey Sonnenfeld, "This Is No Time for Silence," ChiefExecutive.net.

Information on GE's embrace of green energy under Jeff Immelt as CEO comes from author interviews and various public reports, including Dorothy Pomerantz, "CEO Transition: How Jeff Immelt Reinvented GE," GE Newsroom, August 1, 2017; Scott Malone, "GE's Immelt to Unveil New Green Energy Technology," Reuters, May 11, 2009.

For Sonnenfeld's critique of Jeff Immelt ("So much of the job of leadership..."), see Nelson D. Schwartz, "Wall Street's Fading Crush on G.E.," *New York Times*, June 22, 2008.

Reporting on activist investor Nelson Peltz pushing to oust Jeff Immelt as GE CEO comes from author interviews and various public reports, including Rick Clough, "GE Surges on Report That Peltz's Ire May Lead to CEO Change," Bloomberg, March 10, 2017; Charles Gasparino and Brian Schwartz, "General Electric CEO Immelt in the Hot Seat with Trian's Peltz," Fox Business, March 10, 2017.

Regarding Immelt's description of his own tenure as CEO in his book *Hot Seat*, see author interviews and reviews, including Charles Gasparino, "GE's Immelt-Down: Harsh Light on in-the-Dark CEO's Failure," *New York Post*, February 20, 2021; "Ex-GE Boss Jeff Immelt Bares His Singed Soul in 'Hot Seat,'" *New York Post*, March 6, 2021.

Background on Sonnenfeld's CEO Summits comes from author interview with Sonnenfeld.

Information on former SEC chief Harvey Pitt's belief that Sonnenfeld's summits were going woke beginning in 2020 comes from author interviews with Pitt and others, and Charles Gasparino, "Yale CEO Summit Strikes Nonpartisan Tone Despite Biden Remarks, Racial Injustice Conversations," Fox Business, June 6, 2020, and Sonnenfeld's published work, including "Corporate America Got Woke on Race," *Politico*, May 23, 2021.

Reporting on Ukrainian president Zelenskyy and his meetings with Wall Street executives and appearance at Sonnenfeld's summit comes from author interviews and public reports, including Charles Gasparino, "Wall Street Has Its Eyes Set on Ukraine," *New York Post*, February 25, 2023; "Zelensky Wines, Dines with the World's Richest in the Hopes of Rebuilding War-Torn Ukraine," *New York Post*, September 23, 2023.

Information on Sunbeam board member and corporate governance expert Charles Elson's defenestration of "Chainsaw Al" Dunlap as CEO comes from author interviews and public sources, including Daniel Kadlec, "Chainsaw Al Dunlap Gets the Chop," *Time*, June 29, 1998.

Details on Sonnenfeld's fraught relationship with Donald Trump come from author interviews and Molly Ball, "How Big Business Got Woke and Dumped Trump," *Time*, November 1, 2021.

Sonnenfeld's positions on ESG and woke capitalism are explained in author interviews and news reports, including Jeffrey A. Sonnenfeld, "CEOs Shouldn't Be Afraid of Politicians Who Cry 'Woke,'" Yale Insights, September 15, 2022.

Reporting on CEOs condemnation of Trump's January 6 activities and Ken Frazier standing up to Trump after Charlottesville comes from author interviews and news reports, including David Gelles, "The CEO Who Stood Up to President Trump: Ken Frazier Speaks Out," *New York Times*, February 19, 2018; Tom Krishner and Paul Wiseman, "Top CEOs Met to Plan Response to Trump's Election Denial," AP News, November 13, 2020; Molly Ball, "How Big Business Got Woke and Dumped Trump," *Time*, November 1, 2021; Lucy Bayly, Haley Messenger, and Emily Pandise, "CEOs and Business Leaders Condemn 'Appalling Events' at Capitol, Push for Unity," NBC News, January 6, 2021.

Information on CEOs signing a petition opposed to the Georgia voting law comes from author interviews and David Gelles and Andrew Ross Sorkin, "Hundreds of Companies Unite to Oppose Voting Limits, but Others Abstain," *New York Times*, May 27, 2021.

Details of Delta's opposition to the voting law, and its CEO's salary, come from author interviews and published reports, including David Gelles, "Businesses Face Backlash for Criticizing Georgia Voting Law," *New York Times*, April 1, 2021; Kristin Majcher, "Highest-Paid US Airline CEOs in 2022," Skift, June 13, 2023.

Reporting on the pressure on MLB commissioner Rob Manfred to move the All-Star Game out of Atlanta in 2021 and its impact on minority businesses in the city with the highest number of Black-owned businesses comes from author interviews and public reports, including Charles Gasparino, "MLB Swings and Misses in Political Debacle to Move All-Star Game from Georgia," *New York Post*, April 10, 2021; "MLB, Players' Union Facing All-Star Lawsuit for Pulling Game out of Atlanta," Fox Business, May 31, 2021; Michael Ruiz and Andrew Murray, "Dem-Backed MLB All-Star Game Move Cost Majority-Black Atlanta Tens of Millions of Dollars," Fox Business, July 13, 2021; Maggie Davis, Dan Shepard, and Pearly Huang, "Atlanta Is Nation's Hub for Black-Owned Businesses," LendingTree, February 6, 2023.

On Colorado voting laws having more restrictions than Georgia's, see Nicole Fallert, "Colorado, Site of New MLB All Star, Also Has Some Restrictions," *Newsweek*, April 6, 2021.

Chapter Five: Woke and Broke

Mark Cuban's contention that woke is good for business comes from author interview with Cuban, and various public sources, including Conor Murray, "Mark Cuban Calls Going Woke 'Good Business'—and Conservatives and Fellow Shark Kevin O'Leary Bite Back," *Forbes*, June 14, 2023.

Cuban's sale of Broadcast.com was good for him but terrible for the acquirer, Yahoo. It is considered among the worst internet acquisitions of all time, according to reporting by Verne Kopytoff, "5 Worst Internet Acquisitions of All Time," *Fortune*, May 21, 2013.

On the success of Nike's Kaepernick ad, see various public sources, including Soo Youn, "Nike Sales Booming After Colin Kaepernick Ad, Invalidating Critics," ABC News, December 21, 2018; "Nike's 'Dream Crazy' Advert Starring Colin Kaepernick Wins Emmy," *The Guardian*, September 16, 2019.

On LeBron James wearing a hoodie after the death of Trayvon Martin, and the background of Martin, see Roy Burton, "LeBron James, Trayvon Martin and When a Picture Is Worth More Than 1,000 Words," Bleacher Report, March 23, 2012; Lizette Alvarez, "Defense in Trayvon Martin Case Raises Questions About the Victim's Character," *New York Times*, May 23, 2013.

The Michael Jordan incident and "Republicans buy sneakers, too" line is from Tim Bontemps, "Michael Jordan Stands Firm on 'Republicans Buy Sneakers, Too' Quote, Says It Was Made in Jest," ESPN, May 4, 2020.

On Gen Z becoming less woke, see David McLennan and Whitney Ross Manzo, "Why Generation Z Might Not Be as 'Woke' as Most Think," *The Hill*, October 11, 2022.

Information regarding NFL TV ratings taking a hit over the Kaepernick one-knee issue and as the league embraces progressive politics, and owners' dismay over commissioner Roger Goodell's progressive positions, comes from author interviews with various team owners, and published reports, including Charles Gasparino, "NFL Drops the Ball as TV Ratings Take Hit over 'Woke-ism,'" *New York Post*, December 28, 2020; Michael McCarthy, "Shock Poll: A Third of NFL TV Viewers Boycotting Games Because of Colin Kaepernick-Led Protests," *Sporting News*, October 5, 2016; Brian Schwartz and Charles Gasparino, "In the Battle over NFL Player Protests Trump Wins with the Fans, Easy," Fox Business, September 25, 2017; Shalise Manza Young, "Juicy New Details Revealed in Growing Feud Between Roger Goodell and Jerry Jones," Yahoo Sports, November 17, 2017.

Reporting on the NBA's success despite its embrace of progressive politics comes from author interview with Mark Cuban, and Yussuf Kahn, "2022–23 NBA Season Proves 'Go Woke, Go Broke' Is an Absolute Joke," First and Pen, May 26, 2023.

The percentage of NFL players who are African American comes from Walter Sharp, "What Percentage of NFL Players Are Black?," Sporkskeeda, February 8, 2021.

Details of the NFL owners' 2023 meeting come from author interviews with two people who were present.

On the new management of the Washington Commanders looking to change the lyrics of "Hail to the Redskins," see Ivan Lambert, "Commanders Suggest New Lines to 'Hail to the Commanders,'" Commanders Wire, July 27, 2022.

Details on the pressure faced by former Redskins owner Dan Snyder to change the team's name amid criticism over racism come from author interviews with people close to Snyder and public news accounts, including Emma Bowman, "For Many Native Americans, the Washington Commanders' New Name Offers Some Closure," NPR, February 6, 2022.

Former SEC chair Jay Clayton's dealings with CAP and HRC come from author interview with Clayton; CAP and HRC had no comment after the author provided them with this excerpt from the book.

On salaries for working at CAP, see Sam Dorman, "Biden OMB Nominee Neera Tanden Received $731 G over 2 Years from Liberal Nonprofit," Fox News, January 12, 2021.

Details on CAP's corporate donors and its power in Washington come from author interviews, its website, and various public sources, including Ken Silverstein, "The Secret Donors Behind the Center for American Progress and Other Think Tanks," *The Nation*, May 22, 2013; Greg Sargent, "Center for American Progress, Poised to Wield Influence over 2016, Reveals Its Top Donors," *Washington Post*, January 21, 2015.

Gary Gensler's background, including his personal life, is from author interviews and various public sources, including Peter Henn, "Who Is Gary Gensler? SEC Chair Leading America's Anti-crypto Charge Once Offered to Work as Adviser to Binance," CCN, June 14, 2023.

Details on Gary Gensler's relationship with Sam Bankman-Fried come from author interviews and reporting, including Charles Gasparino, "SEC Chairman Gary Gensler Met with Head of FTX Months Before Collapse," Fox Business, November 14, 2022; "How Sam Bankman-Fried 'Madoff' with Regulators," Fox Business, December 31, 2022; Lydia Moynihan, "SEC Boss Gary Gensler Faces Ethics Scrutiny over Sam Bankman-Fried Meeting," *New York Post*, June 22, 2023.

Reporting on Sam Bankman-Fried and effective altruism comes from author interviews and Gideon-Lewis Kraus, "Sam Bankman-Fried, Effective Altruism, and the Question of Complicity," *New Yorker*, December 1, 2022.

Details on Gensler's desire to expand SEC rulemaking into areas such as corporate diversity come from an online chat with Lloyd M. Johnson Jr., publisher of the *Black In-House Counsel Annual Report*, as in "A Mission for Inclusion: In Conversation with Gary Gensler," on the SEC website, November 22, 2023.

Chapter Six: The Fight Begins

Much of the reporting in this section is from author interviews with retired McDonald's CEO Ed Rensi, people close to Disney CEO Bob Chapek, and various published reports about McDonald's looking to expand franchise ownership to African Americans and Disney's opposition to the Florida sex education law.

Background on the pressure faced by Chapek from board members and employees comes from people close to Chapek and published reports, including Alex Sherman, "Disney's Wildest Ride: Iger, Chapek and the Making of an Epic Succession Mess," CNBC, September 6, 2023.

Milton Friedman's conversation with Ed Rensi is from author interview.

Information on Ray Kroc's hiring of Robert Beavers and his legacy at McDonald's, including his role in expanding African American franchises, comes from author interviews and published reports, including Graydon Megan, "Robert Beavers, Former McDonald's Executive, Dies at 71," *Chicago Tribune*, August 31, 2015; "The Legacy Continues for The First Black Owned McDonald's," McDonalds.com.

Details on Herman Petty becoming the first of eventually three hundred African American McDonald's franchisees come from author interviews and published reports, including "Herman Petty," Honorary Chicago, February 25, 2022.

Background on the Reedy Creek Improvement District comes from various public sources and reports, including the "About" page of the Central Florida Tourism Oversight District's website; Central Florida Tourism Oversight District, report on "Past Practices of the Reedy Creek Improvement District," December 4, 2023; Hannah Sampson, "Disney's Special Tax District in Florida, Explained," *Washington Post*, April 25, 2022.

Background on Bernie Marcus and his Job Creators Network comes from author interviews and published news reporting, including Charles Gasparino, "Here's Why Home Depot's 94-Year-Old Co-founder Bernie Marcus Says He's 'Particularly P–ssed Off,'" *New York Post*, November 4, 2023; Alexandra Ma, *Business Insider*, February 22, 2019.

Chapter Seven: "Who the Fuck Are These People?!?!"

Descriptions of Larry Fink's reaction to the Consumers' Research attack ads come from author interviews with Larry Fink and the creator of the ads, Will Hild.

Background on Leonard Leo and his connections to Consumers' Research and the history of the organization comes from author interviews and published reports, including Kenneth P. Vogel, "Leonard Leo Pushed the Courts Right. Now He's Aiming at American Society," *New York Times*, October 12, 2022.

Consumers' Research's description as a "dark money" group comes from author interviews and published reports, including Eamon Javers, "Conservative Group Launches Ad Campaign Against 'Woke Capitalism,' Targeting CEOs by Name," CNBC, May 18, 2021.

The description of Will Hild's activities and work from his home in Bethesda, Maryland, comes from author interviews and published reports, including Saijel Kishan, "The Little-Known Group That's Battling Wall Street over ESG," Bloomberg, June 7, 2023.

Reporting on Consumers' Research targeting Larry Fink and BlackRock but also Brian Moynihan of Bank of America comes from author interviews, published reports, and Gabriel Hays, "Watchdog Group Accused Bank of America of Using Bank as 'Political Club' Against Americans," Fox News, June 7, 2023.

Larry Fink moderating Gary Gensler's climate disclosure proposal comes from author interview with Fink and from BlackRock's submitted public comment letter to the SEC.

Larry Fink's "behaviors are going to have to change" comments come from published reports, including Aubrie Spady, "BlackRock CEO Slammed for 'Force Behaviors' Comment After 2017 Interview Re-emerges About DEI Initiatives," Fox Business, June 5, 2023.

The description of Larry Fink and his personal attributes and desire to be US Treasury secretary come from author interviews and various public reports, including Fink's biography and credentials on Influence Watch's website; Charles Gasparino, *The Sellout: How Three Decades of Wall Street Greed and Government Mismanagement Destroyed the Global Financial System* (New York: Harper Business, 2009).

Fink's conversation with David Solomon comes from author interview with Fink.

Details of Larry Fink's work for the government following the 2008 financial crisis come from author interviews and various published reports, including Suzanna Andrews, "Larry Fink's $12 Trillion Shadow," *Vanity Fair*, March 2, 2010.

Reporting on Larry Fink's tenure at First Boston and the reasons behind his departure comes from author interviews and various published reports, including Gasparino, *The Sellout*.

Information on Steve Schwarzman's "mistake" in allowing Fink to leave Blackstone comes from author interviews with people who have heard the comment, and various public reports, including Devin Banerjee, "Schwarzman Says Selling BlackRock Was 'Heroic' Mistake," Bloomberg, September 30, 2013.

Details of Schwarzman's departure from Lehman and the creation of Blackstone come from author interviews and published reports, including Kenneth N. Gilpin, "Ex-Lehman Official Joins New Venture," *New York Times*, October 22, 1985; James B. Stewart, "The Birthday Party," *New Yorker*, February 4, 2008; Ken Auletta, *Greed and Glory on Wall Street: The Fall of the House of Lehman* (New York: Warner Books, 1987).

The description of Fink's departure from Blackstone comes from author interviews with Fink and people close to Schwarzman as well as published reports, including Devin Banerjee, "Schwarzman Says Selling BlackRock Was 'Heroic' Mistake."

The description of Blackstone's Hilton Hotels deal comes from author interviews and published reports, including Gillian Tan, "Blackstone Exits Hilton, Earning $14 Billion After 11 Years," Bloomberg, May 18, 2018.

The description of BlackRock's purchase of Barclays' investment arm and expansion into ETFs comes from author interviews and published reporting, including Svea Herbst-Bayliss, "BlackRock to Buy BGI, Becomes Top Asset Manager," Reuters, June 12, 2009.

Details on the explosion of "passive investing" during this time come from author interviews and news reports, including Adrienne Buller and Chris Hayes, "The Passive Revolution," Common Wealth, August 4, 2022; Robin Wigglesworth, "Passive Attack: The Story of a Wall Street Revolution," *Financial Times*, December 20, 2018.

Information on the 2008 financial crisis, Occupy Wall Street, and the rise of populism contributing to corporate wokeism comes from author interviews and various published reports, including James A. Anderson, "Some Say Occupy Wall Street Did Nothing. It Changed Us More Than We Think," *Time*, November 15, 2021.

Reporting on Fink's 2016 edict to push ESG firm-wide across BlackRock comes from author interviews with people on the global conference call and published reports, including "ESG Integration Across Asset Classes," High Meadows Institute, September 2019; Stephen Andrews, "ESG Investing at BlackRock," BlackRock.com, November 2019; and BlackRock's 2016 Annual Report.

On the size of blue-state pension funds compared to those in red states, see Ross Kerber, "Blue State Pension Funds Invest More Money," Yahoo News, September 20, 2023.

On the growth of sovereign wealth funds and the use of ESG, see Hazel Bradford, "ESG Moves Up on Sovereign Wealth Funds Priority List," *Pensions & Investments*, February 13, 2023; Libby George and Hadeel Al Sayvegh, "Sovereign Wealth Funds Struggle to Turn Their Trillions to Climate Finance," Reuters, December 6, 2023.

Details of Fink's relationship with Donald Trump are from author interview with Fink and published reports, including "Remarks by President Trump in Strategy and Policy Forum," Trump White House Archives, February 3, 2017.

Details on Hartford Funds putting the word "sustainable" into its title and the boost in investor inflow come from author interviews with people in the money management business and Shane Shifflett, "Wall Street's ESG Craze Is Fading," *Wall Street Journal*, November 19, 2023.

On Senator Elizabeth Warren's criticism of Fink and BlackRock over oil company investments, see Lauren Hirsch, "Elizabeth Warren Pushes Larry Fink on BlackRock's Pledge to Fight Climate Change," CNBC, February 26, 2020; Francine McKenna, "Why Warren Would Bar Execs from BlackRock, and not Goldman, from a Clinton Administration," Market Watch, September 26, 2016; Oscar Williams-Grut, "BlackRock Accused of 'Greenwashing' $85bn Coal Investments," Yahoo Finance, January 12, 2021.

Details on criticism of BlackRock "greenwashing" investments come from author interviews and published reports, including Oscar Williams-Grut, "BlackRock Accused of 'Greenwashing' $85bn Coal Investments."

Reporting on left-wing protests in front of BlackRock's offices, including environmentalists, comes from author interviews and various published reports, including Aleese Kopf, "Protesters Fined for Using Megaphone," *Palm Beach Daily News*, May 22, 2016.

On BlackRock exiting the thermal coal business, see Jasper Jolly, "BlackRock Holds $85bn in Coal Despite Pledge to Sell Fossil Fuel Shares," *The Guardian*, January 13, 2021.

Information on how BlackRock's AUM exploded to record levels amid the ESG embrace, and Fink's boasting of it, comes from author interviews and published reporting, including Cam Simpson and Saijel Kishan, "How BlackRock Helped Make ESG the Hottest Ticket on Wall Street," BNN Bloomberg, December 31, 2022.

Details on BlackRock's hiring of former Obama aide Brian Deese to lead its ESG effort come from author interviews and published reports, including Trevor Hunnicutt, "BlackRock Hires Former Obama Climate Adviser: Memo," Reuters, October 10, 2017.

Information on Brian Deese's role inside the firm comes from author interviews with BlackRock execs who dealt with him.

Information on Fink prodding portfolio companies to adopt diversity measures, particularly on corporate boards, comes from author interviews and public sources, including Lyuba Goltser, "BlackRock's Larry Fink Delivers Annual Message to CEOs," Weil, Gotshal & Manges LLP, January 22, 2019.

International Women's Day document obtained by the author through BlackRock sources.

The Rachel Lord Zoom call details come from a copy of the call that was circulated internally and shared with the author.

Dimon's criticism of Fink comes from author interview with a senior JP Morgan official.

Details on Fink setting up an office in Washington, DC, in anticipation of being named Hillary Clinton's Treasury secretary and his remarks that he could do more "good" as head of BlackRock come from author interviews and Michael Neibauer, "BlackRock Pays $183.9M for Downtown D.C. Office Building," *Washington Business Journal*, July 27, 2015.

The comparison of Larry Fink to Henry Luce is from Lance Morrow, *The Noise of Typewriters: Remembering Journalism* (New York: Encounter Books, 2023).

Former Merrill Lynch CEO and BlackRock board member David Komansky's assessment of Larry Fink's politicization as CEO comes from author interview with an executive who spoke to Komansky directly.

The letter to Fink from American Water comes from a copy of the letter obtained by the author.

Chapter Eight: The Boys from Brazil (and Belgium)

Details of Daniel Blake's role in handling the fallout of the Dylan Mulvaney controversy come from author interview with a representative for Blake and published reports, including Isabel Keane, "Second Bud Light Marketing Exec Placed on Leave After Dylan Mulvaney Backlash," *New York Post*, April 24, 2023.

Senior management downplaying and being unaware of Dylan Mulvaney's hiring comes from author interviews and published reports, including Ariel Zilber, "Anheuser-Busch CEO Shifts Blame on Bud Light Dylan Mulvaney Ads: 'Not a Formal Campaign,'" *New York Post*, May 4, 2023.

The information that Mulvaney was among many AB InBev influencers is from author interviews with AB vendors and published reports, including Emily Stewart, "The Bud Light Boycott, Explained as Much as Is Possible," *Vox*, June 30, 2023.

Details of Mulvaney's "365 Days of Girlhood" social media spots are from reviews of the spots themselves and published reports, including Samantha Riedel, "Dylan Mulvaney Gives Tampons to People Who Need Them. Transphobes Are Mad," Them, December 9, 2022; Amelia Harvey, "Who Is TikTok's Dylan Mulvaney and Why Did Drew Barrymore 'Kneel' Before Her?," The Things, March 16, 2023.

That Dylan Mulvaney was being repped by CAA comes from published reports, including the Creative Artists Agency website.

Details of Mulvaney's interview with President Biden come from author interviews and published reporting, including Edie Heipel, "In Interview with Trans Activist, Biden Condemns States Banning Sex Changes on Kids," Catholic News Agency, October 24, 2022.

Anheuser-Busch CEO Brendan Whitworth's comments on Dylan Mulvaney and background come from various published reports, including Lisa Fickenscher, "Anheuser-Busch CEO Refuses to Say Whether Bud Light Will Work with Dylan Mulvaney Again," *New York Post*, June 28, 2023; Blake Stilwell, "Anheuser-Busch CEO and Marine Vet Answers Hard Questions About Bud Light Marketing," Military.com, June 28, 2023.

Information on Blake and Heinerscheid being placed on leave comes from author interviews and published reports, including Amanda Holpuch and Julie Creswell, "2 Executives Are on Leave After Bud Light Promotion with Transgender Influencer," *New York Times*, April 25, 2023.

Blake's reaction to being put on leave and AB's rationale behind it are from author interview with a person with direct knowledge of the matter. Blake has been given excerpts of the book that involve him, as has Alissa Heinerscheid, the other marketing executive put on leave. AB InBev also has been given chapters of this book involving the matter and has not commented other than to downplay the description of the AB InBev CEO as a "Davos Man."

Details of Daniel Blake's career are from his LinkedIn profile.

Blake's description of the typical Budweiser beer drinker is from Diana Pearl, "Busch Reminds Small-Town Family What Their Dad Really Wants for Father's Day," *Adweek*, June 15, 2018.

Blake's role in marketing Kirin beer is from author interview.

Heinerscheid's comments about "fratty" culture are from her Facebook feed and from published reports, including Harriet Alexander and Alex Hammer, "Bud Light's Under-Fire Marketing VP 'takes LEAVE OF ABSENCE' After Dylan Mulvaney Controversy—and 'Is Replaced by Budweiser Executive,'" *Daily Mail*, April 21, 2023, and Heinerscheid's comments on the *Make Yourself at Home* podcast, Episode 21.

Heinerscheid's background is from author interviews with former AB execs and published reports, including Giulia Carbonaro, "Who Is Alissa Heinerscheid? Bud Light's VP of

Marketing amid Trans Debate," *Newsweek*, April 10, 2023; Heinerscheid's marriage announcement to her husband, Henry Heinerscheid, is from the *New York Times*.

Information about Heinerscheid's role in the *Game of Thrones* commercial and its critical acclaim is from published reports, including Katie Richards, "How the Demise of Bud Light's Bud Knight Came to Be in a Super Bowl Spot for HBO's Game of Thrones," *Adweek*, February 4, 2019; Heinerscheid's interview with Provoke Media; and Matthew Gabriele, "About That Medieval Bud Light/Game of Thrones Super Bowl Ad," *Forbes*, February 6, 2019.

Information about Heinerscheid's role in the Miles Teller Super Bowl commercial is from published reports, including Jameson Fleming, "Keleigh and Miles Teller Dance Through Hold Music Hell in Bud Light's Super Bowl Ad," *Adweek*, February 2, 2023.

Information about cost cutting after InBev bought Anheuser-Busch is from author interviews and published reports, including "3 Years After InBev Deal, a New Anheuser-Busch," *Columbus Dispatch*, November 29, 2011, and "The Battle Is Over: InBev Buys Anheuser-Busch," *IndustryWeek*, July 14, 2008.

Details of AB InBev management's need to cut costs because of debt and merger activity and the impact on marketing are from author interviews and various published reports, including "AB InBev's New CEO Will Inherit Debt Hangover," Breakingviews, May 10, 2021; Philip Blenkinsop, "InBev Cost-Cutting Measures Set for U.S. Export," Reuters, July 8, 2008; Seb Joseph, "AB InBev Cuts Marketing Spend After Sales Slump," *Marketing Week*, April 1, 2013; Carlos Alberto Sicupira, Jorge Paulo Lemann, and Marcel Hermann Telles, "Belgium: AB InBev's Cost-Cutting Had Its Days," Inside Beer, March 6, 2019.

Details about AB moving its advertising and marketing to New York City following InBev's deal come from author interviews and published reports, including "Anheuser-Busch Moves Marketing and Advertising to NoMad," Kew Management, April 7, 2015.

Details on the Anheuser-Busch St. Louis HQ are from published reports, including Tripp Mickle, "Anheuser-Busch InBev Moving U.S. Sales, Marketing Hub to New York," *Wall Street Journal*, December 9, 2014.

Background on the Busch family is from author interviews and published reports, including Acacia Squires, "The 'Bitter' Tale of the Budweiser Family," NPR, December 22, 2012; Susan Berfield, "The Fall of the House of Busch," NBC News, July 17, 2011; Kristin Stoller, "For This Anheuser-Busch Heir, Trouble Followed," *Forbes*, June 21, 2019.

Details on the "Frankie and Louie" Budweiser commercial are from author interviews and published reports, including "Budweiser—Ferret Gets the Job," *AdAge*, January 31, 1999, and "Budweiser—Frogs' Final Act," *AdAge*, January 31, 1999.

Details of InBev's purchase of AB are from author interviews and published reports, including Daniel Roberts, "The Biggest Beer Merger Ever Was Never Supposed to Happen," Yahoo Finance, September 30, 2016.

Information on Anheuser-Busch's dominant market share and decline comes from author interviews and various published reports, including Kenneth Musante, "This Bud's for You: Anheuser-Busch Looks Like a Stock That Could Hold Up Well During Tough Times for the Economy," CNN, January 28, 2008; Joshua M. Bernstein, "The Mystery Of Bud Light," *The Atlantic*, July 21, 2023.

On AB InBev's CEO receiving initial accolades, see published reports, including "Profiles of the World's Best CEO's," *Barron's*, March 26, 2011.

InBev's description as a culture of cost cutting comes from author interviews with former executives and distributors and this published report, among others: Seb Joseph, "AB InBev Cuts Marketing Spend After Sales Slump," *Marketing Week*, April 1, 2013.

Reporting on Michel Doukeris becoming AB InBev's CEO and his relationship to Davos is from author interviews and public reports, including the World Economic Forum's bio page for Michel Doukeris; Doukeris's public comments on ESG; Lisa Johnson, "Michel Doukeris Named AB InBev CEO," *Consumer Goods*, May 6, 2021; Simon Mainwaring, "Purpose at Work: How AB InBev's New CEO Michel Doukeris Is Brewing Up a Future Full of Cheer," *Forbes*, February 7, 2022; Klaus Schwab, "Davos Manifesto 2020: The Universal Purpose of a Company in the Fourth Industrial Revolution," World Economic Forum, December 2, 2019.

Background on Davos and Klaus Schwab, including his net worth, comes from author interviews and various public sources, including Peter S. Goodman, "He Has an Incredible Knack to Smell the Next Fad: How Klaus Schwab Built a Billionaire Circus at Davos," *Vanity Fair*, January 18, 2022; David Boyd, "Klaus Schwab's Net Worth," Finty, June 16, 2023; Marilyn Haigh, "Bono: Capitalism Is a 'Wild Beast' That If Not Tamed Can Chew Up a Lot of Lives," CNBC, January 24, 2019.

On the relationship between Klaus Schwab and Henry Kissinger, see Klaus Schwab, *The World Economic Forum: A Partner in Shaping History; The First 40 Years, 1971–2010* (Cologny/Geneva, Switzerland: World Economic Forum, 2009).

For Schwab's comments about former president Trump, see Goodman, "He Has an Incredible Knack to Smell the Next Fad."

Doukeris being listed on the Davos 2022 agenda is from "World Economic Forum Annual Meeting List of Participants as of 17 November 2021," Politico.com.

On Ezgi Barcenas providing an update on AB InBev meeting its sustainability targets, see Doukeris's public comments on ESG at Davos, and public reports, including Jessica DiNapoli and Philip Blenkinsop, "Budweiser Brewer AB InBev 'Off Track' on Non-alcoholic and Low-Alcohol Beer Goal," Reuters, May 25, 2022.

On Doukeris adopting the "Davos Manifesto" at AB InBev, see Simon Mainwaring, "Purpose at Work."

On Doukeris unveiling ESG strategies, see the 2021 Environmental, Social & Governance Report from Anheuser-Busch, February 24, 2022.

On Doukeris talking about his ESG agenda at AB InBev, see "AB InBev CEO Talks Sustainability, Global Recession Risk, and Beer Pricing," Yahoo Finance, February 17, 2023.

On Krause Fund Research's criticism of AB InBev's business, see research report from Krause Fund Research, April 15, 2021.

Chapter Nine: This Bud Is Not for You

Background on the "This Bud's for You" commercial comes from published reports, including Nicolette Baker, "Budweiser Plans Regional Super Bowl Ad with 'This Bud's for You' Tagline," VinePair, January 31, 2023.

On AB InBev's employing DEI in beer ads using transgender actors and overtly supporting LGBTQ+ issues in commercials, see Brooke Sopelsa, "Bud Light Debuts Trans-Inclusive TV Ad," NBC News, August 15, 2016; Glenn Garner, "Transgender Runner CeCé Telfer Felt 'Seen' by Other Athletes After Olympic Trials Ineligibility," *People*, August 30, 2021; Chaitra Krishnamurthy, "Bud Light Canada Launched Rainbow Cans in 2022 to Celebrate LGBTQIA2S+ Community," HITC, April 5, 2023.

Reporting on Daniel Blake and Alissa Heinerscheid speaking at the distributors' convention and details of upcoming Bud Light commercials comes from author interviews with attendees and published reports, including Ginger Adams Otis, Lauren Weber, and Jennifer Maloney, "Bud Light Brewer Puts Two Executives on Leave After Uproar over Transgender

Influencer," *Wall Street Journal*, April 22, 2023; Jennifer Maloney and Lauren Weber, "How Bud Light Handled an Uproar over a Promotion with a Transgender Advocate," *Wall Street Journal*, May 22, 2023; Jennifer Maloney, "How Bud Light Blew It," *Wall Street Journal*, May 21, 2023.

Details of Dylan Mulvaney's hiring come from author interviews and published reports, including Owen Myers, "'Panic And Rash Decision-Making': Ex-Bud Light Staff on One of the Biggest Boycotts in US History," *The Guardian*, September 19, 2023.

Details of the first Dylan Mulvaney Bud Light social media ad on February 11, 2023, come from published reports and her personal Instagram page.

Details of the Dylan Mulvaney March Madness ad come from published reports and her personal Instagram page.

On Travis Tritt boycotting Bud Light, see published reports, including Yaron Steinbuch, "Travis Tritt Boycotts Anheuser-Busch After Bud Light Teams Up with Dylan Mulvaney," *New York Post*, April 6, 2023.

On Kid Rock firing on cans of Bud Light, see published reports and his Instagram feed.

Details on the initial response of AB to go silent come from author interviews with people close to the company.

The story of the construction worker demanding his beer not be poured into a Bud Light glass comes from an eyewitness account.

On Budweiser and Bud Light beer sales in free fall following the Mulvaney controversy and consumer boycotts, see various published reports, including Breck Dumas, "Bud Light Sales Fall Further, Modelo Extends Lead as Best-Selling US beer," Fox Business, August 29, 2023; Dee-Ann Durbin, "Bud Light Parent Says US Market Share Stabilizing After Transgender Promotion Cost Sales," AP News, August 3, 2023.

The Blake part of the post-Mulvaney cleanup team story comes from author interview with a Blake representative.

On the "Backyard Grunts" commercial post-Mulvaney, see Aimee Picchi, "After Dylan Mulvaney Backlash, Bud Light Releases 'Grunts' ad with Kansas City Chiefs' Travis Kelce," CBS News, June 4, 2023.

Details on the strategy behind Brendan Whitworth's first public statement post-Mulvaney come from author interviews with people involved in the discussion; details of his statement come from various published reports, including Haadiza Ogwude, "Anheuser-Busch CEO Releases Statement amid UC Grad Dylan Mulvaney, Bud Light Backlash," *Cincinnati Enquirer*, April 14, 2023.

Information on Donald Trump Jr.'s support of Whitworth and its backfiring comes from author interviews with people close to AB and various published reports, including Emma Colton, "Trump Jr., GOP Under Fire for Going Soft on Bud Light Boycotts: No Interest in 'Pushing Back,'" Fox News, April 17, 2023.

Information on the Mercury PR agency being hired by AB comes from author interviews with people who work with AB.

Reporting on Whitworth's interview with Gayle King and AB InBev's continued support of LGBTQ causes comes from author interviews and Dean J. Hampton, "Anheuser-Busch CEO Says His Company Will Continue to Support the LGBTQ Community," NBC News, June 28, 2023; "Bud Light and the NGLCC Continue to Empower LGBTQ+ Owned Small Businesses Across America," Anheuser-busch.com, May 30, 2023.

On Michel Dourkeris's comments to analysts about the Mulvaney controversy, see various published reports, including Eri Sugiura, "AB InBev Boss Blames Social Media 'Misinformation' for Backlash Against Bud Light," *Financial Times*, May 8, 2023.

On AB producing "unique commemorative cans" for other influencers, see Ryan Chatelain, "Bud Light Partnership with Trans Influencer Infuriates Some Conservatives," Spectrum News NY1, April 6, 2023.

Details of Senator Ted Cruz's investigation of AB and the Mulvaney controversy come from author interview with Cruz and a memo produced by his staff.

Chapter Ten: The Not So Wonderful World of Woke Disney

Details of Sage Steele's firing and controversy come from author interviews with Steele, various published reports, and Megyn Kelly's podcast, *The Megyn Kelly Show*, Episode 610, August 17, 2023.

Information on ESPN's demos comes from author interviews and published reports, including Damjan Jugovic Spajic, "11 Fascinating ESPN Viewership Statistics for Diehard Fans," PlayToday.com, November 21, 2023.

On ESPN's profits and the impact of cord cutting on the bottom line, see Alex Weprin, "How Profitable Is ESPN? Disney Breaks Out Figures for First Time," *Hollywood Reporter*, October 18, 2023.

Details on ESPN copying its business model from Deadspin come from author interviews and published reports, including Kerry Flynn, "ESPN and Competitors Ditch Their 'Stick to Sports' Mantra. Politics Is Now Fair Game," CNN, September 1, 2020.

On Deadspin's bankruptcy filing after the Hulk Hogan case, see Noah Frank, "The Rise and Fall of Deadspin: How 'Jerks in Brooklyn' Changed Sports Journalism," *The Guardian*, July 21, 2022.

Information on the top Disney shows of the 1990s comes from author interviews with Disney executives and published reports, including Phil Pirrello, "Ranking Disney's 10 Best Animated Movies from the '90s," Atom, June 12, 2019.

On Chris Berman's stature at ESPN during the 1990s, see ESPN's press room on its official website.

Disney's profits in 2023 and before are from Macrotrends.net.

On ESPN's declining viewership, see published reports, including Colin Dixon, "What ESPN Says About the Declining Traditional TV Industry," NScreenMedia, January 24, 2023.

On former Disney CEO Michael Eisner revising and hosting *The Wonderful World of Disney* in the late 1980s, see Julie Hyman, "Former Disney CEO Michael Eisner: 'I've Always Worked at Companies Where I Have Fun,'" Yahoo Finance, April 7, 2021.

Information on Disney's successes during the Eisner years and his vision for the company with the Capital Cities/ABC deal is from author interviews and published reports, including Kim Masters, "The Epic Disney Blow-Up of 1994: Eisner, Katzenberg and Ovitz 20 Years Later," *Hollywood Reporter*, April 9, 2014; THR Staff, "Michael Eisner on Former Disney Colleagues, Rivals and Bob Iger's Successor," *Hollywood Reporter*, July 27, 2016.

Details of Disney's deal to buy Capital Cities/ABC come from published reports, including, Laura Landro, Thomas R. King, Elizabeth Jensen, and Jeffrey Trachtenberg, "That's Show Biz: Walt Disney's Merger with Cap Cities/ABC Stuns Global Industry," *Wall Street Journal*, August 1, 1995.

Information on Eisner modeling Disney after GE as a conglomerate comes from author interviews with media CEOs who know Eisner.

Details on Eisner's resignation come from author interviews and published reports, including Merissa Marr, Mylene Mangalindan, and Joann S. Lublin, "Disney Turns to Insider Iger to Take CEO Reins from Eisner," *Wall Street Journal*, March 14, 2005.

The conversation with Ace Greenberg comes from author interview and Charles Gasparino, "If Wall Street Were Olympian, He'd Ace the Marathon," *Wall Street Journal*, March 8, 1999.

Details of Sage Steele's career at ESPN in this section come from author interviews with Steele and ESPN officials.

Jason Whitlock's description of ESPN comes from his interview with Megyn Kelly on her podcast, *The Megyn Kelly Show*, Episode 273, March 3, 2022.

Examples of politics front and center at ESPN and coverage of George Floyd's death come from author interviews and published reports, including Carly Ortiz-Lytle, "Stephen A. Smith Walks off Set After Celtics Promote White Head Coach and Not Black Candidate," *Washington Examiner*, June 3, 2021; Ben Strauss, "ESPN Has Tried to Focus More on Sports, but That Changed with George Floyd," *Washington Post*, June 6, 2020.

Information on Sage Steele being denied a role in ESPN's Floyd special comes from author interview with Steele, ESPN officials, and Joe Flint, "ESPN Anchor Sage Steele Claimed Black Colleagues Excluded Her from Race Special," *Wall Street Journal*, July 21, 2020.

On ESPN staffers holding a moment of silence over the Florida sex ed law pushed by Ron DeSantis, see Brittany Bernstein, "ESPN Broadcasters Hold Moment of Silence to Protest Florida's Parental-Rights Bill on LGBT Ed," *National Review*, March 19, 2022.

On Former ESPN host Jemele Hill calling Trump a "white supremacist," ESPN's reaction, and Trump's reaction, see Aris Folley, "Jemele Hill Says Calling Trump a White Supremacist Is Like 'Saying Water Is Wet,'" *The Hill*, December 27, 2018; Nolan D. McCaskill, "White House Suggests ESPN Fire Jemele Hill over 'Outrageous' Trump Comments," *Politico*, September 13, 2017; German Lopez, "Donald Trump's War with ESPN and Jemele Hill, Explained," *Vox*, October 10, 2017.

Details of the Rachel Nichols incident at ESPN are from author interviews and Kevin Draper, "A Disparaging Video Prompts Explosive Fallout Within ESPN," *New York Times*, August 25, 2021.

Information on Sage Steele's comments on Jay Cutler's podcast and the subsequent fallout comes from a review of the podcast based on her interview with Megyn Kelly, her lawsuit against ESPN, author interviews, and published reports, including Minyvonne Burke and Diana Dasrath, "Sage Steele and ESPN Part Ways After Settling Lawsuit," NBC News, August 15, 2023; Joe Morgan, "Sage Steele Opens Up Following ESPN Exit: 'This Is So Much Bigger Than Me,'" Fox News, September 1, 2023; Leah Asmelash, "ESPN's Sage Steele Apologizes for Controversial Comments About Obama's Racial Identity and Vaccine Mandates," CNN, October 6, 2021.

Details of Disney CEO Bob Chapek's banning of plastic straws come from author interviews, Disney's public statements, and various published reports, including Genevieve Shaw Brown, "Walt Disney Company to Eliminate Plastic Straws and More by 2019," ABC News, July 26, 2018.

On the average cost to attend Disney World, see Joshua Powell, "How Much Does It Cost to Go to Disney World? Average Park Visit Prices 2023," Magic Guides, May 31, 2023.

Details of the Bob Iger succession race at Disney come from author interviews with people close to the matter and various published reports, including Ben Fritz, "Disney Overhaul Sets Stage for Succession Race," *Wall Street Journal*, March 14, 2018.

Background on Chapek comes from author interviews with people close to the former Disney CEO. Chapek did not refute this description through a spokeswoman and declined further comment.

Details of the differences between Iger and Chapek come from author interviews with current and former Disney employees and studio executives who know them both.

Information on Bob Iger's dealmaking spree and the debt overhang left to Chapek come from author interviews and published reports, including Thomas Buckley and Lucas Shaw, "Bob Iger Shifts from Building an Empire to a Disney Yard Sale," Bloomberg, July 16, 2023.

Details of Iger and Disney's embrace of sexually diverse characters come from author interviews with people with direct knowledge of the matter and various published reports, including Mey Rude, "A Brief Timeline of Disney's 17 'First Gay Characters,'" *Out*, September 16, 2022.

On trigger warnings on old Disney programming, see "Content Advisory Message Now Shown on Old Disney Films," *The Urban News*, October 14, 2022.

Reporting on Disney's Reimagine Tomorrow program to introduce more diverse characters comes from author interviews and "Disney Launches Digital Destination to Amplify Underrepresented Voices," Walt Disney Company website, September 1, 2021; information on how this filtered down to hiring decisions is from an internal memo, "Disney General Entertainment Content, Inclusion Standards," confirmed by Disney.

Information on Disney's "Gay Days" and warnings to parents come from various public reports, including Eve Chen, "What Days Are Gay Days at Disney World? Everything to Know About the Red Shirt Tradition," *USA Today*, April 17, 2023; Ted Johnson, "New Florida Laws Spark Concern Among Organizers of Gay Days Events at Walt Disney World and Other Sites," *Deadline*, May 31, 2023; Jess Colopy, "Disney Once Officially Warned Guests About 'Homosexuals' Gathering at Magic Kingdom," Inside the Magic, August 22, 2022.

Details of the *Mulan* controversy and Disney's business interests in China come from author interviews and Dr. Ewelina U. Ochab, "Why Is Disney Under Fire over Mulan?" *Forbes*, October 22, 2022.

Details of John Lasseter's messy #MeToo exit from Disney come from author interviews and Kim Masters, "John Lasseter's Pattern of Alleged Misconduct Detailed by Disney/Pixar Insiders," *Hollywood Reporter*, November 21, 2017.

Information on Chapek's new, less woke direction for the company upon taking over as CEO comes from author interviews of people with direct knowledge of the matter and various published reports, including Jim Geraghty, "At Disney, Woke Strikes Back," *National Review*, November 21, 2022; Alex Sherman, "Disney's Wildest Ride: Iger, Chapek and the Making of an Epic Succession Mess," CNBC, September 6, 2023.

Details of Chapek's misstep with Scarlett Johansson, and Alan Horn's reaction, are from author interview with media executive who spoke with Horn, and various published reports, including Joshua M. Patton, "Scarlett Johansson's Black Widow Lawsuit Doomed Bob Chapek's Disney Career," Comic Book Resources, November 22, 2022; Anthony D'Alessandro, "Disney CEO Defends Studio Amid Scarlett Johansson's 'Black Widow' Lawsuit: 'Our Talent Is Our Most Important Asset,'" *Deadline*, September 21, 2021; J. Clara Chan, "Disney CEO: Talent Deals Undergoing 'Reset' After Scarlett Johansson Lawsuit," *Hollywood Reporter*, September 21, 2021; Beatrice Verhoeven, Umberto Gonzales, and Diane Haithman, "Scarlett Johansson's Lawsuit and Disney Brand 'Carnage': Is CEO Bob Chapek to Blame?," *TheWrap*, August 2, 2021; Dominic Patten, "Disney & Scarlett Johansson Resolve Bitter 'Black Widow' Profits Lawsuit; Big $$$ Win for Oscar Nominee," *Deadline*, September 30, 2021.

Information on Chapek shifting blame on the Johansson controversy to Iger and heightening frictions between the two come from author interviews with media executives, and published reports, including Sherman, "Disney's Wildest Ride."

Details of the DeSantis-Chapek fight over the Florida sexual education law come from author interviews and various published reports, including Ron DeSantis's book *The Courage to Be Free: Florida's Blueprint for America's Revival* (New York: Broadside Books, 2023); Alexandra Steigrad, "Ex-Disney CEO Chapek Griped to DeSantis About 'Pressure' to Slam Fla.'s 'Don't Say Gay' Bill: Book," *New York Post*, February 27, 2023; Tal Barak Harif and Felipe Marques, "Disney Versus DeSantis: A Timeline of the Florida Feud," Bloomberg, April 27, 2023; Tom Hudson, "How Disney and DeSantis Clashed over Power and Policy, and What It Means for Business and Politics in Florida," WLRN, May 10, 2022.

Reporting on academic studies purporting to show positive benefits from teaching children about gender fluidity comes from author interviews and various published reports, including "Experts: Sex Education Should Begin in Kindergarten," Montclair State University, College News and Events, December 19, 2020; Eva Goldfarb and Lisa Lieberman, "Three Decades of Research: The Case for Comprehensive Sex Education," *Journal of Adolescent Health*, October 12, 2020.

On the percentage of children who grow out of gender dysphoria, see Jon Brooks, "The Controversial Research on 'Desistance' in Transgender Youth," KQED, May 23, 2018.

On Gina Carano being fired by Disney, see Ryan Parker and Aaron Couch, "'The Mandalorian' Star Gina Carano Fired amid Social Media Controversy," *Hollywood Reporter*, February 10, 2021.

Iger's initial tweet opposing the Florida sex ed law is from Bob Iger's official Twitter/X account.

Details of Chapek's discussion with the Brunswick Group on the initial response to the DeSantis sex ed law come from author interviews with people involved in conversations, and published reports, including Selome Hailu, "Disney Employees Slam Bob Chapek's Memo on 'Don't Say Gay' Bill: 'Silence Is Unacceptable,'" *Variety*, March 7, 2022.

On Disney the executive adding "queerness" to programming, see Twitter feed of the Manhattan Institute's Chris Rufo and published reports, including Alexandra Steigrad, "Disney Exec Cops to Advancing 'Gay Agenda' by 'Adding Queerness' to Shows," *New York Post*, March 30, 2022.

Background on the pressure faced by Chapek from board members and employees comes from people close to Chapek and published reports, and see Sherman, "Disney's Wildest Ride."

Chapek's conversation with DeSantis is from Ron DeSantis's book *The Courage to Be Free*.

Details on Chapek changing course on the "Don't Say Gay" law after being attacked by employees and left-wing group come from author interviews with past and former Disney executives; his official statement on Disney's support for the LGBTQ+ community; and public reports, including Alex Weprin, "Disney CEO Bob Chapek Addresses Company's Response to Florida's 'Don't Say Gay' Bill," *Hollywood Reporter*, March 7, 2022; Jennifer Maas, "Disney CEO Received Letter from LGBTQ Staff Pleading for Support Before 'Don't Say Gay' Bill Passed Florida Senate," *Variety*, March 10, 2022; Selome Hailu, "Disney Employees Slam Bob Chapek's Memo on 'Don't Say Gay' Bill: 'Silence Is Unacceptable,'" *Variety*, May 7, 2022; Bob Chapek, "Statement on Disney's Support for the LGBTQ+ Community," Walt Disney Company website, March 11, 2022, and Sherman, "Disney's Wildest Ride."

Details of Disney chairwoman Susan Arnold telling Chapek to apologize come from author interviews with Chapek reps, Disney executives, and published reports, including Sherman, "Disney's Wildest Ride."

On Chapek getting a contract extension, see Brent Lang, "Embattled Disney CEO Bob Chapek Gets Contract Extension," *Variety*, June 28, 2022.

On Chapek restoring a same-sex kissing scene in *Buzz Lightyear* and starting to put similar scenes in other content, see Abbey White, "'Lightyear' Producer Says Disney Was 'Supportive' of Lesbian Characters, but There Was 'Definite Pushback' to Kiss," *Hollywood Reporter*, June 15, 2022; Caroline Miller, "Lightyear Gets Warning Sign for Gay Kiss Scene at Oklahoma Theater, Sparking Backlash," Movieweb, June 26, 2022.

On Disney's *Strange World* flopping at the box office, see "Disney's 'Strange World' Flops, LGBTQ Character to Be Scapegoated?," TMZ, November 27, 2022.

The information on DeSantis stepping up attacks against Disney following Chapek's U-turn on the Florida sex ed law, including dismantling the Reedy Creek deal, comes from author interviews and published reports, including Julia Malleck, "DeSantis's Disney District Board Launched a New Attack on the Company," *Quartz*, August 22, 2023.

Iger attacked the Florida same-sex law in an interview with Chris Wallace on CNN+, March 31, 2022.

On Chapek, fighting for his job, meeting with employees and growing a beard, see Avidan Grossman, "Disney CEO Bob Chapek Is Rocking the Rare Corporate Power Beard," *GQ*, September 9, 2022; Brooks Barnes, "At Corporate Pep Rally, Disney C.E.O. Pitches Warmer, Fuzzier Side," *New York Times*, September 11, 2022.

Details on Disney's stock tanking, being among the worst performers in S&P for the first half of 2022 and on track for its worst performance since 1974, putting increasing pressure on Chapek to resign, come from author interviews and published reports, including Bradford Betz, "Disney Stock Tumbles amid Florida Bill Controversy," Fox Business, April 22, 2022; Caitlin Huston, "Disney Stock Fell 44 Percent in 2022 amid Tumultuous Year," *Hollywood Reporter*, December 30, 2022.

On activist investors circling Disney amid poor performance, see published reports, including Kim Masters, Alex Weprin, "Behind Disney's Activist Investor Battle: A Marvel Mogul's Revenge Play," *Hollywood Reporter*, January 17, 2023.

Details on Chapek's firing and Iger's return are from author interviews with company insiders and published reports, including Brooks Barnes, "Disney Brings Back Bob Iger After Ousting Chapek as C.E.O.," *New York Times*, November 20, 2022.

Chapter Eleven: The Biggest Woke Target in the World

The opening scene comes from my dinner with Morgan Stanley CEO James Gorman.

Details on the fed funds rate increases to combat inflation come from author interviews and various public reports, including Benjamin Curry, "Understanding the Federal Funds Rate," *Forbes*, November 1, 2023; James Royal and Brian Beers, "Biggest Winners and Losers from the Fed's Interest Rate Decision," Bankrate, December 13, 2023.

On Biden's approval rating sinking because of inflation, see Jed Graham, "Biden Approval Rating Sinks to New Low on Economic Issues," *Investor's Business Daily*, October 2, 2023.

Information on ESG contributing to inflation comes from author interviews with top Wall Street CEOs, BlackRock's Larry Fink, and published reports, including Inigo Fraser Jenkins, Alla Harmsworth, Robertas Stancikas, Harjaspreet Mand, and Maureen Hughes, "The Intimate Linkage of ESG and Inflation," AllianceBernstein, May 23, 2022.

Details on Consumers' Research's attacks against Fink and BlackRock becoming more multilayered come from author interviews with its executive director, Will Hild, Larry Fink himself, and various published reports, including Zachary Evans, "Non-profit Releases Ad Attacking BlackRock over China Investments," Yahoo News, October 28, 2021.

Information on Consumers' Research's letter to governors about BlackRock comes from author interview with Hild, a copy of the letter obtained by the author, and Thomas Catenacci, "Consumer Group Issues Alert over BlackRock's Woke Crusade: 'No Regard for American Families,'" Fox Business, August 17, 2022.

Details on states boycotting BlackRock over ESG come from author interviews and Eric Revell, "Kentucky Warns BlackRock, JPMorgan Chase over 'Energy Boycotts,'" Fox Business, January 3, 2023; Tsvetana Paraskova, "Republicans Withdraw $1 Billion from BlackRock Due to Its ESG Policies," *Oil & Gas 360*, October 10, 2022.

Details on Tennessee suing BlackRock come from author interview with BlackRock officials and Sandy Mazza, "Tennessee Sues New York Investment Giant BlackRock over Climate-Based Policies," *Nashville Tennessean*, December 20, 2023.

On former VP Mike Pence attacking BlackRock over ESG, see op-ed by Pence, "Republicans Can Stop ESG Political Bias," *Wall Street Journal*, May 26, 2022.

Information on BlackRock's support for ESG through the placement of the firm Engine No. 1 on the board of ExxonMobil comes from author interviews with Larry Fink and other top Wall Street executives, and published reports, including Matt Phillips, "Exxon's Board Defeat Signals the Rise of Social-Good Activists," *New York Times*, June 9, 2021.

Details on Will Hild's additional attacks comparing Fink to various dictators come from author interviews with Hild, Fink, and published reports, including Timothy Nerozzi, "Consumers' Research Deploying Mobile Billboards, New Ad Linking BlackRock CEO to China," Fox News, March 28, 2022.

The description of Larry Fink's position on the need for a "transition" to a green economy and his criticism of Modern Monetary Theory comes from author interviews with Fink and published reports, including Fink's 2021 Letter to CEOs; Sissi Cao, "World's Largest Money Manager Says Liberals' Favorite Economic Theory Is 'Garbage'" *Observer*, March 7, 2019.

On Vanguard announcing withdrawal from the Net Zero Alliance, see published reports and the company's announcement on its official website.

Details on NYC comptroller's Brad Lander's letter to Larry Fink and Fink's reaction come from author interviews with reps for Lander and Fink, the letter published on the New York City comptroller's website, and published reports, including Charles Gasparino, "It's Only a Matter of Time Until the ESG Movement Will R.I.P.," *New York Post*, August 26, 2023.

On George Soros's criticism of Larry Fink, see Soros, "BlackRock's China Blunder," *Wall Street Journal*, September 6, 2021.

Details on the broadening attacks against Fink and BlackRock over ESG come from author interviews and published reports, including Evan Harper, "Is BlackRock's Larry Fink Blowing It for the Climate?," *Washington Post*, May 7, 2023.

BlackRock's 2021 and 2022 earnings are from published reports, including "BlackRock Net Income 2010–2023," Macrotrends.net.

Information on BlackRock moving away from ESG comes from author interviews with BlackRock officials and published reports, including Charles Gasparino, "Investment Titan BlackRock Mutes ESG Talk amid Backlash," *New York Post*, October 7, 2023.

Information on BlackRock overhauling its lobbying department amid ESG pushback, including Republicans, comes from author interviews with people directly involved in the matter and various published reports, including Brooke Masters, "BlackRock Steps Up Spending on US Lobbying in Face of Anti-ESG Attacks," *Financial Times*, January 28, 2023; Rob Kozlowski, "BlackRock Recruits Former SEC Investment Management Head Blass," *Pensions*

& Investments, May 13, 2021; Ross Kerber, "BlackRock Names New Corporate Affairs Chief," Reuters, June 15, 2023; "Dalia Blass to Conclude Tenure as Director of the Division of Investment Management," SEC website, December 22, 2020.

Information on BlackRock no longer mandating PMs' use of ESG screens in non-sustainable funds comes from author interviews and published reports, including Gasparino, "It's Only a Matter of Time Until the ESG Movement Will R.I.P.," *New York Post*, August 26, 2023.

Details of BlackRock's ad campaign come from author interviews with BlackRock officials and published reports, including Silla Brush, "BlackRock Debuts Ad Campaign to Burnish Image as It Faces ESG Scrutiny," Bloomberg, June 6, 2022.

On Fink's attendance at the COP28 climate conference, see Alastair Marsh, "Larry Fink Leads CEOs Back to COP Talks They Snubbed Last Year," Bloomberg, October 19, 2023.

Information on climate activists targeting BlackRock comes from author interviews and published reports, including Davide Barbuscia and Ross Kerber, "BlackRock's President Faces Climate Questions at New York Event," Reuters, February 16, 2023.

Background on BlackRock president Rob Kapito comes from author interviews; his views on inflation and "pampered" younger generations from Ariel Zilber, "'Entitled' Millennial Generation 'Never Had to Sacrifice': BlackRock Exec," *New York Post*, April 15, 2022.

Reporting in this section BlackRock on president Robert Kapito being targeted by Hild's organization, on Kapito being targeted by left-wing activists at the energy conference in Austin, and Kapito leading the firm's messaging comes from author interviews with Hild and BlackRock officials. Information was also gleaned from various published reports, including Alexandra Tremayne-Pengelly, "BlackRock President Robert Kapito Is the Latest Target for Climate Protesters," *Observer*, February 17, 2023; Brad Johnson, "BlackRock President Denies Accusations of Fossil Fuel Divestment at Texas Oil and Gas Convention," *The Texan*, March 29, 2022.

BlackRock's Mark Wiedman's comments about ESG at the Semafor conference are from author interviews and published reports, including Gasparino, "Investment Titan BlackRock Mutes ESG Talk amid Backlash," *New York Post*, October 7, 2023.

Chapter Twelve: Woke Is Finally Broken

Details of the Jack Dorsey dinner are from author interviews with people who were present.

On Twitter's market capitalization rising to a high of $61 billion, see Bill Alpert, "Twitter and Jack Dorsey Proved Investors Wrong. Now the Stock Looks Expensive," *Barron's*, February 26, 2021.

The number of Twitter's active daily users is from published reports, including Stacy Jo Dixon, "X/Twitter: Number of Monetizable Daily Active Users Worldwide 2017–2022," Statista, November 6, 2023.

Reporting on the controversy surrounding Twitter's Section 230 privileges comes from author interviews with members of Congress, published reports, and Lauren Feiner, "House Republican Staff Outline Principles to Reform Tech's Liability Shield," CNBC, April 15, 2021.

Additional details about Dorsey's New York meeting are from author interviews with people who were present.

Details of Elon Musk's purchase of Twitter come from author interviews and various published reports, including Charles Gasparino, "Twitter on the Cheap: Is Elon Musk Eyeing a Discount?," *New York Post*, July 30, 2022; "Elon's Musk-See Fight for Twitter," *New York Post*, July 16, 2022; "With Intrepid Twitter Bid, Elon Musk Is in Battle with Naysayers," *New York*

Post, April 24, 2022; Thomas Barrabi, "CNBC's David Faber Argues Elon Musk Could Face Jail Time over Twitter Deal Exit," *New York Post*, July 11, 2022; Michelle F. Davis, "Goldman, JPMorgan Could Get $133 Million for Advising Twitter on Musk Deal," Bloomberg, May 17, 2022.

Details of Twitter management's censorship of right-leaning voices on the release of the Twitter Files come from author interviews and various published reports, including Farnoush Amiri and Barbara Ortutay, "Ex-Twitter Execs Deny Pressure to Block Hunter Biden Story," AP News, February 8, 2023; "Twitter Suppressed Covid-19 Info, Suspended Top Experts, Allege Twitter Files," *The Economic Times*, December 27, 2022; Benjamin Wallace-Wells, "What the Twitter Files Reveal About Free Speech and Social Media," *New Yorker*, January 11, 2023.

Information about Twitter's business model that mostly lost money over the years comes from author interviews and various published reports, including Elizabeth Napolitano, "Musk Reveals Twitter Ad Revenue Is Down 50% as Social Media Competition Mounts," CBS News, July 17, 2023; Timothy B. Lee, "Twitter Stock Fell After Weak Third-Quarter Results. Here's Why the Company Is Struggling," *Vox*, October 27, 2015.

On Netflix standing behind comedian Dave Chappelle despite controversy over *The Closer*, see Julian Mark, "Netflix CEO Argues That Chappelle's New Special, Criticized as Transphobic, Is Too Popular to Cancel," *Washington Post*, October 12, 2021.

On Spotify standing with Joe Rogan, see Wendy Lee, "With New Joe Rogan Deal, Spotify's Exclusive Big-Name Podcasting Era Is Done," *Los Angeles Times*, February 2, 2024.

Ed Rensi's comments are from author interview.

Details of Job Creators Network meetings and ad campaigns come from author interviews with Ed Rensi and Alfredo Ortiz and the Job Creators Network's press release regarding its "No Mouse in My House" campaign.

The reference to Glenn Loury and John McWhorter's changing beliefs on George Floyd and Derek Chauvin's guilt are from Glenn Loury and John McWhorter, "The Truth About George Floyd's Death," *The Glenn Show* podcast, December 2, 2023; the reference to George Floyd as "Saint George" is from a Gerard Baker column.

On the MLB All-Star Game returning to Atlanta, see published reports, including Mark Feinsand, "Braves to Host 2025 All-Star Game at Truist Park," MLB.com, November 16, 2023.

Details of AB InBev's Cesar Vargas meeting with reporters are from author interviews with people directly involved in the matter.

On the decline in AB InBev beer sales, see Jordan Valinsky, "Bud Light Sales Keep Sinking," CNN, October 31, 2023.

Details on AB InBev's partnership with UFC and "Power Slap" come from author interviews with UFC's Dana White, and Charles Gasparino, "Budweiser's Power Slap Venture Is a Knuckleheaded Bid to Turn Its Brand Around After Dylan Mulvaney Fiasco," *New York Post*, December 16, 2023; Stefan Sykes, "Anheuser-Busch and UFC Strike Multiyear Partnership, as Brewer Tries to Turn Around Bud Light Sales," CNBC, October 24, 2023.

On Anheuser-Busch's Super Bowl ad spending and the use of non-woke characters, influencers, and the Clydesdales, see Eleanor Terrett and Charles Gasparino, "Budweiser Attempts Rebranding with Super Bowl Ads," Fox Business, January 30, 2024, and Aislinn Murphy, "Budweiser's Clydesdales Return for Super Bowl LVIII," Fox Business, January 31, 2024.

On Bud Light's year-over-year sales decline, see Breck Dumas, "Bud Light Sales Down Nearly 30% Year over Year," Fox Business, January 31, 2024.

Details of Disney's woke business model taking a toll on the company's stock price and finances and the company disclosing that wokeness could hurt its bottom line come from author interviews and various published reports, including Joe Flint, "Disney's Bob Iger Plays Down Asset Sales, Vows to Build Modern Version of Company," *Wall Street Journal*, November 28, 2023; Ariel Zilber, "Struggling Disney Hints Its Woke Politics 'Present Risks to Our Reputation and Brands,'" *New York Post*, November 28, 2023; Samantha Delouya, "Disney Is in Trouble. Bob Iger Has 5 Big Problems to Solve," CNN, November 8, 2023.

Information on media industry Democrats' increasing frustration with the leftism of the Biden administration thwarting deals comes from author interviews with top media executives who spoke on a not-for-attribution basis.

Details on BlackRock and other big money managers shutting down ESG funds come from author interviews and published reports, including Silla Brush, "BlackRock, State Street Among Money Managers Closing ESG Funds," Bloomberg, September 21, 2023; Brian Boyle, "ESG Funds Shrink for the First Time Ever," *The Daily Upside*, November 19, 2023.

On concerns that ESG could lead to antitrust violations and investigation by GOP congressman Jim Jordan, see Saul Elbein, "Jordan Subpoenas Climate Group for Alleged 'Collusion' and Antitrust Violations," *The Hill*, November 11, 2023.

Information on the demise of general green investing is from author interviews and various published reports, including Krystal Hur, "Clean Energy Stocks Have Fallen out of Favor. They Face More Challenges Ahead," CNN, December 3, 2023.

On Hertz dumping its EVs, see Allysia Finley, "Hertz, Tesla and the Perils of CEO Group Think," *Wall Street Journal*, January 14, 2024.

On Fink calling Bitcoin a "store of value," see Charles Gasparino, "Crypto-Hating Gary Gensler Bites the Bullet by Aiding the 'Wild West' of Investing," *New York Post*, January 13, 2024.

Fink explaining where he went wrong on ESG is from author interview.

On Fink doing business in Texas again and Lieutenant Governor Dan Patrick calling him the "king of Wall Street," see Amanda Albright, "Texas Lauds BlackRock's 'King of Wall Street' in Change of Tune," Bloomberg, February 6, 2024.

The information on Texas demanding that its municipal bond underwriters do no business that curtails the sale of firearms, impedes oil drilling, or threatens Israel's right to exist is from a copy of a letter to potential bond underwriters from the attorney general of Texas.

On Goldman and Citadel leaving high-crime and taxes in blue states for Texas and Florida, see Shelly Hagan, "Goldman Sachs Descends on Dallas in Wall Street's Latest Move West," Bloomberg, May 2, 2023, and Ariel Zilber, "Ken Griffin Moved Citadel out of Chicago After Colleague Robbed at Gunpoint," *New York Post*, September 21, 2022.

On Coca-Cola disassociating itself from BLM after the group's pro-Hamas support, see Ariel Zilber, "Coca-Cola Has Quietly Scrubbed References to Hamas-Supporting BLM from Its Website," *New York Post*, October 23, 2023.

Details on Target closing stores over "organized retail crime" are from author interviews and published reports, including Julie Coleman, "Target CEO Says He's Pleased with the Progress That's Been Made Against Retail Theft," CNBC, November 15, 2023.

Information on Jay Clayton's appointment to the Amex board and its impact on Amex backing off of its use of CRT in employee seminars comes from author interviews.

Details of DEI officers losing their jobs amid the backlash to corporate wokeism come from author interviews and Kiara Alfonseca and Max Zahn, "How Corporate America Is Slashing DEI Workers amid Backlash to Diversity Programs," ABC News, July 7, 2023.

Reporting on Sam Bankman-Fried and "effective capitalism" is from author interviews and Jennifer Szalai, "How Sam Bankman-Fried Put Effective Altruism on the Defensive," *New York Times*, December 13, 2022.

Ed Rensi's comments are from author interview.

On George Soros handing operational control of his activist work to his son, see Gregory Zuckerman, "George Soros Hands Control to His 37-Year-Old Son: 'I'm More Political,'" *Wall Street Journal*, June 11, 2023.

Reporting on Jamie Dimon praising Donald Trump in Davos is from author interviews and Kevin Breuninger, "Jamie Dimon Praises Trump; Warns MAGA Criticism Could Hurt Biden," CNBC, January 18, 2024.

Information on Jamie Dimon stating he wasn't taking a knee in support of BLM back in 2020 and his explanation of stakeholder capitalism comes from author interview with a JP Morgan press official.

On how DEI and wokeness led to antisemitism, see Barton Swain, "How 'Antiracism' Becomes Antisemitism; Demonizing People in Racial Terms Because They're Successful Turns Out to Have Consequences," *Wall Street Journal*, December 29, 2023.

Details on Wall Street executives fighting back against campus wokeism as it devolved into antisemitism come from author interviews with CEOs and various public reports, including Charles Gasparino, "Apollo CEO Marc Rowan Hits Back at UPenn Leadership After Antisemitism on Campus," *New York Post*, October 28, 2023; "Where Is the CEO Outrage During the Ongoing War Between Israel and Palestine?," *New York Post*, October 14, 2023.

Claudine Gay's reasoning for her resignation is from her resignation letter.

On critics of Claudine Gay saying DEI was the reason for her appointment to run Harvard, see Melissa Koenig, "Billionaire Bill Ackman Claims Harvard President Was Hired Because of DEI Initiative," *New York Post*, December 7, 2023.

On donations by Marc Rowan and Bill Ackman to Penn and Harvard, see Charles Gasparino, "Feminist Leaders, Democrats Are Radio Silent on the Rape, Torture of Jewish Women," *New York Post*, December 9, 2023.

The remarks by Bernie Marcus are from author interview.

On Qatar as a major source of American university endowment money, see Ashley Carnahan, "Funding from Arab Countries to US Universities Raises Questions," Fox Business, November 14, 2023.

Index

AB InBev
alienating traditional customers, 185
Anheuser-Busch acquisition, 172–173, 175
Blake, Daniel, 163, 167–170, 182, 186
Bud Light (*See* Bud Light beer)
Budweiser (*See* Budweiser beer)
Clydesdales commercials, 169, 173, 186, 249
Cruz and, 188
damage control, 186–188
declining sales, 176
DEI hiring guidelines, 170–171
digging out of branding disaster, 247–248
distributors and wholesalers convention, 182
Doukeris, Michel, 166, 176, 178–180, 187–188
ESG goals, 178–180
founders, 173
Frankie and Louie ad, 174
Heinerscheid, Alissa, 164–165, 167–168, 170–171, 182
Kid Rock and, 248–249
Mulvaney fiasco (*See* Mulvaney, Dylan)
nationwide boycott, 164
original headquarters, 173
"Power Slap" competition and, 248
prioritizing growth through acquisitions, 175
progressive leanings of, 171–172
reducing marketing spend, 175–176
revenues, 180
Spuds MacKenzie commercials, 169, 173–174
subscribing to the Davos Manifesto, 178
Super Bowl ads, 169, 181, 249
UFC and, 248
Whitworth, Brendan, 21, 166–167, 186–187, 248–249
"About BlackRock" ad campaign, 235
Abrams, Stacey, 111, 246
Ackman, Bill, 259–260
Adams, Eric, 87
affirmative action
in college admissions, 53–54, 244, 253, 260
as corporate priority, 51
DEI vs, 53
in employee recruitments, 13
African Americans. *See* Black people
Aggregated CEO-to-worker compensation ratios, 45
Agrawal, Parag, 241–242, 243
Alibaba, 42

American Express, 29–30, 109, 255
American Legislative Exchange Council, 233
American Water, 160–161
Anheuser, Eberhard, 173
Anheuser-Busch. *See* AB InBev
antisemitism, 65–66, 108, 244, 260–261, 262
anti-woke mass movement, 68
Apollo Group Management, 259
Apple, 43, 206, 251
Arbery, Ahmaud, 73
Arnold, Susan, 217, 219
assets under management (AUM), 150
Auletta, Ken, 148

Baby Boomers, 116
Baker, Gerard, 11
Bank of America (BofA), 83, 88–89, 90–93
banking crisis. *See* financial crisis of 2008
Bankman-Fried, Sam, 124–125, 255–256
Barcenas, Ezgi, 178
Barclays Global Investors, 150
Bastian, Ed, 110
Bates, Richard, 218–219
bathroom bill, 91
Bear Stearns, 197
Beavers, Robert, 132
Becker, Greg, 71. *See also* SVB
Ben & Jerry's ice cream, 56, 114
Biden, Hunter, 76–77, 243
Biden, Joe, 39, 48–49, 75, 166, 250–251
Biden administration, 49, 223, 250–251
Bitcoin, 253
Black Lives Matter
  as anti-American, 25
  as anti-Israel, 26
  core mission, 25
  corporate donations to, 3
  description of, 24
  founding members, 24
  ideology, 25–26
  as "radical chic", 26
  underpinnings of, 24–25
Black National Anthem, 117–118
Black people. *See* people of color
Black Widow (film), 210–212
BlackRock. *See also* Fink, Larry
  "About BlackRock" ad campaign, 235
  alpha, 153–154
  assets under management, 153, 233
  Barclays Global Investors purchase, 150
  business model, 142
  CEOs caving to ESG edicts, 151
  China business dealings, 43, 226–227
  as Consumers' Research target, 137–141
  energy and gas investing, 156
  engaging corporation board diversity, 157–158
  Engine No. 1 and, 228
  ESG as way of life, 3–4, 152–154
  ESG fund business, 151
  ESG metrics and, 37–38
  ESG Pillars, 153–154
  formerly Blackstone Financial, 149
  founders, 144
  Kapito, Rob, 235–236
  marketing strategies, 56–57
  Net Zero Alliance, 230
  redeploying resources, 253
  re-messaging, 235–237
  shutting down ESG funds, 251
  stock value, 234
  success in ESG, 154–155
  sustainable investing, 143
Blackstone Financial. *See* BlackRock
Blackstone Group, 147, 148, 234
Blake, Daniel, 163, 167–170, 182, 186
Blankfein, Lloyd, 11–12, 151
Bloomberg, Michael, 85, 123
Boardroom Initiative, 135, 245, 261
Boeing, DEI hiring goals, 52
Bogle, Jack, 155
Bok, Scott, 258–259
Bollea, Terry Gene "Hulk Hogan", 194

Bono, 176
book writing, act of, 1
Bragg, Alvin, 85–87, 256
brands, politicization of, 55–56
Brito, Carlos, 175
Broacast.com, 114
broken windows theory, 85
Bronitsky, Jonathan, 2, 5
Brown, Michael, 23
Brunswick Group, 216
BU Center for Antiracist Research, 94
Bud Light beer, 2–4, 60, 176, 183–184, 249, 255
Budweiser beer
  boycott of, 184–185
  branding as key to success, 172
  Dylan Mulvaney ad, 55
  image of, 169
  Mulvaney fiasco, 164–168
  re-rebranding of, 168
  slogan, 174, 181
Burr, Bill, 244
Busch, August, III, 173, 174
Busch, Adolphus, 173
Busch, Augustus, IV, 173, 174–175
business leaders. *See* CEOs
Business Roundtable, 31, 40, 101, 103

CAA talent agency, 165–166
Capital Cities/ABC, 196
Capitol Hill riot, 106–107
Carano, Gina, 215
Carlson, Tucker, 248–249
carried interest, 148
Case, Anne, 90
Cathy, Dan, 9, 21–22
Cathy, S. Truett, 8–9
cause marketing, 56
Cavallari, Kristin, 200
Center for American Progress (CAP), 35, 66, 121–123
Center for Antiracist Research, 94
Center for Corporate Governance, 104–105
CEO Summits, 101–103, 105, 108
CEOs
  caving to BlackRock's ESG edicts, 151
  caving to progressive mob, 21
  farming out politics to HR, 47–48
  Friedman's views of, 33
  indirect report to Human Rights Campaign, 65
  main function of, 35
  as masters of the universe, 21
  political shift, 50
  posing as social justice warriors, 130
  setting woke agenda, 48
  shaping political/social debate, 81–83
  Sonnenfeld, Jeff, 105, 108
  Sonnenfeld and, 101–103
  taking eye off the ball, 32–34
  thrive on power, 148–149
  using companies for social/cultural change, 11
  veering into progressive politics, 102
Chapek, Bob, 21. *See also* The Walt Disney Company
  banning plastic straws, 204
  challenges inherited by, 210
  contract extension, 219
  cultural differences between Disney infrastructure and, 128–129
  DeSantis and, 210, 213, 215, 218, 220
  "Don't Say Gay" law, 129–130, 214–217
  edge in getting CEO job, 205–206
  Iger feud, 212–213
  Iger's choice as his successor, 209
  lacking emotional quotient, 206
  managerial flaws, 209–210
  ousted from Disney, 221
  political ambitions, 128
  Rensi on, 126–128, 130
  supporting LGBTQ+ employees, 217–218
  using shareholder money for social engineering, 127–128, 217–218
Chappelle, Dave, 244

Chauvin, Derek, 79, 246
Chenault, Ken, 30, 109
Chetty, Raj, 88–89
Chick-fil-A, 7–10
China
  BlackRock's business relationship with, 43, 226–227
  Disney's business dealings with, 208
  exempt from ESG mandates, 154
  Nasdaq listings standards exemptions, 42
Chinese Communist Party (CCP), 42, 43, 208
Citadel investment empire, 78
Citigroup, 34
Civil Rights Act, 53–54
Clayton, Jay, 37, 120, 123, 234, 255
Clinton, Bill, 74, 122
Clinton, Hillary, 74, 122, 155
Coca-Cola Company, 255
Cohan, William, 12
Cohn, Gary, 11–12
Cohodes, Marc, 125
Collage Group, 58
college admissions, affirmative action in, 53–54, 244, 253, 260
college campuses, antisemitism on, 108, 258–262
Communications Act, Section 230, 240
consumer behavior, shift in, 67–68
Consumers' Research, 137–141, 226–227
Cook, Tim, 230–231
Coors, 175–176
Cornell, Brian, 62–63, 66, 255
corporate America
  adopting zero-emissions standards, 143–144
  ESG investing in, 37–38
  as foot soldier to progressive movement, 1–2
  productivity and, 34
corporate boardrooms. *See also* CEOs
  board gender diversity compared to firm performance, 40–41
  Elson on, 105
  as increasingly progressive, 75
  politicization of, 33
  priorities of, 3
  supporting corporate wokeism, 48
corporate governance, 21, 31–32, 36–37, 41, 101, 104–105
corporate harassment, forms of, 18–19
corporate sensitivity sessions, 95
corporate social responsibility, 17–18, 100
corporate wokeness
  CRT and (*See* critical race theory)
  Cuban rationalizing, 113–115
  description of, 11
  diversity, equity and inclusion (*See* DEI)
  employees encouraged to admit their inner racism, 95
  ESG and (*See* ESG)
  failing of, 19
  infusing corporate decision making, 24–25
  phases of, 56
  rationales for, 113
  Rensi's ve, 138
  Rensi's views on, 245, 247
  in retreat, 254–255
  as well financed, 21
corporate-social-political action, 55–56
Corzine, Jon, 11–12
The Courage to Be Free (DeSantis), 217
Covid pandemic
  DEI-tailored handouts, 88
  economic implications of, 77–78
  lock-down mode, 79, 80
  Trump facing, 73–74
  White House Covid meeting, 77–79
Credit Suisse First Boston, 147
Crenshaw, Kimberlé, 27
critical race theory (CRT)
  defining characteristics, 15
  systemic racism and, 27
  in the workplace, 15
crony capitalism, 50–51
Cruz, Ted, 188

C-suite. *See* CEOs; corporate boardrooms
Cuban, Mark, 43, 107, 113–116, 119–120
Cullors, Patrisse, 24
cultural marketing, 56–59
Cummings, Whitney, 244
Cutler, Jay, 200–201

Dallas Cowboys, 117
Dallas Mavericks, 114
Daly, Mary, 72
Damore, James, 44
Daniels, Stormy, 85
Davos Manifesto, 178
de Blasio, Bill, 26
Deadspin, 193
Deaton, Angus, 90
Deese, Brian, 157
"defund the police" movement, 84–87, 255
DEI (diversity, equity and inclusion). *See also* ESG (environmental, social and governance)
  affirmative action vs, 53
  DEI-tailored handouts, 88
  at Goldman Sachs, 12–14
  as illegal, 53
  politicization of brands through, 55–56
  power of, at major companies, 51–52
  SEC's enforcement of, 125–126
Delta Air Lines, 110
DeSantis, Ron
  in battle against wokeism, 28
  BlackRock's business relationship with, 227
  Chapek and, 210, 213, 215, 218, 220
  The Courage to Be Free, 217
  Covid pandemic and, 81
  Disney and (*See* The Walt Disney Company)
  Don't Say Gay legislation (*See* Parental Rights in Education Act)
  exposing Trump's weaknesses, 81
  Fink and, 142
Diageo chain, 59
Dimon, Jamie
  Business Roundtable and, 31–32
  Chinese market, 43
  on fighting racism, 89
  Fink rivalry, 158–159
  on Georgia's voting laws, 110
  goes woke, 36
  on shareholder capitalism, 31–34
  "taking a knee" photo, 3–4, 83–84, 256–257
  Trump and, 78, 257
  at World Economic Forum, 177
Disney. *See* The Walt Disney Company
Disney, Roy E., 196
Disney, Walt, 133
Disney+, 207
"Don't Say Gay" law (Florida), 129–130, 214–217
Dorsey, Jack, 94, 239–241
Doukeris, Michel, 166, 176, 178–180, 187–188
Dunlap, Chainsaw Al, 104
Durkan, Jenny, 80–81

effective altruism, 255–256
Eisner, Michael, 195–197
Electronic Data Systems, 134
Elson, Charles, 104–105, 106
Ely, Robin, 41
emotional quotient, 206
Engine No. 1, 228
Enriquez, Daniel, 86
entertainment, unwoke, 244–245
Environmental Social Governance, 4
EPCOT (Experimental Prototype Community of Tomorrow), 133–134
equity, fairness vs, 53
ESG (environmental, social and governance). *See also* DEI
  countries exempt from mandates, 154
  description of, 16–17
  downside of, 38
  ESG investing models, 153

ESG *(cont.)*
Fink's views of, 45, 226–229
global acceptance of, 36
greenwashing, 155–156
as illegal, 251–252
mainstreaming, 35–41
as proxy advisers, 37
social part of, 40
taking environmentalism to extreme, 39
United Nations and, 36
ESPN
business model, 192–193
demographics, 192–193
Disney's purchase of, 194
Hill, Jemele, 199–200
navigating woke politics of, 197–200
programming, 193
racial justice movement coverage, 199
ratings, 192–193
SportsCenter, 198
Steele, Sage, 191–192, 197–203
The Undefeated Presents Time for Change, 199
V Foundation fundraiser, 202–203
vax mandate, 201
ESPN+, 193
Evans, David, 58–60
exchange-traded fund (ETF), 150
ExxonMobil, 228

The Fall of Minneapolis (documentary), 246
Fauci, Anthony, 81
federal government
Biden administration, 49, 223, 250–251
debt growth, 224–225
DEI-tailored handouts, 88
Obama presidency, 51, 75–76, 99
pressuring corporate wokeism, 50
racial and gender diversity mandates in, 48–49
Federalist Society, 139
Fidelity, 155
financial crisis of 2008, 12, 17–18, 34, 70, 91, 98, 146–147, 150
Fink, Larry. *See also* BlackRock
assets under management (AUM), 150, 161
background of, 145
as BlackRock founder, 137
board diversity commitment, 157–158
as Consumers' Research target, 137–141
contacts network, 145–146
dealmaking, 150
Deese and, 157
Dimon rivalry, 158–159
as ESG's biggest defender, 44–45, 226–229
as force on policy issues, 143
growing PR problem for, 228–229
Haley and, 253–254
Lander and, 231
love of gossip, 145
market power of, 142
media attention, 146–147
moderate transformation, 253–254
Obama and, 152
passive investing, 150–151
personal politics of, 152
pressure from the left, 231–232
receding into the background, 235
on renewable energy business, 143
as risk manager, 146
Schwarzman and, 147, 149, 233–234
as securitization founding father, 146
seeking allies, 232–233
Solomon and, 146
SVB and, 69
as Trump's money manager, 155
Utopian aspirations, 160
Wiedman's dig at, 236–237
at World Economic Forum, 177
Zelenskyy and, 102–103
Finley, Allysia, 252
First Boston Corporation, 145, 146–147
First Republic, 72

Florida Power & Light, 28
Floyd, George. *See* George Floyd's death
Ford, Henry, 34
Frazier, Ken, 109
Freedman, Bryan, 203
Friedman, Adena, 43–45
Friedman, Milton, 31, 33, 131
FTX, 124–125

Garza, Alicia, 24
Gawker media, 193–194
Gay, Claudine, 17, 259–260
Gaza, 261
GE Asset Management, 95
GE Capital, 98
Geithner, Tim, 146
Gekko, Gordon, 38
General Electric (GE), 14–15, 51, 96–100
Gensler, Gary, 37, 44, 123–125, 143
Gen-Zers
  anti-woke mass movement and, 68
  conservative element within, 116
  embracing wokeism, 58
George Floyd's death
  background of, 79–80
  Chick-fil-A franchises under attack after, 21
  documentary on, 246
  follow-on effects from, 84–85, 88
  increase in DEI mandates after, 52
  protests, 80
  systemic racism and, 26
Georgia voting legislation, 109–111, 246–247
Gianforte, Greg, 227
Gillen, Andrew, 52–53
Gillette, 32
Giuliani, Rudy, 85
Glass, Lewis & Co., 37
globalism, 100
Glocer, Tom, 106, 108, 109
Go, Michelle, 86
Goldman Sachs
  Chick-fil-A debate, 7–10
  culture, 13
  diversity, equity and inclusion (DEI) at, 12–14
  embracing corporate wokeism, 12–13
  ESG money managers and, 17–18
  gender pronoun guide, 14
  Solomon, David, 12–13, 19–20
  speaker list, 15
  stock market value, 19
  top partners for, 11–12
Goodell, Roger, 117–118
Google, speech codes, 44
Gore, Al, 38, 177
Gorman, James, 223, 224
Gray, Joe, 169
Gray, Jon, 148
The Great Recession, 18
Great Recession, 151
green economy, 38, 39, 151, 152, 253
Greenberg, Alan "Ace", 197
Greenhill & Co., 258
greenwashing, 155–156
Griffin, Ken, 78

Haley, Nikki, 253–254
halo effect, 59, 63, 166
Hamas massacre, 4, 26, 108, 254, 258
Handy Dan, 134, 135
Harris, Josh, 118
Harris, Kamala, 24, 49
Harvey, Ian, 181
Heinerscheid, Alissa, 164–165, 167–168, 170–171, 182
Hertz rental car company, 252
Hild, Will, 139–141, 144, 226–227, 228–229
Hill, Jemele, 199–200
Hilton Hotels, 149–150
hiring quotas, 3
Hispanics, BlackRock's marketing strategy for, 57
Hochul, Kathy, 227

Hoffman, Liz, 236
Home Depot, 134–135, 261
Horn, Alan, 212
Hughes, Coleman, 93–94
human capital disclosures, 125
human resource (HR) departments
  DEI training and, 29, 246
  as politically woke, 29
  politics farmed out to, 47–48
  power of, 16
  quota machine of, 53
Human Rights Campaign, 35–36, 65, 121, 218

Iger, Bob. *See also* The Walt Disney Company
  as Apple board, 206
  butting heads with Trump, 207
  Chapek feud, 212–213
  choosing Chapek as his successor, 209
  on DeSantis "Don't Say Gay" legislation, 215–216, 220
  as Disney CEO, 128, 196, 221–222
  instilling progressivism at Disney, 128–129
  overpaying a series of acquisitions, 207
  retirement, 213
  stepping down as CEO, 205
  taking politics out of Disney, 249–250
Immelt, Jeff, 51, 98–99, 100
InBev. *See* AB InBev
India, exempt from ESG mandates, 154
inflation
  bankrupting working class with, 68, 126
  under Biden's presidency, 39
  ESG creating, 4, 32–33, 39, 229
  Gorman and, 223–224
  Inflation Reduction Act, 223–224
  Kapito on, 236
  as regressive form of taxation, 46
  transitory inflation, 223–226
Inflation Reduction Act, 223–224
Ingraham, Laura, 116
Institutional Shareholder Services, 37
intersectionality, 27
iShares Global Clean Energy, 252
Israel, 26, 111, 258, 261. *See also* Hamas massacre

Jackson, Ketanji Brown, 49
James, LeBron, 111, 115, 116
James, Tony, 148
Jenner, Kendall, 63
Job Creators Network, 135, 245–246, 261
Jobs, Steve, 206
Johansson, Scarlett, 210–212
Jones, Jerry, 117
Jones, Paul Tudor, 78
Jones, Reg, 96
Jordan, Jim, 251–252
Jordan, Michael, 116
JP Morgan, 36, 242

Kaepernick, Colin, 23, 114, 116–117
Kapito, Rob, 144, 235–236
Katzenberg, Jeffrey, 195, 196
Kelly, Megyn, 191
Kemp, Brian, 109, 246
Kendi, Ibram X., 93–95
Kid Rock, 164, 185, 248–249
King, Gayle, 187
Komansky, Dave, 160
Kornbluth, Sally, 260
Kroc, Ray, 132
Kudlow, Larry, 78
Kushner, Jared, 102

Ladapo, Joseph, 81
Lagarde, Christine, 177
Lander, Brad, 231–232
Langone, Ken, 134–135
Lasseter, John, 209
Latinx, defined, 89
Lehman Brothers, 148
Leo, Leonard, 139
Levine, Rachel, 49

Levy, Gus, 11–12
Lew, Jack, 154
LGBTQ+ community. *See also* trans people
  BlackRock's marketing strategy for, 57
  books aimed at children, 61, 64
  business side of appealing to, 61–62
  China's oppression of, 42
  Parental Rights in Education Act and, 214–215
  SEC hiring requirements, 123
  state of emergency for, 36
Loeb, Dan, 78, 221
Loeffler, Kelly, 78
Lord, Rachel, 158
Loury, Glenn, 246
Luce, Henry, 159–160

Ma, Jack, 42
Mac Donald, Heather, 82
Mack, John, 48
The Magical World of Disney (television show), 195
Magill, Liz, 258–259
Major League Soccer, 117
Manfred, Rob, 111
Manhattan Institute, 82
Manzo, Whitney Ross, 116
Marcus, Bernie, 4, 48, 134–135, 245, 250, 260–262
marketing
  cause marketing, 56
  charity vs, 131
  halo effect, 59, 63, 166
  politicization of brands, 55–56
  racialized image making, 67–68
marketing tribalism, 58–60
Martin, Trayvon, 115
Matagrano, Scott, 174
Mayer, Kevin, 205, 210
McDonald's USA, 47, 131–132. *See also* Rensi, Ed
McLennan, David, 116
McMaster, Henry, 227
McWhorter, John, 246
The Megyn Kelly Show, 191–192
meme stock, 124
Merck, 109
Mercury Public Affairs, 187, 247
Meredith College, 116
Merrill Lynch, 150
microaggressions, 26–27, 54
Millennials, 58, 68
Miramax, 195
Mnuchin, Steve, 78
Modelo, 248
Modern Monetary Theory, 230
Moon, Keith, 141
Moore, Lecrae, 21
Morgan Stanley, 224
Morgenthau, Robert, 86
Morningstar, 252
Morrow, Lance, 159
Moynihan, Brian, 83, 88–89, 91–92, 140
Moynihan, Lydia, 8
Mulvaney, Dylan
  March Madness video, 184
  AB InBev recruitment, 163, 182–183
  Biden and, 166
  bubble bath ad, 183–184
  Bud Light bath video, 183–184
  Bud Light commercials, 247–248
  Doukeris's spin on fiasco, 187–188
  response to March Madness video, 184–186
  social media feed, 188–189
  as social media influencer, 55, 165–166
Murdoch, Rupert, 128
Musk, Elon, 230–231, 241–242. *See also* X (social media platform)
Myers, John, 95–96

Nasdaq Stock Market
  exemptions to listing standards, 42
  listing standards, 41–45, 124
  obsession with ESG, 41–42
National Economic Council, 12, 78

Navy SEAL Foundation, 24–25
NBA (National Basketball Association), 43, 115, 117
Net Zero Alliance, 38–39, 230
net zero emissions, 38–39, 230
Netflix, 244–245
Netzel, Brian, 29–30
New York City, 85–87
New York Times, 1619 Project, 68
NextEra Energy, 27–29
NFL (National Football League)
  annual revenues, 117
  Black National Anthem and, 117–118
  fan base, 116–117
  Goodell, Roger, 117–118
  Kaepernick and, 23, 114, 116–117
  racial politics of, 116–118
Nichols, Rachel, 200
Nike, 56, 114, 116, 117
North Carolina bathroom bill, 91
NYU Langone, 135

Obama, Barack
  Facebook Town Hall guest, 75–76
  Fink and, 152
  Podesta and, 122
  presidency, 50–51, 75–76, 99
  Robinson and, 35
Ocasio-Cortez, Alexandria, 11
Occupy Wall Street, 18–19, 151
organized retail crime, 84–85, 255
Ortiz, Alfredo, 245
Ovitz, Michael, 196

Parental Rights in Education Act (Florida), 129–130, 214–217
Partnership for New York City, 85–86
passive investing, 150–151
Patrick, Dan, 253
Patten, Dominic, 212
Paul, Ron, 253
Paulson, Hank, 11–12, 146
Paycheck Protection Program (PPP), 88
Peltz, Nelson, 99, 221
Pence, Mike, 77–78, 106, 227–228
Penny, Daniel, 85
pension funds, 19, 41, 71, 122, 141, 146, 153, 156, 227, 229
people of color
  BlackRock's marketing strategy for, 56–57
  hiring quotas, 53, 90
  Latinx, 89
PepsiCo, 62–63
PepsiCo Positive (pep+), 62–63
Perot, Ross, 134
Peterson, Jordan, 107
Peterson, Peter, 148
Petty, Herman, 132
Pitaro, Jimmy, 193
Pitt, Harvey, 102, 108, 124
PNC bank, 149
Podesta, John, 121–122
Powell, Jerome, 223
"Power Slap" competition, 248–249
private equity firms (PE), 148
progressive, academia destroying meaning of, 103
progressive movement, 1–2, 11, 50, 75, 106, 231, 250–251
proxy process, 21, 50, 150
Publishers Clearinghouse Consumer Insights, 247

Qatar, 261
queer fashion, 61

race-based hiring, 56
"A Racial Equity 21-Day Challenge" controversy, 92–93
racial justice movement, 199
racial wealth gap, 89–90, 257
Ramaswamy, Vivek, 12
Raveneau, Latoya, 216
Reedy Creek Improvement District, 133–134, 220

Rensi, Ed. *See also* McDonald's USA
background of, 47, 130
on CEOs involved in social engineering, 134
on Chapek, 127–128, 130
on charity vs marketing, 131
on ending corporate wokeness, 245, 247
fighting corporate wokeness, 4
Friedman and, 131
hating corporate wokeness, 138
on inclusion, as good for business, 132
introducing Black-owned McDonald's franchises, 132
Marcus's Job Creators project and, 135
predictions, 256
Robinson, Kelley, 35, 121
"Rock the Woke" campaign, 245–246
Rogan, Joe, 244
Rogan, Seth, 181
Rogers, Kenny, 197
Ronald McDonald House, 131
Rowan, Marc, 259
Rubin, Robert, 11–12, 124
Rufo, Chris, 92, 216

Sandberg, Sheryl, 176
Sanders, Bernie, 11
Sarandos, Ted, 244–245
Schumer, Amy, 181
Schumer, Chuck, 155
Schwab, Klaus, 177
Schwarzman, Steve, 78, 87, 147–150, 233–234
Scott, Stuart, 202–203
SCOTUS. *See* U.S. Supreme Court
Section 230 of the Communications Act, 240
Securities and Exchange Commission, 37, 120–126
securitization, 18, 146–147
shareholder capitalism, 31–34
Sherman, Alex, 212
shoplifting, 84–85
Silicon Valley Bank, 2, 69–72
Six Sigma management theory, 97
slavery, 68
small business, 88
Smirnoff Vodka, 59
Snyder, Dan, 119
social justice
Moynihan on need for, 88
NBA and, 43
overt displays of, 115
Pepsi, 63
racial diversity increased by, 101–102
Rensi and, 131
Sonnenfeld and, 101–102
through race-based hiring, 56
violence disguised as, 80–82, 84
social media
influencers, 165 (*See also* Mulvaney, Dylan)
Twitter, 239–242
as window to American psyche, 183
X, 231, 241–244
social media companies, censorship by, 76–77
socially responsible investing, 35
Solomon, David, 12–13, 19–20, 82–83, 145–146, 254–255
Solomon, John, 65
Sonnenfeld, Jeff
CEO Summits and, 101–103, 105, 108
defending C-suite wokeism, 105
Elson and, 104–105
on ESG fads, 105
on Georgia's voting laws, 109–110
Immelt and, 98–99, 100
Peltz and, 99
social justice and, 101–102
Trump and, 105
Welch and, 96–97
Zelenskyy and, 102–103
Soros, George, 35, 65–66, 86, 232
sovereign wealth funds, 153
Spacey, Kevin, 176–177

SportsCenter, 198
Sprecher, Jeff, 78
Squeri, Stephen, 30, 255
St. Patrick's Cathedral, 135
stakeholder capitalism
  Business Roundtable and, 101
  CEO-to-worker compensation ratio and, 45
  corruption of, 255
  description of, 32
  as fashionable, 97
  mainstreaming ESG, 34, 151
  rise of, 18
Starbucks, 83
Starkman, Eric, 62–63
State Street, 37, 38, 155, 227–228
Statista, 45
"stay awake", 23
Steele, Sage
  beginning of downfall, 191–192
  cut from key assignments, 202–203
  ESPN's investigation into, 201–202
  ESPN's ultimatum, 202
  lawsuit against ESPN, 203
  ousting at ESPN, 197–199
  racial identity of, 201
  on *Uncut with Jay Cutler*, 200–201
Stefanik, Elise, 259
Stitt, Kevin, 227
Stokes, Patrick, 173
Strange World (film), 219
Sullivan & Cromwell, 121
Summers, Larry, 124
Super Bowl ads, 169, 181, 249
Supreme Court. *See* U.S. Supreme Court
SVB, 2–3, 69–72
Swaminathan, Vanitha, 55–56, 69
systemic racism, 26, 73–74

Tanden, Neera, 122
Target, 3, 4
  boycott of, 67
  customer base, 63–64
  LGBTQ+ books for children, 64
  marketing tribalism, 60–61
  Pride Month celebration, 61–64, 255
target marketing, 56–58
Taylor, Breonna, 73
television advertisements, 67–68. *See also* marketing
Teller, Miles, 171
Tesla, 242–243
thermal coal production, 156
Thernstrom, Abigail and Stephan, 89
Thiel, Peter, 194
Thomas, David, 41
TikTok, 165
Time Inc., 159
Title VI of the Civil Rights Act, 53–54
Title VII of the Civil Rights Act, 54
Tlaib, Rashida, 11
totalitarianism, 103–104
toxic masculinity, 32
trans movement, 189
trans people, 59
transitory inflation, 223–224
Tritt, Travis, 184–185
Trump, Donald
  2020 election, 76, 106–107
  Bragg and, 85
  Capitol Hill riot, 106–107
  CEOs' views of, 106–107
  Dimon and, 257
  Fink and, 155
  Hill on, 199
  Iger butting heads with, 207
  low points of, 81
  presidency, 12, 73–75, 77–79
  Sonnenfeld and, 105
  at World Economic Forum, 178
Trump, Donald, Jr., 21, 187
21 Century Fox, 128, 207
Twitter. *See also* Dorsey, Jack; X (social media platform)
  Agrawal, Parag, 241–242
  content moderators, 240

Musk targeting, 242
Musk's purchase of, 231, 241–242
political bias of, 239–241
regulatory quirk, 240

UFC (Ultimate Fighting Championship), 248
Ukraine, 102–103
unconscious bias, 26–27
Uncut with Jay Cutler podcast, 200–201
United Airlines, DEI mandates, 52
United Nations, 36
United Way, 92–93
University of California, Berkeley, DEI statements at, 52–53
unwoke entertainment, 244–245
US Public Health Service Commissioned Corps, 49
U.S. Supreme Court, 49, 139, 244

V Foundation, 202–203
Vanguard, 37, 38, 155, 227–228, 230
Vargas, Cesar, 247–248
Veterans Administration, 27
violence, disguised as social justice, 80–82, 84
virtue signaling, 22, 70, 115

The Walt Disney Company. *See also* Chapek, Bob; Iger, Bob
brand damage, 249–250
Buena Vista Worldwide Home Entertainment, 206
Buzz Lightyear animated film, 219
Capital Cities/ABC purchase, 196
China and, 208
declining shares, 250
Eisner's vision, 195–197
enforcing diversity mandates, 207–208
EPCOT, 133–134
ESPN purchase, 194
excusing China's human rights abuses, 42–43
Florida and, 3, 133
Gay Days at theme parks, 208
grading managers on wokeness, 126
Iger and (*See* Iger, Bob)
Johansson and, 210–212
making streaming profitable, 212
plastic straws ban, 203–205
Reedy Creek Improvement District, 133–134
same-sex characters introduced in Disney movies, 207, 219
setting racial quotas for Disney characters, 207–208
stock chart, 220–221
stock price, 195
Strange World (film), 219
theme parks, 133, 208
21 Century Fox purchase, 128
woke hypocrisy of, 208
Warren, Elizabeth, 19, 123–124, 151, 156
Washington Commanders, 118–119
Washington Redskins, 91, 119
wealth gap, 89–90
Weill, Sandy, 34
Weiss, Bari, 13
Welch, Jack, 14–15, 48, 96–97, 100
White, Dana, 248
White House Covid meeting, 77–79
white man's guilt, 30
white privilege, 27
Whitehead, John, 11–12, 48
Whitlock, Jason, 198
Whitworth, Brendan, 21, 166–167, 186–187, 248–249
Wiedman, Mark, 236–237
WikiLeaks, 122
woke, defined, 23
woke investing, 251–252
wokeism/wokeness. *See* corporate wokeness
Wolfe, Tom, 26
women, BlackRock's marketing strategy for, 56–57
The Wonderful World of Disney (television show), 195

World Economic Forum, 36, 176–178, 257
Wylde, Kathryn, 85–87

X (social media platform). *See also* Twitter
firing work workforce, 243
mission, 241
Musk's management style, 242
Musk's purchase/renaming Twitter, 231, 241–242
"The Twitter Files" release, 243–244

Yahoo, 114
young consumers, 114–115
Youngkin, Glenn, 60, 214

Zelenskyy, Volodymyr, 102–103
zero-emissions standards, 38–39, 100, 143–144
Zimmerman, George, 115
Zuckerberg, Mark, 75–76

About the Author

Charles Gasparino is a Fox Business Network senior correspondent and *New York Post* columnist who has covered business for CNBC, *Newsweek*, and the *Wall Street Journal*. He is the author of five books, including the *New York Times* bestseller *The Sellout*, which chronicled the causes of the 2008 financial crisis.